URBAN POVERTY,

POLITICAL

PARTICIPATION,

AND THE STATE

Lima 1970–1990

URBAN POVERTY,

POLITICAL

PARTICIPATION,

AND THE STATE

Lima 1970–1990

....

Henry Dietz

UNIVERSITY OF PITTSBURGH PRESS

Published by the University of Pittsburgh Press, Pittsburgh, Pa. 15261
Copyright © 1998, University of Pittsburgh Press
Manufactured in the United States of America
Printed on acid-free paper
10 9 8 7 6 5 4 3 2 1

Library of Congress Cataloging-in-Publication Data
Dietz, Henry A.
    Urban poverty, political participation, and the state : Lima,
1970–1990 / Henry Dietz.
    p. cm. — (Pitt Latin American series)
Includes bibliographical references and index.
ISBN 0-8229-4063-9 (cloth : acid-free paper)
ISBN 0-8229-5667-5 (pbk. : acid-free paper)
    1. Urban poor—Peru—Lima—Political activity. 2. Political
participation—Peru—Lima. I. Title. II. Series.
    HN350.L5 D54 1998
    306.2'0985'25—ddc21   98-9054
                                                            CIP

A CIP catalog record for this book is available from the British Library.

TO ANNE

CONTENTS

ACKNOWLEDGMENTS

Anyone who has ever undertaken a lengthy research project knows all too well how debts pile up. In this case, keeping a project alive over twenty-five years has meant my receiving significant assistance of many types from a great many people. In the first place, financial support came from numerous sources, including the following: the Social Science Research Council (1970); the Stanford University Center for Research in International Studies (1970); the Ford-Rockefeller Foundation's program of social science and legal research on population policy (Grant RF-73070, 1973); the American Philosophical Society, Philadelphia (1975, 1980, 1993); the Tinker Foundation (1982); the Policy Research Institute of the University of Texas (1985); the Hogg Foundation of the University of Texas (1985); the Heinz Foundation (1990); and the Institute of Latin American Studies (1970 to the present) and the University Research Institute (1974 to present), both of the University of Texas at Austin.

In Lima I received invaluable assistance and institutional support from many sources, among them the Pontificia Universidad Católica and the Universidad del Pacífico. Many faculty members at both universities gave of their time and expertise and encouragement; students at the Catholic University were instrumental in administering the surveys in 1982, 1985, and 1990. I would also like to thank numerous individuals at Apoyo S.A. and from several ministries and government agencies over the years for making data available to me. I benefited a great deal from innumerable conversations with individuals associated with the Instituto de Estudios Peruanos, with DESCO, with the Centro de Investigaciones at the University of the Pacific, and with the Escuela Superior de Administración de Negocios.

Individual thanks are impossible to enumerate completely. My special thanks go to Marcia Koth de Paredes of the Fulbright Commission and her husband, Ernesto; to Fernando Tuesta; to Ofelia Montes and to Olga Paredes; to the family of Federico and Enriqueta Sanchez, for thirty years of friendship; to Orlando Llontop, Padre Jeff Klaiber S.J., and Padre John Sima S.J. There is no way to thank the hundreds of working-class people across Lima who gave of their time as re-

ix

spondents to the surveys. Many individuals read the draft of the book manuscript or parts of it: Mark Jones, Folke Kafka, Cynthia McClintock, Scott Palmer, Aldo Panfichi, Gonzalo Portocarrero, Fernando Tuesta, and Franco Uccelli deserve all thanks and none of the responsibility. All translations are mine unless otherwise noted.

My wife, Anne, has been an integral part of the project since 1970 and has done far more than her share of coding questionnaires and participating in the whole life of the enterprise, which simply would not have been completed without her encouragement and support. Gillian and Allison were not born when it started. Gillian is now about to start graduate school while Allison is more than halfway through Stanford. This study has, for better or worse, been a part of their entire lives, and it is high time for it to come to an end. *Fini.*

URBAN POVERTY,

POLITICAL

PARTICIPATION,

AND THE STATE

Lima 1970–1990

Lima's Districts in 1990

Notes: Districts in bold type are sites of surveyed neighborhoods. Districts 42–47 constitute Callao, Lima's port city and a distinct jurisdiction.

Key:

The Central City
1. Barranco
2. Breña
3. Jesús María
4. La Victoria
5. **Lima-Cercado**
6. Lince
7. Magdalena del Mar
8. Miraflores
9. Pueblo Libre
10. Rimac
11. San Borja
12. San Isidro
13. San Luis
14. San Miguel
15. Santiago de Surco
16. **Surquillo**

The Northern Cone
17. Carabayllo
18. **Comas**
19. Independencia
20. Puente Piedra
21. San Martín de Porres

The Eastern Cone
22. Ate
23. Chaclacayo
24. **El Agustino**
25. La Molina
26. Lurigancho
27. San Juan de Lurigancho

The Southern Cone
28. Chorrillos
29. **San Juan de Miraflores**
30. Villa El Salvador
31. Villa María del Triunfo

Peripheral Districts
32. Ancón
33. Santa Rosa
34. Cieneguilla
35. Lurin
36. Pachacamac
37. Pucusana
38. Punta Hermosa
39. Punta Negra
40. San Bartolo
41. Santa María del Mar

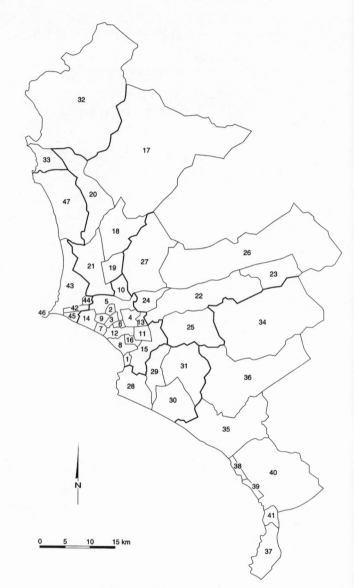

1

....

THIRD WORLD
URBAN POVERTY
AND POLITICAL
PARTICIPATION

THE LAST HALF of the twentieth century has witnessed enormous and fundamental changes throughout the Third World. World War II saw colonialism
replaced by frequently fragile and unsustainable efforts at independence and
nation-building. Socialism and communism collapsed, leaving economic and
political systems groping to find replacements. Capitalism and democracy both
flourished, at least rhetorically, but their shallow roots often became painfully
clear, as the dependent status of many nations and their poverty and inequitable
distribution of resources (education, income, wealth, power) made the futures
of both democracy and capitalism uncertain. Demographic changes—especially
the growth and redistribution of populations—forced national and global agencies to address often related issues of international and internal migration and
their simultaneous causes and effects: poverty, massive urbanization, unemployment, underemployment, and the widening disparity between mushroom-
ing demands, needs, and expectations on the one hand and the all-too-frequent
inability of states to respond adequately to such demands on the other.

This book examines these social, economic, and political processes and
changes as they occurred during a two-decade period in Peru. Peru offers an
unparalleled observational laboratory for investigating a wide range of critical socioeconomic changes: massive poverty and extreme income inequality,
a burgeoning primate urban setting (Lima), sustained and severe macrolevel
socioeconomic crisis, a regime change from military to civilian rule, a brutal insurgency movement, the growth of a massive and complex urban informal sec-

tor, and a state that has become increasingly irrelevant for much of its citizenry. All these topics have been the subject of much scrutiny, and no single study can encompass all of them. The focus of this book is political participation, which during the 1970–1990 period developed two distinct but related faces: formal political participation (basically, voting and electoral involvement) and informal political participation (politics on the neighborhood and community grassroots level).

Political participation is still too broad a focus, however. Individual citizens do not all participate in similar ways. For example, the presence of well-defined social-class differences creates distinct patterns of political involvement, both formally and informally, as upper and lower classes have separate political goals, access to power, and knowledge about the political process. A severe economic crisis can change patterns of political involvement across class and income lines. Many other factors could in like fashion affect behavior.

A case can thus be made for focusing on a specific class or stratum of society, rather than trying to take on society as a whole. I concentrate on the formal and informal political participation of Peru's low-income urban working class, specifically the individuals and families who inhabit Lima's central-city tenements and peripheral squatter settlements. These people comprise the segment of Lima that has, in the past thirty years or so, become the majority of the city's population.

Lima's poor not only make up the city's majority, however; individually and as a group, they are more vulnerable to macrolevel economic shifts (especially declines) than perhaps any other group in Peruvian society. Why is this the case? After all, the rural poor in Peru (and in any Third World setting, for that matter) are poorer in absolute terms than their urban counterparts (Glewwe and de Tray 1989). First, the urban poor depend upon a monetary economy and have no ability to shield themselves from, for instance, the ravages of high levels of sustained inflation, rises in prices, or diminished purchasing power. The rural poor may operate within an economy that includes barter; they may also practice subsistence farming or other strategies to provide themselves with food and clothing. Neither of these alternatives is a viable survival mechanism in a large city. Second, not only are the urban poor more vulnerable to economic downturns; they may also be much more open to political stimuli from newspapers, radio, television, the actions and persuasions and propaganda of political parties, labor unions, and neighbors. They may therefore perceive the effects of poverty and economic crisis more immediately and more acutely than do the rural poor.

Yet this vulnerability to economy vicissitudes has not prevented an enormous rural-urban migration from occurring throughout Third World nations, and Lima has been no exception. Lima's demographic and physical growth—from a population of about 600,000 in 1945 to one exceeding 7 million by the early 1990s—has been dictated by the arrival of millions of migrants, the majority of whom are low-income. By 1990 most estimates agreed that well over one-half of Lima's total population lived in the city's squatter-origin settlements, while another quarter resided in central-city tenement rental slums. The sheer weight in numbers, which brings with it not only ever-increasing demands for jobs, housing, and schools but also involvement in formal and informal political processes, makes the poor an appropriate focus for this book.

Concentrating on this segment of Lima's population also provides the book with some boundaries. Any investigation that sets out to look at how several macrolevel factors have affected individual-level political participation over a period of twenty years requires a variety of different types of data and information. Macrolevel aggregate data are necessary, for example, to sketch in the broad trends in Lima and throughout Peru during the 1970–1990 period. Somewhat more specialized data are needed to understand the characteristics, growth, and development of specific districts and neighborhoods in Lima. Descriptive and historical information can enrich economic and social statistics on both these levels, while census and secondary data are useful in coming to grips with the growth and complexity of the informal sector. And electoral data can illuminate how Lima and its forty or so districts voted in the several elections that have taken place since 1980, when Peru returned to civilian rule. But all these data, alone or in combination, cannot provide the dynamics necessary to follow individual-level constancies and changes in political participation over a twenty-year period. Longitudinal data would be ideal, especially survey data that could follow specific individuals and/or small neighborhoods over time. Such longitudinal data are hard to come by.

The core of this study consists of four separate surveys that were carried out over a twenty-year period in six lower-class neighborhoods in Lima. The first was conducted in 1970, during the heyday of General Juan Velasco's self-styled Revolution of the Armed Forces. The second occurred in 1982, shortly after Peru returned to civilian rule in 1980 and about a year and a half into the Fernando Belaúnde administration. The third took place in 1985, immediately after the election of Alán García; and the fourth in 1990, shortly after Alberto Fujimori won his surprising landslide victory. Each survey consists of between 450 and 600 interviews. At the time of each survey, I collected a good deal of ethnographic, informant-interview, and observational material in each neighborhood. I returned to the same communities to replicate the surveys and, whenever pos-

core
of the
surveys

sible, to the same individuals and families to gather more of the same sort of information.[1]

Although political participation is the basic dependent variable of the book, I also undertake to address a related and tricky question: participation for what? Political participation may be an end in itself, but surely such a view is too constrained, since participation has multiple impacts. The most obvious may come from electoral participation; when people vote, their actions produce an outcome (excluding the effects of fraud and other such manipulations of outcomes), and I spend a good deal of time examining the results of voting in Lima. Another broader but perhaps less obvious impact has to do with the construction of democracy. Much of the literature concerned with democratic transition and consolidation at least mentions the need for newly democratic societies to establish and nurture a thriving civil society. I do not mean to anticipate here the more detailed discussion that follows in this chapter and in chapter 2, but virtually all observers concur that a strong civil society is an essential component of a democracy, and that civil society rests upon vigorous voluntary associational life (Hall 1995; Diamond, Linz, and Lipset 1990, 29). I have included activities such as community involvement and cooperation in what I call informal participation; and the book has a great deal to say not only about how the urban poor participate but also about how their particular patterns of participation over time have shaped Peru's civil society.

Political Participation

Political participation has been defined in innumerable ways, and it is probably not possible or essential for any single study to provide a definition that would be applicable to all settings and situations. In general terms, "political participation" refers to activities by citizens designed to influence government and its policies or personnel in some fashion (Verba and Nie 1972; Verba, Nie, and Kim 1978; Nagel 1987; Booth and Seligson 1978). However, to define what political participation is precisely may not be as critical as to discover why and how people become involved in it.

The analysis here employs the notion of modes of participation established some years ago by Verba and Nie (1972). Briefly stated, the concept of modes of participation has its theoretical roots in the idea that people involved in political participation do not range from inactivists to activists along some single dimension, but rather that, when people do in fact undertake political activity, different people choose to become involved in different kinds or modes of activity. Some may never become involved at all; others may vote but do nothing more; others may involve themselves in campaigns, participate in neighborhood projects, or petition authorities for individual or communal needs or benefits (anything from a stop sign on a corner to petitions for police protection or to running water).

Citizens in all countries will in one way or another, and for one reason or another, become involved in politics in different ways. But it takes only the slightest reflection to realize that the type of regime plays a critical role indeed in determining what modes will be present or acceptable in a given society. Yet to say that a democratic regime allows a wide range of political activity, while an authoritarian regime does not, comes close to being a tautology, given that the breadth and depth of political involvement is commonly cited as a defining characteristic of democracy itself (Dahl 1971).

The fact that Peru was under military rule from 1968 to 1980 and then returned to civilian governance throughout the decade of the 1990s allows for an empirical examination of what happens to patterns of participation when regimes change. To predict that modes of involvement change if regime types change is to predict relatively little. But how do they change? Are some modes replaced by others? Are some modes retained regardless of regime type? The underlying idea here is that any definition or discussion of political participation must take into account regime type.

In an authoritarian regime, definitions of political participation derived from liberal democracies are clearly inapposite, since no meaningful elections are held and all political decisions flow from a highly centralized, nonrepresentative source of power. Few if any mechanisms exist for influencing the selection of government officials or for having a regular, constitutional vehicle for expressing an opinion about such officials or their policies or performances. Such a regime can make political participation: (1) nonexistent or illegal; (2) severely controlled and almost entirely ceremonial; or (3) informal and largely bureaucratic in nature, consisting of efforts at self-help or at petitioning government bureaucracies for aid.

On the other hand, democratic political participation involves behavior that is intended to affect "the decisional outcomes of government" (Verba and Nie 1972, 2) as well as to influence "the selection of governmental personnel and / or the actions that they take" (Weiner 1971, 164–65). Voting, campaigning, and all the other activities that accompany electoral politics come to the fore, of course, but to conclude that political participation has one face under authoritarianism and another under democracy may be unwise. For the urban poor in particular, political participation is generally instrumental in nature, regardless of the type of regime in power, since their participation is aimed at influencing the distribution of valued material resources, generally collective goods. When a transition occurs from authoritarian to democratic rule, authoritarianism's repressive controls that constrain political involvement are inevitably replaced by new avenues of involvement, most notably a whole range of electoral activities (voting, campaigning, party involvement, and so on). Yet previous modes of authoritarian participation involving activities such as community involvement and demand-making aimed at governmental bureaucracies cannot be expected to disappear, since the material needs and expectations of poor groups transcend regime types and certainly do not magically materialize because democratic procedures have replaced authoritarianism.

Quite the contrary: even though a transition from military to civilian rule occurs, political participation may become increasingly multifaceted or pluralistic, with citizens not only voting and becoming involved in electoral activities but also continuing to pursue individual- and neighborhood-level needs and wants that require the allocation of extremely limited resources. In such a situation, elected officials from the president down to the most local district council representative will predictably encounter petitions, requests, negotiations, bargains, threats, and attempts to defeat them for two not necessarily related reasons: failure in their performance to provide what the populace wants and needs, and opposition from a political party that seeks their removal regardless of performance. In other words, political participation under democratic rule (and compared to authoritarian rule) will become more complex as elected officials, candidates for office, political parties, government agencies, and the mass of citizens all attempt to influence the allocation of values.

If a democratically elected administration cannot or does not respond to the pressures and demands created by these several avenues of political participation, the citizenry has the option of voting against that administration and turning it out of office. A more serious problem arises for a democracy, however, if dissatisfaction not with a particular administration but with the system as such starts to take hold. Systemic alienation or delegitimation, especially if it becomes widespread, poses a crucial dilemma for democracy, especially given the likely alternatives, which generally consist either of a return to military rule or of a turn to a radical or revolutionary option. It is here that Hirschman's (1970) three options come to mind: the citizen can be loyal to the system, can voice his complaints about it, or can exit from the system either by opting out or by favoring the creation of a new system.

All of this being said, a working definition of political participation for this book is going to have to be flexible or at least multifaceted, if for no other rea-

son than that authoritarian rule prohibits or makes moot certain types of involvement permitted by civilian regimes. One specific definition of participation
for the urban poor involves individual or collective efforts to supply themselves
and their immediate neighborhoods with public goods, sometimes but not always through attempts to obtain a favorable distribution of governmental resources.[2] Such participatory activities I call *informal political participation*. Under
democratic governance this notion of participation remains operative but is aug-
mented by the addition of *formal political participation,* which consists of voting,
campaign or political party involvement, and other similar activities aimed at
influencing the selection or policy decision-making of governmental personnel. For the purposes of this book, full political participation combines the formal and the informal.[3]

polit. partic. Def.

By using a broad definition of participation that goes beyond the electoral
and includes the communal, I avoid what Larry Diamond has labeled the "electoral fallacy" (1996, 22). Diamond argues against

> privileging electoral contestation over other dimensions of democracy and ig-
> noring the degree to which elections, even in genuinely competitive elections,
> may deny significant sections of the population the opportunity to contest for
> power or defend and advance their interests, or may leave significant arenas of
> decision-making beyond the reach or control of elected officials. (22)

Bringing in informal participation allows us to observe how a significant sec-
tion of the population defends and advances its interests, regardless of whether
electoral procedures are operative or not.

It could be argued that both parts of my operational definition deal largely
with procedural and not with substantive democracy.[4] That is, they are concerned more with how people participate and less with the outcome(s) of that
participation. Is this focus on procedure justifiable when poverty and people
caught up in poverty form the heart of the study? As Cohen and Dawson (1993)
and many others (Pateman 1988; Herzog 1989) have observed, a society cannot
reasonably be considered democratic unless and until that society includes
basic economic and physical security for its citizens. Can or should a society be
perceived as democratic if, for example, its members have no feeling of attach-
ment to it because it is unresponsive to their needs or because a combination of
poverty and inequality leave the majority of its citizens with only the most
meager chances at securing food, employment, housing, and medical care
(Cohen and Dawson 1993, 287)?

To accommodate such an argument, informal political participation explicitly includes direct efforts to obtain material public goods, through either indi-

vidual or collective efforts at the grassroots level. Indeed, such efforts lie at the heart of informal participation. Attempts and strategies employed by the poor to increase the amount of or to influence the distribution of nonneighborhood material resources or to provide neighborhood collective goods through their own efforts thus incorporate the need for determining not only how people participate but what happens when they do.

In addition, the multilevel, longitudinal nature of the study and of the data permits a partial answer to the question of whether the procedures by which people participate have any substantive effect on their lives, welfare, and surroundings. Informal participation can (hypothetically at least) produce a collective or public good. For example, neighborhood cooperation might result in the construction of a new community center, or petitions directed at a government agency might spark action from the state. If these efforts succeed, then it is possible (but by no means certain) that they could lead to additional efforts using the same techniques of neighborhood cooperation or state-directed petitioning. In the formal political arena, large numbers of poor citizens might switch their votes, split tickets, abstain, turn to radical alternatives, or become alienated if parties and candidates are seen as ineffective in making good on electoral promises to deliver goods and services. Whatever the specific example, bringing together data that unite various levels of analysis (the individual, the neighborhood, the district, the city, the metropolitan area, the nation, and the nation's position in the international context) across a twenty-year period affords an unparalleled examination of political participation not only as procedures and mechanisms but also as a means of obtaining (or at least trying to obtain) substantive ends and goals.

Rational Political Participation

The notion of rationality can be linked to political participation through a model that treats democracy as a collective good and that introduces the idea of shifting preferences both within and vis-à-vis democracy. I start from the assumption that when a shift occurs from authoritarianism to democracy, democracy can be thought of as a collective or public good, that is, a good which cannot provide benefits to one individual without simultaneously providing the same benefit to others (Olson 1965; Abrams 1980). Such goods are characterized as having nonexcludability (individuals cannot be excluded from consuming the good) and jointness of consumption (benefits can be provided

Collective good = clean air [handwritten annotation]

to more than one individual simultaneously). The usual examples of a collective good are national defense or clean air.

Democracy is a collective good insofar as all citizens can participate in exercising this good (with some few exceptions, such as prisoners or noncitizens) and insofar as the benefits derived from the presence of this good are nonexcludable. If democracy is perceived as a collective good, then the notions of elasticity and marginal cost and marginal utility can be applied. This application might appear farfetched at first, since democracy cannot be purchased in any usual sense. Moreover, it might appear moot to apply marginal utilities and costs to democracy, since democracy is usually seen as either present or absent.

However, at the moment of its establishment as an operative political system (T_I), democracy is an inelastic public good. The "amount" of democracy is the same for each citizen simultaneously (at least in procedural terms); in addition, the amount remains constant even if its cost(s) may vary. Part of the costs of democracy at T_I (its start-up costs) may be characterized as the sum of the efforts made by all citizens to contribute or participate (minimally, to vote; maximally, to run for office) in its initial establishment. If at T_I all benefits of democracy (the franchise, popularly elected officials, ideological choices) are simultaneously available to all citizens, then these benefits are democracy's total utility, and the notion of future marginal utility does not apply. That is, it is not logical to expect that more democracy will be provided because it is completely provided at T_I. For most citizens in a nation undergoing the transition from authoritarianism to democracy, the total utility of democracy at T_I is greater than its costs.

At T_I two basic dimensions define preferences—and therefore utilities and costs—for an individual citizen. The first preference dimension deals with *political* preferences and concerns a dimension best described as a preference for democracy versus any other alternative. The second preference dimension deals with economic *well-being* and can best be described as a preference for well-being versus material discomfort or deprivation. Each of these preferences has its own utilities and costs.[5]

As time moves beyond T_I, the total utility of democracy remains constant, but under certain conditions the costs associated with its maintenance (its marginal costs over time) may become more burdensome. The key phrase here is "associated with." While the fairly narrow and largely political costs of establishing democracy at T_I (that is, the costs of voting, campaigning) may remain largely the same, additional marginal costs that are perceived to be linked with democracy may start to emerge.

These costs are either political or economic in nature. For the former, citizens may perceive democracy as allowing or even encouraging conditions (corruption, public dishonesty) viewed as costly. For the latter, citizens may perceive democracy as costly (whether correctly or not makes no difference) because of poor economic conditions or performance. Both economically and politically, therefore, increasing marginal costs may start to approach democracy's total utility until a threshold is reached, at which point the sum of democracy's marginal costs equals or surpasses democracy's total utility.

Questions about which preference dimension ranks first in importance in the mind of a citizen may arise if the citizen perceives the costs of preferring democracy as diminishing the probabilities of maintaining well-being. If this is perceived to be the case, then a citizen may use one or more of the mechanisms of democracy (voting ideologically, for example, or switching candidate or party support) in protest or may perceive that his preference for democracy means his welfare will be at an unacceptable level. In other words, if democracy is present but its marginal costs start to exceed its total utility, then democracy as a system provides mechanisms for its own downfall. If individual citizens perceive or undergo decreasing welfare, their preference for democracy may weaken. Thus the presence of democratic mechanisms (the vote, the right to protest or to demand attention to grievances) can paradoxically threaten not only a regime but ultimately the system itself.

Contextualizing the Model: Motives, Bounded Rationality, Poverty, Individual Behavior Options, and Constraints

These ideas need fine-tuning to focus upon the particular context of this book, and later chapters advance some specific hypotheses about how a decline in well-being can bring about shifts in both formal and informal political participation. Yet some aspects require immediate elaboration. As an illustration, I make the assertion that people will participate in politics. Yet this assertion avoids the question of why people become involved in politics, which itself has been the subject of extended inquiry.

MOTIVES FOR PARTICIPATION

Individual citizens have a variety of reasons for becoming involved in politics, and these different reasons produce different types of political involvement. For example, when it comes to formal (electoral) participation, some citizens may decide to vote because they wish strongly for a particular candidate or party to

[handwritten margin note: People have variety of reasons for becoming involved in politics]

win; and, regardless of the rational-choice argument that one vote cannot matter and that a truly rational voter will not vote, such citizens will go to the polls.
Other citizens may wish to see a particular candidate defeated and will vote
strategically in hopes of seeing that enemy defeated. Other citizens may vote
out of a spirit of civic duty or because the law obligates them to do so. Probably most individuals vote as a result of a mixture of motives.

In Peru citizens are required to vote; they are fined if they do not. Under
such rules motives for voting become muddied, primarily because (it can be argued) the underlying cause for everyone's voting is to obey the law and avoid
punishment.[6] Yet sanctions cannot by themselves explain all voting, even if they
are enforced. In the first place, and most obviously, abstention exists; not every
citizen votes in Peru (Pareja Pflucker and Gatti Murriel 1993). Moreover, in
addition to voting, which is in most countries the most common and easiest
political act, Peruvians become involved in other types of political activities, including campaign and party activities, not to mention a whole panoply of nonelectoral informal participation (neighborhood politics, petitioning the state).
Yet no positive or negative societal sanctions exist for such informal involvement;
incentives or disincentives for such involvement come from the individual.

It is safe to say that the great majority of Peruvian citizens vote for reasons
other than to avoid a fine. But if mandatory voting laws are, in effect, what is in
many societies a fundamentally important question—Why do people vote?—
has little meaning (Verba and Nie 1972, 103). What does become salient is why
people vote for a specific candidate. Why might they switch their votes over
time? And why do patterns of informal political behavior change over time? Addressing these questions means addressing the general question: What does it
mean to act rationally in a social context such as Peru's?[7]

BOUNDED RATIONALITY

A rational view of behavior assumes that people do things to achieve a goal. In
general, behavior is rational if it is appropriate to specified goals in the context
of a given situation. Over time this postulate has been subjected to much criticism and refinement. In the mid-1980s Herbert Simon proposed his idea of
"bounded rationality" (bounded in the sense of limited or constrained) in response to arguments that an individual can never act in an optimally rational
fashion if such rationality assumes perfect knowledge (Simon 1985; also Miller
1986; Bennett and Bennett 1986; Grofman 1987). An individual, whatever his intentions, cannot obtain perfect knowledge, because of constraints of time or
money or will (Simon 1982). In his seminal statement in 1985 Simon sketched in
a "subjectively rational actor" who not only has limitations on his abilities to ac-

quire knowledge but also adapts his behavior to and because of external situations and constraints.

The concept of such an individual is especially appropriate here for two reasons. In the first place, Lima's urban poor make their calculations about both formal and informal political participation based, at least in part, on the nature of relevant formal institutions (political parties, state agencies, the state itself) and informal institutions (neighborhood circumstances, local group dynamics). They judge how well they think these formal and informal institutions have done in confronting macrolevel problems such as economic conditions, poverty, and state-society relations. Lima's poor undoubtedly take such constraints and circumstances into account when making their decisions about how to vote and whether to become involved in community affairs. In the second place, Simon notes that "before the methods of economic reasoning [can be applied] to political behavior, we must characterize the political situation, not as it appears 'objectively' to the analyst, but as it appears subjectively to the actors" (Simon 1985, 298). If one of the principal tasks of political science is to carry on painstaking empirical research at both the macro and micro levels, Simon warns that arriving at a reasonable specification of a situation is no easy matter (303). It is precisely the intent of this book to undertake such research on both the macro and the micro levels by describing as fully as possible just what the circumstances of the 1970–1990 period were for the urban poor of Lima, and how the poor behaved under those circumstances.

POVERTY AS BOUNDING RATIONALITY

Simply the condition of being poor—the inability to obtain necessary or scarce goods because of insufficient purchasing power—exerts a major role in defining what for poor people will be rational political behavior, formally as well as informally. If resources such as time, money, and physical effort play major roles in determining how much and in what ways people participate in politics, then the poor anywhere will operate at a disadvantage compared to their better-off counterparts. In the United States, for example, recent work by Brady, Verba, and Schlozman (1995) has convincingly argued that major constraints on political participation do indeed include resources (time, money, civic skills), engagement (lack of interest, minimal concern), and recruitment networks (mobilizational networks that operate by leaders, issues, or opportunities).

Brady, Verba, and Schlozman make use of a national sample for their work, thus allowing for maximum variation in socioeconomic status; but since I am confined to the lower classes of Lima, money in particular and other resources in general operate within severe limitations. Whereas some socioeconomic variations occur within and across the samples, all of the respondents are either lower class or charitably (even by Peruvian standards) lower-middle class. Yet, because monetary income is more or less constant does not mean that all other resources available to Lima's poor either do not vary or are universally scarce (see chapters 5–8). Education, for example, shows greater variation than does income. Disposable time is for most individuals and groups a scarce resource but perhaps especially so for the poor, who struggle constantly to find work or some means of generating income. Despite poverty as a constant, Lima's poor nevertheless show significant variation in the amount of time they are able and willing to put into politics, as well as the degree to which they mobilize around political leaders, issues, and opportunities.

Although the Lima data are confined to one social class, this limitation is an advantage, thanks to the longitudinal nature of the entire study and to the fact that the intensity and scope of poverty in Lima and Peru varied significantly over time (see chapters 3–5). Thus, poverty can be treated as a variable, as something that changes, not as something that is either present or absent, which thereby makes it possible to investigate whether changes in poverty are accompanied by changes in the political behavior of the poor. Hypothetically, for example, if poverty becomes increasingly acute, formal and informal political participation could both change: formally, vote-switching behavior and/or movement toward support for nontraditional candidates and political movements might increase; informally, demand-making addressed toward the state might initially increase and then (given a lack of response) might diminish as it is replaced by self-help coping tactics and strategies.

INDIVIDUAL BEHAVIOR OPTIONS

One general way to think about individual-level responses by poor people to changes in poverty comes from Hirschman (1970), who posits three alternative behaviors for consumers faced with deciding which firm to patronize. A customer may (1) remain loyal to a firm, (2) voice complaints about a firm, or (3) leave (exit) the firm and go to another. The options are (in opposite order) exit, voice, loyalty. Exit has traditionally been a topic of interest to economists, who are curious about why a customer leaves a firm, thereby using the market "to defend his welfare or to improve his position" (Hirschman 1970, 15). The concept of exit is attractively clear-cut: the customer either stays with the firm or leaves it. Political scientists, on the other hand, have been more concerned with voice, which in contrast to exit is for Hirschman a graduated, "messy" concept that ranges "all the way from faint grumbling to violent protest" (16). Exit is economic activity par excellence; voice is likewise political action. But

Hirschman also offers a third option: loyalty, which applies to individuals who stay with a firm and who either "actively participate in actions designed to change . . . policies and practices" (38) or "simply refuse to exit and suffer in silence, confident that things will soon get better" (76). Hirschman's treatment of these three generates a whole range of propositions and hypotheses: "exit drives out voice" (16), for example, or "loyalty holds exit at bay and activates voice" (78).

Each of these behavioral options can be found in formal and informal political situations and in political behavior patterns. First, in the informal arena, for example, a citizen can show loyalty to his neighborhood (and his nation, for all that) by dutifully working on communal problems with his neighbors, by petitioning state agencies in time-honored and nondisruptive fashions, and by being cooperative in general. In the formal arena, a voter can show loyalty to a candidate or party even if that candidate or party is unable to slow or reverse a decline in the voter's well-being. For a political party, of course, loyalty over time is a quality sine qua non to be devoutly nurtured among its adherents and those independents or undecideds it wishes to attract to its causes and its candidates.

Second, a citizen voter may choose to voice dissatisfaction. Voice consists of attempts to change, rather than escape from, an objectionable state of affairs. Informally, neighborhood members can utilize voice merely by being willing to complain out loud and publicly. Or they can become more demonstrative and assertive in articulating their demands or in the nature and content of those demands. Formally, adherents of a political party can attempt to practice voice through complaints or threats to abandon the candidate or party if it does not or cannot respond to their needs. Nonmembers (either individually or acting as a group), in contrast, may find it frustrating, time-consuming, and difficult to try to persuade a party to listen to their complaints.[8]

Third, exit is the most dramatic response for the dissatisfied citizen. Informally, a citizen can decide to drop out of neighborhood activities and petitioning activities, seeing them as useless or as activities whose marginal costs outweigh their benefits. In the formal arena, a citizen may exercise the exit option by switching his vote from one party to another. A citizen may also opt for more extreme exit options: by not voting for traditional parties, by not voting at all, or by sympathizing with or actually joining a radical group whose aim is the destruction of the whole political system.

These three options will not be equally attractive at any given time; their relative attractiveness may change as circumstances change. Under good economic conditions, for example, loyalty may dominate. If conditions deteriorate, voice and exit may each rise. Hirschman's claim that under many conditions exit tends to drive out voice is based on the idea that if it is easy for people to leave (that is, if there are no reprisals for leaving), they will not participate in efforts to change an unsatisfactory situation (Hirschman 1970; also Nagel 1987, 45). Conversely, difficulty of exit fosters voice, if not loyalty.

These generalizations need some refinement under the assumption that political participation exists in both formal and informal terms, since what holds for one type of participation may not hold for the other. For example, under economic crisis, loyalty (and perhaps voice) may dominate in the informal arena, since refusing to cooperate in neighborhood survival efforts may become personally irrational (that is, counterproductive). But formal participation may generate rapid and widespread increases in voice (complaints) and in exit, as citizens reject one party or one incumbent after another in their search for someone who can demonstrate an ability to ameliorate the crisis.[9] In the case of successive failures by different parties and rulers to correct the situation, an extreme exit option (that is, a move to a radical or violent alternative) may grow increasingly attractive to greater numbers of people who see no another option, unless the costs or risks (in the form of reprisals) for becoming loyal to such an alternative are too great.

I return to Hirschman later and examine formal and informal behavior patterns in considerable detail (see chapters 7, 8). But economic changes are not the only cause of changes in individual behavior. A change in political regime types also can bring about changes in individual participation, for at least two reasons. First, democracy allows certain ways of participating (most notably voting) that authoritarianism does not. Second, a new democracy must persuade its citizens to accept and support democratic rules. Authoritarian regimes can, if they must, force compliance, at least over the short run, but democracies must convince the citizens that they have some specific minimum probability of benefiting from democracy itself.

Przeworski (1991) argues that citizens will comply with and support a democratic regime to the extent that they perceive their interests are better met—even if they are on the losing side in a democracy—than their probable gains in some future nondemocracy. A democracy must not only provide a higher minimum welfare "floor," it must also provide the possibility of a higher ceiling, meaning that citizens can have "real opportunities to improve their material welfare" (32). But such gains are never automatic or guaranteed; a transition to democracy means at heart that political actors must be willing to accept "organized uncertainty" (13). Democracy may allow individual players to decide how they will act and to understand the rules of the game, but the outcome of a particular contest is never assured. When uncertainty arises in the economic sphere

reasons for personal
changes of behavior
— economic
— regime – political

it may increase uncertainty in the political sphere as well, not only in terms of the outcome of a specific election but also in terms of how enduring support for democracy itself may be (see below).

As an illustration of the minimum welfare floor that a democracy putatively provides, Przeworski (1991) claims that one thing a democracy can do is provide its citizens "security from violence" (31). In some ways such a claim is true, or it should be; citizens in a democracy should not fear arbitrary arrest or disappearance in the same way they might under authoritarian rule. But consider the case of a democratic nation in which a violent insurgency seeks power through intimidation. "Security from violence" in such circumstances may be difficult for a democratic regime to ensure—as administrations in Peru found out the hard way throughout the 1980s as they confronted the Shining Path.

Both Simon and Przeworski are useful to describe and explain rational behavior for poor citizens in a political system undergoing fundamental changes across time. Simon's rational actor bases his behavior in general on limited knowledge, on external circumstances, and on his subjective perception of the political system. Przeworski becomes relevant when he notes that a democratic transition, if it is to succeed, generates certain specific external circumstances and requirements. These include accepting organized uncertainty and new rules for formal involvement in the political game.

Lower-class citizens may accept these requirements (individual constraints, system uncertainty) in part because of their belief or hope that a democratic system offers opportunities for advancement in material welfare. The poor can thus be said to behave rationally in a democracy if they accept uncertainty and comply with formal rules—but only up to a point. This point is precisely the threshold where material welfare floors collapse (or, in the terminology used earlier, where the welfare-preference dimension outweighs the democracy-preference dimension). At such a point, poverty equates with survival and rational behavior becomes redefined and redrawn.

RATIONALITY AND FORMAL AND INFORMAL BEHAVIOR

I need to distinguish between rationality in the formal political arena and rationality in the informal political arena. In the formal arena, the poor in Peru do not have to decide whether it is rational to vote: given mandatory voting, it is clearly rational to vote and most individuals do. What constitutes a rational choice of whom to vote for is a totally different matter. A first general prediction based on well-established democracies—for example, that voters employ a rationality principle by supporting the party that does a better job of managing the economy—may not take us very far. A study such as Hibbs (1982) (which Simon praises for its finding that "voters evaluate the cumulative performance of the governing party relative to the prior performance of the current opposition" (259) assumes a well-institutionalized democracy with a stable party system that gives voters a chance to make comparisons across time.

Yet in many countries, and certainly in Peru during the time in question, at least two developments obviate transferring or even testing such a conclusion. First, Peru had a multiparty system when democracy was reestablished in 1980. But only one of those parties had ever held the presidency, and it had been overthrown by the military twelve years earlier. This fact alone means that voters had no way of judging prior performance. Second, as the decade proceeded and as one party succeeded another (no party won back-to-back presidential races), low-income citizens in particular rejected one party after another. In effect, as Lima's voters became enmeshed in worsening economic conditions, candidates and parties that had earlier held office became unacceptable. It became irrational to vote for anyone who had already held office, since they had all demonstrated their inability to resolve the nation's problems. In the formal arena, therefore, constant vote-switching became rational, and voters rejected one candidate, party, and ideology after another.

Formal participation (voting) is in many ways only an indirect reflection of political rationality, however, since in casting a vote an individual citizen has no immediate hope of influencing policy or of providing his neighborhood with something it may need. It is in the informal arena that rational behavior becomes more clearly manifest. By definition, informal political participation involves individual and collective efforts to supply public goods, at times through a favorable distribution of state resources. Such behavior is inherently and unabashedly instrumental and coincides with Bryan Roberts's observation that "participation . . . depends on people feeling that they have reason to participate" (1995, 186).

This being the case, informal behavior (whether individual or in the aggregate) becomes a highly sensitive indicator of what the poor perceive to be rational, since much of what constitutes informal behavior comes directly from the poor and their communities and is not scripted or imposed from without. As the poor create their own political structures and modes of informal participation, these structures and modes can be assumed to be rational expenditures of time and resources, or else they would never come into existence in the first place. That such participatory structures (local neighborhood nonpartisan associations, soup kitchens, women's associations, sports clubs, cooperatives) vary over time and from one neighborhood to another simply indicates that rational behavior may be influenced by micro neighborhood factors as well as national contexts.

These and other arguments will be examined throughout the course of this book. The underlying point is that the urban poor operate under a variety of conditions over which they have little or no control. These conditions place severe limitations and constraints on them. The actions of such people are clearly (as Simon might say) "subjectively rational" and can only be understood by taking into account multiple contexts as well as multiple goals. For instance, an ultimate or ideal goal for the poor might be to eliminate the limitations and constraints that keep them poor. But their realistic goals and daily imperatives more likely involve enhancing survival chances, reducing entropy (that is, increasing control over one's life), and lessening the threat of daily material precariousness and uncertainty (Eckstein 1992, 392–93). Just how Lima's poor have participated politically to increase the probability of survival, control, and certainty over a twenty-year period is the stuff of this study.

STRUCTURAL CONSTRAINTS AND RATIONAL BEHAVIOR

Relatively little attention has been paid to how poverty defines or constrains rational behavior for poor individuals, either in the United States or in Third World settings. Indeed, not much is known about the effects of economic stress on the political behaviors of the poor (Cohen and Dawson 1993, 286). But assuming that a lower-class individual has certain goals or needs in mind, how will this individual act in circumstances where alternatives are present, but perhaps severely limited, and where choices (often limited or only minimally satisfying) can or must be made (Popkin 1979, 30–31)?

Some definitions of rationality dictate that people act exclusively in their own self-interests, that is, purely in one's own material well-being and welfare. Yet, Lima's urban poor quite clearly care not only about themselves but also about their families, their immediate physical surroundings, their friends and relatives, their city, and their country. Overall, the urban poor decide to become involved in politics primarily when their direct involvement (through informal, collaborative, or petitioning modes, for example) or their indirect involvement (through formal, electoral modes) has a reasonable chance of providing needed collective goods or of influencing the selection of officials whose public policy decisions might be beneficial in providing such goods. Both formal and informal instrumental political participation are thus aimed at facilitating or improving Przeworski's (1991) "specific minimum probability" that they will benefit materially and otherwise from democracy.

Innumerable factors (macroeconomic conditions, poverty, policies of the state, relations between the state and civil society) all create the objective situations or contexts in which the urban poor live and make decisions about participating. Yet despite the frequently overwhelming presence of such powerful macro forces, a lower-class citizen clearly makes the final decision about whether and how to become involved in informal neighborhood activities, or whether and how and for whom to vote. Informal involvement—deciding to attend a local neighborhood meeting, to contribute physical labor toward the construction of a community center or the installation of a water system, or to petition a government bureaucracy for assistance—has both benefits (the acquisition of goods or a service) and costs (time, money, the possibility of not obtaining a needed good). An individual will weigh the advantages and disadvantages in determining whether and how to participate in such political activities. Formal involvement—deciding whom to vote for or whether to become involved in partisan activities—is an autonomous decision.

It is clear that, for both informal and formal participation, the individual lower-class citizen does not control many of the crucial factors defining Simon's subjective context, in which "rational" decisions are made about whether to participate and how to do so. Four such factors of a priori primordial importance to the urban poor include macrolevel economic conditions, the presence and intensity of poverty, the nature of the state, and relations between the state and its civil society. As these four factors change and interact, two levels of the urban setting act as filters and as mediating devices for the four macro factors. The city at large is affected by these macro factors, but it also affects the individual neighborhood where its poor inhabitants live. Likewise, the local neighborhood and its specific profile of physical needs affects the political behavior of the poor, whose behavior can rebound back up and affect one or more of these several levels of analysis.

STRUCTURATION AND URBAN PRAXIS

Although these four macro and two intermediate factors are viewed as essential for understanding political participation, they do not determine—in some lockstep fashion—political participation among the urban poor or among any other group or social class. These factors and levels influence, filter, mediate, intensify, and constrain behavior but they do not predictably determine it. Ultimately, one by one, individuals decide whom they are going to vote for, whether and how to become involved in campaigns or party activities, when and if to cooperate in community affairs, how to petition government officials. Macro factors may generate, increase, or decrease feelings of inclusion or alienation, of satisfaction or discontent, of being radical, liberal, conservative, or reactionary, but such factors absolutely do not dictate how individuals will behave in response to such feelings and perceptions.

In this sense I agree with the basic arguments found in "structuration" theory (Gilbert and Gugler 1992; Giddens 1984) as well as in "urban praxis" theory. Both these schools of thought counter the overly deterministic nature of neo-Marxist structural analysis (Harvey 1973, 1978; Smith and Tardanico 1987). Structuration theory accepts "the possibility of change within broad structural constraints. Human agency can modify society even when the odds are against it. Hence [for example] social movements may spring up against dictatorships and transform the way that the state acts" (Gilbert and Gugler 1992, 3).

In somewhat similar fashion, urban praxis theory argues for a duality of social structure and human agency. This notion of duality directs attention not only to structural constraints but also to structural opportunities, implying that urban "social structures are simultaneously outcomes and channels of human consciousness and praxis" (Smith and Tardanico 1987, 89). In particular, Castells's treatment of subordinate groups in Third World urban settings calls for incorporating the roles of consciousness and of social action for changing the circumstances of daily urban life (Castells 1983; Smith and Tardanico 1987, 96–98). Castells also identifies three additional dimensions of urban life—cultural, sociospatial, and political—that act as three axes of social conflict or at least as potential flash points between state and society. Whether Castells is correct in all respects here is less important than how his arguments and the basic structuration argument coincide: purely structural analysis is overly deterministic, individual actors make their own decisions, and their decisions affect their surrounding and contexts, just as these surroundings affect them.[10]

The overall perception adopted here of the urban poor and of their political behavior is quite congenial with the ideas of structuration and urban praxis. Individual lower-class citizens are influenced by several macro factors (the economy, poverty, the state, and state–civil society relations), which in turn take on specific forms within an urban context. The lower-class individual per se has, of course, little or no direct control over such factors.[11]

Precisely how these factors influence the individual citizen is not predetermined, meaning that what constitutes a rational response to these factors depends on the individual. Some general hypotheses about the effect of macro factors on individual behavior are suggested throughout chapter 2 and form the basis for much of the analysis in chapters 6–8. Thanks to the longitudinal nature of the data, the change of regimes from authoritarian to civilian, and the onset of economic crisis, in this study hypothesis-generation and hypothesis-testing are not confined to a single point in time. On the contrary, it becomes possible to test hypotheses about how political participation is affected by changes in regime types, by good and bad economic times, by increased intensity of poverty, and by changes in the nature of the state and of state-society relations. In parallel fashion, it also becomes possible to examine hypotheses about the specific influence of these dynamics on the urban setting, in general, and on the effects of age and internal development within neighborhoods, in particular. Carrying out such an investigation means having a framework that specifies the linkages between and among these several variables, contexts, and levels of analysis. I would now like to propose such a model, to clarify these relationships and set the stage for the rest of the book.

about study
changing
aspects

2

MACROLEVEL

CONTEXTS AND

PARTICIPATION

An Analytic Model

THE FOUR MACROLEVEL factors that, a priori, can be assumed to influence the behavior of Lima's urban poor over time are as follows: (1) macroeconomic conditions, (2) the presence and intensity of poverty, (3) the Peruvian state, and (4) state–civil society relations. In addition, two other factors—metropolitan Lima itself and its individual neighborhoods—act as filters or lenses to focus the impacts of these four macro variables in a specific fashion. The four macrolevel factors are obviously interrelated, and one purpose of the model offered here is to identify such interrelationships. But treating each one separately also has advantages; certain data illuminate different aspects of the four variables and of their interrelationships.

Of the four macro factors, the first two (economic conditions and poverty) are largely structural in nature, whereas the other two (the state and state–civil society relations) are more interactional. Each of these factors is substantively described in terms of the Peruvian case in chapter 3; how each affects the others and especially how each affects microlevel political participation make up major themes that appear throughout the book. The point of treating them briefly here is to indicate, in general and hypothetical terms, how these macrolevel factors might influence political behavior.

Although I examine the impact of all four of these macro variables on behavior, I pay special attention to the question of state–civil society relations and how the urban poor have—through informal activities—influenced and in fact created Peru's urban civil society. If civil society is "the space of uncoerced human association and also the set of relational networks—formed for the sake of family, faith, interest, and ideology—that fills this space" (Walzer 1995, 153), and if such uncoerced human association is assumed to be essential for the development and sustainability of democracy, then identifying the patterns of informal participation created and followed by the urban poor is critical for understanding the nature of Peruvian civil society during the period in question. It is for this reason that I give civil society particular notice throughout the book.

Inequality, Distribution, and Political Behavior

One macrolevel economic phenomenon common in Third World nations is a high degree of income inequality. Many developmental economists have examined the effects of inequality on overall development; fewer have speculated about the political effects of inequality. Compared with much of the rest of the Third World, Latin America is relatively well-off, especially when compared to sub-Saharan Africa, for example, where poverty in absolute terms is far greater. But although Latin America might not make the headlines because of mass starvation, as a region it has the unenviable reputation of having one of the most skewed income distributions in the world. And within Latin America, Peru and Brazil rank as having the region's widest gaps between the wealthy and the poor.[1]

A capitalist nation can generate inequality while its political system proclaims equality (Dahl 1971, 78–80). This contradiction can be resolved in a developed, wealthy nation by removing certain goods and services from the market and distributing them to the society in the form of rights both political (freedom of expression, the right to elect and to be elected) and economic (unemployment insurance, access to education and basic health care). These rights place a putative limit or threshold on the level of poverty and inequality in society, thereby protecting against too great a gap between the rich and the poor. The democratic system distributes these rights by assigning part of its resources to the production of public goods and services (Figueroa 1995, 68–69; Okun 1975).

In an underdeveloped capitalist society, however, the amount of income to be distributed within the society is less (in aggregate as well as in per capita terms), the resources available to the state are less, and the distribution of income tends to be much more uneven. Therefore, the economic rights package is more limited, both in resources available and in the scope of distribution of those resources. The *expectations* for such rights may be high, though, because the demand for public goods and services is high (from the overall poverty in the society) and because a democratic system by its very nature promises such goods and services. Such a set of circumstances can, under certain conditions, produce distributive disequilibrium or instability in both political and economic terms. As Sachs (1990) puts it, "a high level of social conflict, rooted in high income inequality, contributes to weak political institutions and a rapid turnover of governments" (11).

According to many neoclassical economists, one possible response to this instability is the populist response whereby "high income inequality . . . contributes to intense political pressure to use macroeconomic policies to raise the incomes of lower-income groups" (Sachs 1990, 68). Dornbusch and Edwards (1991, 1–2) argue for the existence of what they consider a definable pattern of populist macroeconomics in Latin America. They claim that populist regimes in Latin America have in general tried to deal with income inequality problems through the use of overly expansive macroeconomic policies, and that these policies result in major macroeconomic crises that have ended up hurting the poorer segments of society, such that real wages are lower at the end of the populist cycle than they were at the beginning.[2] During 1970–1990, Peru went through two such cycles, first under Generals Velasco and Morales Bermudez (1968–1980) and then again more disastrously under President Alán García (1985–1990).

Thus the first two macrolevel variables I utilize here (economic conditions and poverty) have been the subject of much discussion by developmental economists and political scientists. But many studies of the social impacts of economic populism use purely macrolevel aggregate data (Lago 1991). My study employs additional data that bring in the Peruvian state and state–civil society relations; these data, along with the survey results, describe and analyze microlevel behavior of the urban poor during the two cycles of macroeconomic populism in Peru. Chapters 3, 4, and 5 spell out the impacts of these cycles for the nation of Peru, for Lima, its capital, and for certain of Lima's districts. Chapters 6–8 then examine how the urban poor—putatively one of the major target groups or beneficiaries of populist macroeconomic policies—behaved and reacted *politically* as these populist cycles ran their course. What follows here is a general discussion of these four variables and how each affects political participation.

1. Macroeconomic Crisis

A severe and prolonged economic crisis spells difficulties for any political system —Third World or developed, capitalist or socialist, democratic or authoritarian. In Third World countries, multiple indicators of economic crisis are available. They include runaway inflation, loss of purchasing power, currency devaluation, difficulties in maintaining international creditworthiness because of foreign debt repayment problems, insufficient international reserves, pressures to undertake structural readjustments through austerity budgets, declining governmental revenues, and decreasing state capacity to deliver minimal services.

During the 1970s, most Latin American nations had military governments, but these authoritarian systems chose different economic policies and strategies. Chile in 1973–1989 opted for a dramatic neoliberal free market economy; Brazil in 1964–1989 concentrated on economic growth; and Argentina in 1966–1973 and again in 1976–1983 tried a variety of options, none for any extended period of time. All three of these authoritarian governments instituted severe limitations on human rights. Peru was a notable exception to all of these policies. The Velasco regime experimented with redistributive, reformist, state-led policies, and its human rights abuses were remarkably light. But by the 1980s, all these military regimes were suffering from one combination or other of the several economic maladies mentioned above, and all of them opted (through widely different means) to reestablish civilian rule.

These military regimes had predicated their assumptions of power on promises that they could do better than their civilian counterparts. All of them (with the possible exception of Chile) demonstrated that they could not. In the specific case of Peru, the military's reach far exceeded its grasp; promises to redistribute land, to build infrastructure, to reform education, and to mobilize the populace all ran headlong into a lack of capital, of trained personnel, and of the capacity to meet long-standing needs, let alone keep new promises.

Peru underwent as severe and difficult economic times during the 1970s and then again in the 1980s as any country in Latin America or the world. The populist regime of General Juan Velasco Alvarado (1968–1975) attempted to push economic growth through a massive infusion of state capital and the creation of large state-owned enterprises. But by the end of the military regime (specifically the 1975–1980 administration of General Francisco Morales Bermudez), Peru began to undergo economic crisis, and low-income urban groups suffered in an especially acute way.

The repercussions of populist economic problems are micro as well as macro.

Rising levels of unemployment and underemployment generate, maintain, and accentuate poverty by reducing income, compelling additional members of a household to work, preventing children from attending or advancing in school, and by cutting back on nonessential expenses, which for very low-income groups can eventually come to mean virtually anything other than food. For Lima's lower classes especially, but by no means exclusively, as the state lost its capacity to generate—let alone distribute—material resources, informal solutions became ever more frequent to problems such as employment (the growth of the urban informal sector), housing (the spread of self-help housing and squatter settlements), and simple survival (the creation of neighborhood soup kitchens).

ECONOMIC CRISIS AND POLITICAL PARTICIPATION

Under macroeconomic crisis, the urban poor may continue to participate in the formal political arena (by voting, for example), although precisely which patterns of participation may develop is an empirical question. Various hypotheses are possible. If conditions deteriorate sufficiently, abstention and casting blank ballots as protest may increase, for example. Or vote-switching may become more prevalent, in perhaps two ways: first, by switching support from one party or candidate to another across different elections for the same office (from one presidential election to another, for example); and second, by switching support across elections for different offices (voting one way for the presidency and another for mayor), a pattern roughly akin to ticket-splitting. Informally, involvement in individual activities (taking on extra work, or joining a protest movement) or in communal coping strategies (forming or utilizing soup kitchens) may become more notable, since such activities are rational expenditures of time and energy for low-income individuals whose resources are under constant erosion.

Whatever the specific results, sustained economic crisis makes itself felt in both formal and informal participatory arenas. Ways of participating may disappear, coalesce, or take on entirely new guises or modes as individuals decide each day how to allocate their decreasing resources of money, time, and energy. In Third World cities, poverty acts as a constant presence in this decision-making process, even though the degree or intensity of poverty may vary over time.

2. Poverty

Poverty 2 faces- macro → + indiv.

Endemic poverty in Third World nations has at least two faces: macro and individual. Macro poverty is in general characterized by a lack of resources, inadequate distribution of those resources, long-standing inequities frequently caused or reinforced by racial, ethnic, cultural, and social norms of that society, and an economic system that exploits the poor in order to support the wealthy. The state itself may not have the material resources (taxes), capacity, or political will, because of pressures from elites to maintain the status quo.

Individuals who are poor have, of course, their own characteristics. Their low or inadequate income limits their access not only to the market economy and its consumer goods but also to such things as private sector medical care or education. In addition, the poor do not have access (or at least equal access) to the state and its resources. Politically speaking, the poor do not have the same access to information or to the inner workings of the political system. Moreover, political parties pay little attention to the poor except at election time, and then only to seek their votes. The poor are more likely to be isolated from the formal political process and are more apt to use informal mechanisms to confront their most immediate individual and collective problems. The poor also suffer from significant constraints or bounds on their abilities to accumulate resources.

Both macro- and microendemic poverty are intensified by economic crisis, but just how "normal" or "intense" poverty affects individual political participation remains the subject of much debate and speculation. Although poverty doubtless colors political behavior, general agreement exists that poverty by and of itself is not automatically destabilizing. Beyond that point lies much controversy (Nelson 1979).

Two major schools of thought view the relationship between poverty and political behavior in sharply divergent ways. Relative deprivation theory (Gurr 1970) posits that a significant or widening gap between people's aspirations and achievement can produce instability. Rational action theory (Muller 1980; Muller and Opp 1986; Muller, Dietz, and Finkel 1991) argues that political action (especially illegal action) depends upon an individual's discerning that the cost of participating in such actions outweighs the costs of not participating.

For low-income urban groups to whom poverty is a modus vivendi, predicting what sorts of behavior macroeconomic crises will provoke is problematic. A crisis may well serve to widen the gap between aspirations and achievement through inflation and price increases, but deprivation does not automatically or necessarily lead to frustration, alienation, or protest behavior. In like fashion, economic crisis may spur some previously passive individuals to participate in politics, perhaps in protest mobilizations or in radical movements, but the costs of such involvement include not only the potential of repression by the state but also the extra time, money, and energy that such involvement requires, resources that become especially scarce among the poor during times of crisis.

POVERTY AND POLITICAL PARTICIPATION

All of this is to say that endemic poverty exerts a dominant contextual effect for citizens who are caught up in it. It acts as a severe and ever-present constraint; it also forces the poor to consider political participation from a highly instrumental point of view, since for such people political involvement (especially involvement beyond simply voting) is something of a luxury, to be undertaken only if there is a reasonably good chance of a material payoff. Political participation for its own sake is, for most poor people, an activity that simply does not make sense. Under conditions of endemic poverty, formal participation goes on because the law requires it, and because voting and related activities do make up one general means of trying to influence the choices of governmental personnel and the choices made by them. Under poverty, informal participation goes on because it constitutes one of few means by which the poor can directly ask for assistance. It can also generate and use intraneighborhood resources for direct benefit.

If poverty becomes increasingly acute over time, several results are possible. Levels of formal participation might diminish as the poor see no reason to vote or see no candidate capable of addressing their needs. Or formal participation might increase as candidates and parties try to use the massive numbers of poor in order to be elected. Informally, participation might increase or become more multifaceted as state assistance becomes increasingly unlikely. On the other hand, informal activities might fall off as individuals use all available time for survival. (These are empirically testable hypotheses to be addressed later.)

3. The State

Without worrying too much about a precise definition, I view the state institutionally and instrumentally as an organization that enforces regulations, at least in part through its monopoly on violence. Rueschemeyer, Stephens, and Stephens (1992, 6, 63) employ a similar definition. The state consists of the set of organizations involved in making and implementing binding collective decisions, if necessary by force. Harking back to Weber, the state is an administrative and legal order with binding authority over the area of its jurisdiction. The greater its capacity to act on its environment (social as well as physical) and to impose its own collective goals, the greater the development and sophistication of the state (Badie and Birnbaum 1983, 35; Migdal 1988; Huntington 1968). Viewed in this fashion, any state can be judged (and also compared with another state) by its ability to manipulate certain instrumentalities to make its actions effective.

If the state is a concrete entity or collection of entities that attempts to impose its will upon a defined territory and populace, the effectiveness or efficacy of that state can be measured by its abilities to reach into the lives of its citizens and to make a difference therein, to create and maintain social and political order, and to deliver certain expected or promised goods and resources (material or otherwise) that it distributionally controls. These characteristics—its ability to order society, to penetrate into and to respond to that society, and to distribute within that society—all combine to provide a means for determining the degree to which an organization or cluster of organizations should or can in fact be labeled a state. It might well be that within a specific nation at a particular point in its history, the state therein operates as such for only a portion of its members, while for other members the state and its components are tangential, marginal, or irrelevant.

Such considerations become especially appropriate when dealing with low-income groups whose welfare or survival can depend heavily upon the capacity or willingness of the state to deliver material goods and services. But state capacity and efficacy are ipso facto conditioned by several factors. Two of the most important are (1) the macroeconomic processes described above and (2) the formal duties given to it by the administration or regime in power. If either or both of these change, then the capacity of the state will change as well. Between 1970 and 1990, the Peruvian state underwent change not only because of deteriorating economic conditions but also because of the shift from an authoritarian to a civilian regime in 1980. Since it is virtually an article of faith that a civilian regime must be (because it is expected to be) responsive to demands and stimuli from its society, a civilian government that replaces a military one during deteriorating economic conditions faces a severe test indeed.

THE STATE AND POLITICAL PARTICIPATION

As a regulatory entity, the state has an important if not absolute voice in how political participation will be defined. All regimes, whether authoritarian or civilian, define what sorts of participatory activities can take place. Whether a state can enforce its rules is a very different question. A weak state that promulgates rules governing political involvement may be obeyed only to the degree that its citizens wish to obey, especially if those citizens perceive that the state's ability to implement sanctions is minimal.

In parallel but broader fashion, a state's ability to control economic activity depends upon its capacities to convince its citizens that obeying its rules (paying taxes, for example) is worthwhile. If an economy persists in a state of crisis, or if a state cannot provide sufficient reason—through the delivery or distribution of valued goods and services, for example—for its citizens (especially the poor ones) to conform to its rules, then an increasing gap may develop between what the state can control (the formal economy and its members) and what it cannot (the informal). If enough people either vote only to avoid state sanctions or refuse to vote as a protest, or if a sizable percentage of the labor force is employed in informal, extralegal, and uncontrolled activity, then the state may, from the citizen's perspective, lose its raison d'être. Political participation and its regulation by the state are thus not givens in poor societies, especially for groups in such societies as are themselves poor. Participation and its guises and modes are then much more fluid, a fact that contributes not only to unpredictable individual behavior but also to macropolitical instability.

4. The State and Civil Society

Two principal reasons, one substantive and one theoretical, make state–civil society relations a major theme of this study. For the first, Lima's poor throughout the period 1970–1990 organized themselves to generate, provide, petition for, or demand certain basic collective goods for their neighborhoods. Since civil society consists of voluntary associational life, I return repeatedly to how the poor organized and mobilized themselves and responded to efforts by the state to mobilize them over the two decades in question. For the second, most scholars posit the development of a civil society as a crucial component for democratization. Civil society is generally defined as the independent self-organization of society, the constituent parts of which voluntarily engage in public activity to pursue individual, group, or national interests within the context of a legally defined state–civil society relationship (Lipset 1994; Hadenius and Uggla 1996).

Diamond (1994) enumerates several components of civil society, and among them is the claim that civil society is "bound by a legal order of shared rules" (5). But in many Third World settings, states simply may be unable to impose a legal framework, especially on the masses. As a result, lower-class civil society may in fact be highly organized—but this in spite of or in the absence of (and not because of or thanks to) any efforts by the state to impose any legal order of shared rules or to dictate organizational criteria.[3]

Thus something of a paradox emerges. Civil society exists in part because citizens organize themselves to protect against unwanted encroachments by the state. Yet at the same time, the several interests and goals of such organizations dictate that civil society will attempt to influence the state's policies and its allocation of valued resources.

Relations between a state and its poor citizens depend upon a multitude of factors. Those of special interest here are the economy and the viability of the state itself as an entity. Especially for low-income groups, the performance of the economy will color relations with, and perceptions and evaluations of, the state. On a short-term basis, citizens may blame a particular administration (whether authoritarian or civilian) if macroeconomic conditions are unsatisfactory or if their own economic circumstances are deteriorating. But if citizen petitions generated by economic crisis and directed toward state agencies go unresolved, then dissatisfaction may not be limited to an administration but may instead be generalized to the state or to the political system as a whole.

In parallel fashion (and regardless of economic conditions), if citizens conclude that the basic functions of the state do not work, then the legitimacy of the state may erode, resulting in a civil society whose members view the state as largely useless or irrelevant to its needs, and therefore as something to be avoided. Examples might include the inability of the state to guarantee basic human rights or justice, or to maintain itself free from corruption. Such a perception could also lead to decreasing levels of system support and hence to macrolevel political instability. I return to these and related questions throughout the book. Suffice it to say that a vigorous associational life can support and aid a state but can also exist independent of or in opposition to that same state and its policies, if that state and its policies are perceived as irrelevant or harmful.

STATE–CIVIL SOCIETY RELATIONS
AND POLITICAL PARTICIPATION

If a nation reaches the point where economic crisis has demonstrated to a large percentage of its citizens that the state has become irrelevant (or worse), several different types of political activity may result. Under authoritarianism, citizens frequently undertake mass mobilization to demonstrate their dissatisfaction with specific policies, or with authoritarianism per se. Under civilian rule, a wider variety of manifestations can occur. Electorally, incumbent defeats may take place as opposition parties emerge or strengthen. Voting patterns may reflect increasing polarization because of urban-rural, class, or ethnic, linguistic, religious, or cultural divisions. Informally, if state mechanisms prove ineffective, the poor may retreat to their own neighborhood groups and organizations. Extremist groups may make an appeal to individuals for whom the state has lost all credibility and for whom the electoral process no longer has any legitimacy.

This last point deserves some special mention in the case of Peru. Every country has entities other than the state that exert influence over any one or all four of the factors examined here. These groups can range from labor unions to grassroots social movements, religious movements, or radical political parties and insurgent groups. In the Peruvian case the specific group that must be taken into account is Sendero Luminoso (the Shining Path), whose violent campaign against Peru's political, social, and economic infrastructure started in 1980, just as civilian rule was reestablished. The combination of an extended economic crisis, the deterioration of the Peruvian state, and the presence of the Shining Path made daily life in Peru in the mid- and late 1980s more difficult than it had been at any other time during the twentieth century (and probably since Peru's defeat in the War of the Pacific during 1879–1883).

As would any entrenched, violent, uncompromising revolutionary movement, the Shining Path influenced all of the factors identified here. It exacerbated Peru's economic crisis through bombings and other destructive acts; it forced the state to expend scarce resources for military and intelligence operations; it created an image of the state (frequently deserved) as being unable to control its military and as uncaring about human rights. It increased state–civil society tensions through intimidation, threats, and fear; it focused much of its recruitment efforts and intimidation on the poor, especially the rural poor at the outset of the 1980s, but more and more on Lima as the 1990s approached. And it influenced political participation by its campaigns of subverting the electoral process, through assassinations of candidates and officeholders and through threats against voters.[4]

The Shining Path is not the subject of this book, and it does not occupy a central place. Yet its high salience during the 1980s requires that it be acknowledged as a major political actor and that its impact on all of Peruvian life be taken into account. When a group such as the Shining Path can affect a nation's overall macro economy and its level and intensity of poverty, along with the state itself and the nature of the relations between the state and the society at large, then the political behavior of that nation's poor will necessarily be affected, at least indirectly. In addition to its indirect effects, the Shining Path made every attempt throughout the 1980s to threaten, intimidate, and recruit among the poor as well as to disrupt the electoral process. How all of these efforts affected Lima's low-income groups will be a theme throughout the book, although not a central concern.

The Urban Setting and Political Participation

There is one final factor, and this is physical location. An urban setting by and of itself influences political behavior in a variety of ways, especially when the setting is the capital, primate city of a Third World country. Following the end of World War II, most Latin American and Third World cities found themselves the targets of large-scale cityward migration, a phenomenon that not only produced rapid population growth but an exploding demand for services such as jobs, housing, transportation, and physical infrastructure. Such services might not be essential in rural areas, but in an urban setting, low-income inhabitants —migrants or otherwise—came to expect such services and to react in politically sensitive ways if they were not delivered. The sheer numbers and densities of urban populaces made them especially amenable to urban political stimuli (either self-generated or generated by external actors such as individual leaders, political parties, labor unions), with the result that many of these services became politicized. People began to expect the state to deliver them *(services)* and to blame the state if it did not do so.

Post–World War II Latin American cities thus became vastly heterogeneous. Yet they were frequently divided—either because of legal boundaries or because of income, class, or ethnic cleavages—into rather homogeneous districts or enclaves. Such discrimination did not, however, necessarily produce large-scale predictable patterns of voting. In particular, sometimes dire predictions that the urban poor would automatically support leftist parties or populist candidates were not borne out (Dietz 1985).

In the 1980s, however, the economic crisis of the decade created increasingly difficult conditions and intensified the breadth and intensity of poverty in Latin America's major cities. As a result, at least in part, class-based (or at least socioeconomic-status-based) voting in Latin American cities sometimes became more evident, as did incumbent defeats. In addition to these changes in formal behavior, informal participation in efforts to provide local survival mechanisms such as soup kitchens also became more common. Economic crisis, especially because of high levels of unemployment and underemployment in the formal private sector economy, can affect the entire urban environment by generating a large informal urban sector or economy, whose manifestations include increasing numbers of people employed in informal occupations such as street vending, housed in informal dwellings such as squatter settlements and shantytowns, and transported by informal transportation networks such as extralegal bus lines and pirate taxis (de Soto 1986; Carbonetto et al. 1988; Toledo and Chanlat 1991).

The basic point here is that the urban setting influences how these processes and structures affect the urban populace. An economic crisis affects city dwellers, but this crisis takes on certain specific forms in a city, as does poverty. Likewise, the state affects city dwellers, but the state also operates under constraints established by that city, as do state–civil society relations. I therefore view Lima as a filter, as an agent that is acted upon by macrolevel factors, which in turn acts upon these factors to give them a specifically urban (and a more specifically *limeño*) flavor.

It must also be underscored that, within a city, local neighborhoods develop certain marked characteristics that further influence and shape the general urban environment. I used a specific cluster of such neighborhood-level variables to select the six barrios or communities used in the four surveys. These variables were (1) the age of the neighborhood; (2) the original manner of formation of the community; and (3) the overall development of the community, which in turn is made up of four components: (a) the materials used in the construction of the majority of the neighborhood's dwellings, (b) the overall population density of the settlement, (c) the type of terrain on which the community is located, and (d) the internal cohesion within the community. This last item (d) in turn includes such factors as the level or intensity of conflict within the community, the efficacy of the local association, and the success of communitywide activities. All these factors were taken into account for the selection of the survey sites because of their putative impacts on the community and on the political participation of their inhabitants.

Despite this lengthy list of factors, variables, and multilevel contexts, perhaps it bears underlining once again that the soul of this book concerns the political participation of the urban poor. Macrolevel factors such as economic crises, poverty, the state, and state–civil society relations are all assumed to affect micro participation, as does the presence of a group such as the Shining Path and the fact that the individuals under discussion constitute *urban* poor and not rural poor. In addition, the fact that these low-income individuals inhabit specific neighborhoods with specific characteristics in the specific city of Lima is also assumed to be relevant. Finally, it is assumed that all these factors are individually perceived, experienced, and interpreted by the urban poor, and that they

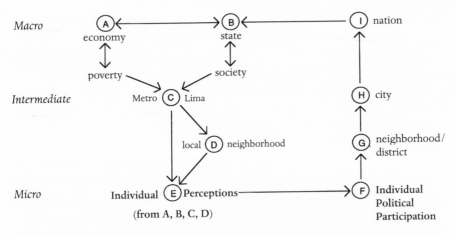

Figure 1. A Multilevel Model of Individual Political Participation

themselves as human beings play major roles in the rational decision of whether and how to participate in politics. Describing, analyzing, and understanding political participation thus remains the goal; other factors are important as they affect participation, not as subjects of inquiry by themselves.

A Model for Examining Political Participation

It would now perhaps be worthwhile to put the various aspects of this discussion into diagrammatic form. Figure 1 indicates the linkages between the several macro and micro factors identified above. Tracing these through will not only clarify the book's general arguments and structure but will also permit the generation of several specific propositions and hypotheses, as well as some initial discussion of the sorts of empirical indicators and data sources that will be utilized for these factors and their interrelationships.[5]

POINT A

Point A indicates the presence of the two fundamental macrolevel processes identified as affecting political participation: economic development (especially economic deterioration and crisis) and endemic poverty (understood here as a macrolevel societal phenomenon). These two processes are obviously interrelated. Data include a wide range of macro indicators concerning economic performance and poverty: inflation, cost of living, unemployment, underemployment, incidence of informality, minimum wage, the gap between wealthy and poor, percentage of household income spent on food, infant mortality, communicable disease incidence.

POINT B

Point B indicates the macrostructural factors assumed to influence participation: the state (which includes its formal rules and its capacities, and their limitations, to affect the distribution of valued goods and services) and the specific regimes that govern and regulate the state. Point B also includes the relations between the state and civil society. These two components of Point B are reciprocally influential, as are Points A and B. Indicators include tax revenues, percentage of citizens paying taxes, budget expenditures for social welfare programs, urban infrastructure, public health, goods and services delivered to low-income districts and individuals, and the degree to which needs are met by the state.

POINT C

Point C is the urban setting, specifically Lima, including not only metropolitan Lima but its legal districts. Data of interest include growth of the city in demographic and physical terms, homogeneity of urban districts by social class (income, education, employment, type of housing), and gaps between wealthy and poor districts. Relevant data also include city- and district-level electoral results over time, and specific policies directed at the poor undertaken by city authorities.

POINT D

Lima is legally divided into some forty or so districts, each with formal boundaries and each with highly restricted political and economic power. Each district is composed of dozens of neighborhoods that are frequently informal in nature and that exist more as local reference points than as juridical entities. Nevertheless (and especially for the poor), neighborhoods are important concepts. People identify with their immediate place of residence and are more apt to be influenced by (and to influence) their immediate neighbors (aside from family members and perhaps friends in the workplace) than anyone else. They are also more apt to donate time or money or energy to projects with immediate and local benefit. Data of utility here include neighborhood self-help survival and coping efforts, the perceived and real influence of state-funded programs on local neighborhoods, and the overall makeup and profile of the residents of specific barrios.

POINT E

Point E concerns micro (that is, individual) perceptions of the macro processes at A and B and as filtered and specified through C and D. Individual-level sociodemographic characteristics (age, gender, status as migrant, income, socioeconomic status, and so on) also come into effect at Point E. Data are largely from surveys that elicit information dealing with individual backgrounds, status, politically relevant perceptions, opinions, evaluations, ideological tendencies, views of the neighborhood of residence, perceptions of local and national problems, and similar issues.

POINT F

Point F is the major dependent variable of the entire investigation—political participation in its formal (electoral) and informal (community-based) modes. It is at Point F that the urban poor as individuals make decisions (sketched in the model in chapter 1) concerning the relative preference weightings for democracy as compared to well-being, and where—on the basis of those decisions—they undertake, change, discard, or otherwise modify their political behavior. Data are again from surveys and include electoral behavior over time, evidence of vote-switching, reasons for voting and changing vote over time, membership in politically relevant organizations, involvement in neighborhood affairs, and demand-making addressed to external authorities.

POINTS G AND H

Points G and H, although not a major concern, approximate a kind of feedback loop. If political behavior has an impact on intermediate (G, or the neighborhood and the city) and on macrolevel (H, or national) stability or instability, such stability or instability will in turn affect the state and state–civil society relations. (The Shining Path is not represented schematically but should be understood perhaps more than anything else as a presence. Throughout the 1980s the Shining Path had the ability to influence all the macro and micro variables in the model.)

To reinforce the earlier argument, making political participation the dependent variable does not assume that macro factors determine in some absolute fashion the behavior of individuals. Patterns emerge when individuals are grouped, of course; like individuals will tend to act in like fashion. But all similar individuals do not act in equal fashion. Individuals can and do have the ability to decide rationally how to act, and the collective weight of those individual decisions can and does affect macro factors.

Some Tentative Propositions and Hypotheses

These several points are connected by a variety of linkages, each of which can be described by a proposition or series of propositions and hypotheses:

AB—a macro-macro reciprocal linkage, which assumes that macroeconomic crisis and poverty mutually affect the state and state–civil society relations. AB posits that economic crisis and deepening poverty simultaneously raise needs and expectations and decrease the capacity of the state to meet these increases, thereby diminishing the regulatory and distributional abilities of the state and hence its potential relevance for the citizenry. The same conditions may make neighborhood-generated associational efforts (such as soup kitchens) essential for survival; the existence of such efforts may also highlight the diminished capacity of the state.

AC—a macrointermediate linkage, which assumes that both poverty and macroeconomic crisis affect the general urban environment of Lima and its components. AC posits that, as economic crisis and poverty increase in severity, city-specific needs and expectations (the ability of the city to provide and maintain its infrastructure, for example, to extract resources such as taxes, to deliver scarce goods and services, to regulate effectively daily life) take on ever greater salience as they simultaneously become more difficult to accomplish.

BC—a linkage parallel to AC that focuses on the state and state–civil society relations. BC posits that, as weaknesses induced by AB lead to the increasing inability of the state to deliver goods to local urban authorities, and thus from these local authorities down to the district or neighborhood level, the city itself undergoes physical deterioration and likely becomes the target and arena for various manifestations of discontent from below.

CD—a linkage that concerns the relationship between the larger urban setting and a specific neighborhood. CD assumes that the city at large and a particular residential setting interact with one another. If, for example, the city incorporates or annexes a previously illegal settlement into a legal district of the city proper, then the change in legal status may make new resources—at least potentially—available to this neighborhood that were unavailable earlier. The ways these resources can be obtained may also affect how the inhabitants of this neighborhood behave politically.

CD and DE—linkages that concern the effect on the individual of the urban setting in general, and of a specific neighborhood. CE posits that residence in a city per se has multiple effects on low-income inhabitants: it intensifies economic difficulties and poverty as well as awareness of the state and its programs, and it expands the number and impact of political stimuli that affect individual citizens. DE assumes that residence in a specific neighborhood makes a separate and discernible difference, based on a wide variety of factors that include the perceived needs of the neighborhood as well as its age, its size and physical location and characteristics, and its overall internal development, political as well as physical.

EF—a micro-micro linkage that involves the relationship between individual perceptions and personal characteristics determined at E and their influence on individual political participation, formal as well as informal (F). Presumably, if economic performance sours, poverty intensifies, the state and state–civil society relations lose relevance. If the urban and neighborhood settings themselves exacerbate all such tendencies, then formal (electoral) behavior might reveal voter abstention, vote-switching, incumbent defeats, and ticket-splitting. Informal behavior might be revealed in increased neighborhood-level involvement and in survival behaviors.

FG, FH, FI—linkages between individual political participation and the neighborhood, the urban setting, and the nation. FG argues that the aggregate of individual formal and informal participation affects the immediate residential environment (for example) by obtaining communal goods. FH posits not only that political participation affects who is elected within the city but also that the city's elected officials may be increasingly under pressures from formal and informal participation. FI carries the same argument as FH to the national level. One specific example might be individual voting behaviors identified at Point F and their effect on national political affairs, specifically on political parties and the national party system. Grassroots support for local candidates and political movements may disrupt national parties and their leaders, leading to increased party fluidity and unpredictability.

IB—one final linkage that posits a relationship between macro instability and the state and state-society relations. As instability (unpredictability) increases, the ability of the state to regulate society diminishes. Contrariwise, the possibility increases that political behavior emanating from subordinate groups may bring about change.

Conclusions

Przeworski (1991) argues that democratic transitions should be viewed as transitions to "organized uncertainty." In other words, one of the major problems facing any new democratic system is how to exact or enforce compliance with the new rules of the game, especially since the outcomes of that game are unpredictable. Przeworski's answer is that political actors will comply and cooperate with the new regime's framework if there is some specific minimum probability that benefits will be derived from such compliance and cooperation:

if some important political forces have no chance to win distributional conflicts and if democracy does not improve the material conditions of losers, those who expect to suffer continued deprivation under democratic institutions will turn against them. To evoke compliance and participation, democracy must generate substantive outcomes: It must offer all the relevant political forces real opportunities to improve their material welfare; . . . from the static point of view democratic institutions must be "fair": They must give all of the relevant forces a chance to win from time to time . . . from a dynamic point of view, they must be effective: They must make even losing under democracy more attractive than a future under nondemocratic alternatives. (32–33)

The data in the book allow several of the propositions and hypotheses contained in Przeworski to be tested and perhaps modified. For example, groups or individuals who suffer deprivation under democracy might turn against it, as Przeworski argues. But they might turn against a specific administration rather than against democracy itself. Or they may simply choose to ignore or to circumvent nonfunctioning institutions rather than actively to oppose them. Or again, whether deprived groups do or do not turn against democracy and its institutions may depend on the alternatives available. The presence of a threatening nondemocratic alternative may work toward maintaining compliance and cooperation. The Shining Path in Peru may be such a case; throughout the 1980s it presented itself as a clear alternative to democratic institutions by almost any standard. But it was so extreme that it may have acted to unite the bulk of society (especially the poor) against it, out of fear.

Przeworski's focus on macro factors in the transition to and consolidation of democracy provides a nice balance to Simon's (1985) concentration on micro behavior as results of such factors. If Przeworski is correct, macrolevel uncertainty should be a prime ingredient in the subjective political situation confronted by the urban poor. One immediate problem might emerge: What could happen if Przeworski's inherent political uncertainty, which is a characteristic of the state and of state-society relations, becomes exacerbated by economic crisis and endemic poverty? Such a combination may prove too much uncertainty for both the society at large and for its most disadvantaged members.

The Structure of the Book

The remainder of the book is arranged so as to examine and analyze the arguments developed in chapters 1 and 2. Chapter 3 examines macro developments in Peru from 1970 through 1990 by analyzing macroeconomic problems, changes in the levels and intensities of poverty, and corresponding changes in the state, its policies, and in state–civil society relations. This latter became especially important when the regime changed from authoritarian to democratic in 1980.

Chapter 4 focuses on the political economy of Lima, examining changes in Lima's urban primacy, unemployment and underemployment rates, the many faces of urban informality, the potential for spatial class polarization, and the appearance of coping and survival grassroots mechanisms among the city's poor. Chapter 4 also presents a quick sketch of politics in Peru and Lima during the period under study, including the transition to democracy that occurred from 1978 to 1980, the several elections that took place from 1980 to 1990, and the impact of the Shining Path. The chapter also describes the districts of Lima where the specific research neighborhoods are located.

Chapter 5 concentrates on the six specific low-income research neighborhoods or barrios, and on the changes they underwent from 1970 to 1990. Changes took place in size, density, physical housing, and infrastructure. In addition, chapter 5 presents some of the basic characteristics of the respondents in each of the four survey samples. Chapter 6 is a quantitative analysis of how identifiable modes of participation evolved over the twenty years in question. As authoritarian rule was replaced by democratic procedures, individual citizens had the chance to expand and modify the ways they became involved in the political process. Then as economic crisis appeared, citizens could react both formally and informally as they attempted to confront a worsening situation. Empirically identifying specific modes of participation allows a more precise description of the formal and informal faces of participation.

Chapter 7 looks at two aspects of informal participation in the six barrios over time: grassroots involvement and barrio-state relations. The term *grassroots involvement* refers to how people in the barrios interacted in attempts to provide themselves with needed goods and services that both the authoritarian and the democratic state could or would not provide. The term *barrio-state relations* refers to the avenues and mechanisms used by the barrios to petition for and extract resources from local and national authorities, again under both military and civilian rule. Chapter 7 presents the survey data as well as observational and informant information. Chapter 8 parallels the previous chapter but focuses on formal political participation, using survey data to examine the role of individual-level electoral politics in the 1978–1980 transition and then the changes in electoral political participation from 1980 to 1990, as Peru faced its extended economic crisis as well as the emergence of the Shining Path.

Chapter 9 returns to the theoretical and analytic concerns of chapters 1 and

2 as well as to the scheme presented in chapter 2. It offers some conclusions about how the model helps us understand the contexts of political participation, as well as some reflections on the substantive results concerning Peru that emerge from the data. Finally, the epilogue, chapter 10, presents a brief update concerning politics in Peru since the completion of the last survey (1990) and on the trajectory of formal and informal participation among Lima's poor.

3

·················

THE POLITICAL

ECONOMY

OF PERU

I HAVE JUST PROPOSED a model and a series of hypotheses to show how several national-level macro processes and structures influence both the urban environment and an individual's political participation. The city reacts to national economic deterioration or improvement, and to the spread or reduction of poverty. It also reacts to, and thereby affects, the state's ability to regulate what goes on within the city and to distribute goods and services to the city and those who live in it. Changes in state capacity in turn affect state–civil society relations. I assume that Lima focuses and often intensifies macro events in ways that are distinctly urban, and that this focusing and intensifying undergoes further specifying on the district level.

I use a variety of aggregate data to illuminate how certain districts within Lima and the metropolitan city as a whole were affected by macroeconomic crisis, increases in the extent and intensity of poverty, and a decline in state capacity during the period of this study, 1970–1990. In addition, fundamental changes in Peru's political system—exemplified in the 1980 transition to democratic rule and a subsequent series of presidential and municipal elections—both affected and were affected by these economic shifts, thus recasting state–civil society relations. As the ability of the state to fulfill its basic roles grew progressively weaker, this deterioration in state–civil society relations was judged and reflected through the electoral process, as well as through informal political participation processes.

Dornbusch and Edwards (1991) argue that the economics of populist leaders and administrations "do ultimately fail; and when they fail it is always at a frightening cost to the very groups who were supposed to be favored" (i). The Dornbusch and Edwards discussion has particular relevance for Peru during the period 1970–1990 for two reasons: first, because Peru went through two cycles of macroeconomic populism with the Velasco and García administrations; and second, because these cycles had a dramatic impact on the urban poor, which was precisely one of the key target groups for each cycle. Here I fill in the Dornbusch-Edwards argument with some appropriate macrolevel aggregate data to create a broad-brush-strokes picture of entrenched poverty, the course of Peru's economy during our period of study, and the impact of macroeconomic populist policies on the urban poor.

Economic Developments, Poverty, and Crisis

BACKGROUND TO 1968

Poverty has been a way of life for the majority of Peruvians ever since Spain formed a colony there in the 1530s, and certainly since the nation won its independence in 1824 (Berry 1990; Thorp and Bertram 1978). Breaking from the Spanish crown was a symbolic act in many ways. Peru remained almost entirely dependent upon its extractive (mining and agricultural) exports to provide manufactured goods, and the rigid class structures in place since the conquest remained in operation, assuring that the elites on top, whether peninsular or criollo in origin, would not have to share their wealth or power. The emergence of an economy based on latifundios allowed Peru to maintain an exportable surplus; latifundio agriculture also provided considerable commercial importance to Peru's coastal cities (Trujillo, Chiclayo, Piura), although at the time of independence Peru was still very much a rural society (less than 10 percent of Peru's populace was urban at the time of independence).

England replaced Spain as Peru's major trading partner in the decades following the Wars of Independence. England's and Europe's needs for raw materials permitted Peru to diversify into guano and nitrates, then later on into cotton and sugar, and later still into oil. But reliance on these raw materials also strengthened Peru's dependence on European economies, making the nation subject to the vagaries of Old World demands and business cycles. In addition, these linkages deepened Peru's poverty and its enormous income discrepancies.

During the same time period, Peruvian politics finally started to consolidate. Peru's first rulers had been a series of so-called Marshalls of Ayacucho, self-designated military heroes who took turns governing and frequently robbing the treasury of the new nation. These men were finally challenged by civilian political parties in the 1850s and 1860s. But the political system that emerged was one dominated exclusively by the traditional civil oligarchy. Mass politics was decades away.

Following the disastrous War of the Pacific with Chile in 1879–1883, the late nineteenth and early twentieth centuries saw what is often called the Golden Age of the Oligarchy. Following the war the extractive agricultural and mineral economy was reestablished, to reign supreme once again. The traditional land-holding elites retained tight control of Peru's economic and political power, despite the first signs of industrialization and a new urban-based elite (Hunt 1985). World War I saw the United States replace England as Peru's principal source of capital and major trading partner, but U.S. corporations not only needed Peru's extractive surplus but also saw Peru as an additional market for their technology and capital goods. Certain advanced extractive enclaves for agriculture, minerals, and (later) oil began to use wage relations and advanced technology, as did urban-industrial coastal cities.

> The sierra, aside from the mineral enclaves, was needed only as a source of cheap wage goods (foodstuffs) to keep wages down in the industrial work force; . . . rapid urban growth and surplus accumulation [occurred] in Lima and the coastal cities, and, in the sierra, continuation of labor-intensive technologies, largely non-wage relations, and price mechanisms. (Wilson 1987, 203)

The twentieth century saw changes take place in Peru's political system. Although civilian dominance was by no means assured, leaders such as Augusto Leguía (1919–1930) began serious steps to modernize Peru through policies of extensive public works, especially road-building programs, and through ambitious efforts to expand and update Lima. Mass politics emerged in the 1920s as a young populist firebrand named Víctor Raúl Haya de la Torre founded his Alianza Popular Revolucionaria Americana (APRA; Popular Revolutionary American Alliance) party, and labor unions and other political parties and movements were grudgingly accepted as participants in the political and economic arenas. Nevertheless, simply holding elections seldom guaranteed that the winner would be able to take or retain office if the military preferred otherwise.

The Great Depression hit Peru hard; its extractive export-based economy suffered badly. One result was the first surge of what was to become a tidal wave of displaced migrants who headed toward Lima in desperation as their rural livelihoods disappeared. World War II brought an end to the depression; Peru's major exports (especially minerals such as copper, lead, and zinc) were in high demand. Following World War II, Peru found itself firmly inserted into the global economic system, but under conditions that distorted the nation's growth and maintained its poverty. Its dependence on raw materials was remarkable, even by Latin American standards. In 1950, for example, industrial production in Peru was only 14 percent of GDP, compared with 17 percent in Colombia and 22 percent in Chile (Thorp 1978, 39), and its income distribution remained among the most skewed in Latin America.

Peru experimented briefly with civilian rule during and after World War II with the administrations of Manuel Prado (1939–1945) and José Luis Bustamante (1945–1948), whose government was cut short by a military coup led by General Manuel Odría in 1948. Odría ruled until 1956, at which time a variety of pressures forced him to hold elections, which Manuel Prado again won. Initially, the 1950s were good to Peru; Odría implemented conservative economic policies that welcomed foreign investment, but by the end of his term a rising cost of living and a falling off of investment created public dissatisfaction. When Prado maintained many of the same conservative policies, by the end of his term he faced the same sort of discontent as had his predecessor.

The 1962 elections saw a tight three-way race between Víctor Raúl Haya de la Torre and his APRA party, General Odría, who ran as a civilian, and Fernando Belaúnde Terry, an architect who had first made his political appearance in 1956 and who represented Peru's urban educated middle classes. No candidate took the mandated one-third of the popular vote in 1962, and when a constitutional stalemate threatened, the military stepped in, annulled the elections, and ruled for a year, then called new elections. The same three candidates ran again, but this time Belaúnde managed to garner 38 percent of the popular vote and was ushered in with much fanfare as the archetypal "new" Latin American president in the Alliance for Progress mold. But Belaúnde was a more successful candidate than he was president; by 1967 significant economic problems had appeared in the form of inflation and devaluation, and Belaúnde—in part hamstrung by an APRA-Odría congressional alliance—was unwilling or unable to take steps to counteract them.

Peru, of course, was not immune to what was going on in the world. The 1960s saw intensified competition among multinational firms as the U.S. world-market leadership declined. Improvements in technology and communications allowed firms to restructure production. Multinationals no longer had to invest directly to serve individual national markets; instead, they could use economies of scale and improved transportation to divide up the production process. Developing countries with low-skilled wage earners began to assemble components for reexport, while research and development and advanced manufacturing took place in the industrialized countries. These countries thus began to compete for shares of this nontraditional export market, and reductions in tariffs and tax incentives became common tactics. Belaúnde imitated many of these policies, but he was unwilling to institute other fiscal and tax policies necessary to sustain overall economic growth.

Throughout Peru's first century and a half of existence as a nation-state, no administration undertook any serious confrontation with Peru's endemic poverty and its huge inequities in income distribution, perhaps because Peru's structural dependence contributed greatly to its record of painfully slow growth. Thorp and Bertram (1978) conclude that per capita income grew at "probably little more than one percent a year over 1890–1975" (321). Given the enormous disparities in income and the abysmal poverty of the masses, such slow growth meant that the state would not have had the resources to redistribute, even had it wanted to do so (which it did not). Berry's (1990) close examination of the linkages between international trade, the state, and income distribution (as an indicator or surrogate for poverty) in Peru since 1870 marshalls an impressive array of data concerning income distribution in Peru over the past century or so. Berry concludes that, in the late 1870s, the top 1 percent of the population received about 25 percent of the total income, while the top decile of the population took about 40–45 percent. In contrast, the bottom 10 percent of the population took in about 4 percent of the income in the 1870s. In 1961 (almost a hundred years later, when data were much more reliable), the top decile's share of national income had climbed to 52.8 percent, whereas the bottom quintile had dropped to just about 2.4 percent (Berry 1990; Webb 1977; Webb et al. 1981).

In sum, Peru's first century and a half saw economic dependence, a marked susceptibility to exogenous boom-and-bust cycles, and constant profound poverty and income maldistribution. In the political sphere, civilian and military leaders distrusted one another; since World War I, only one elected civilian president had been able to turn power over to an elected successor (Manuel Prado to José Bustamante, in 1948). Given the new global economy developing in the 1960s, Peru's disadvantageous position in it, and the plight of the great majority of its population, it became questionable whether any government could make a difference. In 1968, one did appear, however, clearly dedicated to breaking Peru out of its historical patterns. It is not surprising, perhaps, that it was a military government.

The Revolution of the Armed Forces, 1968–1980

Dornbusch and Edwards (1991) argue that macroeconomic populism not only has certain specific characteristics but that it also has certain inevitable results. They sketch in the major policy prescriptions of macroeconomic populism and also identify three phases of the populist economic cycle. The initial policy prescription emphasizes reactivation of a sluggish economy, redistribution of income, and a restructuring of the economy. The heart of the policy thus rests upon "reactivation with redistribution," generally through large increases in real wages. According to Dornbusch and Edwards, phase 1 sees a brief, successful vindication of this policy stance, with growth of output and high real wages and employment. The growth of demand is met by a rundown of inventories. Phase 2 begins when bottlenecks appear in response to expanding demands for domestic goods and decreasing domestic inventories. Price controls, devaluation, and exchange controls become necessary; inflation increases strongly, but wages keep up and budget deficits worsen. In phase 3, "pervasive shortages, extreme acceleration of inflation, and an obvious foreign exchange gap lead to capital flight. . . . The budget deficit deteriorates violently. . . . The government attempts to stabilize by cutting subsidies and by a real depreciation. Real wages fall massively and politics become unstable" (11).

I am not concerned here with providing a close description and history of the economic policies of the Velasco and García periods. Such accounts are readily available elsewhere (Thorp 1987; Kuczynski 1990; Pastor and Wise 1992; Lago 1991). Rather, a brief tracing of the Velasco and García experiences with populist macroeconomics lets me concentrate on the social and political ramifications of populist economics, especially on Lima's urban poor.

When General Juan Velasco assumed power through a military coup in 1968, he vowed to create a Peru that would be less dependent, one in which all its citizens would have the chance to participate. One way the self-styled Revolutionary Government of the Armed Forces chose to attain these goals was through a series of populist economic and social policies that made the state a far more powerful actor in the nation's economy than ever before. The most notable methods to strengthen the state were reforms of ownership. The Velasco administration "assumed that the structural and distributional aspects of the economy were strongly related," and that "the monopolization and misallocation of economic resources by the [domestic] oligarchy and foreign investors were responsible for the economic slowdown, for the growing disequilibrium, and for the failure of benefits to filter adequately through the system" (Fitzgerald 1983, 44).

By many criteria, the Velasco administration enjoyed some significant early successes, primarily because of extremely favorable world conditions (such as world prices for Peru's principal exports) and a slowdown of the growth program undertaken during Belaúnde's first term in office (1963–1968). Budget corrections and a real depreciation taken toward the end of Belaúnde's term ironically allowed the military government to enjoy an initial massive expansion. Real per capita income expanded an average of 3.7 percent annually from 1968 to 1974; in other terms, using 1980 as 100, real per capita income rose from 87 in 1968 to 105 in 1974 (Dornbusch and Edwards 1990, 252).

The Velasco regime also assumed, however, that private and foreign capital would continue to be invested in Peru and that the nationalization of certain strategic resources would yield a profit. What the military sought was a variant of Evans's triple alliance of local, international, and state capital, which had worked spectacularly in Brazil from 1967 to 1973 (Evans 1979). But domestic and foreign capital hesitated, scared off perhaps by Velasco's constant rhetoric about reforms and redistribution. As a result, partly by intent and partly by default, the Peruvian state assumed ever greater salience in the national economy. The aggressiveness of the Velasco government in this area soon became clear: as private and international capital investment shrank, the state's role increased, until by 1976, the public sector accounted for more than half of the total investment in the country (Thorp and Bertram 1978, 309). But the state quickly found it did not have the administrative capacity and personnel to manage the large number of ministries, public enterprises, and new state agencies that were created in the early 1970s. In addition, implementing the many goals of the revolution (several varieties of agricultural cooperatives, industrial cooperatives, state enterprises) absorbed far too many of the limited resources that the military government had at its disposal.

Peru did undergo a remarkable expansion of nontraditional manufactured exports (relative to traditional raw exports) in the 1970s. Wilson (1987) notes that from 1975 to 1980, nontraditional exports multiplied eightfold, and their portion of total exports reached 25 percent in 1980. But these exports were not the assembled goods that became so important in other Latin American countries such as Brazil. Rather, they were for the most part traditional raw materials that underwent some industrial processing before export (for example, cotton thread or cloth instead of raw cotton, copper wire instead of bar copper). As a result, Peru never gained any significant advantage in international trade and lost whatever significance it had once had as the final assembly point for its own internal market. In addition, this increase in nontraditional exports was the only area where results were fairly promising, and the returns to the state were nowhere near enough to be able to finance the many reforms the military leaders had promised.

Politically, strong populist tendencies emerged within the Revolution of the Armed Forces as the state tried to convince the masses of Peru to support its goals, constantly advertised as being implemented in their behalf: "¡La revolución es tuya!" (The revolution is yours!). The most noticeable organizational policy appeared as the Sistema Nacional de Apoyo a la Mobilización Social (SINAMOS; National System for the Support of Social Mobilization), which was set up as a multilevel national agency to promote involvement, especially by Peru's low-income urban and rural masses, in the revolution (Dietz 1980, chap. 8; Delgado 1975; Stepan 1978). But the many rhetorical flourishes that accompanied SINAMOS's birth in 1971 were never backed with sufficient resources. The agency's personnel frequently found themselves holding the tail of a tiger, as its target groups mobilized themselves to protest against both the unkept promises and the economic crisis that became steadily worse as the 1970s progressed.

By 1973 the total consumption of goods and services had started to exceed the total production of the economy. By 1975 expenditures surpassed production by 10 percent, and many of the results predicted by Dornbusch and Edwards came to the fore. The ability to consume was being financed by borrowing petrodollars abroad to finance the massive flow of imports into the country. Indebtedness rose from U.S. $737 million in 1968 to $1,121 million in 1972, to $8,032 million in 1979, 85 percent of which was public sector debt (Thorp and Bertram 1978, 310).[1] Wage increases, which had been positive in real terms up until 1973, declined sharply as government deficits and the money supply both increased rapidly. Conditions continued to worsen until the International Monetary Fund (IMF) stepped in with a series of structural adjustments that eliminated most food and petroleum subsidies, maintained prices with the rate of inflation (in 1978 about 70 percent), and limited wage and salary increases to about 10–15 percent.

It is not surprising that by 1977 the underemployed started to outnumber the employed, while between 1973 and 1979 unemployment rates rose from 4.2 to 8.5 percent (Stallings 1979, 245–48; *Caretas* 1977; Shapiro 1976). But these rates were not evenly distributed within Peruvian society. Outright unemployment in 1979 was 12.6 percent in the nonagricultural sector and only .3 percent in the agricultural, and yet underemployment was 64 percent in the agricultural and 39 percent in the nonagricultural (*Economía y Política* 1980, 7). Such disparities encouraged rural-urban migration, especially toward Lima, since many individuals were more willing to risk urban unemployment rather than underemployment at rural wage levels.

Inflation also increased. In 1974, inflation was at 17 percent, but it rose to 48 percent in 1976, to 95 percent in 1978, and to about 70 percent in 1980 (Banco Central de Reserva, June 1978; *Actualidad Económica* 1980, 6). Likewise, the consumer price index doubled from 1977 to 1978 and again from 1978 to 1979. Both white- and blue-collar wages in Lima began to slip in 1973; using 1973 as 100, white-collar salaries fell to 66.6 in 1977 and to 53.5 in 1980, while blue-collar fared somewhat better, dipping to 77.4 in 1977 and 78.8 in 1980. It should be remembered, however, that blue-collar wages were considerably lower than white-collar salaries. Public employees had perhaps the worst time of all. By 1980 their real incomes were reduced to 37 percent of what they had been in 1973. The minimum wage slipped less than any of the other groups, falling as low as 55.7 in 1978 but recovering to 88 in 1980 (official minimum wage throughout the period was approximately $40–50 per month). Finally, food prices rose very rapidly: "Pursuant to these instructions, prices for edible oils were increased in May [1978] by 130 percent, for dairy and wheat products by 40 percent to 65 percent, and petroleum products by a weighted average of 60 percent," in the rather bland words of an IMF confidential memorandum of 1978 (Sheetz 1986, 96).

The military period still generates strong opinions and debate in Peru. Fitzgerald's overall conclusion about its effects on Peru is harsh, perhaps, but on balance certainly not unfair: "in economic terms, . . . the increased role of the state . . . is [the most] striking" change, but in "the crucial area of distribution and the ability to withstand international economic fluctuations, . . . we can find no progress" (Fitzgerald 1983, 61). By 1980 the military was discredited, and the economy's decline would be sustained throughout the next decade.

What the Peruvian military did during the Velasco period (1968–1975) was attempt to strengthen the state and to make it an active participant in the development process. But Velasco's expectations that both domestic and international capital would form an alliance with a stronger Peruvian state were not realized as they had been in other Latin American nations, most notably Brazil. In the first place, the Peruvian state never developed the capacity to intervene in the economy so as to achieve its own ends rather than the interests of local or foreign capital. One factor that in particular short-circuited the military was an unwillingness of local and international capital to invest, which was in large part because of the military's plethora of rules and constraints on investments. The Peruvian state itself thus became the major investor, but its lack of capital forced it to borrow heavily, thereby creating a new and more egregious form of debt dependency.

Politically, the populist-corporatist SINAMOS experiment demonstrated three things: that it was possible to mobilize sizable portions of Peruvian society, that the Peruvian state could promise a great deal, and that the state was unable to deliver on these promises (Stepan 1978; Dietz 1980). What was up until that time Peru's worst economic conditions since World War II combined with a mobilized, frustrated, and angry populace to launch a series of strikes—first sectoral and then national—that the military was unable to contain. In 1978 the military held a constituent assembly election, and in 1980 national elections returned the country to democratic rule. But what the military left behind was hardly an encouraging or positive legacy for the civilian governments of the 1980s.

Civilian Governance: Orthodox, Heterodox, and Collapse

The Belaúnde and García administrations of the 1980s are remarkable for their apparent differences. Belaúnde exemplified the old generation of political leadership in Peru (he first stood for the presidency in 1956) and ran as the founder of his own party, which was in reality more a political following than an institutionalized party. He was clearly identified as an adherent of orthodox economic policies. García, on the other hand, was young (thirty-four when he was elected) and headed APRA (founded in 1924), Peru's oldest and best-organized political party. He ran on a platform of populism and center-leftist economic heterodoxy. Yet despite these seemingly fundamental differences, both administrations proved disastrous for Peru; the only way Belaúnde might conceivably be seen as a successful chief executive is to compare him with García. In essence, macroeconomic mismanagement and crisis characterized both administrations; each president committed numerous fundamental political errors, which compounded the effects of their economic miscalculations.

THE BELAÚNDE ADMINISTRATION, 1980–1985

Fernando Belaúnde had been elected president in 1963 but was overthrown in 1968 by the Velasco coup. And although he returned to power in 1980 with a strong electoral victory, he confronted a country that had changed dramatically in the intervening twelve years. Not only was the economy showing signs of severe strain when he reassumed office, but the populace was nowhere near as malleable or passive as it had been during his first term. Moreover, the 1978 and 1980 elections gave Peru a political party system that, although still immature and uninstitutionalized, at least offered a wide set of choices ranging from a vocal and frequently fragmented Marxist left to a mature APRA (center-left) to Belaúnde's Acción Popular (AP; Popular Action) center-right party, to a conservative probusiness right in the Partido Popular Cristiano (PPC; Popular Christian Party).[2]

Belaúnde's strategy for combating Peru's multiple economic problems was thoroughly orthodox. It utilized a straightforward neoliberalist *cono sur* (southern cone) model with an IMF stabilization program.[3] The Belaúnde administration's shift away from the statist model of the Velasco years was in fact a return to the norm for Peru, which usually reverted to laissez-faire policies following its infrequent experiments with state intervention (Thorp and Bertram 1978). The IMF and other transnational entities had acquired considerable influence because of Peru's debt problems (Pastor and Wise 1992, 86). Thus, privatizing state enterprises, stimulating domestic and international private investment, opening the economy, reducing tariffs and trade barriers, and eliminating government involvement in pricing and marketing all became the hallmarks of the Belaúnde administration. The hope was to stimulate the economy through new opportunities for national and foreign investments, trade liberalization, state investment into the economic infrastructure, and predictable macroeconomic policies.

Most of these goals were either unattainable or abandoned. For example, neither domestic nor foreign private sector resources had enough capital to make substantial gestures toward the eighty or so public enterprises that were initially to be sold, liquidated, or turned into joint ventures. Although many state enterprises did weaken, few were fully liquidated (Reid 1985, 83–84). And the hoped-for return of foreign direct capital investment did not materialize; the nationalizations, antiforeign rhetoric, and labor disturbances of the late 1970s had all made international investors nervous, so much so that foreign direct investment hit what was then an all-time low of negative $89 million in 1984 (Pastor and Wise 1992, 89). Significant trade liberalization policies implemented at the beginning of the Belaúnde administration resulted in a flood of foreign imports, many of which were luxury items. Manufacturing output dropped by one-fifth between 1980 and 1983, and many firms went into the red because of the increased costs of borrowing.

The role of the state, under orthodox economic policy, was to encourage and support private enterprise and to reinvigorate exports. But the severe recession of 1983, inadequate supplies of state capital, and mismanagement meant that projects took far longer than predicted. State resources and expertise that could have been directed toward coping with the macroeconomy went elsewhere, while incomplete projects became an albatross for the next government. Overall, the 1980–1985 period was a dismal one for Peru. Inflation doubled and by the end of Belaúnde's term was running monthly in double figures. The

overall inflation rate for 1985 was 165 percent (Crabtree 1992, 35). The GNP stagnated, debt rose by over 70 percent, real wages declined by more than 35 percent (Pastor and Wise 1992, 90–91).

The Shining Path, which had been established by Abimaél Guzman while he
was a faculty member of the Universidad de Huamanga in the southern sierra
city of Ayacucho, began its campaign of terror and intimidation on election
day in 1980. By 1985 the movement had spread the length of the Peruvian Andes
and was waging war on Peruvian society as a whole. Political assassinations became increasingly common as did the destruction of development projects and
infrastructure (power lines into Lima were a constant target). Sendero Luminoso thus became a serious threat to Peru's domestic stability.

The Belaúnde administration decided to counter by the quickest means possible, namely military force. But an inadequate, ill-trained, and nervous military found itself accused of human rights abuses as frequently as the Shining
Path. Belaúnde, meanwhile, was unable to mount a long-term program of
economic development for the southern sierra in order to undercut Sendero
Luminoso. By 1985 the Shining Path and the military had together been responsible for an average of twelve hundred deaths a year attributable to political violence (DESCO 1989).

I postpone a full discussion on poverty trends until covering the García administration so as to examine them across the full decade. Suffice it to say at
this point that Belaúnde's orthodox policies heightened Peru's already profound
income disparities and its poverty. Peru's population/income distribution ratios
worsened; the bottom half of the nation's urban populace received 19.7 percent
of the income in 1985, and the rural distribution was only slightly better at 20.3
percent (Webb and Fernandez Baca 1991, 1035–62). Real blue-collar wages fell
further than white-collar salaries by 1985; using 1980 as 100, in 1985 salaries
reached 80 but wages dropped to 64. The subsidies on foodstuffs and petroleum
products in place during the early 1970s never returned, resulting in price structures that left salaries and wages ever further behind.

In the political arena, Belaúnde and his AP party had won the 1980 presidential and legislative races by a comfortable margin, but his coattails proved too
short. In November of the same year, Peru's left showed signs of strength in
Lima in the national municipal elections. Three years later, in another round
of municipal elections in November 1983, the left—now in a coalition called
Izquierda Unida (IU; United Left)—along with a newly resurgent APRA under
Alán García both did well. APRA took one-third of the total popular vote nationwide, and IU finished a close second with 29 percent, evidence of a significant shift from the center-right to the left and center-left. IU won the mayoralty

of metropolitan Lima as well as every low-income district mayoral race in the capital. The 1983 municipal elections were widely viewed as a referendum on Belaúnde's performance in office; if so, then AP had plenty of reason to mourn, as the AP mayoral candidate in Lima finished a dismal fourth and last. By the 1985 presidential race, Belaúnde was widely discredited and his party a shadow of itself as it finished a distant last in a four-party race.

THE GARCÍA ADMINISTRATION, 1985–1990

Alan García's 1985 victory completed APRA's sixty-year quest for the presidency of Peru, and García was determined to make the most of it. His strongly populist style and significant abilities as a public speaker—along with good looks and youth (he was not even thirty-five when he won the presidency)—attracted many erstwhile AP members, some significant leftist support, and the majority of Peru's vast number of unaffiliated voters. As a result, APRA won not only the presidency but also both houses of Congress and (a year later, in the 1986 municipal elections) the mayoralty races in most of Peru's major provincial cities.

In its campaign APRA had promised, in rather vague ways, to reverse Belaúnde's orthodox approach and to dedicate itself to social democratic policies and goals (reduced inflation, income redistribution) in favor of the poor. These promises read in hindsight very much as if they were designed to be the quintessential macroeconomic populist policy perspective outlined by Dornbusch and Edwards (1990). Such goals were not only part of APRA's ideological platform, they were also intended to provide a new means of counterattacking the Shining Path. Because they wished to present themselves in sharp contrast to Belaúnde and to appear to be standing up to the IMF and the debt problem, García's team of economic advisors recommended a heterodox program of economic revival, growth, and distribution (Crabtree 1992, 25–68; Pastor and Wise 1992; Paus 1991).

García declared in his first policy speech that he would limit Peru's debt repayment to 10 percent of export earnings and would seek to mediate repayment with the country's creditors directly, without including the IMF. Although such declarations received the most publicity, other policies—such as wage and price freezes, fixed currency exchange rates, and interest rates pegged more or less to inflation—carried much more substance. The basic assumptions behind such moves were that reducing debt payments would provide more state revenue for investment, that underutilized capacity could be reactivated, and that fiscal accounts would improve through higher taxes on income, consumption, and imports (Crabtree 1992, 32–33).

The heterodox policy worked for about eighteen months, as significant improvement occurred in several key areas in 1986 and 1987. GDP expanded from 1.5 percent in 1985, to 10.1 percent in 1986, and 7.8 percent in 1987; consumption and investment both rose appreciably, and annual rates of inflation, although still high, were cut in half from 1985 to 1986, from 165 to 78 percent (Crabtree 1992, 35). Peru's urban sector, both formal and informal components, enjoyed some prosperity as income and employment levels both reduced some of their previous losses. Real wages increased by an average 9 percent in 1986; open unemployment fell from 8.9 percent in 1984 to 4.8 percent in 1987, while underemployment also decreased (43 percent to 35 percent), meaning that for the first time in some years, those people fully employed represented the largest block in the labor force (INEI 1992). What had happened was that demand for labor had increased in the formal sector, as had the demand for informal sector goods (Graham 1992, 177).

In addition, four major organizational innovations by the García administration in addressing employment and income issues among low-income groups had also come on-line. These four—the Programa de Empleo (PROEM; Employment Program); the Instituto para Desarrollo del Sector Informal (IDESI; Institute for Informal Sector Development); the Programa de Apoyo Directo (PAD; Direct Aid Program); and the Programa de Apoyo de Ingreso Temporal (PAIT; Program of Temporary Income Assistance)—all had distinct but related populist goals. PROEM encouraged hiring outside of Peru's enormously restrictive job security regulations, for example, while IDESI promoted access to credit for micro enterprises in urban areas. PAD worked with urban communal soup kitchens and provided infrastructure in Lima's squatter settlements. At its height, PAIT employed about five hundred thousand squatter *pobladores* (inhabitants) at minimum wage (at that time, about $36 per month) for three-month periods to collect trash, build sanitation facilities and access roads, and clean up the notorious litter on Lima's beaches (Graham 1992, 176–81). All these programs, especially PAIT, were inaugurated with great fanfare by APRA, all of them had a good deal of initial success, and all of them (with the partial exception of IDESI) encountered severe funding difficulties when the economy started to collapse in 1988. PAD in particular became highly politicized, as it tried to co-opt or replace existing communal programs and organizations, some of which had been originally organized by the left during Alfonso Barrantes's term as mayor of Lima in 1983–1986.

In general, by mid-1987 many of the imbalances and tensions inherent in the whole heterodox model had appeared. In trying to balance mutually incompatible objectives, the government "found itself trying to reconcile competing objectives: rectifying worsening external imbalances, remedying the problem of deteriorating public finance sectors, and getting the private sector to invest, all within the context of keeping inflation down and production up" (Crabtree 1992, 38). Domestic private investors and the state eyed each other with increasing wariness, and Peru's major commercial creditors and the government were frozen in positions of no retreat and no flexibility. Plans to effect income redistribution and to continue or increase PAD, PAIT, IDESI, and PROEM all folded as the economic good times of 1986 and early 1987 deteriorated. Their demise was caused by the inadequacies of the state's administrative apparatus as well as by the politicized and frequently clientelistic and patronage-laden nature of APRA's attempts to impose control over existing local-level popular organizations and movements in rural as well as urban areas. Despite such obstacles and some outright failures, García carried forward plans begun under Belaúnde to restructure Peru's existing departments (states) into new legal regions. But by mid-1987, the heterodox model had collapsed, and García realized that he would have to do something to rescue his popularity and his nation's economy.

All observers agree that García's decision in July 1987 to nationalize the private banking industry separates the first years of his administration from the hyper-inflation accompanied by hyper-recession that characterized the 1988–1990 period. Much has been written about this period (Graham 1992; Crabtree 1992; Pastor and Wise 1992), and it is not necessary to go into great detail here. García's decision to nationalize the private sector banking industry was in large measure an individual decision that had not been thought through. Not only did García seriously underestimate the public reaction and resistance to such a move, he also miscalculated opposition within his own party (Crabtree 1992, 121–27). The attempt at nationalization (which ultimately failed) was at heart a political move aimed at regaining the political upper hand in his party and with public opinion. It did neither. Rather, it alienated the business community, put many APRA politicians on the defensive, and failed to rally the Peruvian public.

By late 1987, the nationalization attempt had been superseded by a serious erosion of the whole economy. Inflation reappeared, the trade deficit grew because of a surge in imports, and public sector revenues declined. In desperation, the García administration contacted the IMF and the World Bank, thereby giving public notice that the heterodox model was no longer operative. A series of readjustment policies appeared throughout the first half of 1988, culminating in severe shock treatments in September and November. These policies (especially September's) had extreme effects on Peru's economy and produced a whole raft of social repercussions. Inflation rose overnight; in the ten days after the announcement and prior to its implementation, the overall consumer index rose 114 percent, at the same time that price controls were being discarded (Crabtree 1992, 135). But once it was implemented, the shock treatment did not stop inflation (prices rose another 40 percent in October).

Overall, the year 1988 was calamitous, and 1989 and 1990 were no better. The economy contracted by 9 percent in 1988 and in 1989 by an additional 12 percent. Average real income dropped by almost one-quarter (22 percent) from 1987 to 1989, meaning that most consumers, especially low-income, did not have enough money to afford basic goods. Using 1979 as 100, the average figures for wages for 1987 were 75 for minimum wages, 69 for government employees, 109 for private sector white-collar workers, and 91 for blue-collar workers. By December 1988 these levels had collapsed to 48 for minimum wage, 28 for government workers, and to 60 and 46 for white- and blue-collar private sector employees. According to Ministry of Labor household surveys, the percentage of the labor force of metropolitan Lima that was adequately employed (60 percent in 1987) was 19 percent in 1989, and 11 percent in 1990. Agricultural production fell, for a variety of reasons, causing shortages to develop in urban areas and forcing the government to spend dollars it could not afford to import staples such as rice and potatoes. The state's antipoverty programs either were discontinued because of a lack of money or were overwhelmed by the scope of the economic collapse.

Poverty throughout the nation and in its urban areas became more acute than ever, and its social effects more dramatic. Javier Abugattás (1990) estimated that a basic basket of staples cost $48 per month, and that half of the country received less than this amount in wages or earnings. The amount necessary for minimal caloric intake was $31; almost 30 percent of Peru earned less than this. Crabtree (1992) cites a Prisma-Cayetano Heredia study done in Lima's southern cone of squatter communities that is especially revealing. Nutritional status among children underwent an abrupt fall subsequent to September 1988, caused in large part by declines in income. Two household studies in March 1988 and June 1989 showed that, in those fifteen months, family income in the households surveyed fell 56 percent in real terms, meaning that half the families could not cover basic caloric requirements. Child mortality increased for all age groups up to five years of age.

At the same time, the APRA government and the state provided far less than necessary to combat such poverty-related problems. As just one example, by 1990 Peru's social security system had undergone enormous decapitalization in real terms through negative real investment yields (from minus 21 percent to minus 28 percent), high state debt, much employer evasion and payment delays, and vast administrative costs (52 percent of total expenditures in 1986).

Moreover, only one-third of the labor force was covered and only one-fifth of the total populace (Mesa-Lago 1994, 133). One of the state's major safety nets obviously offered no assurance to the poor, even if (as was unlikely) they were putatively covered.

As Peru faced what was undoubtedly its worst economic and social crisis of the twentieth century, Sendero Luminoso continued its terrorist attacks on individuals as well as on the whole social, political, and economic fabric of society. Deaths from political violence rose steadily following 1985—especially around election time, when Sendero Luminoso tried to intimidate candidates and undermine the whole electoral process through threats and assassinations. Such deaths numbered about 1,150 in the 1985 national elections, for example, and totaled almost 2,000 in the 1989 national municipal elections, at the depth of the recession. In addition, between 1986 and 1989, the National Election Board estimated that 166 mayors abandoned their campaigns, resigned from office, or were killed. Judges called upon to try suspected members of the Shining Path were frequently threatened and intimidated; not a few were killed (DESCO 1989). The García administration's early policies of promoting agricultural development in the sierra deteriorated after 1987, thereby eliminating any hopes of a long-term developmental effort to counter the presence of Sendero Luminoso.

By 1988 the Shining Path had begun to move into metropolitan Lima in a serious way, recruiting in low-income areas and doing everything it could to subvert and destroy industrial unions as well as local community organizations. But Sendero Luminoso was not the only disruptive force that emerged in Peru in the late 1980s. The litany seems endless: drug-trafficking, and the violence and the money accompanying it; the presence of another insurgent movement in the Movimiento Revolucionario Tupac Amaru (MRTA, or Tupac Amaru Revolutionary Movement); street violence because of economic desperation; strikes in various sectors of the economy; racial and ethnic tensions; abuses of the military in the country's declared Emergency Zones (where the state could not guarantee citizen safety because of the presence of the Shining Path); corruption within the police force; the appearance of right-wing death squads rumored to be affiliated with APRA; and loss of confidence in the judicial system. It was against this backdrop that municipal elections were held in November 1989, and presidential elections in April and June of 1990 (two rounds, with the two candidates who finished first in April competing against one another in June).[4]

The Shining Path increased violence around elections to undermine the whole process, and although the three elections in five months went off smoothly, all of the major parties were in difficulty. APRA presented candidates, but García's disastrous performance in office made campaigning difficult for any candidate who represented the party. García's public opinion polls during his administration reflected his administration's performance; he ran a 45 percent approval rating in July 1988, but less than 10 percent gave him a favorable rating in December, and he never rose above 15 percent for the rest of his term (Apoyo 1993). Peru's left arrived in 1989 badly divided over ideological and personal issues. IU was unable to overcome its historical tendencies to splinter, despite (or even because of) Alfonso Barrantes's 1983 Lima mayoral victory and others elsewhere. Barrantes had been defeated in his reelection bid in 1986, and the left never really recovered. Splits and divisions became ever more difficult to paper over, and the multiplicity of parties and movements could not agree on whether to support Barrantes again for a 1990 presidential bid and how to treat APRA and Sendero Luminoso:

> The schizophrenia of the left was the impulse, on the one hand, to build alliances towards the right in a bid to bolster existing forms of parliamentary democracy and to win the 1990 elections by moving toward the center; and on the other, the impulse to create and defend popular power by occupying a political space to the left, which, increasingly, was being contested by Sendero Luminoso, the MRTA, and their respective political allies. (Crabtree 1992, 169)

Two different and bitterly opposed factions finally appeared in the forms of IU and ASI (Acuerdo Socialista de Izquiera, or Leftist Socialist Alliance); each ran candidates for all offices in 1990, each took votes from the other, and many voters—confused and disenchanted with the endless bickering and inability to maintain a united party—simply turned away from the left altogether in search of an alternative.

Two such alternatives became apparent, one sooner and one later. The first came from the right when two groups—Fredemo and Movimiento Libertad— began in 1987 to generate considerable interest and support. Movimiento Libertad attracted attention primarily because of the presence of Mario Vargas Llosa, Peru's most famous living novelist. A onetime staunch supporter of Castro, Vargas Llosa had by the 1980s moved well to the right and had become a fervid Thatcherite. Aligning himself with Hernando de Soto and his neomercantilist interpretations of Peru's massive informal sector, Vargas Llosa saw García's bank nationalization as the perfect chance for him to lead a rightist movement backed by Lima's traditional business sector.

The Frente Democrático (Fredemo) became a coalition of three center-right parties and movements: Belaúnde's AP, the PPC under Luis Bedoya Reyes, and Movimiento Libertad. The coalition had a difficult time agreeing on rules; ideological differences caused tensions, and Vargas Llosa actually walked out on two occasions. But the pressures holding Fredemo together overcame those splitting it apart. In addition, Fredemo enjoyed considerable backing in the Lima media. And, at least as important, the nature of the economic crisis convinced some of the populace that more conservative rather than radical policies were called for.

Vargas Llosa's campaign speeches went further than was perhaps advisable, publicly promising the electorate that he would indeed institute a shock economic treatment to confront hyperinflation, reduce the state bureaucracy, and privatize most state enterprises. APRA in particular, along with the left, leapt upon such talk, claiming that Vargas Llosa would bring the economy to its knees and making pointed references to the social impact of the shock adjustment experience of Bolivia during the mid-1980s. *Los informales* of Lima (the small-scale informal business sector)—who comprise anywhere from 35 to 50 percent of the city's labor force (de Soto 1986; Carbonetto et al. 1988)—were from several accounts severely discomfited by what they perceived as threats to their well-being, and instead of turning toward Fredemo, whose platform was ostensibly in their favor, began to seek out another option.

This second alternative was much later in appearing. Alberto Fujimori, first-generation Peruvian-Japanese agricultural engineer and onetime rector of Peru's agricultural university, La Molina, but a national political nonentity, entered politics in 1989 on a vague platform of "Work, Honesty, and Technology." In public opinion polls of January and February 1990 (the first round was scheduled for April 8, 1990) Fujimori's party—Cambio 90—was not even listed as a separate party but was instead bunched with several parties under "Other." At the time, conventional wisdom held that Fredemo would take a plurality and that APRA was the only political force that might possibly prevent a first-round Vargas Llosa victory. But the thorough discrediting of García and APRA for all but the most loyal APRA party members; the hopeless divisions within the left; and the combination of fear generated by shock economic adjustment and of distrust of Vargas Llosa as a candidate of Peru's traditional, white, Lima elite—all came together to create some significant political space for nontraditional candidates, which Fujimori certainly was.

The municipal elections in 1989 had been something of a bellwether for the 1990 contest, especially in Lima. Ricardo Belmont, a popular television personality with no political experience whatsoever, won Lima's mayoral race handily, taking 45 percent of the popular vote while running as an independent with no backing from any established political party. Perhaps taking a cue from Belmont's success, Fujimori played on his nonaffiliation and his image as an honest, hardworking *técnico* (technician) to generate extraordinary momentum for the month or so prior to April 8, 1990, accumulating about a point a day for three weeks to finish a strong second (24 percent) to Vargas Llosa's 28 percent. APRA finished third with only one-fifth of the popular vote; IU and ASI together took 11 percent; null and void ballots totaled about 14 percent (Tuesta 1994).

The second round runoff between Fredemo and Cambio 90 was foreordained; Fujimori swept to a 60–40 percent victory. I delve into the specifics of Fujimori's election, and of voting among the urban poor in general, in chapter 8. Here let me note only that Cambio 90 drew substantial support from rural and urban lower-middle- and lower-class sectors. It is ironic that the so-called urban *informales* and the *microempresarios* (individuals engaged in small-scale informal business) that De Soto and Vargas Llosa had been assiduously courting turned out in great numbers for Fujimori. It is more ironic still that in less than a month following his inauguration Fujimori instituted one of Latin America's most drastic shock adjustment policies ever, eliminating subsidies, allowing prices to rise, and curtailing most state programs designed to assist the lower class.

During the 1970–1990 period, Peru went through two distinct yet similar populist cycles whose macroeconomic policies were strikingly similar and whose results were similarly disastrous. Both the first (driven by a reformist military) and the second (undertaken by the leader of Peru's largest political party) failed to make their redistributive policies work; each left its successors with a considerable mess. Fernando Belaúnde was faced with the severe economic problems left by the Velasco period; Alberto Fujimori confronted the worst socioeconomic conditions Peru had seen in the twentieth century.

This overview of the political economy of Peru from 1970 through 1990 has linked macroeconomic events with the transition from military to civilian rule and with the several presidential and municipal elections. Overall, Peru's political economy had an extraordinarily difficult time; the downturn that began in the late 1970s under the military was never fully arrested, the orthodox policies of Belaúnde created further tensions and difficulties, and García's brief honeymoon with heterodox policies abruptly degenerated into wholesale economic freefall. But precisely how these macro developments were intensified, mitigated, focused, and otherwise changed within Lima itself remains to be explored.

4

....

METROPOLITAN
LIMA AND
ITS DISTRICTS

LIMA HAS BEEN the capital city of Peru since its founding in 1532, but it has always been much more than that. Lima is Peru's economic, social, cultural, and financial center; it dominates the rest of the country.[1] As a result, the province of Lima, which contains the city and its surrounding suburban, exurban, and rural areas, has been overwhelmingly Peru's wealthiest and most advanced.

Studies on the distribution of poverty in Peru (Cruz Saco 1992; Glewwe 1988; Glewwe and de Tray 1989) all agree that the metropolitan Lima area ranks far higher in poverty than any other part of Peru.[2] By any and all standards and indicators, metropolitan Lima is richer, better serviced, and healthier than all other regions of the country. In sharp contrast, traditional highland indigenous Peru (especially the so-called *mancha india* departments of Cuzco, Puno, Ayacucho, Apurimac, and Huancavelica) fall behind by sometimes extraordinary margins (Cruz Saco 1992). For example, in the mid-1980s, Lima contained only 3.4 percent of the nation's poorest decile, although it held over one-quarter of its total population. In abrupt contrast, the rural sierra was home to 60 percent of the nation's poorest decile while it held only 30 percent of its total population (Glewwy 1988, 38).

Such national figures would appear to argue that people are better off in Lima, and in many ways they are. Perhaps most important, people, including low-income groups, perceive themselves as better off in the city. Yet (as has been endlessly pointed out), urban poverty is qualitatively different from its rural counterpart. Not only is the city more expensive in almost all aspects, but

63

survival in the city requires a monetary income; subsistence agriculture is not a viable option. Employment and participation in the labor force (especially for heads of households) is thus obligatory, and the official minimum wage, the cost of living, and inflation become real-life issues that take on a crucial, immediate importance that they may not have in rural areas.

As Peru passed through the 1920s, the Great Depression, World War II, and the massive changes of the postwar period, one thing never changed: Lima's dominance over the rest of the nation. The 1940 census showed that Lima had 590,000 inhabitants, which made it ten times larger than Arequipa, the nation's second city. Such a 10:1 ratio has been basically maintained up through 1990 and into projections for the year 2000—Lima, 8.3 million; Arequipa, 940,000 (Varillas Montenegro and Mostajo de Muente 1990, 411).

Lima's ability to maintain itself as a primate capital arises from several interconnected factors. Since World War II, Peru has developed small modern enclaves in the extractive (mining) and manufacturing (textiles, food-processing, some consumer durables) sectors of the economy. Until the 1968 reforms of the military government these enclaves were under the control of either domestic or international elites, which influenced Peru's labor force in a multitude of ways. In the extractive or agricultural sector of the economy, the modern enclaves enjoyed access to capital and often produced raw or partly finished commodities for export. But much of the rural labor force necessarily became landless wage labor, while others (minifundistas, or independent small farmers) were forced to survive through subsistence agriculture. Small rural artisans, displaced minifundistas, and landless farmworkers, however, could not compete with advanced agricultural techniques or with capitalist manufactured goods and were thus unable to maintain a viable place in the rural economy. This situation, compounded by rising population growth rates and severely limited arable land (about 5 percent of Peru is presently cultivable), led tens of thousands of rural individuals to migrate into urban areas—and especially into Lima —in search of alternative employment. As migration became more common and more people flowed into Lima, the city profoundly changed its physical form and makeup but maintained its demographic hegemony.

Lima's dominance is revealed even more tellingly in other areas. Throughout the period in question, Lima's grip on virtually all indicators of economic, social, and physical well-being remained solid. In the mid-1980s Lima produced 69 percent of the nation's industrial output and 80 percent of its consumer goods. Lima generated 87 percent of Peru's tax revenues; consumed 98 percent of its private investment; received 83 percent of its bank deposits; and contained more than half its public employees, half its hospital beds, three-quarters of its telephone subscribers, while being home for 28 percent of its population (Allou 1989, 9).

Urbanization and Economic Crisis

Lima's primacy has thus been unchallenged for decades, even centuries. But does severe and sustained economic crisis have an impact on urbanization? on a city's growth, for example, or on the distribution of its populace by social class? or on its labor force? That Lima experienced an economic crisis during the late 1980s is not open to debate. Open unemployment rose from 4.8 percent in 1987 to 8 percent in 1990; underemployment (defined as either working less then thirty-five hours a week or receiving less than the minimum wage) increased over the same two years from 35 to 81 percent (Crabtree 1992, 143). By the end of the 1980s, income inequalities had become more profound than ever: the poorest decile received 2.5 percent of the city's income, and the bottom half received 24 percent; the top decile received 28 percent (INEI 1992, 103–10). The incidence of poverty in metropolitan Lima (defined as the inability to purchase the basic minimum of food, health, education, housing, transportation) increased from 30 percent of all households in June 1985 to 47 percent by mid-1988 (*Perú Económico* 1990, 11–13).

The spatial distribution of poverty in Lima is far from even (as will become abundantly clear throughout this chapter). By the end of the 1980s, the residents of the wealthiest district in Lima had an average annual expenditure for food, health, and education that was three times that of the poorest district. Yet the residents of the wealthiest district spent about 32 percent of their total annual expenditures on food; in sharp contrast, the poorest district's residents spent about 71 percent on food. In absolute numbers, the residents of the wealthiest districts spent about half again as much for food as did the poorest residents (INEI 1992, 103–10).

In the late 1980s Portes (1989) raised the question of whether certain well-established urbanization patterns that developed during the 1960s and 1970s held true during the "lost decade" of the 1980s. All of the literature that examines the 1960s and 1970s agrees that these decades saw accelerating primacy rates, spatial polarization within the cities by social class, and high informal employment. Portes proposed that Latin America's 1980s macroeconomic crisis was caused in significant part by the region's subordination to external factors and constraints. For example, as multinational corporations took over import-sub-stitution industrialization (ISI) plans in many countries, urban workers were displaced by increasingly capital-intensive technologies. In parallel fashion, agri-cultural labor displaced by technological advances in the countryside migrated to the cities but found few openings in the formal urban economies. Given such changes, Portes asked if primacy, residential homogeneity, employment, and informality differed during the 1980s as compared with the 1960s and 1970s. To address this question, Portes examined the growth and development of several Latin American cities, Lima among them.

Portes was unable to dedicate full attention to any one of these cities, how-ever, since he was attempting to draw generalizations about Latin American urban areas overall and was thus forced to use only a few indicators common to all of the urban settings he examined. I use Portes's factors—primacy, residen-tial homogeneity, employment, and informality—as a framework to look at Lima's development over the period 1970–1990, since each of these factors had a major impact on the lives of the city's poor populace. But I also have the luxury of using a wider and more precise range of indicators than Portes employed.

PRIMACY

Up until 1980 Lima and Peru matched the general profiles of Latin American regional growth and urban development. Nationally, Peru's GDP made mod-est, steady progress until the oil shocks of the 1970s, increasing foreign loans and debt payments, declining terms of trade, and the imposition of readjust-ment policies all led to near stagnant or negative economic growth rates and declines in GDP and in wages. Many of these downturns could, according to Dornbusch and Edwards (1991), be attributed to and perhaps even predicted by the nature of the macroeconomic populist policies of the Velasco period. But throughout the twentieth century, regardless of specific administrations, Lima was (even by its Latin American neighbors) a late industrializing city whose de-mographic growth after World War II soon outstripped its capacity to provide jobs in the formal blue- and white-collar sectors.

The growth patterns of Lima from 1940 to 1990 are quite clear. The city grew from 591,000 (1941) to 1.8 million (1961), 3.3 million (1972), 4.6 million (1981), and finally to 6.5 million (1993). Its index of primacy (Lima's size vis-à-vis the com-bined populations of the second, third, and fourth largest cities) first acceler-ated and then slowed—a ratio of 4.27:1 in 1941 reached 5.55:1 in 1961, declining gradually to 4.03:1 in 1993. Yet Lima's percentage of Peru's total population rose throughout the post–World War II period, jumping from 8.3 percent (1941) to 17.6 percent (1961), 23.3 percent (1972), 25.9 percent (1981), and 29.4 percent (1990).

Finally, Lima's percentage of Peru's total urban population also grew, rising from 26.9 percent (1941) to 41.8 percent (1990).

Overall, the 1940–1960 period showed a significant increase in primacy. This growth then declined modestly first across the 1970s and then more sharply across the 1990s (Webb and Fernandez Baca 1992, 173–202). Altogether, these figures show steady increases in the percentage of Peru's total and total urban population that inhabited Lima, although the slowdown in primacy during the 1980s in particular substantiates Portes's general hypothesis of primacy decrease in times of economic crisis.

SPATIAL SOCIAL-CLASS POLARIZATION AND HOMOGENEITY

Portes was concerned with class polarization, by which he meant the degree to which a city is divided—either by formal legal divisions or by more ad hoc income and market mechanisms—into areas that are homogeneous in terms of social class. Portes hypothesized that prior to the 1980s Latin American cities experienced decreasing center city densities. Not only did the wealthier classes move out to new suburban areas during this time, but advances in public transportation made it possible for the inhabitants of even low-income housing areas (for example, squatter settlements) to locate relatively far from the central city as well. Thus densities should decrease in the older core if and/or when the city spreads. Yet Portes's data indicated that such was not the case in most of Latin America's major cities. He based his conclusions on data showing that densities increased steadily. In the case of Lima, Portes's data showed that density rose from 24 inhabitants per square kilometer (1941) to 60 (1961), 104 (1972), 144 (1981), and 187 (estimated in 1990).

These figures are misleading, however. Portes employed data for the entire state or department of Lima, which includes many small towns, isolated rural areas, and considerable highland sierra in addition to the province of Lima, which contains the city. Using density figures for metropolitan Lima—that is, only the province of Lima—provides a more accurate idea of truly urban density. Metropolitan Lima's density increased dramatically from 1941 to 1972, growing three times from 1941 to 1961 (from 210 to 653 people per square kilometer), and another 1.8 times (to 1,172 people per square kilometer) from 1961 to 1971. But from that time on, the city's density continued to grow at a diminished pace, 1.4 times from 1972 to 1981 and the same again from 1981 to 1990, arriving at an estimated 2,281 people per square kilometer in 1990 (Allou 1989). An even more precise picture of density growth emerges by examining specific districts (see below).

But urban density is at best an indirect measure of class. Fortunately, in the case of Lima, much more direct aggregate indicators of social class are available. Indeed, several attempts have been made to classify Lima's districts by social class, or at least by a variety of aggregate-level indicators that are a priori assumed to stand for social class. In an early effort, Powell (1969) used the percentage of population inhabiting squatter settlements; Dietz (1985) later elaborated on Powell by using district-level census data, including percentage of blue-collar, employer, independently employed, illiterate, unemployed, or classified squatter population. García (1985) likewise employed several variables to rank Lima's districts by relative poverty, including number of households per dwelling unit and number of occupants per dwelling unit, percentage of population living in squatter settlements, or that are members of the labor force between six and nineteen years of age, that are illiterate, that are unskilled or semiskilled blue collar, and percentage of dwelling units without electricity, drinking water, and sewerage (see also Cameron 1991a, b; Durand 1996).

All these studies agree that if the variables used are in fact reasonably valid operationalizations of social class, then probably throughout all of its history and certainly since World War II Lima's legal districts are, with some few exceptions, remarkably homogeneous in two crucial ways. First, the social class of their inhabitants is homogeneous, and second, the compositional nature of the districts is also uniform.[3] Among the indicators that are most valuable as operationalizations of social class are housing, age distribution, municipal finance, income, and informality.

HOUSING

Housing is for Lima one of the most crucial and precise indicators of social class and of poverty, low-income levels, and homogeneity. Low-income housing exists in a variety of forms in Lima as elsewhere in Latin America; the two basic types are, first, slum or *tugurio* environments and their several manifestations (*callejónes, correlones, azoteas*), which are generally found in Lima's central city as well as in its older blue-collar areas, and second, its much more famous squatter settlements (known variously across the years as *barriadas, pueblos jóvenes,* or *barrios marginales*), which are communities or whole districts of self-help autonomous housing, almost always illegal in origin and in general located on the periphery of the city (Grompone et al. 1983, 57; see also Leeds 1969).

How has the growth of Lima's squatter settlements manifested in the overall legal structure, development, and growth of the city? In 1960, a year before the 1961 census, Lima had twenty-seven districts; by 1993 it had forty-two. Twelve were added between 1960 and 1981. The question to be asked is how homogeneous these twelve new districts were. In terms of housing, five—Villa María del Triunfo (created in 1961), Comas (1961), Independencia (1964), San Juan de Miraflores (1965), and El Agustino (1965)—all had more than half of their dwelling units classified as squatter in the 1981 census.

In sharp contrast, three more of the new districts—La Molina (1962), Jesús María (1963), and San Luis (1968)—were all middle-class and higher; they had no squatter housing whatsoever in 1981. Four more districts were also added: Santa Rosa and Santa María del Mar (1962) were small outlying beach resort districts; Cieneguilla (1970) was a largely rural district, and San Juan de Lurigancho (1967) had about one-quarter of its 1981 population classified as squatter. It is worth noticing that after 1981 two more districts were formed: Los Olivos (1987), a lower-income district, and Villa El Salvador (1983), an immense self-help community created by the Velasco government following a massive land invasion in 1971, which in 1990 was estimated to be 100 percent squatter.

García's (1985) calculations show, not surprisingly, that the five new squatter-intensive districts ranked among the thirteen poorest districts in the city. Thus if type of housing (in this case, percentage squatter) is a meaningful operationalization of social class, then during the 1960–1990 period the new districts created in Lima were extraordinarily homogeneous: they were either largely squatter or largely not. This conclusion is buttressed by additional data from the Instituto Libertad y Democracia (ILD 1989a), which calculated from census and other data that approximately 45 percent of Lima's population in 1982 lived in what it termed "formal" housing—that is, housing built in accordance with the norms of property rights, legal transactions, and contracts.[4] About 47 percent lived in "informal settlements" (squatter settlements of a wide variety of descriptions), while 7 percent resided in rental slum housing. What is notable about the distribution of these latter two types of housing is that there was very little overlap between the two. Twelve of Lima's districts in 1982 contained higher than the mean of slum housing; ten contained higher than the mean in squatter housing. Yet no single district was higher than the mean in both. Barranco was the highest in slum housing, with 22 percent; several districts were over 95 percent squatter; Rímac had the highest combination of the two types of housing, with 14 percent slum and 31 percent squatter. It is clear that those districts of Lima that contained high concentrations of squatter housing did not have large percentages of people living in rental slum housing. Squatter housing was concentrated in what are (or were, at the time of their creation) marginal, outlying areas; low-income rental slum housing was located either in the older areas such as the central city (Barranco, Magdalena, Rímac, Lima Cercado) or in blue-collar districts (La Victoria, Surquillo, Breña). No district was then—nor is today—predominantly rental slum to the degree that several districts were predominantly squatter. For example, Barranco had the highest slum incidence, but only slightly more than one-fifth of its inhabitants lived in such housing (ILD 1989a, 24), whereas several districts in Lima had two-thirds or three-quarters of their populations living in squatter housing.

As for overall densities, those areas of Lima that were densely crowded in 1960 or 1970 remained so throughout the 1980s. As would be expected, the central city and older districts that had the highest concentrations of slum housing have the highest densities within the metropolitan area. In 1990 Cercado de Lima, Barranco, Breña, La Victoria, Lince, Magdalena, Rímac, San Luis, and Surquillo all had estimated population densities of more than 20,000 people per square kilometer. Yet over the period 1960–1990 their densities increased only modestly, generally 25–35 percent for the period. In other words, they were densely populated in 1960 and they remained that way; none of them showed any decrease across the thirty years (Allou 1989). In contrast, San Martín de Porres, which was created through invasions and underwent extremely rapid growth in the early 1950s, saw its density multiply sixfold since 1961. Comas, Independencia, Villa María del Triunfo, and San Juan de Miraflores, all classic invasion squatter districts, saw their populations double or treble from the 1960s to 1990, although in comparison with the central city areas of Lima, these squatter districts still had relatively low density levels, ranging anywhere from 4,500 to 10,000 people per square kilometer (Webb and Fernandez Baca 1991, 60, 112).

AGE DISTRIBUTION

An additional indicator has to do with age distribution. As a rule, low-income families tend to be larger than wealthier (for many reasons and motives), and while the data concerning population pyramids are sometimes incomplete, it is clear from both the 1981 and the 1993 censuses that Lima's squatter-intensive districts had noticeably younger populations overall. At least 40 percent of the total populations of Comas, Villa María del Triunfo, Independencia, San Juan de Miraflores, and El Agustino were under the age of fifteen, whereas Lima's wealthier districts (San Isidro, Miraflores) had less than one-quarter under age fifteen (Driant 1991, 132–34).

MUNICIPAL FINANCE

Figures dealing with Lima's municipal finances offer a further idea of the overall scarcity of resources confronting Lima, especially its lower-class districts, as well as the striking comparisons between wealthy and poor districts within the city.[5] In 1981 metropolitan Lima's budget totaled about $76 million for a city whose official population was 4.1 million people, which works out to approximately $17.50 per capita for that year. By 1985, with inflation taking its toll, the total budget dropped to $42 million, with the average per capita expenditure decreasing to $8.36.

Low as these figures may be, differences across districts are even more striking. In 1981 the six lowest per capita districts (Villa María del Triunfo, Comas, San Juan de Lurigancho, El Agustino, San Juan de Miraflores, and Independencia) averaged $5.40 income per capita in their municipal budgets, ranging from $4.09 to $6.89; the two wealthiest districts, Miraflores and San Isidro, averaged $44.35, about an 8:1 difference. By 1985 the same six lower-class districts, because of inflation, had dropped in real terms to $2.16 (ranging from $1.67 to $2.94); Miraflores also dropped (to $23), but San Isidro managed to hold even ($45), meaning that the difference between the six lowest and the highest had become about 21:1 (Allou 1989, 139–40). The spread of averages among the poorest districts is remarkably tight in both years, another sign of homogeneity: poor districts are not only poor, they are poor in like degrees.

Thus across a wide range of indicators—age, employment, occupation, housing, population density, financial resources—Lima has shown itself to be remarkably homogeneous by social class insofar as its formal divisions are concerned. Such divisions are by no means accidental; Lima's wealthy have always made great (and successful) efforts to keep themselves isolated from the city's *masas populares,* and to see that these masses in turn are relegated to slum environments or squatter-intensive areas. Whether in good economic times or bad, since World War II and the period of Lima's fastest ever expansion (1960–1970) and its subsequent lesser though steady growth, the city's political economy and those who manage it have seen that the migrants and the poor have been forced either to reside in rental slum neighborhoods or, in most cases, to fend for themselves by creating self-help housing through land invasions, which are subsequently incorporated into the city as large homogeneous chunks of poor people with minimal financial resources to meet their endless needs.

INCOME

Up until 1980 or so, open unemployment was relatively low in most Latin American cities, primarily because people, especially lower-class individuals, had no choice but to find some income-producing activity, even if they "invented" their own work (Portes et al. 1989). For the same reasons, underemployment and informal employment were also high. Given the onset of economic crisis, it would be logical to predict an expansion of the informal sector as well as growing unemployment and underemployment as formal wage and salary labor contracted.

The data for the 1970–1990 period in metropolitan Lima provide more than enough material for a vivid picture of wages, salaries, and employment. (Some national-level data have already been presented in chapter 3.) Insofar as Lima is concerned, income levels through the first part of the 1970s (that is, during the Velasco administration) more or less held their own. The official urban minimum monthly wage, which was worth about $50 in 1968 (and which, it should be emphasized, many people do not receive or are not guaranteed to receive), had risen to $78 by the end of 1974, which was as high as it would go. By 1977 it had declined to $35, when it rose again to about $60 by the time of the Belaúnde administration in 1980. But it then suffered a steady decline, dropping to $38 by the end of his term. The minimum wage rose briefly during the García heterodox period, reaching $45 by 1987, but then fell disastrously, to $29 in December 1988 and to $22 only two months later—that is, with 1979 as 100, by February 1989 the minimum wage was 37. By the end of calendar 1990, the official minimum wage was worth $17 (Webb and Fernandez Baca 1991, 524).

Wages for private sector blue-collar and white-collar workers fell as well. With 1979 as 100, wages for these two groups reached 52 and 49 respectively by early 1989. More dramatic still, according to the Ministry of Labor, using 1988 as 100, in December 1989 the real purchasing power of the average wage in metropolitan Lima was 51. Lima's workforce lost an average of 4.3 percent in purchasing power in the month of April 1990. From February 1989 to February 1990, state employees lost 43 percent of their purchasing power while receiving wage increases worth 22 percent (*El Comercio,* 1990, E.1). Nominal wages, of course, showed extraordinary increases: whereas for most of 1986 the official minimum monthly wage was about 700 intis, by December 1989 it was 435,000 intis, and by December 1990 it was 25 million intis (Webb and Fernandez Baca 1991, 524).

Inflation in the Peruvian economy has been a sometime thing; over certain periods of time it has been reasonably well under control, while at others (especially the late 1980s) it has been among the highest in the world. Losses in purchasing power naturally accompany high inflation, since state policies designed to match wages with inflation almost always fall short of their goal. Inflationary pressures began to take hold during the latter part of the military government in the late 1970s, and although there was some relative respite during Belaúnde's term and the first eighteen months or so of the García administration, the 1988–1990 period saw inflation completely out of control, reaching about 7,500 percent in the twelve-month period between June 1989 and June 1990.

Lima's urban populace in general and its urban poor in particular were thus faced with developing survival and coping strategies to overcome the ravages of what was by the late 1980s daily and even hourly inflation. Shopkeepers and businesses raised prices constantly, of course, and often large items (not only real estate but other durable goods) publicly carried price tags in dollars. The usual tactic for the consumer was to change any national currency immediately into hard currency (almost always U.S. dollars), a need that during the 1980s created astounding street brokerage operations. The most famous of these circulated around Jiron Ocoña in downtown Lima, where hundreds of young men (and some women) clutching packets of U.S. currency and hand calculators carried on a vigorous, noisy business buying and selling currency. Anyone who could not manage to make such transactions to preserve purchasing power was, of course, left far behind.[6]

INFORMALITY

Lima's informal sector is the most studied in Latin America and perhaps the world.[7] Conceptually, the best known work on Lima is undoubtedly de Soto (1986; see also ILD 1989a, 1989b, 1990a), although Carbonetto et al. (1988) is more sophisticated and empirical. Trying to do justice either to de Soto or to Carbonetto (and to their critics) is not feasible here; suffice it to say that their approaches are quite distinct. De Soto proposes a legalistic approach to informality, arguing in effect that overlayered bureaucracies and stifling legal restrictions of the formal sector of the economy force many hundreds of thousands of people (for the most part low-income) to use extralegal survival tactics to generate jobs, to secure housing, to manufacture, to engage in commerce, and in general to survive and cope with an urban economy that has highly restrictive entry mechanisms (de Soto 1986). Carbonetto, in contrast, argues that the informal sector has two major origins: first, a structural origin because of the gap between the demand for employment within the formal sector and the growth of the labor force; and second, a more cyclical and variable origin that is based on economic cycles that regularly exclude a fraction of the workforce in times of recession (Carbonetto et al. 1988, 59).

Regardless of the approach, any study of the informal sector must define the concept, a task that has caused much difficulty, although in macro terms the problems are certainly surmountable. Portes and Castells provide a representative definition: the informal sector refers to a set of economic activities characterized by (1) the absence of an explicit and written labor contract, (2) a lack of

state regulation of wages and working conditions, and (3) a clear separation between ownership of labor and capital (Portes and Castells 1989, 12). Yet the informal economy is best understood in terms of income generation and not in
terms of individual condition. That is to say, an individual worker may well
switch between the two sectors frequently, even in the course of the same day,
as in the case of a worker with informal part-time work. The critical feature of
the informal economy is that it is unregulated by the institutions of a society
that can and do regulate similar activities within that society.

De Soto (1986), Carbonetto et al. (1988), and others (for example, Toledo and
Chanlat 1991) have generated a wealth of empirical information dealing with
Peru's—and especially Lima's—informal economy. Rather than attempt to
summarize their conclusions here, simply let it be said that Peru may have the
world's largest informal economy relative to population size. Whether it be
manufacturing, commerce and sales, transportation, or housing, Peru and Lima
in particular have seen informality grow to huge proportions (de Soto 1986; ILD
1989a; also Carbonetto et al. 1988, esp. chap. 4 and tables 14–19). Regardless of
theoretical and technical arguments over the quality of de Soto's data (Bromley
1990; Rossini and Thomas 1990), the basic point has been made in thoroughly
convincing fashion: Lima's informal economy has grown to enormous size and
scope, the numbers of individuals involved within it have increased dramatically since the 1960s, and its contribution to Lima's overall economy and to the
survival of hundreds of thousands of its families is incontestable.

Cameron utilizes a common means of operationalizing the informal sector:
"The method consists of separating from the total economically active population all extractive sectors, all professional occupations, and all firms with over
4–9 workers. . . . What remains is the informal sector" (Cameron 1991a, 308).
Using this technique Cameron identified four major occupational groups
(workers, employers, white collar, and informal); he also divided the labor force
into rich, middle, poor, and informal groups. He then calculated the percentage
of informales in each of Lima's districts. As would be expected, the five squatter-intensive districts created between 1961 and 1981 (identified above) all contain high numbers of individuals working in the informal sector. All of them
are over 40 percent informal, and three of them (Villa María del Triunfo, Independencia, and El Agustino) are over half, with El Agustino having the highest
concentration in all of Lima at 63 percent (Cameron 1991a, 309).

CONCLUSIONS

While the 1970–1990 period saw Lima's growth and primacy slow in comparison with the 1960s, the city continued to retain its centuries-old primacy. Spatial

polarization by social class continued unabated, as the older, central districts of Lima with significant slum housing maintained their population densities, despite the movement of enormous numbers of people (mostly lower class) to increasingly distant marginal areas, which, as their populations increased over time, became legally incorporated into Lima as homogeneously poor districts, whether measured by type of housing, age distribution, municipal finance, income, or informality. The economic crisis of the 1980s put a halt to its previously explosive growth, but one characteristic never changed: residential social-class homogeneity, which remained constant despite extraordinary rises in inflation, unemployment, underemployment, and the size and complexity of Lima's informal sector.

Five Lower-Class Districts in Lima

To this point the focus for the most part has been on metropolitan Lima as a whole. Although I have emphasized the city's lower-class areas and populace living in poverty, specific districts have not received much attention. Each one of the six neighborhoods in which my sample surveys were administered, however, is located within a certain district, and it is now useful to look at more general, district-level information, and to describe the larger, formal, legal contexts.[8] Yet, however specific, even district-level data do not describe the sample neighborhoods. Some of Lima's districts have upward of half a million people; and among the dozens of neighborhoods that make up a district, each one has its own characteristics and history. (I therefore spend a good deal of time in chapter 5 providing historical descriptions and analyses of the sample neighborhoods.) Nevertheless, it is critical to examine the districts in which these neighborhoods are located, if for no other reason than that municipal government in Lima operates on the district level and therefore neighborhood groups must necessarily interact with district-level officials.

COMAS

Comas is located about fourteen kilometers from downtown Lima, north of the city. It is composed of a series of broad, sandy, desert valleys between spurs of Andean foothills that were, until 1958, unpopulated. Comas is a relatively new district of Lima; it was officially created in 1961, entirely because in 1958 it was the site of the then largest and most publicized land invasion in Lima's history. Most newspaper and eyewitness accounts estimate that ten thousand people moved onsite within the first forty-eight hours of the invasion, and the area grew rapidly from there on. The 1972 census gave Comas a population of 173,000, which grew to 283,000 in 1981, and to 404,000 in 1993 (Webb and Fernandez Baca 1991, 131; INEI 1994, 16). Comas's population density also increased over the years, from 92 people per hectare (1972), to 151 (1981), and to an estimated 221 (1990), or about two and a half times from 1972–1990 (Webb and Fernandez Baca 1991, 131; Allou 1989, 14).

Housing in Comas is almost entirely informal in nature. ILD (1989a) estimated that over 90 percent of the houses in Comas in 1982 were owner-built, ranging in materials from straw mat to brick and mortar. A great many households contain small businesses of a wide variety (convenience stores, restaurants, cottage industries). By the 1980s Comas's burgeoning population and its location on the major highway leading north from Lima began to attract businesses from outside the district. Branch banks, clothing stores, places of entertainment (the most noticeable being two large movie theaters), and a wide variety of commercial establishments all appeared during the 1970s and 1980s as businesses realized how much aggregate demand can be generated by a quarter-million people.

Comas placed eighth in García's poverty ranking of Lima's districts (García 1985, 127), and by the mid- to late 1980s was clearly showing signs of the economic crisis that gripped the entire country. Cameron (1991a) calculated that slightly less than three-quarters of its labor force was poor in 1986–1987 and that almost one-half (47 percent) was employed in the informal sector. One partial explanation for such conditions lies in the size of place of employment. Comas in 1984 had approximately 500 manufacturing establishments (Allou 1989, 30), but of these, 440 had four or less employees. The great majority of these establishments were thus small cottage industries that were likely to be informal, have low wages, and provide few if any benefits to their workers.

In the early 1980s over 40 percent of Comas's population was under the age of fifteen, and one-quarter of its total population older than fifteen had less than a complete primary education—two facts that together meant Comas's population was young and lacking access to education, something that is absolutely critical for economic progress in the case of Peru (Glewwe 1988). In 1986 Comas had about 150 soup kitchens, but a few years later the economic crisis had hit hard, and more than 1,300 communal kitchens were preparing in excess of 167,000 portions a day (Webb and Fernandez Baca 1991, 280). One final social indicator: in the late 1980s Comas had a total of 21 medical establishments of all descriptions (public and private hospitals, clinics, health centers, medical outposts), with a total of 301 beds, for 340,000 people (Allou 1989, 67).

All in all, Comas in 1990 represented a classic case of a semiconsolidated squatter-origin district. Formed through an initial massive land invasion, followed by other, smaller invasions, Comas was among the half-dozen largest districts of Lima. The community selected for sampling, Primero de Enero, was one of these smaller invasions: begun in 1968, it grew to full size (about 2,500 families) within a few years. In 1970 Primero de Enero represented a recent invasion-formed neighborhood. Like most of its surroundings in Comas, it consolidated over the years and by 1990 had reached a point where the great majority of its housing was permanent.

SAN JUAN DE MIRAFLORES

Prior to the mid-1950s, in what is now known as Lima's southern cone, whatever population existed was widely scattered across an immense semidesert and desert area. In the late 1950s, however, the Prado administration began a small experimental lower-class housing project known as Ciudad de Dios, a move that rapidly opened up the entire area for a variety of low-income housing, and for large numbers of people—who invaded land, who were victims of urban demolition projects in the central part of Lima and who were transferred to the area, or who were members of housing cooperatives that purchased land for their members in the area. Whatever the specific causes, the legal district of San Juan de Miraflores was created by 1965. The district had a population of 107,000 in 1972, which expanded to 168,000 in 1981, and to 284,000 in 1993 (Webb and Fernandez Baca 1992, 180; INEI 1994, 16). Given the size of the district, however, its population density remained relatively low over the years, although the density was higher than that of Comas (274 people per hectare as compared with 221 for Comas) in 1991. Such a difference is predictable in light of the larger number of two- and three-story houses in San Juan de Miraflores.

Because of the multiple reasons for its foundation and consolidation, San Juan became far more heterogeneous than Comas and its neighboring poorer districts such as Villa María del Triunfo or Villa El Salvador (which is perhaps Peru's most famous self-help settlement).[9] Parts of San Juan de Miraflores were (from almost any Peruvian perspective) lower-middle- to middle-class housing; parts were classic squatter communities. Some areas had paved streets and sidewalks since their inception; others waited for decades for such amenities.

The whole district was also, from the beginning, under much firmer control of the municipality and the state, meaning that, although land invasions did take place, the district did not grow haphazardly. Shortly after its inception, San Juan became the locus of a good deal of commercial investment, both by its inhabitants and by outside interests. The community built schools and market areas, and some of the squatter-initiated neighborhoods such as Pamplona Alta (the area sampled for this study) had considerable success throughout the 1970s and 1980s with self-help community projects such as neighborhood centers.

San Juan de Miraflores clearly ranks among the poorer (the bottom third) of Lima's districts on virtually any dimension of social well-being. According to García's (1985) study, San Juan de Miraflores ranked ninth on a poverty scale of all of Lima's districts, coming right after Comas. By the middle of the 1980s, Cameron (1991a) estimated that 44 percent of the labor force of San Juan de Miraflores was employed in the informal sector and that 71 percent of the labor force could be classified as poor, figures that were a slight improvement over those of Comas. In 1985 San Juan had a total of thirteen medical establishments, but not one of these had any patient beds; all of them were small medical posts (Allou 1989, 67). The district had approximately 40 soup kitchens in 1986 (Allou 1989, 74); this figure had risen dramatically by 1990, to more then 350, producing 167,000 portions, indicating an enormous need for such communal assistance (Webb and Fernandez Baca 1991, 280).

The neighborhoods sampled in San Juan de Miraflores are four areas within Pampa de Arena—San Francisco de la Cruz, Virgen de Buen Paso, Nuevo Horizonte, and Alfonso Ugarte—all of which date from the mid-1960s and all of which were formed through relatively small land invasions. At the time of the first survey in 1970, Pamplona represented a squatter neighborhood in a fairly early stage of consolidation. Some of the houses had begun to be built with brick and mortar, but most were either straw matting or some combination of brick and less durable materials. The four neighborhoods were selected on the basis of internal organizational differences, since all four were at that time physically similar. Some of the barrios had well-established community associations that were able to organize their neighborhoods and generate a considerable amount of self-help activity, whereas others were languishing, either because of internal conflicts or because of moribund associational life.

CERCADO DE LIMA

Lima Cercado (understood today to mean downtown Lima; the literal meaning is "walled Lima") is the heart and soul of old Lima. It is the Lima that Francisco Pizarro founded in 1532, and it has been the center of the city since Independence was declared in 1821 when it officially became a district of the city. For centuries it housed both the wealthiest and the poorest of Lima's inhabitants, and in it were concentrated all the city's riches and power. The Plaza de Armas, its main square, epitomizes this convergence: it is the site of the presidential palace, the cathedral, the archbishop's palace, and the city hall.

Since the middle of the 1800s, the city has grown, of course, and much of what was previously upper-class residential housing has deteriorated. What were once elegant homes became rental housing, as the city became more crowded and roads and development opened new, more desirable areas for the wealthy. These rental units were frequently subdivided into ever smaller units; landlords and owners paid decreasing attention to maintenance, which finally resulted in blocks of severely dilapidated housing. At the same time, the latter part of the nineteenth and the first part of the twentieth centuries saw so-called *callejón* (alleyway) housing built specifically as low-income housing. These were alleyways with small two- and three-room apartments running off them; a central spigot and two or three public toilets comprised the hygienic facilities.

Even as housing became less desirable, Lima Cercado managed to hold on to its reputation as the heart of business and commercial Lima. This meant that major streets were widened and modern office buildings appeared, especially during the 1920s and again following the end of World War II. By 1960 or so, Lima Cercado was a combination of governmental and ministry buildings, offices, cramped alleyway housing, many small businesses as well as large commercial and financial establishments, an immense amount of sidewalk and street vending, and heavy and congested traffic.

For decades Lima Cercado had an area of 2.2 square kilometers (about 5,600 acres). Its population was about 339,000 in 1961, which grew to 354,000 in 1972 and to 371,000 in 1981, and then diminished slightly to 340,000 by 1993 (Webb and Fernandez Baca 1992; INEI 1994, 16). This slow rate of growth (about .5 percent per year) is because of the scarcity of housing, new or old, and the density of the population (about 168 people per hectare in 1981). Ever since census data have been collected, Lima Cercado has been metropolitan Lima's (and the nation's) largest district in population. This dominance finally changed in 1981, when San Martín de Porres, an invasion-formed district dating from the 1950s, surpassed Lima Cercado, only to be surpassed itself by San Juan de Lurigancho in the 1993 census.[10]

Lima Cercado fell about midway in García's (1985) ranking of Lima's districts by poverty. About one-quarter of the district resided in squatter settlements in 1981; 14 percent of its population fifteen years or older had an education of less than complete primary; about 45 percent of its labor force was composed of unskilled manual labor (García 1985, 120–23). This last figure compares closely with Cameron (1991a), who calculated with 1986–1987 data that 43 percent of Lima Cercado's labor force was informal and that 64 percent was poor. In 1990 Lima Cercado had some 260 informal communal kitchens, serving approximately 52,000 rations daily to low-income individuals, numbers that place it among the top third of all of Lima's districts. Lima Cercado also had nearly

50 medical establishments with more than 2,500 hospital beds, because virtually all of the city's major public hospitals are in this district (Allou 1989, 67).

The specific neighborhood selected for sampling in Lima Cercado—28 de Julio—lies well beyond the downtown central core (about twenty minutes by bus) and it is a relatively quiet, ordered part of Lima Cercado. It was created through a series of small invasions in the late 1940s and, over the years, developed into what might be considered the ideal end point for a squatter settlement. By the late 1970s it was indistinguishable from any other part of lower-middle-class Lima Cercado and had been taken from the list of officially recognized squatter settlements of Lima because it no longer required or merited state assistance.

EL AGUSTINO

East of the downtown center of Lima and close by the major central highway that climbs into the Andes mountains are three hills: Cerro San Cosme, Cerro El Pino, and Cerro El Agustino. During World War II, Lima constructed a new wholesale-retail market, universally known as La Parada, on what was then outlying, marginal land near the highway, where trucks from the highlands could unload their produce. As a result, the city expanded toward these hills and the nearby land, which had been haciendas for many years. Cerro San Cosme, the smallest of the three, was the first of these hills to be invaded (in 1956), since it was located within a few blocks of La Parada.

In the late 1940s a hacienda at the foot of Cerro El Agustino was abandoned by its owner, but many of the hacienda workers stayed on and gained employment in and around La Parada, where there was a great need for large numbers of unskilled workers. Over the next decade or so the flat areas of the hacienda gradually filled in through mini-invasions and accretion, as did the lower parts of the hillsides. In 1965 the district of El Agustino was created.

El Agustino from its inception has been poor and crowded; much of its populace originally depended on work in and around La Parada, and although its labor force has become more heterogeneous over time, the area continues to project stark poverty. For many years Avenida Riva Agüero, the main street of the district, was a rutted packed-dirt road given to enormous congestion and potholes; it was finally paved during the 1970s but remains virtually the only surfaced major street. Both the flat areas and the surrounding hillsides became crowded with housing, some makeshift and some partially finished, but all enveloped in a gray unrelieved by any vegetation. Streets are frequently nothing more than pedestrian alleyways. Although a significant effort at urban renewal and renovation in some of the neighborhoods on flat land took place during the Velasco administration, the whole district is still very poor.

El Agustino's population grew from 117,000 (1972) to 168,000 (1981) and then dropped off slightly to 154,000 (1993), primarily because district lines were redrawn (Webb and Fernandez Baca 1992, 180; INEI 1994, 16). García's poverty ranking of Lima's districts that uses 1981 census data placed El Agustino as the second poorest district in the city (García 1985, 127), second only to Caraballyo, a much more rural district well to the north of Comas. Perhaps the most striking characteristics of El Agustino are its population density and the nature of its labor force. In 1972, the population density was about 115 people per hectare; by 1990, this figure had more than doubled to an estimated 240 people per hectare, many of whom live on steep hillsides and most of whom live in single-story dwellings (Webb and Fernandez Baca 1991, 131).

El Agustino's labor force has always been poor. Data from 1986–1987 (Cameron 1991a, 96) show that about three-quarters of El Agustino's workforce could be classified as poor (ranking the district seventh in the city), but that nearly two-thirds (63 percent) was employed in the informal sector, by far the highest percentage in all of Lima (only three others of a total of twenty-five districts had over half their labor forces in the informal sector). With a population of 170,000 in 1986, El Agustino had twenty medical establishments. One of these was a large state hospital with 637 beds, but it was dedicated largely to tuberculosis patients and to children, and it served all of metropolitan Lima. The district had no other establishment with any patient beds.

Overall, El Agustino exemplifies the poorest parts of Lima and those facing a set of intractable problems. Demand to live in and around La Parada has sustained population pressures in El Agustino, but the labor force drawn to La Parada has a strong tendency to be poorly educated and unskilled or semi-skilled. And the physical terrain makes regularizing and installing infrastructure difficult and expensive.

Two separate neighborhoods in El Agustino were selected for sampling. These are Zones A and B of 28 de Julio, which are relatively small (six or seven hundred households) contiguous neighborhoods on level terrain on opposite sides of Avenida Riva Agüero. At first glance they appear to be much the same in size and overall development: houses tend to be half-finished brick and mortar dwellings along crowded, narrow streets. In fact, their major attraction in 1970 was caused by their similarities, and their one outstanding difference: Zone A had severe internal associational difficulties and strife, whereas Zone B was well organized behind a single neighborhood group that had accomplished a good deal. The two zones thus offered a chance to see how organizational differences affected the political behavior of the citizenry.

SURQUILLO

In the years following World War II, Lima began to spread from its central core, filling in once green areas of haciendas and farms as development followed the major arterial roads built during the Leguía administration of the 1920s. In like fashion, the Odría (1948–1956) administration spent much money in public infrastructure, including highways, state office buildings, a national stadium, and elementary and secondary schools. One of the arterial roads that saw a great deal of activity along it was the Paseo de la República, which ran from one of downtown Lima's central plaza areas south toward the Pacific Ocean.

Development along the Paseo de la República included light industry, markets, and a proliferation of blue-collar and middle-class neighborhoods, and so substantial was this growth that in 1949 a new district named Surquillo was created. The 1961 census found 71,000 people in Surquillo, a total that expanded to 90,000 (1972), 134,000 (1981), and then diminished rather significantly to 88,000 (1993), because district lines were redrawn (Webb and Fernandez Baca 1991, 180; INEI 1994, 16). The district's population thus grew slowly following 1971, at least in comparison with any of Lima's squatter-intensive districts. But it maintained a significant blue-collar flavor, in terms of both employment and housing, although many of its neighborhoods would be classified as middle to upper middle by Lima standards. In addition, Surquillo was estimated in 1990 to have the highest population density of any district in the city, with 41,508 people per square kilometer (INEI 1992, 1). More than one-third of Surquillo's workforce in 1981 was either manual labor or independently employed; less than 3 percent of the labor force was classified as employer (Allou 1989, 18). In 1984 Surquillo had a total of 850 industrial enterprises, although well over one-half of them (535) employed four people or less. But in contrast to Comas and San Juan de Miraflores, Surquillo did have some major factories: some 33 establishments employed more than 3,400 workers (Allou 1989, 30).

By the late 1980s, Cameron (1991a, 96) calculated that only slightly more than half of Surquillo's labor force was poor, and that about one-third of it was employed in the informal sector, both figures that are well below the other sampled districts reported on here. Indeed, Cameron found that 30 percent of Surquillo was middle class and 18 percent upper class, in sharp contrast to Comas, San Juan de Miraflores, and even Lima Cercado, for example. García (1985, 127) ranked Surquillo twenty-first in his study of Lima's districts, making it easily the wealthiest of the five sampled districts.

Yet Surquillo's poor always have been poor. Many residents of the district's numerous slums and substandard housing environments are frequently migrants or simply low-income individuals who earn a precarious living in Surquillo's factories and commercial areas. Some of these lower-class households view Surquillo only as a temporary stop on the way to something better, whereas others have lived in such housing for years and intend to keep on doing so. Surquillo's relative proximity to downtown Lima (more or less twenty minutes by bus), its potential as a source of jobs, and its highly urban ambience all combine to make it attractive for many people, regardless of its drawbacks and problems.

Surquillo ever since its creation as a district has never been an area of squatters or of squatter housing. In the mid-1980s, only a tenth of the population lived in squatter housing (Allou 1989, 120). But the total percentage of substandard housing in Surquillo was much higher. About one-quarter (23.6 percent) of the 27,000 housing units in the district were classified "substandard" (*inapropiadas*), including what the census called "improvised housing," "housing in tenements," "housing in buildings not designed to be housing," and "other." Over 90 percent of this substandard housing existed in the form of *callejones* and *correlones*, Lima's generic terms for crowded alleyway rental housing, one of the highest percentages for any of Lima's districts (Allou 1989, 17). In another study using data from 1982, the ILD (1989a, 24) estimated that about one-fifth of Surquillo's housing was slum housing, giving the district the second highest percentage of such housing in metropolitan Lima (the highest was in Rímac). By the mid- and late 1980s, Surquillo was suffering along with the rest of Lima. Despite its population of 140,000 or so, the entire district had only four medical establishments (no hospital at all) and no patient beds.

The neighborhood sampled in Surquillo is a rental slum enclave known locally as Sendas Frutales, or more colorfully as Chicago chico (little Chicago) for the barrio's putative high crime and murder rate. This neighborhood has had an ongoing legal-designation struggle with the state ever since 1972 and its formal status has been in limbo. One result of this status has been an extreme difficulty in creating or maintaining any sort of community organization.

Aggregate Voting Results in Five Lima Districts

I do not intend here to go into electoral results by district in any significant way. In the first place, considerable analysis of the subject is already available (Dietz 1985; Tuesta 1991, 1994; Durand 1996), and there is no reason to repeat or to duplicate these discussions. In the second place, the focus of the book is on individual political participation; thus how a district voted as a whole is a question with only tangential value. Nevertheless, it is still useful to provide some basic

information about voting results in the five districts so that the individual results discussed later will have some larger, more general context.

The five districts show relative uniformity across the several elections that
have occurred since 1980.[11] In the three presidential elections of 1980, 1985, and
1990, all of the districts voted for the winning presidential candidates (AP in
1980, APRA in 1985, and Cambio 90 in 1990). But the margins of victory varied
from the total Lima vote. In general, Comas and El Agustino have considerably
higher levels of leftist support than the other three. APRA has steady support
that varies only slightly across all districts, whereas support for the right (PPC
and CODE, Convergencia Democrática, or Democratic Convergence) is significantly higher in Surquillo and Lima Cercado than elsewhere.

In the four municipal races (1980, 1983, 1986, 1989), results are somewhat
more mixed. The left enjoyed substantial support from 1980 through 1986, in
general doing better in these five districts than in Lima overall. The leftist vote
in Comas, El Agustino, and San Juan de Miraflores was remarkably high and
sustained. By 1989 this pattern was becoming more diffuse; the left maintained
a plurality only in Comas, while a resurgent right (Fredemo) and independent
candidates showed strength in the other districts. As with the presidential elections, Lima Cercado and Surquillo show a more evenly distributed vote, with
the right capturing in each of these districts about the same level of support as
it did in metropolitan Lima. (I take a closer look at voting in chapter 8, using the
survey data from the six neighborhoods, and make some comparisons of neighborhood versus district results.)

Conclusions

The data presented here speak very much for themselves, and summarizing
them would serve no purpose. Overall, metropolitan and district aggregate
data present clear evidence that the poor have since the 1960s achieved numerical superiority in Lima, and that the city's legal expansion has not only reflected the physical growth of the city but has also assured that the lower classes
live with one another and not with the middle and upper classes. The older
parts of central Lima continue to be densely crowded, with people living in
rental slum housing, while the new poor parts of Lima are less crowded but
more uniformly poor. Whether measured by type of housing or monetary resources, by income levels or presence of informality, Lima's poor districts, especially the newer ones composed of uncontrolled squatter sites, are uniformly
poor.

The economic crisis of the 1980s did not disrupt these patterns. Lima's over-

Table 1. Voting Results in Five Lima Districts, 1980–1990

Election and Party	Comas	San Juan	Lima	El A.	Sur-quillo	Metro. Lima
1980 Presidential						
IU	20.1	16.2	12.0	19.1	12.5	12.5
APRA	22.4	21.1	25.1	18.4	23.3	22.9
AP	50.3	50.6	44.5	52.3	47.8	47.1
PPC	5.0	9.2	16.4	6.6	14.1	15.4
1985 Presidential						
IU	34.0	28.9	24.4	36.4	21.1	23.9
APRA	54.9	52.8	51.9	50.4	53.0	50.6
AP	4.0	5.1	4.5	4.2	4.7	4.4
CODE	5.3	11.1	17.2	6.3	19.4	19.2
1990 Presidential 1[a]						
Left	16.2	12.3	12.8	14.0	9.3	11.0
APRA	17.3	14.9	15.2	12.1	14.9	13.8
Cambio 90	43.6	42.2	33.0	49.7	32.0	34.4
Fredemo	21.1	21.8	38.6	22.0	42.9	39.5
1990 Presidential 2[a]						
Fredemo	29.0	37.5	46.3	29.8	51.5	46.7
Cambio 90	72.0	62.5	53.7	70.2	48.5	53.3
1980 Municipal						
IU	43.1	36.7	28.0	41.4	28.3	28.3
APRA	16.0	14.2	17.0	19.3	15.5	16.4
AP	32.0	35.8	32.8	29.5	36.2	34.7
PPC	9.0	13.3	22.2	9.8	20.1	20.6
1983 Municipal						
IU	53.8	47.3	35.1	55.3	36.8	36.6
APRA	28.3	26.1	29.1	24.4	27.8	27.1
AP	7.5	9.2	11.6	8.5	12.2	11.9
PPC	8.0	13.4	21.3	8.7	19.3	21.2
1986 Municipal						
IU	46.5	43.0	33.5	47.3	31.8	33.5
APRA	45.1	42.9	38.7	43.0	39.7	38.7
PPC	8.4	14.1	25.7	9.5	28.3	25.7
1989 Municipal						
IU/ASI[b]	38.6	20.6	24.9	30.7	17.9	24.9
APRA	21.4	38.3	16.0	18.0	14.4	16.0
Fredemo	25.0	28.4	40.2	22.7	47.5	40.2
Other	14.8	17.1	18.9	28.6	20.2	18.9

Source: Tuesta 1994.

Notes: Figures are percentages. Totals do not necessarily sum to 100 percent because of rounding and/or missing data. Totals are for valid votes cast and exclude null and void ballots, blank ballots, and abstentions.

a. Presidential 1 = first round of the presidential race; Presidential 2 = second round.

b. Combined totals of IU and ASI, the two major leftist parties.

all population growth did decline in percentage terms during the 1970s and 1980s compared with the 1960s, but its sheer size and primacy continued to attract hundreds of thousands of migrants every year. As a result, inner-city districts with high levels of rental slum housing continued to be densely populated despite continued growth in the city's outlying northern, southern, and eastern areas.

Chapters 3 and 4 have focused on macro problems and processes—the difficulties in establishing and maintaining democratic procedures amid a collapsing economy, changing and deteriorating social conditions, and the presence of a violent insurgent group that by the end of the 1980s was attempting to move its theater of war into Lima. But before the discussion moves on to an examination of the political participation of Lima's poor, there is still one level of context that affects their behavior, and this is their immediate neighborhood. Thus I now turn to the specifics of the six communities I researched in Lima, to see how they developed and coped with the extraordinary changes that occurred in Peru and metropolitan Lima from 1970 to 1990.

5

....

SIX POOR BARRIOS

AND THEIR

INHABITANTS

IT IS NOW APPROPRIATE to focus in on the six specific neighborhoods that were the sites for the surveys carried out in 1970, 1982, 1985, and 1990. In Lima, as in many other Third World nations, there are two broad classifications of low-income housing (Grompone et al. 1983, 57; Driant 1991; Dietz 1980): (1) rental housing in and around the central city core and in working-class districts (or tugurios); and (2) self-help autonomous squatter settlement housing (or pueblos jóvenes), almost always illegal in origin and in general located on the periphery of the city. Any representative study of Lima's poor must therefore include samples from both types of neighborhoods.

Many observers have differentiated between these two types of settlements (Delgado 1975; Dietz 1980, 36–38). One of the more provocative recent discussions comes from Nugent (1992), who argues that, although both tugurios and pueblos jóvenes are undeniably poor, their social and cultural (and, I would add, political) meanings are fundamentally different. The generalized deterioration of the turgurio environment is largely because of neglect, but this deterioration does not by and of itself change the physical or spatial definition of the city. In sharp contrast, the squatter phenomenon by its urban expansion has absolutely and irrevocably changed the face of the city;

> it is a question of the transformation of the city by and because of poverty, and not as a product of planning controlled by the centralized power of the state . . . if we view the concept of progress as linked to ideas such as bettering the con-

ditions of life, then the creation of [squatter settlements] and the perspective of progress are inseparable. (Nugent 1992, 31–2)[1]

Lima's Squatter Settlements

Attention in Lima is quite naturally first drawn to the city's squatter settlements, which have been known by a variety of local names: barrios marginales, barriadas, and pueblos jóvenes. In 1970, when this study commenced, census data estimated that about one-third of Lima's then 3.5 million or so people resided in the squatter settlements. By 1990 Lima had reached about 7 million, and about half this population lived in these settlements.

As many observers have argued, Third World squatter settlements have one basic common characteristic: they are virtually all of illegal origin. Other than that, they may differ from one another along more lines than they are similar. Thus they may differ by size, age, density of population, location vis-à-vis the city center, size of internal labor market, local geography, manner of formation, internal political cohesion, or materials used in house construction (Leeds 1969, 48–49).

Given such a limitless range of variables and the number of settlements in metropolitan Lima (more or less three hundred), any study that sets out to be approximately representative of these settlements must have clear criteria in mind for picking specific communities. In 1970 I chose three major factors to be a priori of paramount importance for site selection. These three factors were deemed particularly important for understanding informal participation, since at the time there were no formal (that is, electoral) mechanisms for political participation.

First, the age of the settlement was a vital consideration, since it would likely have a considerable impact on political participation, especially informal participation: ceteris paribus the younger the community, the greater the level of participation. In a new community, much remains to be done. Moreover, a new community inhabited by recent arrivals excited about de facto landownership and the possibility of building a house should have a populace with high levels of informal participation. Contrariwise, as a community ages and as local needs susceptible to community efforts are completed, informal participatory levels should tend to fall off. After 1980, when formal (electoral) involvement became an important consideration, a young settlement with less experience in dealing with the state and its agencies and hence lower levels of frustration might have less tendency to vote for non-incumbents or for radical alternatives.

In addition, residents in a newly settled community might well want to demonstrate to the authorities that they are not radical and do not want to rock the boat by supporting radical candidates or parties.

Second, the manner of formation of the settlement was an especially relevant factor for informal participation in 1970. Assuming a onetime massive land invasion, residents might display high levels of cohesiveness and community participation as a spinoff of the successful invasion. In contrast, a community settled by slow accretion might begin its existence with a much lower level of community-based involvement. Or, as another example, if a community formed by invasion was initially met with significant government resistance (as is often the case), then state-community relations might be difficult and strained from the start.

Third, the overall development of the community was deemed an important factor. This factor is a combination of four subfactors: (1) the materials used in construction of the houses, which might vary from straw mat huts *(chozas de estera)* to brick and mortar two- or three-story houses; (2) the overall population density, which derives from lot size, number of people per dwelling, size and regularity of streets and walkways; (3) the type of terrain, or local geography, which can range from flat land near the city or a highway to river-bottom land, to hillsides, to the distant periphery of the city; and (4) the internal cohesion of the community, which is made up of intracommunity conflict, the efficacy of the local association, and the success of communitywide activities.

Lima's Rental Slums

Lima's central city slum areas mark a frequently sharp contrast to the universe of its squatter settlements. Often consisting of older dwellings (some going back to before the turn of the twentieth century), these rooms and apartments range widely in character (Driant 1991, 95) and contain housing that varies from the modestly acceptable to the truly egregious. Low-income rental units are scattered throughout most of metropolitan Lima but are concentrated in the old central city core. They are especially noticeable in downtown Lima in areas such as Barrios Altos, the environs of La Parada (Lima's huge wholesale-retail market), the districts of Rímac, Barranco, and La Victoria, blue-collar districts such as Surquillo and Breña, and the old working-class areas of Ate-Vitarte. The crucial characteristic that defines them all is the rental market landlord-tenant relationship. No administration, military or civilian, has been willing to become embroiled in this byzantine world of decades-old tenant law, and aside from a few efforts made by the Velasco administration to redress the worst abuses of the system (which allowed for throwing tenants out in the street with no warning or reason, for example), individuals living in Lima's tugurios and callejones were by and large ignored and left to their own devices.

Such devices are few and far between. If the physical condition of a dwelling is deteriorating or if a landlord raises rents, there is little an individual renter can do. Likewise, few renters are willing to fix up their dwellings since all such improvements revert to the owner. Thus any sense of community in these areas is apt to be low or nonexistent, especially when compared with Lima's squatter settlements.

So now we come to some crucial questions. In 1970, what did the six research communities look like? And how did they change over the years?[2]

The Research Communities

PRIMERO DE ENERO

At the time of the initial survey, Primero de Enero was the newest of the six barrios; it was then less than three years old. Located about fourteen kilometers northwest of downtown Lima in the district of Comas, it had been founded through a large-scale, well-planned invasion of about six hundred families on January 1, 1968. About six months before the invasion, several families contacted students at the National Engineering University to come out to the piece of land they had in mind and to survey the land and to lay out streets, lots, and open spaces, all in accord with the criteria of the then National Housing Board. The idea was that once the invasion had been recognized by the government, individual families could begin to build houses out of permanent materials immediately, rather than waiting for the government to come out and survey the area and assign approved lots.

The land itself and its location were, from the point of view of the invaders, quite desirable. In the first place, no private individual had clear title to it; instead, only a vague claim existed, by an absentee landowner. In the second place, the land was located near a large existing squatter settlement (Pampa de Comas) that had been formed through an invasion in 1958. There were bus lines running near the invasion site as well as markets and other sources of supplies nearby. Finally, the invaders obtained the covert assistance and support of the then mayor of Comas, who was a member of the opposition party and who had no reluctance in seeing a land invasion embarrass the administration.

The invasion itself went smoothly; about six hundred families moved onto

the unoccupied land, and after a brief initial confrontation with police the set-
tlers were allowed to remain. But any dreams that the government would move
quickly to adopt the invaders' plans and thereby permit the permanent construction of individual housing disappeared in a series of bitter and seemingly
intractable land and boundary disputes with a nearby housing cooperative.
These debates went on for some years, and for the residents the major frustration arose from the refusal of the government to approve of existing lots or to
survey new ones until the dispute was settled. In addition, the original six hundred or so invasion families were soon followed by many more, so that, within
six months or so, Primero de Enero had somewhat more than two thousand
families, a number that grew only incrementally during the 1980s.

The debate with the neighboring cooperative was finally resolved, and over
the years the community developed and consolidated. Many houses moved
from estera huts to one- or two-story brick and mortar dwellings. A large market complex grew up and elementary schools (frequently built by the community and then staffed by the Ministry of Education) appeared, along with other
public facilities such as a post office and some paramedic clinics.

As is usual in all such communities, time and socioeconomic status differences brought divisions to Primero de Enero. Houses belonging to those
pobladores who had higher incomes and more stable employment showed
early signs of improved construction. Most such houses were located on the
level land nearer the highway, where lots were larger (generally 160 square meters) and more regular. In sharp contrast, estera huts located on the hillsides
often remained rudimentary for years. In addition, leaders of the local association, who were for some years generally members of the original invasion
group, frequently disparaged latecomers as trespassers and as detracting from
the original scheme and intentions of the invasion. Small subneighborhoods of
Primero took on importance; people sometimes began to identify themselves
as belonging to such small units instead of to Primero de Enero as a whole, a
process that inevitably created divisions within the community.

Nevertheless, Primero de Enero by and large managed to hang together
over the years and to wring some services and improvements from the state.
Improved streets (crushed rock roadbeds, not pavement), for example, and
some sidewalks were built incrementally. Electricity appeared (but only well
into the 1970s); lampposts were installed and wires strung up, with individual
connections made to houses (many families on the outlying hillsides still obtained electricity by illegally tapping into nearby power lines). Water was for
years delivered by tank trucks that circulated through the area; potable water
and sewerage were much delayed, since installing pipes and pumping equip-

ment required not only substantial capital outlays by the community and the state but also considerable disruption caused by excavating main and branch trenches along existing streets and into existing houses. By 1990 more than half of the houses in Primero de Enero were hooked up to water pipes; however, given the overall shortage of water in metropolitan Lima, water was severely rationed, especially in the summertime, when it was sometimes available for only three or four predawn hours a day.

Additional goods from the state were slow to arrive. Land titles, for example, were delayed interminably, despite many loud rhetorical promises on the part of SINAMOS and the military regime. The Belaúnde administration accomplished relatively little in Primero de Enero, and the García administration's efforts to promote PAIT and other emergency programs in the area in response to the economic crisis of the late 1980s were superficial and short-lived.

By 1990, Primero de Enero was a well-established Lima squatter settlement. It had long been officially recognized as such by the state and was no more marginal or isolated than any of the several hundred barrios of Lima. Its location near a principal highway and other squatter settlements, its formation through a large-scale invasion, and its relatively flat terrain, all allowed the community to proceed ahead with relatively few difficulties.

PAMPA DE ARENA

Pampa de Arena had its start in the early 1960s as the site for a number of families who were made homeless because of a fire in the Tacora area around Lima's marketplace.[3] These families were transferred from downtown Lima to a sandy area about eight or ten kilometers south of the center of the city, where the Prado government had built an experimental low-income housing development called Ciudad de Dios. The displaced families were located on the outskirts of this development, and over the years other families moved in either through fairly small-scale invasions or because of urban renewal projects in Lima that forced the state to find housing, or at least vacant lots.

Over the late 1960s and 1970s Pampa de Arena continued to grow until it had some fifteen distinct zones, some quite small (eight or ten blocks of a dozen or so houses each) and others much larger (a hundred or more lots). Intracommunity cooperation varied. Perhaps because of the overall size of Pampa de Arena or perhaps because of its pattern of incremental growth through small invasions and relocations, Pampa de Arena pobladores—much like their Primero de Enero counterparts—tend to identify with a specific small subcommunity or neighborhood within Pampa de Arena rather than with the overall settlement. Many neighborhood events take place within and concern only one separate neighborhood at a time; for example, one Sunday afternoon in the 1970s, many of the residents of an area known as San Francisco de la Cruz were cooperating in several activities, including the construction of a new community center, a vaccination program for preschool children sponsored by the Ministry of Health, voting for local delegates to the neighborhood association, and playing games of chance for small prizes (soft drinks, beer, cookies), the proceeds of which went to buy more building materials for the community center. But this effort was strictly for San Francisco; no other areas were involved. Other neighborhoods might or might not have the degree of internal cooperation of San Francisco; indeed, both a smaller and a larger contiguous neighborhood were traditionally unable to generate anything like what San Francisco was able to do on a regular basis.

Over the 1970s and 1980s Pampa de Arena became noticeably consolidated; houses with few exceptions turned from straw matting to brick and mortar, streets became regularized, electricity appeared, and other infrastructural improvements were installed. The district of Lima within which Pampa de Arena is located—known as San Juan de Miraflores—grew and consolidated as well. San Juan comprises part of Lima's southern cone, a multidistrict sprawl that is home to at least 1.5 million people, the great majority of whom are poor. In this larger universe, Pampa de Arena is neither the poorest nor the richest.

In recent years Pampa de Arena has encountered some new problems. Virtually all of the community has its fair share of small convenience general stores or *bodegas*, bakeries, cottage industries, and the like, and some of the neighborhoods' central streets are now crowded. Some of the houses built twenty years ago are now stores with families renting rooms above them, despite laws that prohibit renting rooms or houses in officially recognized squatter settlements. Parents complain of delinquency, crime, and the presence of drug users and pushers, and petty theft and assaults are more common than before. Whether because of age, the overall economic collapse of the late 1980s, or the erosion of community spirit because of the increased presence of newer inhabitants with no recollection of the invasions and excitement of twenty or thirty years ago, Pampa de Arena is showing distinct signs of age as well as maturity.

SANTIAGO

Santiago occupies a long narrow strip of land about four blocks wide by twenty blocks long on the southern side of the Rímac River, which divides Lima. This narrow strip used to be the old riverbed; the river was channeled and redirected in the 1920s. In the 1930s the landowners worked it as a quarry for cobblestones, and following the end of World War II some of the quarry workers began to set up houses as squatters, as is still evident in the irregular small blocks at the eastern end of the community. A series of relatively small land invasions filled in the rest of the land during the early 1950s, and by 1952 most of the blocks had been laid out and the lots occupied.

It was about 1952 as well that a strong neighborhood association come into being, and from all accounts the strength of this association was instrumental in preserving the street layout and preventing overcrowding. People who arrived during the mid-1950s had to deal with this association, which controlled the available land and lots and sold rights to occupy the land, although it had no legal basis for doing so and certainly could not provide any legal title to the land. The association also undertook the installation of electricity, water, and sewerage networks, an effort that was in part successful. But a good deal of criticism developed in the late 1950s as the association became less responsive to the community, and reports of mismanagement and disappearing funds became common. As a result, another community organization formed in opposition to the original group, and throughout the late 1960s and early 1970s the two organizations spent as much time battling each other as they did in working for the community.

By 1970 the military government and SINAMOS had intervened, created a new neighborhood organization, and begun to distribute official land titles. Perhaps the most fundamental change occurred in 1973, when Santiago was taken from the list of official squatter settlements and became de facto another part of Lima Cercado. By the end of the late 1970s Santiago was the same as any other lower-middle-class neighborhood in Lima. Most of its streets were paved, and virtually all the houses (two- and three-story brick and mortar, stuccoed) had electricity and running water. The community had two elementary schools and a secondary school, two churches (one Catholic and one Evangelical), a police station, three bus lines servicing it, and a soccer field. Its location next to one of Lima's largest industrial zones was a major concern; fumes from a petrochemical plant were blamed for environmental problems and certain seemingly recurrent skin and pulmonary problems.

Santiago represents in many ways the ideal end point for a squatter settlement. It has progressed about as far as it can; its internal ability to maintain order and coherence over the years kept it under control and allowed infrastructure to be installed without major disruption. But its location away from major sources of ready unskilled and semiskilled employment such as markets also helped to attract (eventually) lower-middle-class inhabitants and to prevent its becoming overcrowded from pressures to subdivide lots or to allow rental housing to overwhelm homeownership.

28 DE JULIO, ZONES A AND B

Lima built a new wholesale-retail market complex in the 1940s, which universally became known as La Parada.[4] As with any such complex, to make it work La Parada depended on large numbers of stall owners, sellers and buyers, warehouse owners, and *cargadores* (people who load and unload produce trucks). Likewise, the presence of the market generated a whole range of secondary industries such as garages, stores, restaurants, and repair shops, along with street vendors and other itinerant entrepreneurs. At the same time, of course, La Parada also created a need for cheap housing, which led to squatting and trespassing on nearby land. Three hills in the immediate vicinity—Cerro San Cosme, Cerro El Pino, and Cerro El Agustino—were all successfully invaded and built upon after the end of World War II.

The hills were unoccupied, and although building on hillsides makes for significant difficulties, the land was available and convenient. In the 1950s the land was still in private hands as a hacienda, but two events took place that changed the area permanently: first, the owners lost interest in maintaining the hacienda and allowed the irrigation system to deteriorate; second, the area as a whole became more attractive for cheap housing near La Parada. The hacienda workers stayed where they were and began a cycle of selling the land (extralegally) to friends and relatives, who bought lots and subdivided them. The physical layout of 28 de Julio thus coalesced over time in a highly irregular manner; the footpaths from the old hacienda became streets and alleyways, and the housing units became small and overcrowded. In addition, the hillsides around the flat areas became covered with houses as well, creating an overall dense and overpopulated impression.[5]

By 1970 houses in Zones A and B—the two neighborhoods used in the survey—were largely either of adobe or of brick and mortar, but many of them were only one story high, making crowding severe. The average size of a dwelling in Zones A and B was about 35 square meters (350 square feet); the average family size was slightly in excess of six people. Zones A and B were both located on flat land adjacent to Avenida Riva Agüero, the major street that runs through El Agustino. This street is almost entirely commercial in nature, with large numbers of car and truck repair shops and shops selling stolen auto parts, restaurants, schools, a movie theater, two small branch banks, and many stores. The community benefited immensely when this street was paved and sidewalks installed in the mid-1960s. However, Riva Agüero remains the only paved street in the area; the side streets in Zones A and B barely permit vehicular traffic, and many of these streets are cul-de-sacs.

The attractions of 28 de Julio as a research site were several. In the first place, in 1970 it was an old community with multiple physical, infrastructural, and organization problems. Perhaps its major built-in difficulty came from its location. Being so close to La Parada, it was a natural target for recent rural-origin migrants and for the unskilled labor force that depended for a livelihood on La Parada. The whole area thus began poor and remained poor; its inhabitants were clearly worse off on average than those of Primero de Enero, Pampa de Arena, and Santiago. Not only were overall physical conditions worse, but the chances of neighborhood improvement were much diminished because of crowding. Indeed, in 1971, Delgado (1975) classified 28 de Julio as a *barriada tugurizada* (roughly, a "slummified" or deteriorating squatter settlement).

Both Zones A and B had tried during the 1960s to undertake basic neighborhood improvements by installing electricity, water, and sewerage. These efforts were partially successful, but putting in the water system involved much more than digging trenches. In several places streets had to widened, meaning that houses had to be demolished—or, in some cases, dismantled and moved, adobe by adobe, a meter or so—to allow room for the water pipes. This construction took several years, and the streets were constantly torn up while it was under way.

By the late 1960s the military government concluded that it would attempt a basic restructuring of Zones A and B. The state made about fifty-five nearby hectares available and announced that between one-third and one-half of each zone would have to be relocated, that much of the remaining housing would be demolished and the streets widened, and that the pobladores who remained as well as those who moved would be given assistance in rebuilding their houses. By 1975 the relocation and renewal of both zones had taken place, and the changes were impressive. The housing on the new land had progressed, but Zones A and B had undergone considerable change. The new housing was almost entirely brick and mortar, and the streets had been regularized, widened, and surfaced (not paved).

Both zones are still densely crowded compared with Lima's more traditional squatter settlements, because lots are smaller and streets are narrower. But for those residents who had lived in either zone for twenty or thirty years, the changes were remarkable and welcome. By the 1980s Zones A and B had become much more decent to live in, although the problems associated with their locations and with overwhelming tendencies toward overcrowding would always remain.

When my initial survey was undertaken in 1970, Zones A and B appeared twins. They were about the same size, had the same population, were the same age, and had about the same overall level of development and the same set of intractable physical problems. But their organizational life was quite different. Zone A had experienced years of internal associational strife and lack of coherent leadership, whereas Zone B had had a series of strong leaders able to count on neighborhood support in their community and petitioning efforts. By most accounts, the state's decision to remodel Zones A and B came as a result of endless petitioning and pestering on the part of Zone B's leaders. Zone A was included largely because it is contiguous with Zone B. At the time of the original survey, therefore, it was possible to hold a wide variety of neighborhood variables constant and examine the differences that a viable local association can make on political involvement.

SENDAS FRUTALES

Sendas Frutales is the single sample that represents a tugurio or urban slum environment. Access to such neighborhoods is harder than it is for a squatter settlement, where a local organization exists and where, in many instances, the pobladores are at least accustomed to the presence of outsiders (if not foreigners). But in the central city and working-class districts of Lima, the rental slum and tenement environments are smaller and more atomized, and their residents are not used to having outsiders around.

Sendas Frutales as an identifiable neighborhood dates back to the immediate post–World War II years. At that time the area was well outside the urban limits of Lima, and its absentee landowners developed it as a nursery for fruit trees, cut flowers, orchards, and truck farming (hence its unofficial name, which means approximately "fruited paths or trails"). Three streets in the form of a square U—with each longer leg of the U about a hundred meters long—housed the workers who lived on the site.

In 1950 the area was incorporated into a new district of Lima called Surquillo, and Sendas Frutales found itself near the intersection of two major thoroughfares. The landowners ceased agricultural production; some of them stayed in the neighborhood and became renters, whereas others sold their land to new individuals who also rented space. As Surquillo grew rapidly into a blue-collar district, the housing found along the three streets came into demand, and the whole area soon became crowded. Some landowners, in search of profits, built callejones with more but smaller apartments and rooms. The end result by the early 1970s was a densely inhabited enclave of approximately eighteen hundred rental housing units (total population of around ten thousand) owned by about fifteen different landlords. The quality of housing varied from the modestly acceptable to the execrable. One family had three rooms (about 60 square meters) with concrete floors and brick and mortar walls and roof, running water and electricity, and in 1970 paid about $6.50 monthly rent. Twenty meters down the street, however, one landlord had divided about 200 square meters into ten separate tiny lots of 20 square meters apiece; each tenant paid rent for the land only, about $20 apiece, and had to buy secondhand adobe from the landowner to build their own houses. None of these rooms had any sanitary facilities.

Although almost purely residential, Sendas Frutales has a local reputation as being a dangerous area and is known locally as "Chicago chico," in reference to its supposed high crime rate. Bars draw a rough crowd and some prostitutes frequent the area, but the crime that does exist is almost entirely because of nonresidents. Most of the pobladores are poor, many are fairly recent migrants, and turnover is high, as new arrivals move in and others move out. Some residents have lived in Sendas Frutales for years, but the more common pattern is for recent migrants to rent a room for a short time until they can find somewhere else cheaper or of better quality or they can make a move to a squatter area. Indeed, the 1970 survey found a small group of families in Pampa de Arena whose previous residence had been Sendas Frutales.

Until 1970 the pobladores of Sendas Frutales had few alternatives available to them if they ran into a problem with their landlords: they could complain to the landlord, they could complain to one level or another of the state (district, city, or national authorities), they could try to do something on their own, or they could leave. All these options had limitations. Complaining to the landlord generally led nowhere, as those owners who wished just to collect rents had no intention of making improvements and said so openly. Going to the authorities encountered delays or no response; local officials either ignored complaints or were bought off by the owners, and national agencies (the Ministry of Housing, for example) had no authority to intervene. The pobladores were unwilling to invest their meager resources in improving their dwellings when all such improvements would revert to the landlord. Many did in fact leave, but others who either had no alternative or were tied to the area through their jobs and other considerations found themselves in a difficult situation.

In late 1972, however, matters changed. One of the most notorious of the landlords forcibly evicted a renter; this renter and his family and neighbors just as forcibly resisted. The owner sought, and obtained, the protection of the municipal police and proceeded to level about a hundred small rooms with the intention of constructing low-rise middle-class housing. The pobladores sought the assistance of Msgr. Luís Bambarén, then Lima's officially designated bishop to the squatter communities of metropolitan Lima. Msgr. Bambarén in turn contacted the colonel in charge of the local office of SINAMOS. After a series of threats, counterthreats, armed confrontations between the owner and the tenants, many meetings, and numerous lengthy open letters in Lima newspapers from both landlords and pobladores appealing to President Velasco, the SINAMOS colonel decreed (with dubious authority and legality) that Sendas Frutales was a squatter settlement and thereby protected under the law.

The repercussions of this decree were several, immediate, and long lasting, since the pobladores, the owners, SINAMOS, President Velasco, and the Ministry of Housing all found themselves in a classic showdown. The landlords and the renters published accusatory, inflammatory letters in Lima newspapers; Velasco issued a formal revocation of the SINAMOS decree and turned the whole matter over to the Ministry of Housing; the SINAMOS colonel delayed in implementing the president's order and was transferred; the pobladores twice marched on the SINAMOS office; and the landlords issued notices of eviction that were countermanded by SINAMOS. The final result was that the SINAMOS decree was revoked and Sendas Frutales was reclassified as an *urbanización popular*, an ambiguous classification at best.

The pobladores rejected such a classification, and matters remained unsettled, even after President Velasco was replaced in 1975 by General Francisco Morales Bermúdez. The battle over the legal status of Sendas Frutales dragged on throughout the rest of the 1970s and well through the 1980s. Many people moved out of the area, either unaware or unmindful of the problem, which remained an issue basically for the landowners and some older residents. Houses were torn down and new ones built, and some new modern office buildings appeared near the entrance to the area, but the main streets that make up Sendas Frutales remained much the same in appearance.

The Neighborhoods Compared

It is now appropriate to pull together this descriptive information and compare the six neighborhoods with one another. The communities can be classified along the three basic dimensions used to select them in the first place in 1970, and each one can be followed over twenty years. It should be self-evident that the sites offer a range of different types of communities. In 1970 they ranged from the new (Primero de Enero) to the settled (Pampa de Arena) to the highly consolidated (Santiago) and the troubled (28 de Julio). They included classic invasion sites (Primero de Enero) as well as accretion settlements (28 de Julio) and atomistic slums (Sendas Frutales); they were flat (Pampa de Arena, 28 de

Julio) or hilly (Primero de Enero), organized (Pampa de Arena) or otherwise (the two zones of 28 de Julio, Santiago); they contained housing that ranged from precarious (Pampa de Arena) to complete (Santiago).

As twenty years passed, some of these differences blurred. The physical location and topographic conditions remained the same, of course, although what had been considered the outskirts of Lima in 1970 (Pampa de Arena) was now perceived as reasonably close in and relatively convenient. Physically, Primero de Enero and Pampa de Arena were quite similar in appearance in 1990, especially along their main streets; the two zones of 28 de Julio were still virtual twins. Santiago remained noticeably more advanced than all the others. Sendas Frutales was still largely a hodgepodge of modest to repulsive housing.

I have sketched in some important characteristics of and changes in the research communities, but all this information does not reveal much at all about the people who live there. Who are they? Where do they come from? How old are they? What kind of jobs do they have? Do the residents of these communities, as well as the communities themselves, make up the urban informal sector that de Soto (1986) and others have described? Although the following chapters say a great deal about modes of involvement as well as informal and formal behavior, it is appropriate here to present some descriptive demographic information about the pobladores of the six neighborhoods and some idea of how these characteristics changed over twenty years.

Barrio Residents

PLACE OF BIRTH

In 1970 slightly more than four out of five survey respondents had been born outside of Lima; this figure changed only moderately by 1990, when about three-quarters were of provincial origin. To be specific, in 1970 Primero de Enero and Pampa de Arena, the two recent invasion-formed communities, had the highest level (over 85 percent) of provincial-born occupants. In 1990 this was still the case; these two communities were the only ones of the six whose provincial-origin inhabitants were greater than 80 percent. More broadly speaking, however, it is noteworthy that all the communities had consistently high levels of migrants. All of them were more than 60 percent migrant.

LENGTH OF RESIDENCE AND SIZE OF HOUSEHOLD

Comparing length of residence across time does two things; it permits a rough idea of how many people move into an area once it is settled, and it shows how permanent the population is over time. In 1970 somewhat less than one-half of the entire sample (44.1 percent) had resided in their communities for less than five years, whereas in 1990 more than four out of five had been in the areas for over ten years (one-quarter had been there for between eleven and twenty years, and over half for more than twenty years). These data indicate that once people arrive in these low-income neighborhoods they tend to stay. The communities tend to reach their physical dwelling capacities quickly; and once this limit is reached the only way that the communities can expand is by increasing the density of occupancy.

Such an increase appears to have happened over the decades; the modal household was five or six inhabitant members in 1970, which grew to seven or eight by 1990. It is noteworthy that the size in both 1970 and 1990 was lower in Sendas Frutales than in any other neighborhood, indicating perhaps that the size of the dwellings and the necessity of paying rent in Sendas Frutales may place constraints on family size. When families leave such a dwelling environment, larger family size may become more feasible.

EDUCATION

The four surveys show a steady increase in the level of education for heads of household across the twenty years, a finding that reflects the very considerable growth in available public education on all levels (primary, secondary, and higher) in Peru and especially in Lima during that time. About two-thirds of the 1970 sample had completed primary education or less; less than one-third had gone on to or had completed secondary, while only a handful had university/technical/vocational training. By 1990 more respondents had some or all secondary (45 percent) than primary (39 percent), and 15 percent had at least some advanced education. These figures argue that Lima's working poor do take advantage of the city's educational infrastructure.

Of the six settlements, Santiago was clearly the best educated. Even in 1970 it had the highest percentage of residents with secondary and higher education, and in 1990 more than one-quarter (27.6 percent) of its residents had higher education, almost twice the percentage of any other community. In contrast, Pampa de Arena in both 1970 and 1990 had the lowest level of education: more of its pobladores had stopped at the primary level than any other community in both years (78 percent in 1970 and 49 percent in 1990). Overall, the data paint a picture of people whose educational achievement is relatively low (by Lima standards, not by Peruvian provincial standards), but whose desire to move ahead with formal education meets with some success.

AGE

In 1970 more than one-third (36.6 percent) of the total sample was between the ages of thirty-one and forty; the next highest cohort was under thirty (26.9 percent), meaning that well over one-half of the sample was under forty years old. In 1990 the age distribution had shifted. Over 60 percent was more than forty years old, and one in five respondents was over sixty. These figures correspond with the length of residence data, which show that people tend to stay in the communities once they arrive.

It should be emphasized that these data are for heads of household. The age distribution for Lima's squatter settlements as a whole has for many years shown a young population; census data and projections indicate that the median age is about fifteen or sixteen. This median has itself changed over time: in the 1960s and 1970s Lima's poblador population was somewhat younger than it was in 1990. This modest decline is probably because of Peru's overall decline in population growth. It may also be a result not only of decreased migration from the provinces into Lima but also, unfortunately, of rising infant mortality rates during the late 1980s.

EMPLOYMENT AND INCOME

Lima's squatter and slum areas house, in very large part, the city's working poor. The 1970 sample was primarily, and more or less evenly, involved in skilled and unskilled manual labor or blue-collar employment; anything higher than this was rare. By 1990 there had been modest change. Only one-quarter of the sample held unskilled jobs, whereas skilled manual and skilled nonmanual workers (roughly speaking, white collar) totaled almost 20 percent. These advances and changes paralleled the increases in education noted above. In 1990 the percentage of individuals who were inactive had tripled; the great majority of these were retired, not unemployed, in accordance with the aging of the communities. Throughout the twenty years the great majority of the respondents (over three-quarters) said that they worked more than forty hours a week; a somewhat smaller percentage in both 1970 and 1990 said that they had held their current job for longer than they had lived in their current neighborhood, indicating considerable occupational stability.

Throughout all six barrios, certain kinds of work dominated. In 1970 more of the men had jobs in construction than anything else (17 percent), although skilled and unskilled service workers totaled 19 percent. One in ten was a transportation worker (bus, truck, and taxi drivers), while another 8 percent apiece worked as small merchants (typically a stall owner in a market) or as street vendors, perhaps the stereotypically classic poor migrant job. Office and technical workers together totaled 4 percent. By 1990 this profile had shifted somewhat. Construction (13 percent) and transportation (6 percent) work were still much in evidence, as were small merchants (12 percent) and street vendors (6 percent), but office workers and technicians had tripled (to 13.5 percent).

In specific neighborhoods, these changes were even more marked. In 1970 Pampa de Arena had only 1.8 percent (two individuals) and Primero de Enero 3.2 percent who were truly white collar (professionals, semiprofessionals, managers, office workers). Santiago, on the other hand, had 41 percent (in real numbers, thirteen out of thirty-two). In 1990, 11.4 percent of Primero de Enero's residents and 17.9 percent of Pampa de Arena's were white collar; however, 27.8 percent of Santiago were also in the same category.

Demographically, therefore, the neighborhoods had a populace that was largely working class. Open unemployment was almost unheard of, even in 1990, when Lima's labor force had suffered severe blows. Such a rarity (of *admitted* unemployment, it must be emphasized) may not be as surprising as it first appears, given lengthy residence in the barrios and the increases in education. On the other hand, the data do not indicate how many people residing in a house held jobs. Yet in almost all cases an individual respondent's monthly income was surpassed by total household income, indicating that almost all households had two or more wage earners. And it bears repeating that the average household size was larger in 1990 than in 1970, which implies that household expenses would have to be relatively greater in 1990.

Reliable income data are notoriously difficult to gather since they are traditionally underreported. Given this caveat, the 1970 sample indicated that 66.5 percent of all respondents in the sample earned up to (or less than) two minimum wages, which at the time was roughly equivalent to $90 monthly and which was considered to be the bare minimum necessary for urban subsistence. In 1990 (and bearing in mind the increases in education that had occurred), 71.3 percent of all individuals earned up to or less than two minimum wages, which had by that time dropped to about $75–80. It should also be kept in mind that the cost of living in Lima had increased dramatically, and the purchasing power of a minimum wage had dropped substantially during 1970–1990. Over the twenty years, therefore, the pobladores saw their incomes decrease, despite overall increases in educational achievement and type of jobs held.

Residents in specific communities showed income differences. Santiago had more wage earners with more than two minimum wages in 1970 (over half its sample), whereas Primero de Enero and Pampa de Arena each had less than 30 percent in such a category. The same situation applied in 1990, although the gross differences between 1970 and 1990 identified above still held true, that is,

Santiago still had more of its respondents earning over two minimum wages, but only 35 percent were at that income level. Primero de Enero and Pampa de Arena were again the poorest of the six, but in 1990 less than one out of five surpassed the two-minimum-wage mark.

INFORMALITY

One question touched on at the outset that again deserves mention is whether the pobladores in Lima's squatter neighborhoods are part of the so-called informal urban sector. This question becomes problematic the moment it is asked, since there is little agreement about how to define the informal sector, let alone who belongs to it (see chapter 3). Portes and Castells (1989, 12) argue that the informal economy is a process of income-generation and not an individual condition. But regardless of the validity of this argument (and its validity is considerable), more popular usages of the word "informal"—and especially of the Spanish term *los informales*—have rightly or wrongly branded certain occupations and the individuals employed in them as informal.[6] It is thus useful to inquire at least briefly into the existence of informality and of los informales in the survey samples.

That Lima has an extensive, complex, vital informal sector is not a matter for debate here, notwithstanding the thorny theoretical, analytical, and policy-relevant arguments about the concept. But most of the discussion about informality takes place on the macro level; there have been relatively few analyses of microlevel informality. The descriptions in this chapter are not intended to classify the pobladores or their neighborhoods as informal or formal; any argument couched in either/or terms is cast in far too simplistic terms. For example, if a squatter settlement founded through the highly informal—not to say illegal—means of an invasion is officially recognized by the state, its inhabitants counted in the census, and the community itself incorporated into a legal district of Lima, is it therefore no longer informal? Or take the case of a woman from that same neighborhood who is a street vendor; she sells cosmetics from a tray and has occupied a particular street corner for eight years. She is one day given a number by the municipality and told that she can remain at her corner if she pays a nominal monthly fee. Does such an act by the state make her any less informal than she was before?

But then, if the question of what constitutes informal activity is complex and contentious, the questions as to who is "an informal" and what is an "informal neighborhood" are even more opaque. It might be easy to conclude that by definition everyone who inhabits a squatter settlement is an "informal." But what if the community is legally recognized by the Ministry of Housing shortly after its inception? Or what if the invasion site is located within a legal district of Lima? Or what if, after a decade or so, official and full land titles are distributed to its inhabitants? How useful or relevant is the informal/formal distinction?

What about occupation? Relatively few pobladores in the six communities across twenty years ever admitted to being employed in one of the classic informal occupations such as street vending or unskilled manual labor or service sector jobs. Many of the pobladores may well own or work for cottage industries that are not formally registered with the state, or that do not pay minimum wages or contribute to the state social security system, but such information is difficult to obtain. In addition, individuals may move in and out of informal occupations over time.

The great majority of the pobladores in the samples have certainly at one time or another been highly informal, especially if they participated in a land invasion or obtained a lot through extralegal or illegal means. And undoubtedly an equally high percentage of them have contributed to the informal economy by buying from street vendors or from unregistered stalls and shops, or by purchasing from informal firms. But even acknowledging that probably all of the pobladores are involved in one way or another with Lima's informal economy says very little that is distinctive about them, since the great majority of Lima's population is also involved, regardless of social class or income, by residing, working, purchasing, or hiring in or from it.

VOTING AND FORMAL POLITICS

Just as a discussion of barrio respondent attitudes and perceptions will help us to understand informal political behavior (discussed in the next chapter), a brief examination of voting-relevant behavior and attitudes may provide a foundation for understanding the discussion of voting itself later on. (Chapter 8 goes into voting behavior at some length, and I will not anticipate that discussion here.) In 1970, of course, when the first survey was carried out, there were no elections and no campaigns; political parties were in abeyance, and questions (for example) about the efficacy of the military regime in power versus civilian rule would have been inappropriate, to say the least. The surveys of 1982, 1985, and 1990 were, however, conducted subsequent to the restoration of civilian rule in 1980 and thus contain information about formal political participation.

In 1982 the survey was carried out slightly more than two years after Fernando Belaúnde had been reelected president. Reported voting levels were high: close to 90 percent of the respondents said they had voted in the 1978 constituent assembly elections and in both the presidential and municipal elections of the 1980s.[7] But in other activities, participation fell off dramatically. Less than one-third said they had attended a rally for any of the three elections; one in ten said they were members of any political party; and only 7 percent said they had campaigned in any election. Four out of five said there had been no change in their neighborhood since Belaúnde's election (15 percent cited a positive change, 5 percent cited a negative change).

In 1985 when Alán García and APRA triumphed, the survey was replicated immediately following the election. Ninety-six percent reported having voted in the presidential race; 89 percent said they had voted two years earlier in the 1983 municipal elections. Being in a campaign (11 percent) and being a party member (19 percent) were still relatively rare activities. When asked if government affected their daily lives, 31 percent said the national government had much effect and 36 percent said it had none; on the metropolitan and district levels, over half said that each had no effect. Belaúnde himself was ranked as a good president by only 7 percent of the respondents; he was ranked poor or very poor by almost one-half, a sharp decline from his 45 percent popular vote total five years earlier.

In 1990, the survey was repeated one more time following the surprise election of Alberto Fujimori. Ninety percent of the sample said they had voted, and some 93 percent said they had done so some six months earlier in the 1989 municipal elections. The García administration was seen by about one-quarter of the respondents as having done something positive for their neighborhoods; more than half said his administration had had no impact.

Across time, it is clear that Lima's lower classes became actively involved in the formal political process. Their (reported) voting levels were as high as anyone else's, although they took little part in other formal activities such as campaigning or attending political meetings and rallies. They thought that government had relatively little effect on their neighborhoods, for good or for bad, and they viewed both outgoing presidents Belaúnde and García in highly negative terms.

Conclusions

The descriptive data presented here paint a longitudinal portrait of Lima's working poor. The pobladores in these six communities are the blue-collar, semiskilled, working-class people of Lima. They are not (with some clear exceptions) the desperately poor, the unemployed or unemployable, or the destitute. Nor are they criminals, marginalized elements, or social outcasts. In sheer numbers alone, they constitute close to half of Lima's total population. Indeed, it can be said with a good deal of accuracy that Lima's wealthy who live lifestyles similar to upper-middle- and upper-class inhabitants of the United States comprise Lima's truly marginal population.

The pobladores are the people who drive Lima's buses and taxis and trucks; they sometimes work in its factories; they build its buildings, wait on its restaurant tables, sweep its streets, or operate its markets; they are sometimes its policemen or its nation's soldiers, or its poorly paid government workers. They buy its building materials, consume its food and beverages, go to its soccer games and movies, and send their children to its schools. They depend upon the city for their livelihood, but the city just as much depends on them. Lima's wealthy middle-class inhabitants may take the pobladores for granted, or may (if and when they think of them) be fearful of them, or ignore them, or wish they would go away, but the rich and wealthy and the districts they live in could not exist or function without the pobladores.

The pobladores have, in the aggregate over the past twenty years, made progress, in spite of everything. Their level of education has risen, and they have tended to move from unskilled to skilled manual jobs. Their communities have progressed as well; individual families now inhabit permanent houses, which in many cases they built themselves over the years, and although paved streets and sidewalks are still not common, electricity has come to all the neighborhoods, as has running water, either in the house or in standpipes scattered through the neighborhood. The supply of water and its purity remain uncertain, however; the Latin American cholera epidemic that started in Lima in 1991 was transmitted widely and rapidly because of leakages in and insufficient treatment of Lima's metropolitan water system.

By most definitions of the term, the great majority of the inhabitants of Lima's squatter settlements (but perhaps less so of its tugurios) can be classified as *cholos,* a term that in Peru calls for careful usage and treatment. The word *cholo* is a frequently derogatory, exclusively urban term for a recent migrant or "citified" Indian, and it can carry with it a range of negative racist connotations. Yet since it applies or can be applied to such vast numbers of people and to their urban culture and way of life, the term has over the past several decades become very much a part of Lima's argot and has sometimes been used by those to whom it is applied as a term of pride and identification.[8]

Perhaps the most notable and widespread manifestation of cholo culture has occurred in the music known as *chicha,* generally described as a combination of the Andean folk dance known as the *huayno* and the Colombian *cumbia.* And although the music itself is distinctive and very much associated with the emergence of the cholo class in Lima, the lyrics to popular chicha songs are even more reflective of the life and times, the aspirations and struggles, of the cholo.

Themes commonly concern migration to the city, feeling uprooted, life and work in the city, and poverty, as well as love, humor, politics, and other more universal themes. Song titles themselves reveal the content and the appeal of the music: "El Cachuelero" (one who looks for part-time work), "I'm a Street Vendor," "Surviving," "I'm from the Provinces," "My Pueblo Jóven," and the like (Suárez 1995).

One song from 1985 by the then widely popular group called Los Shapis was called "El Serranito" (The little man from the sierra). The song dealt with the difficulties of moving to the city:

> One day I left my land with my poncho and little hat
> When I arrived on the coast they called me *serranito*
> Through the streets of Lima I walked quickly
> With my saddlebag on my shoulder I was looking for work.
> All day I walked and hunger was killing me
> I found no work
> How sad I felt
> Night came on me and I asked for lodging
> But the people of the city denied me everything.

Another song by the same group was called "Los Pobladores":

> They called them invaders
> They denied them a thousand favors
> But at the same time pobladores
> Were opening their streets
> In the sand of the hillsides.
> These men were building
> To crown their efforts
> A little schoolhouse for children
> So that they could very clearly
> See all the way to the horizon
>
> [chorus]
> They're the pobladores
> Who live in the sand
> They're the pobladores of the new times . . .

With such lyrics set to familiar but catchy rhythms, and with huge numbers of people who can strongly identify with the themes, there is little wonder that *la musica chicha* became enormously popular with lower-class Lima (as well as denigrated by the upper classes).

So far I have presented information about the several layers and contexts of economic, social, and political processes, events, and structures that have affected Lima's lower classes and low-income populace during the past twenty years. The data paint an especially grim picture of the 1985–1990 period, when hyperinflation, losses in purchasing power, a violent insurgent movement, deteriorating social conditions, and a weakening and ineffectual state all combined to make life particularly harsh for Lima's poor. But Lima's working poor have struggled, coped, and managed; they have survived. How politics—how community, grassroots involvement, petitions and demands directed at the state, and a range of electoral activities—played a role in all of this remains to be seen, and it is to politics that I now turn.

6

MODES OF
PARTICIPATION

PEOPLE BECOME INVOLVED in politics in several ways and for a wide variety of reasons. My principal aim here is to describe some of the fundamental ways Lima's pobladores participated over two decades. How and why did these ways —or modes—themselves change? and how did the frequencies of poblador involvement in them change? It is useful here to recall the model in chapter 1 that sketched in some of the relationships between democracy, conceived of as a public good, and two preference dimensions—political and economic—that can influence an individual citizen's decisions about political behavior over time.

In brief, the model conceptualized democracy as being an inelastic collective good, with (at T_1, the time of its establishment) jointness of consumption and nonexcludability. Initially democracy has a higher total utility than cost. As time progresses beyond T_1, however, a preference for democracy over any other political system, and a preference for material well-being over material deprivation, two dimensions underlying individual preferences, interact with one another and help formulate decisions for the individual. If, for example, democracy as a political system seems well established, then material well-being as a preference dimension may over time assume greater salience, especially for low-income status. This salience may become more pronounced if economic deterioration accelerates rapidly and if the presence of democracy is perceived as either irrelevant or incapable of reversing such acceleration. That is, under conditions of rapid economic decline, low-income citizens may perceive a strong preference for democracy as less important relative to reversing the deterioration of the economy. If at T_2 such conditions obtain, individual citizens may reveal their displeasure or uncertainty or distress over increasingly high marginal costs of maintaining democracy. That is, as a citizen perceives a move toward material deprivation, this citizen's preference for democracy over any other political system may decline.

This interaction between preferences for well-being and for democracy can result in a variety of outcomes through individual citizen choices. My basic aim in this and the next two chapters is to trace these outcomes over two decades. This chapter does so on a large scale by examining how several modes of participation—each in turn made up of several variables—shifted as the transition from authoritarianism to democracy occurred and/or as economic hardships increased or declined. The next two chapters then examine the same interactions as they changed in terms of informal (neighborhood development and petitioning) behavior and formal (electoral) behavior.

This analysis needs some sort of foundation upon which to rest, however. Although political behavior is influenced by macrolevel factors such as economic crisis, poverty, and the state, participation is also influenced by individual-level demographic and socioeconomic characteristics, along with views of one's surroundings. Especially in the case of informal political participation where the provision of public goods is the overriding goal, understanding why and under what conditions certain patterns of political involvement are rational depends heavily in turn upon understanding how an individual perceives the community in which he lives and on how he thinks such goods can be obtained. The first part of this chapter therefore presents a description of how Lima's poor see themselves and their neighborhoods. This is followed by a description of how their basic modes of participation varied over time.

Barrio Perceptions

OVERALL BARRIO SATISFACTION

In 1970, when the first survey was taken, most respondents had what in hindsight might be judged somewhat overly positive views of their communities. Over one-half said that, overall, they were quite satisfied with their neighborhoods; less than one out of ten (8.8 percent) said they were quite dissatisfied; the remainder said they were more or less satisfied. But this rosy picture faded. By 1982 over 20 percent said they were dissatisfied, a proportion that stayed constant through 1985 and rose to 23 percent in 1990. At the same time, those expressing satisfaction dropped to slightly less than one-quarter, meaning that about one-half (53.7 percent) had adjusted themselves to a view of their neighborhoods as fair.

Santiago had the lowest level of poblador dissatisfaction of all communities (7 percent in 1970, 4 percent in 1990); Sendas Frutales had the highest levels of dissatisfaction throughout (19 percent in 1970, 45 percent in 1990), indicating deep frustration with the decades-long legal problems of the community. It is noteworthy that over 40 percent of the residents of Sendas Frutales in 1970 had considerable satisfaction with their community, a figure that was doubtless inflated by hopes that the SINAMOS decree making the area an official squatter settlement would improve their lives. By 1990 this figure had dropped to only 8.5 percent.

In a related vein, almost four out of five respondents in 1970 said that they considered themselves permanent residents of their neighborhoods and that they had no plans to move. This proportion decreased to three out of five in 1982 and then to about half (53 percent) in 1985, only to rise again in 1990 to 62 percent. High levels of barrio dissatisfaction correlated strongly with a desire to move. The problem by 1990 was that economic conditions had deteriorated so much that most people had to be content with where they were and with coping with daily life, much less think about moving.

Across the years the aspect most liked about residing in the six communities was the overall environment. Respondents said they liked the tranquillity of the areas more than anything else; other positive factors included the location of the community and the fact of homeownership (de facto if not de jure). In the newer communities such as Pampa de Arena and Primero de Enero (in the 1970s, at least), residents complained most frequently about the lack of water or other physical problems. Residents in the older communities saw a variety of problems, including petty crime, lack of police protection, or some physical problem such as unpaved streets.

NEIGHBORHOOD UNITY

Perceptions of the ability of a neighborhood to unify and work together doubtless play a role in the degree to which informal political participation will emerge or be sustained over time. In 1970 about two-thirds of the sample saw their barrios as either very or somewhat unified. Level of perceived unity decreased by age of community in 1970: over 90 percent of Primero de Enero saw their newly acquired invasion site as unified, ranging down to Pampa de Arena (three-quarters) to 28 de Julio (about two-thirds) to Sendas Frutales and Santiago, where somewhat less than one-half saw their communities as unified.

Reasons for this low level, however, differed significantly across communities. In Sendas Frutales, unity was difficult because of the atomistic nature of the community, and despite the hope engendered by the SINAMOS decree, more than one in five saw their area with no unity at all (the highest level of all six neighborhoods). In Santiago, community unity was low because of two factors: the split between the two rival local associations, and the fact that the community had done all it could easily do by itself to provide public goods.

By 1990 community unity across all six neighborhoods had declined precipitously. Overall perceived unity dropped to less than one-quarter, while perceptions of lack of unity (little or none) rose to more than three-quarters. Such a collapse came from a variety of factors. Paramount among them was the overall deterioration of the Peruvian economy and the increasing inability of the state to provide even the most basic resources to increasingly large numbers of increasingly needy people. In addition, all the communities were twenty years older, and the readily solved problems that the pobladores could confront themselves had already been taken care of. Adding to this, community unity—like any other social phenomenon—can erode over time. Residents became tired of constantly being cajoled to participate when the problems they faced appeared less amenable to solution. Finally, although many pobladores had resided in their communities for many years, newcomers (even though few in number) had not been involved in past successful community efforts or were unwilling to participate.

Whatever the specific constellation of motives, community unity in 1990 was much lower than it had been. Primero de Enero and Santiago had the lowest levels of all six, again for very different reasons. Primero de Enero's needs were still basically unmet after more than twenty years, but its inhabitants were the poorest of all and their resources the most reduced. In sharp contrast, Santiago was by all indicators the most advanced and developed community, but its inhabitants had fewer truly vital needs to keep it together.

SOURCES OF ASSISTANCE

More than twenty-five years ago, Alex Inkeles developed a survey item designed to probe respondents' perceptions of various sources of assistance. This item asked individuals the most important sources of aid: themselves and their own labor, the government, or fate. The exact wording was: "What is most important for improving life here in _____: hard work by the pobladores, God's help, the government, or good luck?" This item has been replicated countless times in many surveys; it was asked in all four surveys in Lima.

The respondents in the surveys reveal two basic patterns: first, that self-help ("efforts by the pobladores themselves") and government assistance alternate over time but, overall, remain roughly even over twenty years, and second, that reliance on fate is minimal. In 1970 more than half of the sample said that self-help was the preferred way to respond to community needs, although specific community responses varied widely, ranging from over 70 percent in Pampa de Arena to under 40 percent in Santiago. Over time this preference for self-help declined to 50 percent (1982) and to 40.9 percent (1985) but then rose back to half again in 1990. Governmental aid rose and fell in parallel fashion, reaching its highest point (53.2 percent) in 1985. That self-help had risen again in 1990 is not surprising, given the decline of the Peruvian state throughout the late 1980s, but its salience seems to run against the decline in community unity identified earlier. Yet the two sets of responses are not mutually contradictory: self-help may be viewed as critical to resolving a community's needs, even though the perception of unity within that community is low.

Fatalistic responses in any year in any single community never surpassed 15 percent and were generally at or less than 10 percent. Whether such figures are absolutely low depends on what they are compared with, of course. In his 1993 study of Lima's poor, Parodi found a high reliance on self-help; state assistance and fatalistic responses both finished well back. Other comparisons come from other cities and nations. In 1970 Cornelius (1975) asked the same question in Mexico City in several poor communities, as did Moore in 1974 (Moore 1978) in Guayaquil, Ecuador. The answers they received showed significant variance with the Lima responses. In Mexico City, 28 percent answered self-help, 40 percent answered government assistance, a full 30 percent gave a fatalistic response. In Ecuador, three out of five respondents named the government as most important, only one in five chose self-help, while another fifth selected the help of God or good luck. These data show the Peruvian pobladores to be much more self-reliant and to be far less inclined to leave matters to fate than their Mexican and Ecuadorian counterparts. These rather extraordinary differences may be because of the nature of the political regimes in each country. For example, the urban poor in Mexico and Ecuador (at least during the 1960s and 1970s) were socialized into depending upon the government for assistance (Cornelius 1975, 174–77); in Peru, whatever the poor have, they have in large part provided for themselves.

Of course, there were certain goods the pobladores could not provide by or for themselves. Land titles were perhaps the clearest example, but water, electricity, police protection, and garbage collection all eventually had to come from (or at the least with the assistance of) the state, though the community might assist by providing labor. Nevertheless, the willingness of the pobladores to depend upon themselves is notable and relatively steady; its resurgence in 1990 again implies that the capacity of the state was in considerable doubt. Whether they needed water (much of Primero de Enero and Pampa de Arena) or paved streets and sidewalks (parts of 28 de Julio, Pampa de Arena), resolution of legal status (Sendas Frutales), police protection (Sendas Frutales, Pampa de Arena), or environmental protection (Santiago), the pobladores in every community required some sort of state-provided assistance, but few were naive enough to think that it would be forthcoming rapidly or in sufficient quantity.

Modes of Participation as a Framework

With this information as a foundation, I now turn to the ways in which the pobladores became involved in politics from 1970 to 1990, and whether, how, and why these ways changed over time—as regime shifts occurred, as presidents and mayors of various parties were elected and replaced, as the economy first slowed and then collapsed, and as the presence of the Shining Path continued to grow. I was able to extend the study from its initial investigation of poverty and political participation under military rule to a longitudinal examination of participation across regime types and under severe economic conditions. For this I needed not only to organize the data from each survey but also to compare the findings from the different surveys. Verba and Nie's (1972) notion of modes of participation did both.

The idea of modes of participation proceeds from the assumption that individuals have many ways (both direct and indirect) to try to influence the government. These ways of becoming involved generate empirically discernible modes or sets of activity that differ systematically in how an individual citizen relates to his government (Verba, Nie, and Kim 1978, 51). This is to say that people do not simply range from being inactive to being active along some single dimension, but rather that different people may involve themselves in different sorts of activities. Some people (probably the majority) may not be involved in politics at all or may do nothing more than vote, others may do one sort of activity but not another, whereas a very few may do several.

The concept of participatory modes serves to describe the political involvement of a nation at a specific point in time. Verba and Nie (1972), for instance, limited themselves to participation in the United States in their initial study but were able to answer a wide variety of questions. How many people were voters and nothing more, for example? How many were active in petitioning authorities for a good? How many combined activities across more than one mode? Did political involvement vary by socioeconomic status or by other basic divisions? In a later volume, Verba, Nie, and Kim (1978) expanded their investigation by including seven countries, thereby allowing themselves to determine if certain modes of participation existed regardless of national boundaries and distinct political systems.

Verba and Nie and their associates did not investigate two important areas. They did not look at participation in a nation where democratic procedures had been proscribed; and they did not replicate their surveys over time to see how macrolevel societal, economic, or political changes might produce changes in modes of activity. Citizen involvement in modes of participation might change, disappear, or become modified in response to macro changes of a variety of sorts. The most obvious macro change that might induce modal participatory changes would be a change in the type of regime (from authoritarian to civilian, for example, or vice versa) that would legally either constrain or expand citizen involvement in politics. A military government might well prohibit open elections and campaigning and outlaw political parties, leaving only the most hollow and ceremonial of elections; likewise, a new democratic system would likely make every effort to expand and restore the ways in which citizens may be heard and exert influence.

In a somewhat different way, fundamental changes in macrosocial and macroeconomic conditions might produce shifts in modes of participation. The presence of a sustained economic crisis might produce apathy or alienation among those groups who suffer the most, thereby generating either new forms of participation or at least dramatic declines in involvement in the existing modes. Levels of involvement in existing modes might shift as more individuals see formal participation as nonproductive. Or, as Przeworski would argue, if democratic institutions are unable to demonstrate that the material conditions of losers of distributional conflicts will not continue to deteriorate, then those political forces who are society's losers will see less reason to support such institutions (Przeworski 1991). Whatever the specifics, the concept of modes of participation provides a framework for tracing changes in political behavior not only across a regime transition from military to civilian but also across a twenty-year period that includes Peru's most critical economic crisis of the twentieth century. Even though the sample comes from a single country, and from a subgroup of that country's total population, the Lima data offer us a chance of confronting some of the questions that Verba, Nie, et al. have not addressed.

The Context for Political Participation, 1970

In 1970–1971 the military government of General Velasco Alvarado was perhaps at its height. Its reformist policies, its leftist rhetoric, and its dedication to restructuring Peru's economy and society through the self-styled Revolution of the Armed Forces were all subject to much challenge and debate. But one point is clear: the Velasco regime was not just another authoritarian military dictatorship.

As the government announced, endlessly, its policies were aimed at creating a "society of full participation" that focused specifically on Peru's low-income groups such as the highland peasants and the urban shantytown inhabitants. But such a goal required that the government answer the seemingly insoluble question of whether a military government could simultaneously promote and control participation. A military government has three basic choices when it comes to participation (aside from simply abolishing all participatory mechanisms and ruling by decree and repression): to organize a new official party, to manipulate the traditional party system, or to reject the traditional party and electoral systems and redefine political participation in some new form. The Velasco government chose the last of these three and in 1971 created SINAMOS, as an attempt to construct what Kaska (1993) refers to as an "administered mass organization." This organization tried to recast participation through a complex system of local-level citizen involvement in SINAMOS-directed and SINAMOS-approved organizations (Delgado 1975; Dietz 1980; Stepan 1978).

Prior to the onset of SINAMOS, and only two months following the October 1968 coup, the Velasco government created a centralized authority called the Oficina Nacional de Desarrollo de Pueblos Jóvenes (ONDEPJOV; National Office for Development of Young Towns, the euphemism given to Peru's urban squatter areas by the Velasco government). This agency began a vigorous program of community organization and land title distribution. Thus when the 1970 survey data were collected, the Velasco government had begun thinking about how to address the question of recasting participation but SINAMOS, its major mechanism designed to achieve such a goal, was not in place (and had not yet failed, as it would do within a few years).

The collection date of late 1970 to early 1971 is thus particularly apt. The Velasco government was just beginning its experiments with large-scale state intervention into the Peruvian economy, which was itself in reasonably good condition. Subsequent problems concerning the foreign debt, inflation, currency devaluation, and international trade had not yet arisen. Nor had the social experimentation associated with SINAMOS and other programs involving agrarian cooperatives and so-called social interest firms appeared. Yet the government's major effort at land reform and expropriation had started, and the military had already developed its domestic and international image as an oxymoronic reformist military (Hobsbawn 1971; Lowenthal 1975).

MODES OF PARTICIPATION, 1970

Given this setting, what avenues were open to Lima's poor when they decided to participate, either in state-controlled activities or in non-state-controlled, that is, grassroots community efforts? Bearing in mind that the working definition of informal (that is, nonelectoral) political participation included activities aimed at securing collective goods, the 1970 survey asked a series of questions about the individual's participation in a variety of such activities. These questions included involvement in community affairs such as working on a community center or helping install services of some sort, involvement in the local neighborhood association, and involvement in demand-making directed at extralocal authorities (see table 2). It was reasonable at the time of the survey to hypothesize a priori that these individual acts might group into separate modes: for example, communal involvement, local organizational involvement, and national-level involvement. All these types of involvement had been described by numerous observers as the sorts of behavior in which the urban poor might be expected to take part. Whether they would separate empirically into distinct modes à la Verba and Nie remained to be seen. I used techniques developed by Verba and Nie (see table 3), involving a factor-analytic principal-components unrotated solution using the seven variables from table 2. The first component demonstrates clearly that the seven variables in 1970 comprised a participation dimension. All seven had positive and approximately equal associations to this component, indicating that these seven activities had a common basis or underlying dimension that could be labeled participation.

In addition, the results of a rotated oblique solution (table 3) indicate that urban poor of Lima did indeed, at the time of the survey, cluster their behavior into three separate modes: communal involvement, local organizational involvement, and national-level petitioning. These results offer considerable empirical justification for the working definition of political participation that I use throughout the book. It was clear that individuals who engaged in neighborhood projects and/or who took part in the local neighborhood association were as much involved in politics as those who petitioned national authorities, and vice versa. All three of these modes "aim at the provision of desired needs and goals"; two of them, however, simply did not involve direct interaction with government officials.

Table 2. Frequencies of Participatory Involvement, 1970

1. Recent involvement	73.3
2. Frequent involvement	38.5
3. Attended local meetings	51.4
4. Petitioned local organization	33.1
5. Member of local organization	30.5
6. Visited ONDEPJOV office	37.1
7. Petitioned ONDEPJOV	32.6

Notes: Figures are percentages. N varies from 412 to 422.

Table 3. Modes of Participation, 1970 (Principal and Rotated Solutions)

		Rotated		
	Principal	Factor 1	Factor 2	Factor 3
1. Recent involvement	.66	.89		
2. Frequent involvement	.61	.77		
3. Attend local meetings	.68		.80	
4. Petitioned local organization	.78		.59	
5. Member of local organization	.74		.83	
6. Visited ONDEPJOV	.56			.93
7. Petitioned ONDEPJOV	.68			.73

Key:
Factor 1 = community problem solving.
Factor 2 = local organizational involvement.
Factor 3 = state petitioning.

It appeared, at least in 1970, that the referent or arena toward which political activity was addressed was stronger than the form of the activity. That is, while the pobladores made demands on both local and national levels, they were more apt to do one or the other, not both. Thus the probability of one individual's presenting demands on both levels was mitigated by a tendency not to transcend two different arenas of activity.

A few comments are due about Sendas Frutales, the rental slum neighborhood in Surquillo. Sendas Frutales required special treatment in the survey because many items that were key indicators of participation in squatter areas (most notably petitioning ONDEPJOV and interacting with other state agencies) were not relevant. On the contrary, inhabitants of Sendas Frutales were constrained largely to organizing among themselves and to petitioning the landowners or municipal authorities (who in truth had little power to intervene in tenant-landlord disputes). Using five variables dealing with neighborhood problem-solving and petitioning activities,[1] factor analysis showed that these five variables formed a single dimension of participation and that this dimension subdivided into two modes—community activity and petitioning (see Dietz 1980, 129–31).

The rental nature of the housing in Sendas Frutales undoubtedly played a major role in keeping participation levels so low (see chapter 5). When people do not own (de facto if not de jure) their houses, then a sense of community becomes difficult to generate or sustain. Whereas modes of involvement in Sendas Frutales did exist in 1970, the incidence of participation was much reduced.

Overall, the 1970 data are quite straightforward. Three modes appear, each covers a distinct arena or subject of problem-solving and demand-making, and each is congruent with the working notion of political participation under authoritarian rule. The question of next concern regards what happened to such a clear division of participation after the military stepped down in 1980 and the electoral arena was reestablished.

The Context for Political Participation, 1982

Fernando Belaúnde was reelected president in 1980 (he had been deposed in the 1968 coup led by General Velasco). He and his AP won a substantial victory, taking 45 percent of the popular vote, distantly followed by APRA (27.4 percent) and PPC (9.5 percent) and the several candidates of the left, who together totaled less than 14 percent. Belaúnde's triumph was widely seen not only as a vindication of his ouster twelve years earlier but also as the best chance for democracy to reestablish itself in Peru following the tumultuous dozen years of military governance.

When Belaúnde assumed power in 1980, however, it was as leader of a country that had changed fundamentally and irretrievably since 1968. The old landed aristocracy was gone, its power broken; decapitalization of the agrarian sector had been occurring for years; whatever new investment was being made was aimed at the urban areas. The state had become the nation's largest source of investment capital under Velasco (Fitzgerald 1983, 71–77) but with a paradoxical result: the larger the state grew, the less it could accomplish. The military itself perceived this difficulty; indeed, perhaps one of the principal reasons for the 1975 counter coup that saw General Morales Bermudez overthrow Velasco was the recognition that the state had tried to take on too much too quickly and with too few resources, human as well as economic.

As Peru's foreign debt mounted during the mid- and late 1970s, the economy stagnated. New domestic and international investment slowed dramatically, and the Morales Bermudez government soon made it clear that it was determined to remove itself from power and to return power to civilian hands. But the role assumed by the state did not end with its hegemony as source of capital; its efforts at organizing and motivating political participation through SINAMOS had given the urban as well as rural masas populares a taste of political power —but not as the government had intended.

In the first place, SINAMOS pledged (as did the state overall) more than it could deliver, and the intended recipients of SINAMOS promises frequently saw their hopes never materialize. But the efforts by SINAMOS personnel to organize within Lima's shantytowns and to convince people of the need to participate and to make demands did have a lasting impact. Thus the SINAMOS experience became a double-edged sword. People learned that local organization was a viable means of demand-making; they also learned that the state (which was encouraging and even requiring participation) would not or could not deliver the goods and services it promised as a reward for participation (Dietz 1980; Collier 1976).

Belaúnde therefore found himself elected to govern a society that was prone simultaneously toward participation and toward mobilization, which had come both to need and to expect more from the state (in substantial measure because of promises made by the state itself) but which had been disillusioned by the state's inability to meet those increased needs and expectations. Belaúnde's amalgam of southern cone neoliberal strategies and IMF stabilization policies initiated by the Morales Bermudez government in 1978 (Pastor and Wise 1992, 86–87) produced economic hardships, especially for Peru's lower-income groups. Such disenchantment spilled almost immediately into the electoral arena, where voters found a full array of parties and candidates, especially on the left, that were eager for their support.

MODES OF PARTICIPATION, 1982

What is most germane to examine here is how the reestablishment of the electoral process might change patterns of political participation (I examine electoral behavior in detail in chapter 8, and I shall not anticipate that discussion here). The 1982 survey incorporated not only the previous seven "informal participation" items concerning local participation and demand-making (see tables 2 and 3) but also several new items that dealt with voting and campaign activity. Table 4 lists thirteen items and the frequency of involvement in each.

Voting is far and away the most common act, as would be expected. The fact that voting is mandatory in Peru simply reinforces its salience as the most commonly performed political activity in virtually all societies.

Certain specific changes in individual items across the twelve years between surveys deserve mention. Recent involvement in communal activity increased. The frequency of such involvement diminished, although only slightly, whereas attendance at meetings of the local neighborhood dropped by half. Petitioning activities varied: local-level petitioning remained the same, whereas petitioning directed at the Ministry of Housing rose by a considerable degree (from one-third of the respondents to one-half). About one in five respondents had directed a petition to SINAMOS.

Although such variations across twelve years have much intrinsic interest, the question of whether the items from the 1982 survey constitute a single dimension of participation remains as yet unanswered. To see whether the transformation of Peru from an authoritarian to a democratic system produced changes in the clear-cut three modes of participation uncovered in the 1970 data, table 5 replicates the methodology used previously for the 1970 data set, and it is apparent that the crisp, clear findings from 1970 do not reemerge. The unrotated solution in table 5 argues that three modes of participation do exist, but that there is no single underlying dimension to which all of them belong. In other words, the 1982 modes are not related to one another, as they were in 1970. Intrafactor correlations are extremely weak (factor 1 with factor 2 is .07, 2 with 3 is .11, 1 with 3 is .05, all of which are insignificant). In addition, the 1982 modes are not made up of the same kinds of activities as in 1970. The first seven items in table 5 involve both local and national contacting and involvement in solving communal problems. Voting is a second clear mode (items 6–8), whereas campaign activity is a third (items 9–10).[2]

In terms of modes of participation, the 1982 data differ from the 1970 data in two fundamental ways. First, the 1970 survey revealed sharp distinctions among the three modes of participation, which were communal involvement, local organizational involvement, and national-level petitioning. But in 1982, all three of these activities had coalesced into a more general mode of informal participation. Thus nonelectoral involvement in 1982 was less well differentiated than it had been under authoritarian rule in 1970. At that time, with the military in power, nonelectoral participation was the only form of participation that existed. But by 1982, under electoral rule, nonelectoral involvement was not so nicely refracted. Second, as with the cross-national data from Verba, Nie, and Kim (1978), the 1982 Peruvian data show that voting constituted a separate mode unrelated to either campaign activity or nonelectoral informal participation. It

Table 4. Frequencies of Participatory Involvement, 1982

1. Recent involvement	53.3
2. Frequent involvement	44.1
3. Attended local meeting	26.1
4. Petitioned local organization	39.8
5. Petitioned Ministry of Housing	36.4
6. Petitioned SINAMOS	30.3
7. Voted 1980 presidential election	91.3
8. Voted 1978 Constitutional Assembly	88.3
9. Voted 1980 municipal election	89.1
10. Political party member	11.9
11. Campaign activity	6.1
12. Attended political rally	28.2
13. Member of local organization	28.1

Notes: Figures are percentages. N varies from 622 to 668.

Table 5. Modes of Participation, 1982 (Principal Solution)

	Principal Solution (no rotation)		
	Factor 1	Factor 2	Factor 3
1. Recent involvement	.33		
2. Frequent involvement	.32		
3. Attended local meeting	.51		
4. Petitioned local organization	.68		
5. Petitioned Ministry of Housing	.60		
6. Petitioned SINAMOS	.56		
7. Voted 1980 presidential election		.85	
8. Voted 1978 Constitutent Assembly		.60	
9. Voted 1980 municipal election		.81	
10. Political party member			.53
11. Campaign activity			.56
12. Attended political rally			.50
13. Member of local organization			.27

Key:
Factor 1 = problem-solving/petitioning.
Factor 2 = voting.
Factor 3 = campaigning.

thus appears that, whether voting is mandatory or optional, it remains the easiest political act for most citizens and has apparently little to do with whether a citizen participates in other activities or not.

Sendas Frutales, the rental slum area, in 1982 demonstrated some of the idiosyncracies it had in 1970, but the differences between the two types of settlements (rental versus slum) were not so marked as they had been eleven years earlier. The simple existence of a neighborhood association (despite its considerable disorganization and weakness) allowed people to become involved where they had not in 1971, and although the incidence of involvement for Sendas Frutales was still lower than for the squatter communities, the disparities were by no means as great.[3] Despite these individual differences, three separate modes of involvement existed in Sendas Frutales as they did in the four squatter areas. What is perhaps most striking is that the incidences of involvement in voting and in campaigning show no significant differences across all neighborhoods, regardless of status as rental or squatter. Although equal voting levels might well be predictable (since voting is mandatory), it is more surprising to find that campaign activities were unaffected by type of immediate neighborhood.

The 1980 regime transition in Peru served to upset what had been, under authoritarianism, a rather precise division of political labors. By 1982 the single most common type of participant in the sample was the individual who voted but did nothing else (36 percent of the sample), closely followed (35 percent) by the community activist voter who both voted and became involved in community affairs. Other types—such as the all-around activist involved in everything (4 percent) and the complete inactive (12 percent)—were far less frequent. The transition to democracy tended to modify and perhaps to reduce the tradition of communal involvement that so many observers have seen as a hallmark of squatter neighborhoods.

The Context for Political Participation, 1985

By the time of the 1985 elections and the 1985 survey, conducted in the weeks immediately following the election, the electoral scene in Peru had undergone some dramatic shifts. First of all, APRA, which had a dismal showing in the 1980 presidential and municipal elections, was rejuvenated under the leadership of a young and energetic Alan García. Second, Alfonso Barrantes of IU had won the 1983 municipal race in Lima, the left had taken all the district mayoral races in the city's massive low-income districts, and Barrantes was running as a viable leftist presidential candidate. Belaúnde's AP party had plummeted in the polls as the nation's economy had gone sour. The Shining Path, which had become a considerable presence throughout the country's highland areas, had stymied the military's attempts to counter it and had given the military a black and well-deserved label as a major human rights abuser.

As the 1985 elections approached, García constructed an image of himself as the leader of a new wave of APRA politicians. As a result, García together with the APRA party itself (which had been far and away the best organized political party in Peru since its founding in the 1920s) attracted not only the party faithful but also large numbers of independent or unaffiliated floating voters. García swept into office with an almost two-to-one margin. Indeed, he barely missed taking a simple majority of the popular vote. Peruvian law required a runoff between the two leading vote-getters in such a situation, but Barrantes declined to run and García won without a second round.

The popular vote totals in the 1985 election showed that the electorate had little confidence in Belaúnde and his neoliberal economic policies. APRA and IU, the two major opposition parties during the 1980–1985 period, took over three-quarters of the popular vote between them (AP ended up with 7 percent of the popular vote). One remarkable aspect of this whole period was that the Peruvian military, long a sworn enemy of APRA and deeply suspicious of the left in general, made no effort to influence or subvert the electoral process in any way.

Belaúnde's policies toward Peru's urban sectors consisted largely (as they had in his first term in office from 1963 to 1968) of investment in large-scale housing projects aimed at the middle class. There is no denying that this sector of society needed such housing and benefited from such investment. But low-income urban dwellers received far less attention and were left for the most part to fend for themselves. Velasco-period initiatives such as large-scale distribution of full land titles in the pueblos jóvenes and the installation of basic infrastructure (electricity, water, sewerage) were scaled back. Nor did Belaúnde pay much attention to the urban informal sector generally, aside from periodic and unsuccessful attempts to clamp down on street vendors.

Thus from 1980 to 1985 Peru had undergone the transformation from authoritarian to democratic rule. Peru had also seen an elected civilian president serve one full term and turn power over to an elected civilian successor from an opposition party. This was no mean feat, given the economic problems of the Belaúnde period and the successes of opposition parties in the 1983 municipal elections, not to mention the continued and mounting presence of the Shining Path.

MODES OF PARTICIPATION, 1985

The 1985 survey results do not differ notably from those of 1982 in many ways (see tables 6 and 7), and yet certain aspects deserve discussion. Insofar as individual items are concerned, voting continued to be the most common political act among the 1985 respondents, as it was in 1982; about nine out of ten respondents said they had voted in the two presidential (1980, 1985) and in the most recent municipal elections (1983). Collaborating on neighborhood projects continued to be a common activity as well. Recent involvement and frequency of involvement either rose above or at least stayed at previous levels; membership in the local neighborhood association and petitions directed at local association leaders both increased significantly, as did attendance at local association meetings (when compared with 1982). In sharp contrast, petitioning aimed at national-level authorities (government ministries, SINAMOS) dropped precipitously. In items dealing with nonvoting electoral involvement, the number of individuals who had participated in campaign activities rose moderately, as did those who said they were members of (or who strongly sympathized with) a specific political party, but attendance at political rallies fell by almost half. These results indicate that by 1985 overall greater numbers of low-income urban individuals were turning to a range of informal local activities and away from state-directed petitions, perhaps as a result of the neglect by the Belaúnde administration.

Insofar as the structure of modal participation is concerned, the 1985 results reveal one major change. In 1982 the first six variables that compose factor 1 all showed relatively high loadings on that factor. But by 1985 petitioning activities directed at the state did not load highly on factor 1, and indeed formed an additional factor 4, separate from factor 1. These results suggest not only that petitioning the state dropped off in frequency (as shown in table 6), but also that those few people who did such petitioning did so apart from purely local activities aimed at neighborhood improvements.

In Sendas Frutales, the rental slum area, the changes that had started to appear between 1970 and 1982 had continued into 1985. The same three factors revealed in table 7 appeared in the data for Sendas Frutales, as they had in 1982. What was different is that incidences of involvement in individual activities in Sendas Frutales in most cases were much closer, if still somewhat lower, to those in the squatter communities. Indeed, the number of respondents in Sendas Frutales who said they belonged to the local organization (35 percent) was actually higher than in the other neighborhoods (29 percent)—quite a remarkable accomplishment, considering the state of affairs fifteen years previously, when no organization existed at all.

By 1985 three principal modes of participation still dominated the political arena for Lima's lower classes. Local activities continued to be important and to be rational expenditures of time and energy; voting was something that virtually everyone did, but not necessarily in conjunction with anything else. Cam-

Table 6. Frequencies of Participatory Involvement, 1985

1. Recent involvement	55.7
2. Frequent involvement	80.3
3. Attended local meeting	39.8
4. Petitioned local organization	41.5
5. Petitioned government ministry	16.7
6. Petitioned SINAMOS	15.5
7. Voted 1985 presidential election	96.4
8. Voted 1980 presidential election	88.8
9. Voted 1983 municipal election	89.3
10. Political party member	18.9
11. Campaign activity	10.7
12. Attended political rally	16.3
13. Member of local organization	44.7

Notes: Figures are percentages. N varies from 356 to 412.

Table 7. Modes of Participation, 1985 (Principal Solution)

	Principal Solution (no rotation)		
	Factor 1	*Factor 2*	*Factor 3*
1. Recent involvement	.44		
2. Frequent involvement	.41		
3. Attended local meeting	.61		
4. Petitioned local organization	.62		
5. Petitioned government ministry	.21[a]		
6. Petitioned SINAMOS	.17[a]		
7. Voted 1985 presidential election		.78	
8. Voted 1980 Constituent Assembly		.84	
9. Voted 1983 municipal election		.81	
10. Political party member			.47
11. Campaign activity			.51
12. Attended political rally			.51
13. Member of local organization			.31

a. Loaded .71 and .56 on a separate factor.

paigning and other types of involvement in electoral politics were a separate activity and not one for which many pobladores found time or, by inference, saw as worth their time. What is most striking is that state programs were apparently seen by most pobladores as largely irrelevant to the well-being of their neighborhood: the incidence of involvement dropped off from 1982, and state petitioning actually became a discrete activity. It appeared, to put it bluntly, that state-focused activities had become increasingly irrational, given the constraints under which the pobladores had to decide how they would invest their time and resources in politics.

The Context for Political Participation, 1990

The last half of the decade of the 1980s may well go down in Peruvian history as the most difficult and crisis-ridden five years of the twentieth century. The election of Alan García in 1985 had brought great hope to Peru, and García's first eighteen months or so of populist heterodox economic policy produced significant GDP growth (9.5 percent in 1986), accompanied by relatively stable prices despite stubborn inflation of 63 percent in 1986 and 114 percent in 1987 (Dornbusch and Edwards 1991: 277). However, by mid-1987 heterodoxy had run its course, and several economic problems that had previously been either disguised or ignored now emerged with a vengeance. Inflation escalated past 1700 percent in 1988 to 2700 percent in 1989, then to 7500 percent in 1990; the GDP fell 19 percent in 1988 and 1989 combined, while the real per capita GDP growth (–23 percent) and employment growth (–10 percent) sank even further during the same period. Tax revenues as a percentage of GDP fell from 15 percent in 1985 to 5.4 percent in 1989, meaning that the state had diminishing resources to cope with the mounting crisis that was reflected, for example, in the collapse of real wages, which, with 1979 as 100, went from 79 in 1987 to 29 in 1989 (Lago 1991, 277).

These economic woes created and were paralleled by resurgent social problems in the form of communicable diseases (the 1991 cholera epidemic in Latin America that started in Peru was clearly because of infrastructural deterioration), infant mortality, and multiple hardships associated with survival conditions for millions of people. These economic and social ills inevitably meant that García in particular and APRA in general would suffer as elections were held. After winning the bulk of the municipal elections in 1986 (and unseating the incumbent Barrantes in Lima), APRA saw its popularity slide precipitously following García's ill-fated attempt to nationalize the banking and financial industry in mid-1987. At the same time the IU, which had always been a fragile and suspect coalition, disintegrated in personal and ideological arguments as well as in disputes about why and how the Lima mayoral race had been lost (Roberts 1996). The backlash against García's policies generated new life on the right, led by Mario Vargas Llosa and the hastily organized Fredemo and Movimiento Libertad. The 1989 municipal elections provided (at least in hindsight) considerable foreshadowing; in Lima a television personality named

Ricardo Belmont, a political nobody with no prior experience, won the mayoral race by a wide margin over all other candidates backed by traditional parties and movements.

As the 1990 presidential elections approached, therefore, Peru's and Lima's political stages had once again changed dramatically. APRA was in disarray internally and had been publicly humiliated by the García administration; the left had splintered badly and irrevocably; and AP and PPC, the traditional parties of the center right and right, had moved to support Vargas Llosa, who was himself a political novice. The degree to which the traditional parties were rejected by the electorate became plain during the first round of voting, when Vargas Llosa and Alberto Fujimori, the longest of long shots, finished first and second. Then the degree to which Peru's and Lima's lower classes rejected Vargas Llosa as a representative of the nation's upper classes and traditional power structures became equally plain in the second round, when Fujimori won a resounding victory. In Lima, Fujimori took the city's *distritos populares* by large margins.

All of this electoral activity took place not only in a context of extreme economic hardship but also within a vastly increased presence of the Shining Path, which had by 1990 reached what was perhaps to be its maximum ability to generate fear and disruption. Some hundreds of candidates were killed or attacked in the months prior to the elections; further hundreds were threatened and dissuaded from running for office. The Shining Path was making serious headway in the city of Lima, and especially in the pueblos jóvenes where it either infiltrated existing organizations or attempted to overthrow or assassinate local leaders (DESCO 1989).

MODES OF PARTICIPATION, 1990

Given such circumstances, how did Lima's poor participate in politics in 1990? The data in tables 8 and 9, which replicate the items from 1982 and 1985, show that local, informal activities claimed most of the time and attention of Lima's low-income groups. Most such activities either remained steady or rose compared to 1985 and 1982. State-directed petitioning, which had declined severely from 1980 to 1985, remained low. Voting levels were as high as always, but campaigning and attendance at political rallies dropped to their lowest points over the twenty years. Party identification dropped off notably from 1985 levels to the lowest level of all three postauthoritarian surveys.[4]

In general, by 1990 lower-class people saw local-level involvement as a more viable means of coping and surviving than trying to extract resources from the state, which by 1990 had lost virtually all credibility as a source for assistance or security (see chapter 5). Petitioning the state thus had become an irrational ex-

Table 8. Frequencies of Participatory Involvement, 1990

1. Recent involvement	48.5
2. Frequent involvement	77.9
3. Attended local meeting	50.2
4. Petitioned local organization	42.3
5. Petitioned government ministry	19.3
6. Petitioned PAIT	11.6
7. Voted 1990 presidential election	96.3
8. Voted 1985 presidential election	92.3
9. Voted 1989 municipal election	96.1
10. Political party member	8.6
11. Campaign activity	4.3
12. Attended political rally	9.8
13. Member of local organization	48.3

Notes: Figures are percentages. N varies from 303 to 437.

Table 9. Modes of Participation, 1990 (Principal Solution)

	Principal Solution (no rotation)		
	Factor 1	*Factor 2*	*Factor 3*
1. Recent involvement	.62		
2. Frequent involvement	.56		
3. Attended local meeting	.70		
4. Petitioned local organization	.74		
5. Petitioned government ministry	.16[a]		
6. Petitioned SINAMOS	.20[a]		
7. Voted 1985 presidential election		.83	
8. Voted 1980 Constituent Assembly		.80	
9. Voted 1983 municipal election		.78	
10. Political party member			.54
11. Campaign activity			.49
12. Attended political rally			.51
13. Member of local organization	.66		.31

a. Loaded .73 and .61 on a separate dimension.

penditure of time for the pobladores, although many realized that only the state could provide certain amenities and improvements that their neighborhoods needed. Parodi (1993) found in his study that the legitimacy of the state was extremely low, although the pobladores still believed petitioning the state had to be done, even with low expectations that anything beneficial might result (Parodi 1993, 66–67).

In electoral terms, people continued to vote, not only for partisan reasons but also perhaps because they wished to indicate their opposition to the Shining Path. But beyond voting, participating in the electoral arena (for example, becoming involved in campaign activities, or by attending political rallies) dropped off notably, probably for a variety of reasons. First, such activities take time, money, and energy, all of which are extremely limited resources among Lima's poor; and second, such activities were public and participants could be identified by the Shining Path, which by 1990 had developed a serious presence in Lima, especially in its low-income districts.[5]

Table 9 reveals once again the same three modes that first appeared in the 1982 data and that were then modified in 1985. Local-level petitioning and demand-making (factor 1) result from a cluster of local activities, as in 1985. Visits to state ministries or involvement in state-directed activities such as an emergency employment effort called the Programa de Apoyo de Ingreso Temporal (PAIT; Program in Support of Temporary [short-term] Income) not only remained infrequent activities (see table 8) but were, as they had been in 1985, discrete activities distinct from local involvement.

Sendas Frutales, the rental slum neighborhood, continued its slow progress from an inchoate and atomized area in 1970 to a neighborhood worthy of the term "community." The same factors of participation in the four squatter settlements appeared in Sendas Frutales. Levels of involvement in voting and campaigning showed no difference across all five neighborhoods. More surprising was that the incidence of involvement in petitioning activities in several cases exceeded that in the other neighborhoods. Residents of Sendas Frutales, for example, had higher rates of recent community involvement, of attendance at local meetings, and of petitioning local and ministry authorities.[6]

In general terms, the overall effect of severe economic crisis on political participation had become manifest in 1990 in a number of ways. First, it is clear that local-level involvement reemerged or remained highly salient and was viewed by the pobladores as a rational investment of their time. Frequent and recent involvement in communal activities, attendance at local meetings, and membership in the local association by 1985 and 1990 either had risen to all-time high levels or had at least regained ground lost between 1970 and 1982. The similarities of results between the squatter areas and Sendas Frutales argue that economic and social hardships can act as a massive leveling influence that in essence overwhelms more superficial differences to channel participation into those activities that maximize the probabilities of coping and of survival.[7]

Some of these findings seemingly contradict or at least modify some of my earlier work using neighborhoods of different ages at a single point in time, which found that, as a neighborhood ages and develops, intracommunal activity atrophies (Dietz 1980; see also Goldrich 1970). Such a decline may well occur if (and this is a major qualifier) reasonably steady or improving economic conditions exist over time. I made the argument in 1970 that, as a community ages and progresses, those things its inhabitants can do for themselves are in fact accomplished and local-level involvement starts to drop off. But the 1970 data were collected at a single point in time, and the conclusions came from different communities of different ages, rather than across time. The 1970 data were insufficient to show how longitudinal shifts in macrolevel factors could affect individual behavior over time. But the availability of four data sets collected across twenty years indicates that, if economic conditions worsen and state policies are increasingly perceived as ineffectual, then low-income individuals tend to move away from state-directed petitioning and to invest more of whatever resources they have available in local communal activities.

I also argued that the newer the community, the higher the level of local involvement, not only because there was so much that had to be done (that could be done with local resources), but also because a new neighborhood, especially one formed through invasion, was apt to have high levels of community spirit and enthusiasm. The 1970 data showed this to be the case: Primero de Enero, the then new (three-year-old) invasion-formed research site, had far higher levels of local involvement than any of the others. By 1982 Primero de Enero was no longer much different from the other research communities. Yet the increasingly difficult economic pressures of the mid- and late 1980s tended to produce either steady or rising rates of involvement in informal activities in most of the neighborhoods, regardless of age. (More will be said about changes and shifts over time across the samples and the specific communities in the next chapter, which examines in more detail the patterns of involvement in informal activities.)

Conclusions

The data presented in this chapter indicate that the pobladores of Lima changed their views of themselves and their neighborhoods over time, and that their patterns of political participation also changed. The pobladores of the samples saw themselves as permanent residents of their communities, either because they were basically satisfied or because life offered few alternatives. Their views of their neighborhoods were realistic; they knew that there was much to be done, and they thought efforts that combined their own hard work with state assistance were the most practical ways of getting things done. Their communities had once been viewed as reasonably unified, but for a variety of realistic reasons the pobladores perceived that this unity had declined. In recent years they had come to see the state as less relevant in their lives than it once had been, but they still hoped that the state could help out somehow, sometime. The economic collapse of the late 1980s universally meant hard times; households became more crowded, and worst of all, wages did not keep up with other hardwon progress in education, job status, and community consolidation.

MODES OF PARTICIPATION

The modal analysis of political participation developed by Verba, Nie, Kim et al. constitutes a rigorous yet flexible means for examining political participation at a single point in time. It serves also for comparing and tracing changes in participation over time. What are the principal results of using this analytic technique on the four data sets from Lima?

The most obvious result occurred in the reconstruction of participation as regime change took place. There can be little doubt that the Velasco government and its authoritarian state encountered the inevitable impasse that any nonelectoral regime encounters in its attempt both to encourage and to confine participation (or mobilization) for its own purposes. In 1970 the electoral process had been suspended indefinitely and political parties were irrelevant insofar as participation was concerned (they had not been outlawed, but they had no power and there was no reason to pay attention to them). At the same time, the government attempted to woo the nation's poor through claims that Peru's traditional elites had ignored them (which was true) and that the Revolution of the Armed Forces was being waged for them (which was questionable, or at least only partly true).

Lima's urban poor reacted as they always had: they continued their local-level neighborhood efforts to provide themselves with the goods and services they needed, they organized themselves to that end, and they interacted with the state when and if they thought it worthwhile and rational to do so. When the state and its resources and willingness to distribute them are unknowns (as was the case during the early Velasco years) but when prior experience dictates caution and low expectations, self-help and communal mutual assistance become highly rational acts. But the state remained a monopoly in various ways: as the source of certain desired goods (official recognition of the settlement, distribution of land titles), provision of certain services (police protection, garbage collection, mail delivery), and infrastructure (potable water, sewerage). Lima's poor thus had also to petition and interact with the state up to the point where, from their perspective, the expenditure of time, money, and effort to conform to state expectations exceeded the goods and services provided. Thus the 1970 sample displayed a clear division of labor (that is, participation) based on rational calculations of what sorts of activities could satisfy needs and demands.

After 1980 and the reestablishment of civilian rule and electoral procedures, participation became more diffuse for two basic reasons: first, because multiple avenues of participation had come into existence, and second, because the individual citizen had to decide which avenues were worth spending resources on (or in a word, which avenues were rational). The act of voting can never be targeted exclusively at the provision of goods; deciding whether to vote (not a pressing question for the vast majority of Peruvian citizens) and, more important, whom to vote for hinges upon much more than asking oneself whether voting will provide a concrete good. Most citizens of any nation would not argue that, because they voted for candidate A or party B (and always assuming that such a candidate or party won), they would receive a specific good, or even that expectations of receiving a good would dictate their voting preferences. Voters choose whom to vote for because of ideological, personal, and a whole panoply of idiosyncratic reasons that may have little or nothing to do directly with the provision of collective goods.

Electoral participation became mandatory starting in 1980, in part because the state realized that one fundamental building block of democratic consolidation is the routinizing of the electoral process and having the citizenry become accustomed to voting on a regular basis. But for the poor, such formal involvement was, even during the best of times, a civic duty that bore only indirectly on the provision of goods or services. During economic crisis, voting became less relevant to survival, whereas investing time, energy, money, and other resources in informal grassroots community involvement became far more rational.

Thus a transitional democratic state's preoccupation with and insistence on voting can diffuse or deflect direct government-directed petitioning and demand-making. Given the highly limited resources available to the poor to become involved in politics, voting (especially when obligatory) may take time away from more direct participatory activities that are, from the poor's perspective, ultimately more instrumental. Indeed, the willingness of the populace to continue to vote in presidential and municipal elections throughout the course of the 1980s is quite remarkable, given the growing presence of the Shining Path.

Yet the fear and intimidation that Sendero Luminoso by 1990 had instilled throughout Peru ironically worked against that movement. One of Sendero Luminoso's goals was to subvert the whole electoral process, primarily by violently dissuading potential candidates from running, as well as by preventing the electorate at large from voting at all. Sendero failed almost entirely in this effort, except in Peru's most remote regions. Indeed, many Peruvians saw voting as a way of repudiating Sendero Luminoso. On the other hand, the economic crisis of the late 1980s may have produced an ultimate irony: the state encouraged precisely those modes of participation (formal, mandatory voting) that, from the lower-class perspective, were least likely to satisfy basic needs directly, while those modal activities that were most likely to be directly instrumental (informal community efforts, for example) received less attention and resources.

7

....

INFORMAL

PARTICIPATION

Grassroots Involvement

and State Petitioning

To undertake an examination of informal political participation over time, it is useful to return again to the model sketched in chapters 1 and 6 which characterized democracy as a collective good, and which argued that individual citizens make choices about how they will participate in politics based on two preference dimensions: a *political* preference dimension for democracy over any other political system, and an *economic* preference dimension for material well-being over material deprivation. If, over time, democracy is perceived by low-income citizens as being either responsible for or unable to prevent increased material deprivation, then the preference for democracy may weaken or diminish. At the same time, deteriorating macroeconomic conditions and intensifying poverty may find the state unable to meet the poor's increasing demands and needs. Such a weakening could be manifested informally in a variety of ways: the poor could adopt self-help behavior that utilizes the household or the immediate neighborhood and that turns away from the state; they could adopt demonstrative or protest behaviors; or they could look for solutions by sympathizing with or joining a group that advocates radical change or violence.

Two more general ways of considering behavioral options for an individual citizen lie in Hirschman's notions of exit, voice, and loyalty and in Olson's arguments concerning the key role that the size of the group plays in determining whether people will participate in that group's activities or not. Hirschman (1970) posits three basic responses for an individual in his relationship with a firm whose performance is not satisfactory: he can remain loyal to that firm, he can voice complaints, or he can exit and search for an alternative. The exit option has traditionally concerned economists, dealing as it does with competition; the voice option has occupied political scientists, since, as Hirschman puts it, voice "is a far more 'messy' concept because it can be graduated all the way from faint grumbling to violent protest; it implies articulation of one's critical opinions, and . . . is roundabout rather than direct and straightforward." Voice is "any attempt at all to change, rather than to escape from, an objectionable state of affairs, whether through individual or collective petition . . . [or] through various types of actions and protests" (1970, 16, 30).

I would propose here that the very imprecision of the voice option may make it especially applicable in the informal political arena. After all, informal participation consists of community-based activities (collaborating with neighbors, participating in the local association, petitioning local, municipal, or state authorities). These multiple voluntary activities involve a wide range of actions, all of which are subject to high levels of individual choice frequently based on individual constraints: "Do I have time to go to a local meeting? Is it worthwhile to go? Can't someone else go to the Ministry of Housing, since I went last time?" How to articulate a grievance or demand is also open to much debate: "If we go to the ministry, should we ask for assistance or demand it? If we demand it, will we risk sanctions in some form, or will we scare or force bureaucrats into providing what we need?"

In contrast, I would propose that the exit option (here understood as deserting one party or candidate for another, not as deciding not to vote) may be much more applicable and empirically more frequent in the formal or electoral political arena. For example, voting in Peru is an act that involves limited, clear choices: "Should I vote or not vote, yes or no? Should I vote for Party A, B, or C? If I vote for Party A and am disappointed, should I stay with it (loyalty), try to help fix it (voice), or vote for someone else (exit)?" In a time of extended and severe crisis, it is likely that poor voters will opt for the exit option more commonly than the other two (a hypothesis I return to in detail in chapter 8).

Informally, when an economic crisis strikes, low-income citizens must make choices whether to act, and then how to act in order to cope and survive. These decisions can involve choices about (for example) remaining loyal to traditional tactics in presenting petitions, or becoming more aggressive in making demands, or seeing neighborhood problems as less (or as more) worthy of time and effort, or joining a radical movement, or dropping out of informal political participation altogether. As the individual citizen makes decisions among Hirschman's three options, other factors will also influence whether and how to participate.

One such consideration has to do with the size of the group involved, since it is much harder to get people to participate in a large group than in a small one. Olson's (1965) theory of collective action is useful here. In its simplest form, his argument is that rational individuals are unlikely to act spontaneously to advance goals shared by large numbers of people, whereas people in small groups more often act to further common ends.[1] I am not concerned with presenting a rigorous operationalization of what small and large may mean in the context of Lima, but the question of size and of its effect on involvement does become important in discussing Lima in the late 1970s and early 1980s, when numerous efforts were made to create regional, citywide, and even national federations of squatter neighborhood associations.

In this chapter, I provide a detailed description and analysis of informal (non-electoral) participation within and across the neighborhoods, over time. In so doing I also take on the question of whether or to what degree the pobladores in Lima became involved in or created new social movements during the 1970s and 1980s. From the conclusions of chapter 6 we know that certain political activities formed stable modes of involvement over twenty years. Voting, for example, comprised an identifiable, discrete mode after it came on-line in 1980. On the other hand informal involvement, which is to say community participation, changed over time.[2] From a tight, cleanly defined package of three modes of involvement in 1970, community involvement and various forms of petitioning blurred together subsequently into a catch-all problem-solving mode, while voting and campaigning became additional, separate activities.

Political Participation and Rational Behavior

To begin, it is necessary to reintroduce two points from chapter 1: first, the definition of informal political participation adopted at that time, and second, the nature of rationality. Informal participation by the urban poor involves individual or collective efforts to supply themselves and their neighborhoods with public goods, sometimes but not always through attempts to obtain a favorable distribution of governmental resources. This purposely instrumental definition sees political participation not as an end in itself but as a means for material gain and improvement. This underscoring of instrumentality is no great surprise; after all, people in general and the poor in particular seldom become involved in politics for the sheer sake of participating. But to link informal involvement with the literature on new social movements, understanding this materialistic emphasis becomes essential.

This instrumentalist conceptualization of participation is intimately related to the specific characterization of procedural or bounded rationality set forth in chapter 1. In Simon's view, bounded rational behavior is the behavior of a person

> who is limited in computational capacity, and who searches very selectively through large realms of possibilities in order to discover what alternatives are available, and what the consequences of each of these alternatives are. The search is incomplete, often inadequate, based on uncertain information and partial ignorance, and usually terminated with the discovery of satisfactory, not optimal, courses of action. (Simon 1985, 295)

The key element of this characterization of informal participation that connects it to rational behavior should be readily apparent. Poblador informal participation constitutes the most direct and most sensitive reflection of what the urban poor themselves think will actually assist them in obtaining material goods and/or a favorable distribution of governmental resources. The pobladores are always limited by Simon's multiple constraints surrounding them. Patterns of informal political involvement therefore comprise empirical manifestations of what for the pobladores is rational behavior. Grassroots activities are generated from within a community; the forms they take, their persistence over time, and the degree to which people become involved in them, are all related to whether they succeed or not. Reciprocally, whether they succeed will play a large part in people's decisions about whether to continue to become involved in them or not.[3] All of this is to say that informal behavior provides the most realistic portrayal of what the poor consider to be worth their time and effort, since these activities are first created and then sustained (or not, depending upon their perceived success) by the poor themselves.

Simon defines bounded rational behavior as behavior "that is adaptive within the constraints imposed by both the external situation and by the capacity of the decision-maker" (1985, 294).[4] Thus, it becomes essential to identify both internal and external constraints that define the boundedness of rationality. The most obvious constraint here is poverty. Individually or in a group, the urban lower classes are simply poor. They lack the money and resources (time, access to or attention from authorities, autonomous political power, knowledge, organization) that other urban groups might have.

Individual poverty and collective poverty are not the only limitations on the pobladores, however. Again in Simon's terms, they are constrained by external circumstances. For example, the local neighborhood itself can influence how its inhabitants become involved. Individual or group agents external to the community may provoke or initiate types of participation (demonstrations, for instance) that would not otherwise occur except for their presence. Likewise, the Peruvian state is itself poor, meaning that it does not have either the material resources or the political will to respond to all petitioning or demand-making activities that a neighborhood might produce. Finally, a regime can itself act to constrain and to define rational behavior. For example, a regime (authoritarian or democratic) may proscribe certain forms of violent political participation. It is possible, of course, that pobladores may go against such prohibitions, but even if (or because) they do, they may reduce the chances that the state will respond favorably to such behaviors.

Individual Participation and New Social Movements

The notion of informal political participation adopted here is obviously linked to the concept of new social movements. The study of social movements in Latin America in general and in Peru in particular has generated a vast amount of work over the past two decades or so. It is both necessary and appropriate to see how the analysis of informal involvement and rational behavior intersects with the more general topic of social movements.

Many scholars—including Foweraker (1995), Foweraker and Craig (1990), and Escobar and Alvarez (1992)—distinguish between social movement theories that are concerned with strategy, on the one hand, and those that are concerned with identity, on the other. The former, generally labeled resource mobilization theories, highlight "questions of strategy, participation, organization, rationality, expectations, interests, and the like," whereas "identity-centered theories . . . emphasize the processes by which social actors constitute collective identities as a means to create democratic spaces for more autonomous action" (Escobar and Alvarez 1992, 5; also Foweraker 1995). But this materialist-mobilization/identity-creation dichotomy is at best academic and analytic; real life is seldom so clear-cut. Arguments in favor of one to the exclusion of the other may well be at the core counterproductive.[5]

This debate parallels many others in the new social movements literature, which include quantitative versus qualitative data and methodologies, clientelistic versus aggressive poblador-state relationships, or endogenous versus exogenous theories concerning the original stimulus for social movement formation.[6] Both sides of these debates occur throughout this chapter, especially the quantitative-qualitative debate. I use both sorts of data extensively, since I assume that neither approach is by itself sufficient for describing or analyzing informal political behavior, whether individual or in the aggregate.

Treatments of the other debates are also woven throughout the chapter. For example, Stokes's (1991, 1995) research on Lima's urban poor argues that over the years poblador behavior (at least among certain segments of the poblador population) has shifted from strategic resource mobilization employing polite, clientelistic tactics to more overtly ideological goals using assertive, confrontational tactics. Yet regardless of the tactics employed, Stokes readily notes that material resources continue to be a major if not dominant rationale for mobilization among Lima's poor. Foweraker (1990) argues that, in the Mexican context, the demands made by popular movements are of a "welfarist" kind that focus on wages, security, and services of all kinds, that they are "immediate, pragmatic, and concrete," and that "they must seek above all to acquire a *capacidad de gestion*—the ability to get their demands met" (5–6). More broadly Touraine notes that, whatever definition or conceptualization of social movements is adopted, if the form of their participation in the political system is not included, the definition will be inadequate (Touraine 1987, cited in Foweraker and Craig 1990, 302).

The question of whether social movements depend upon internal or external stimuli to form and to function has come under considerable discussion (Salman 1990, 173–74). Whether these external agents are religious groups (Mainwaring 1986), leftist organizations (Eckstein 1989), or charitable institutions (Rodriguez et al. 1973; Riofrio 1978), debate about the need for such agents to provoke or form social movements has continued for decades. And while these issues come under discussion throughout this chapter, my major concern is not with the goals or behavior or involvement of an aggregation of individuals *as* a social movement, but with disaggregated individuals and their individual participation *in* a social movement. Survey data do not offer direct empirical information about the behavior of a group, although they can reveal a good deal about the participation of individuals in such groups. This perspective thus offers a good deal that group-level analysis cannot. The examination of group behavior requires data based on the group as a unit of analysis; the analysis of individual behavior, which is the focus of this book, requires individual-level data either from surveys or from informants. The two units or levels (the individual and the group) are not completely separate; they obviously inform one another intimately. But the emphasis here is on the individual poblador and his behavior; if he belongs to a group or to something that can be labeled a social movement, the survey data can reveal a good deal about his participation in that movement or group. The study of the social movement as such remains a subject area at least analytically separable from the study of individual political participation. Nevertheless, social movements in Lima have for generations created the means for individual participation, and a brief sketch of their development over the twentieth century is necessary for understanding shifts and changes in individual participation.

State-Poblador Relations in Lima, 1900–1968

If social movements are defined as poblador-initiated, grassroots, bottom-up efforts dedicated to organizing within (and much less frequently across) neighborhoods with the intent of obtaining material resources or improvements, then Lima's poor have been creating and participating in social movements for decades. Numerous sources have explored either specific communities or Lima as a whole and have identified certain general chronological patterns of social-movement development over time. Understanding these patterns is essential for analyzing individual participation.[7] I concentrate on the decades 1970–1990, but a short description of earlier times can give an idea of the growth of lower-class Lima and of the changing nature of barrio-state relationships prior to 1970. In terms of the analytic framework offered in chapter 2, the major concern here is the link between point B (state-society relations) and point F, as mediated at points C, D, and E.

THE PREWAR YEARS 1900–1945

Prior to World War II, Lima was a small city that contained less than a tenth of Peru's total population. The 1876 census counted 125,000 people in the city. After the disastrous War of the Pacific with Chile, during which Lima was occupied by Chilean forces, Peru saw modest advancement as agrarian exports and the early beginnings of industrialization gained in importance. Such expansion was not only economic; Lima's city walls finally came down as trolley and light rail lines connected the downtown with outlying suburban areas and with Callao, Lima's port city.

Nevertheless, it was not until the 1920s and the administration of Augusto Leguía that Lima started to grow significantly. Leguía was determined to make Lima a modern city through expanded infrastructure and the construction of new housing and commercial developments. Such investments quite naturally attracted labor and produced the beginnings of a rural-urban migration flow that has continued up until the end of the twentieth century. Yet this low-income populace found itself shut out by a housing market that catered to the city's middle class and by increasingly crowded conditions in central city rental slum areas.

These conditions helped to generate Lima's first modern barriadas or squatter settlements in the 1920s, and by 1945 at least twenty such neighborhoods had come into existence.[8] Most were in marginal or difficult areas (chiefly hillsides), where services were minimal or missing altogether. Under such circumstances, neighborhoods could do little more than undertake grassroots efforts to supply their own needs, since the Peruvian state assumed no official responsibility for these communities.

THE YEARS 1945–1948

This short period covering the truncated term of President José Luis Bustamante y Rivero is essential, since it saw the start of what was to become a long series of large-scale land invasions in and around Lima. The first of these was the 1946 San Cosme invasion, which occurred on a low hill near the then new, central, wholesale-retail market complex universally known as La Parada. San Cosme was followed shortly by similar invasions on nearby hillsides (Cerro El Pino, Cerro El Agustino). Such large-scale takeovers offered strong evidence, then and now, that Lima's poor were capable of mounting well-organized, clandestine, and sophisticated mass movements to supply a demonstrated need (land). If such movements were illegal, then this was a risk or cost that had to be weighed against the benefit of obtaining land.

These land invasions did not escape the attention of the state. Bustamante passed Decree Law 10722, which created the Corporación Nacional de la Vivienda (National Housing Association), Peru's first national state agency dedicated to urban problems and planning. But Bustamante's term came to an early end in 1948, when General Manuel Odría deposed him in a coup.

THE YEARS 1948–1968

This period includes three presidential administrations: Manuel Odría (1948–1956), a general who took power in a coup; Manuel Prado (1956–1962), a member of one of Peru's wealthiest and most conservative families; and Fernando Belaúnde Terry (1963–1968), a young, centrist-reformist architect who headed his own party, AP. It also includes a brief episode of military rule (1962–1963). Each of these administrations made a specific mark upon squatter-state relations.

The Odría administration was notable for its repressive stance against the APRA party; conservative economic policies toward (in particular) foreign investment, especially in the mining sector; an extreme concentration of agricultural land in the hands of a few wealthy owners; modest steps toward import substitution industrialization; and significant expenditures on public works and infrastructure. The combination of these several factors gave enormous impetus to the already existing rural-urban migration, especially toward Lima, as thousands of farmworkers and laborers found themselves either without land or without the means to earn a subsistence living. The figures for the growth of Lima provide ample evidence of this migration: Lima had 645,000 people in 1945, 1,850,000 in 1961, and 3,330,000 in 1972. In other words, the city first tripled in sixteen years, then doubled again in the following eleven. This massive growth was not met by corresponding efforts either by the formal economic structures or by the state apparatus; and by the mid-1960s the barriada had become the principal source of housing for Lima's low-income populace, outstripping central city rental slum environments.

From and because of this growth emerged another salient characteristic of the Odría period: its paternalism toward low-income urban groups. Odría saw the urban poor as a source of potential political support, and he and his wife, who headed the so-called Centro de Asistencia Social (Center for Social Assistance), spent much time and money providing highly paternalistic and clientelistic material aid and comfort to squatter settlements. In many (perhaps a majority) of the cases, Odría himself acted as official sponsor for newly formed communities (Collier 1976), most notoriously the settlement known originally as 27 de Octubre (October 27, which is now the district of San Martín de Porras, one of Lima's largest districts), named after the date of Odría's coup.[9]

After the creation of this settlement, a special law was passed that allowed the local residents' association to enroll members who would settle in the district. The association was headed by Odría's backers and close friends; a person had to join the association in order to move into the settlement. Later on, as 1956 neared and Odría considered running for the presidency (something he eventually did not do), members of the settlement association were forced to become members of Odría's political party. By the end of his term, Odría and his wife had awarded almost nine thousand land titles to the inhabitants of 27 de Octubre. In return, the association often organized marches in support of Odría and his wife, frequently demonstrating in downtown Lima on their birthdays and on the anniversary of the coup (Collier 1976, 59–60).

Odría clearly realized that neither the private sector nor the state could or would attempt to provide low-income housing, and that the best and perhaps only tactical response was to neutralize this expanding sector of Lima by incorporating it. Odría thus brought the support of the masas populares over to his side by demonstrating that he was the one who was on their side and their champion. Odría used the state to help organize groups of invaders, or to indicate that a land invasion in a certain place would not provoke state repression or retaliation, or to make land available to central city slum dwellers who were evicted, generally to allow urban redevelopment by one of the nation's oligopolistic real estate and development companies. Odría also made efforts to assure that local associations emerging during and after the creation of a settlement would be under his control, not only because he sought their support but also because he very much wanted to prevent APRA from penetrating and organizing in the barriadas and gaining their political support. Finally, the Odría administration created the Fondo de Salud y Bienestar Social (Health and Social Welfare Fund) as its agency to coordinate the state's efforts in the barrios marginales.

The Odría administration thus stressed clientelism, paternalism, and state dependence for Lima's poor, especially its squatter population. Its strategy of incorporation was not in the least subtle; it cajoled, persuaded, coerced, and bribed the poor to support an authoritarian regime. It also attempted to blur rather than intensify class differences (in direct contrast to APRA's bottom-up mobilizational strategies) and, in so doing, to limit pluralism. But as Collier notes: "Odría . . . created a new urban sector, one that future political leaders could ignore only at great cost in terms of loss of political support—and perhaps also of political control" (1976, 64).

The Prado administration (1956–1962) was a civilian government that succeeded Odría. Manuel Prado had already been president from 1939 to 1945. He was a member of Peru's aristocracy, and highly conservative in his views, but won largely because he had accepted the support of APRA, the political party Odría had so much repressed. From the start of his administration Prado confronted several major land invasions, the most famous of which was the Comas invasion of 1958.

Newspaper accounts of the time indicate that in about forty-eight hours some ten thousand people moved onto a piece of land north of downtown Lima. Partly as a result of such unprecedented actions Prado and Pedro Beltrán, the aristocratic and influential editor of Lima's La Prensa newspaper who eventually became prime minister under Prado, introduced several new policies for Lima's barriadas. An Agrarian Reform and Housing Commission issued a path-breaking study of the problem (Córdova 1958), as did the Fondo de Salud y Bienestar Social (1960). Beltrán and Prado encouraged the creation of savings and loan cooperatives and attempted to modernize and make more efficient the construction industry in general while allowing vast new private sector housing developments throughout the city.

The Agrarian Reform and Housing Commission gave rise in 1961 to the landmark Decree Law 13517, which had several major parts affecting Lima's squatter population directly (Martínez 1965; Collier 1976, chap. 6; Manaster 1968). It regularized the process whereby squatter communities could be recognized officially and thus become eligible for assistance; it prohibited the formation of new settlements and banned state assistance to all such settlements; it established guidelines for remodeling and legalizing settlements; it required that the pobladores help pay for state assistance; and it introduced the whole concept of self-help as part of the state's official vocabulary and policy tools (as if the pobladores had not been practicing self-help by themselves from the start). Finally, Decree Law 13517 created the Corporación Nacional de la Vivienda (National Housing Board), a state agency empowered to carry out cadastral planning work and to make full and legal land titles available to pobladores in approved settlements.

Law 13517 was obviously breakthrough legislation. It not only gave the state a major role in the squatter communities of Lima, it was also de facto recognition by the state that these communities had to be officially recognized and dealt with. The Prado administration thus changed the paternalistic and clientelistic stance of dependence upon the state of the Odría government to a more neoliberal policy that stressed independence, self-help, autonomy, and property ownership for the squatters. This policy also gave the Peruvian state a justification to allocate fewer resources to the poor, and a means to defuse poblador mobilization by other political groups, especially APRA and the left.

Prado's administration ended with a coup. The military took over when the presidential race of 1962 ended in a constitutional deadlock, and when it seemed possible that APRA might win. The military kept power for only one year, but it replaced the National Housing Board with a Junta Nacional de la Vivienda (National Housing Agency), which began to implement Law 13517.

Fernando Belaúnde Terry (1963–1968) came to office trained as an architect and planner, as someone involved in building and construction all his life. But his interests were in large state-sponsored middle-class housing projects (such as San Felipe and Santa Cruz in Lima) and highways. Urban squatters and their communities were low on his list of priorities and remained so throughout his term. Belaúnde's preference was undoubtedly reinforced by the fact that much of AP's electoral support came from rural areas as well as from Lima's middle class and not from the city's poor.

Although Belaúnde paid little attention to the poor, some of his policies created far-reaching effects. Among other things, he believed that Peru was developmentally constrained by the historical overcentralization of power in Lima.

He consequently undertook what was in the Peruvian context an unprecedented program of decentralization. One result of this program was to make local government elective instead of appointive. This innovation (local elections were held in 1963 and 1966), coupled with the creation of several new districts in Lima that were largely squatter in origin and populace, created an energetic sense of local political activity and involvement in squatter neighborhoods. Local inhabitants could now run for office, and the major political parties found it necessary to compete for the votes these districts could supply by addressing local needs in their campaigns.

As such activity increased, Belaúnde's position as president with a minority in both houses of the Peruvian congress created policy problems. The opposition majority coalition—composed of two old enemies of the 1950s, APRA and the Unión Nacional Odriísta (UNO; National Odría Union), the personalist followership of General Odría—cut funding for the Junta Nacional de la Vivienda and for implementing many of the more expensive aspects of Law 13517, such as remodeling the existing settlements and installing all basic services as prerequisites for awarding land titles. But the junta nevertheless continued to act as a sponsor for new settlements through municipal governments. APRA, which enjoyed some district-level mayoral victories of its own in 1963 and 1966, could also sponsor settlement formation. As a result, the Belaúnde years saw relatively few land invasions in Lima (Collier 1976, 91–92). AP created an organization called Cooperación Popular, designed to facilitate grassroots development throughout the country, especially in rural areas, where it built roads, bridges, water systems, and other infrastructural projects. The Belaúnde period also coincided with the Alliance for Progress years, when foreign financial assistance from the Agency for International Development and other aid from the Peace Corps and similar groups became available for the first time.[10] Belaúnde's administration started in 1963 with great optimism and broad popular support, but a combination of intense political opposition from the APRA-UNO coalition, slowly deteriorating economic conditions, and various episodes of mismanagement and corruption finally brought an early end in 1968, when the military seized power about six months before the scheduled elections of 1969.

Overall, the Belaúnde administration was the first since the end of World War II (and perhaps the first ever) in which party politics became the primary means of power acquisition, and each major party played the game in its own style and at least occasionally by what appeared to be its own rules. APRA, which had previously been forced to operate either clandestinely or in coalition with other parties, was able to use its formidable organizational strength to penetrate Lima's lower classes, to mobilize, recruit, and take control of numerous local neighborhood associations. APRA's superior organization and the faith of its adherents in the party and in its leader, Haya de la Torre, gave it the capacity to socialize and train new party members and to establish linkages between the grass roots and the party structures. UNO focused on developing patron-client relationships, both to develop bases of support for its leader and to counter the mobilizational efforts of APRA. Belaúnde's AP did relatively little in Lima's barriadas and concomitantly won little support. Cooperación Popular did some work in Lima, but its small urban budget and its rural focus did not win many adherents.

Yet as Peru's elites and political parties each tried to develop a strategy for gaining support from Lima's burgeoning populace during the 1950s and 1960s, the pobladores of the squatter settlements of Lima and other cities were not idly waiting for the state or various political parties to act on their behalf. The pobladores themselves formed local neighborhood associations (either with or without the aid of parties or the state), which became common throughout urban Peru. Pobladores created these associations so that a specific neighborhood could organize itself to work toward a common goal through self-help or could approach a state agency to ask for help with legal recognition, *lotización* (surveying the land and regularizing lots and streets), land titles, infrastructure, and police protection. Although the state was committed to helping with the formation of such associations under Law 13517, many communities formed their own organizations and then asked that they be recognized.

The first instance of such associations joining together to form a citywide federation was in Arequipa, Peru's second largest city located in the south. The Asociación de Urbanizaciones Populares de Arequipa (AUPA; Association of Popular Urbanizations of Arequipa) was created in 1956 to act as an umbrella organization and to allow that city's poor neighborhoods to speak with a collective voice and identity. A similar federation appeared in 1963 in Ayacucho, to be followed by other cities as the 1960s progressed (Tovar 1982b, 38–39). The sheer size of Lima's squatter populace and the hundreds of squatter communities created in Lima during the 1960s made (and have continued to make) citywide federations problematic and unwieldy. Attempts to create districtwide federations occurred many times, although most have met with indifferent success (see below).

Each of the three major political parties thus had its own individual goals and tactics insofar as Lima's poor were concerned. Likewise, the urban poor of Lima and of other cities attempted to organize themselves, sometimes independently and sometimes at the urging and with the help of outside assistance from the state, political parties, or external agencies. But this period came to an abrupt end in September 1968, when a military coup led by General Juan Velasco launched a whole new period of state-led mobilizational activities aimed directly at Lima's poor. It was two years after this coup that I carried out the first survey.

The Context for Poblador Participation, 1970

The seven years of Velasco's government, 1968–1975 (he was overthrown in a countercoup), had both immediate and long-term consequences for Lima's poor.[11] Upon taking office, Velasco made it immediately and abundantly clear that the military intended to govern the country indefinitely, and that civilian politicians and parties would have little or no influence (although they would not be outlawed). The country's poor, urban as well as rural, would be the main target for what the military called its Revolution of the Armed Forces and for the creation of *una socieded de plena participación* (a society of full participation).

In December 1968 the Velasco government made one of its first policy moves with the creation of ONDEPJOV. The change in official name or nomenclature was not simply a euphemism, nor was it trivial, either for the military state or for the urban poor. *Pueblo jóven* (young town) was the new name applied to squatter settlements nationwide, for at least a couple of reasons. First, the old label, "barriada" was deemed derogatory. More important, the new name was meant to express the idea that the squatter communities were incipient (if not necessarily young in terms of age) towns in which the inhabitants and the state had an equal stake. In addition to this name change, ONDEPJOV also made it clear from the start that it would encourage and support *organizaciones vecinales* (neighborhood organizations) organized on a lot-by-lot, block-by-block basis. Although ONDEPJOV only operated for two years until it was subsumed under the larger umbrella organization called SINAMOS, its mere creation and existence indicated that the military took the urban poor seriously and that it hoped to count on them for support as the Revolution of the Armed Forces further developed its policies and goals.

Chapter 6 showed that three distinct modes—communal involvement, local organizational involvement, and national-level involvement—existed in 1971 in the squatter neighborhoods.[12] That these three modes would dominate in this era makes sense, given the context of the times. The military state had begun to emphasize community organization and had established a central agency to address barrio concerns (as well as to persuade pobladores to support the policies of the government). Given such policy initiatives and urgings, a rational response on the part of the pobladores would consist not only of continued self-help efforts (to demonstrate to the state that the community was willing to help itself as well as do for itself everything that it could without waiting for supposedly forthcoming state aid) but also of involvement in the local organization and its restructuring and in demand-making addressed to the state (that is, ONDEPJOV). This latter participation would allow the pobladores to see if the initial promises of the revolutionary government were indeed true, that is, whether cooperation would be instrumentally rewarded.

INTERNEIGHBORHOOD DIFFERENCES, 1970

Decisions about rational behavior are influenced by a variety of contexts; they certainly do not occur in a socioeconomic or physical vacuum. One immediately meaningful context that influences participation is the local neighborhood, especially since each community has its own profile of needs. To see if and how levels of participation varied across communities requires going beyond the modal analysis set forth in chapter 6, which dealt only with the overall sample. Thus the most relevant and revealing question to pursue here is whether each neighborhood had particular patterns of involvement, that is, whether the pobladores in each neighborhood became involved in politics in ways distinct to that community.

In 1970 individual pobladores distributed themselves in markedly varied ways by modes of involvement as well as by neighborhood (see table 10). As might be expected, not all pobladores became equally involved, and not all communities showed the same rates of involvement across the three modes. To be sure, certain broad patterns hold across all four neighborhoods. For example, in all of the squatter neighborhoods, communal involvement was clearly the most common activity, and thus the most salient mode of involvement was community problem-solving. About one in five respondents had had frequent and recent involvement in their neighborhoods. "Cross-modal" participants (that is, individuals who ranked high in any two modes) were relatively common; one-quarter of the sample had engaged in such combinations. People who participated exclusively in either local- or state-petitioning activities were scarce. One-third of the pobladores were inactives (individuals who had participated minimally in only one activity); at the other extreme, one-eighth showed high levels of involvement in all three modes.

The disaggregation of the modes of participation into their individual items and a comparison of frequencies across neighborhoods reveals sometimes considerable variation. For example, Primero de Enero and Pampa de Arena—the two communities that were the youngest and that had the greatest material

Table 10. Intercommunity Differences in Participatory Activities, 1970

	Community				
	Primero de Enero (N=92)	Pampa de Arena (N=107)	Santiago (N=101)	28 de Julio (N=112)	Total (N=412)
Modal Involvement[a]					
1. Communal problem-solving	9.8	27.1	25.7	26.8	21.1
2. Local petitioning	1.1	2.8	2.0	5.0	2.6
3. State petitioning	—	0.9	5.0	8.1	3.5
Participant Types					
1. Total activists	26.1	8.4	3.0	14.7	13.2
2. Inactives	22.8	30.8	55.4	29.8	34.7
3. Cross-modal participants	40.2	29.8	9.0	21.5	25.2
Participation Items					
1. Recent involvement	30.4	51.9	5.9	14.2	20.8
2. Frequent involvement	32.3	25.5	13.6	10.5	20.0
3. Attend local meeting	76.3	49.0	8.7	46.9	37.0
4. Petition local org.	54.8	32.7	12.5	34.5	32.1
5. Member, local org.	54.3	27.3	12.7	30.1	25.0
6. Visited ONDEPJOV	55.2	39.8	29.3	43.2	41.5
7. Petitioned ONDEPJOV	46.2	25.6	16.3	38.7	32.6

Notes: Figures are percentages.

[a] Number of individuals who actively participated in each mode but not in others.

needs in 1971—were uniformly highest in levels of involvement. On the other extreme, Santiago's inhabitants were far less likely to participate. Such participatory differences are not random. On the contrary, there are reasons why such rates of participation differ across modes as well as across communities.

In the first place, intermodal differences occur because neighborhood pressure is the most intense (and successful) when it comes to influencing, coercing, and prodding an individual to contribute manual labor or money toward a community project of some sort. Indeed, in 1971 one of the research neighborhoods (a zone of Pampa de Arena) had a system of fines in place for families if contributions were not forthcoming. But attending local assembly meetings is easier to avoid, and families cannot be forced to be a member of the local association. Becoming involved in state-level petitioning clearly also requires considerable sacrifice. In 1970–1971, ONDEPJOV maintained only one central office where all petitions, grievances, and requests had to be presented during working hours, meaning that representatives from a neighborhood had to have the free time and money available to travel to the office, to wait their turns, and to make sometimes innumerable return visits (Dietz 1977). To take part in such activities therefore meant that the individual needed to have flexibility in his work schedule, extra money for travel, and above all the dedication and determination to become involved.

Second, patterns of modal participation also varied significantly across neighborhoods. What was at the time of the survey a young, recently formed invasion site (Primero de Enero) had the highest number of complete activists (26 percent) as well as the lowest number of inactives (23 percent) of all the neighborhoods. As a rule, the older the community and the higher its overall level of development, the lower the percentage of complete activists and the higher the percentage of inactives. But it must be emphasized that age by itself was a less than perfect indicator: 28 de Julio—the old, crowded, poorly developed neighborhood near Lima's central marketplace—had a much higher percentages of activists (14.7 percent) than did Santiago (3 percent), a neighborhood of equal age but of much higher socioeconomic status and infrastructural development. It is noteworthy that Santiago had the highest level of inactives of all neighborhoods (55 percent).

Additional individual items from the questionnaire further illuminate interneighborhood variations. In particular, a comparison of the newest and least-developed neighborhoods (Primero de Enero and Pampa de Arena) with the long-established and well-developed community of Santiago presents some sharp contrasts. For example, well over 80 percent of the inhabitants of Primero de Enero and Pampa de Arena characterized the unity of their neighborhoods as good or strong, whereas only 45 percent of Santiago did so. Two-thirds of the pobladores in Primero de Enero and Pampa de Arena saw hard work as the best way of solving community problems; only 40 percent of Santiago felt this way. Over one-half of Primero de Enero and Pampa de Arena characterized their neighbors as willing to help one another, compared to one-quarter of Santiago. And finally, nearly half (46 percent) of Primero de Enero and Pampa de Arena said that no outside aid was necessary to solve their communities' problems, whereas less than one-quarter of Santiago felt this way. For example, an original land invader of Primero de Enero who worked part-time in a Lima paint factory said:

> Living here means that everyone has to work and help out. Not only does everyone have to build his own house, but we all have to keep trying to make the government come out here and make a decision about the land situation so that final [house] lots can be drawn. And if we don't keep pestering the government

they won't do it. So we all take turns going and asking for help. Does it work? Well, we've only been here three years and already we've done a lot for ourselves. If the government would just pay attention to us we could get along a lot faster.

In sharp contrast, a twenty-year resident of Santiago who drove a taxi for one of Lima's major hotels had a very different perspective:

Why bother? We all worked hard when we first came here, but now everything's done—at least everything that we can do—and there's no reason to. And besides, the neighborhood's divided, and all anyone wants from politics is to fill his own pocket or be a big shot. I have other things to do.

These findings, and these opinions, help to explain the significant differences in levels of community involvement across neighborhoods.

Sendas Frutales, the central city rental slum neighborhood, had its own set of problems and responses to them. The inhabitants of Sendas Frutales did develop patterns of political participation, but these concerned local, not widespread, interactions and some petitioning to municipal authorities. Levels of such involvement were, when compared to the squatter communities, much lower all around: only 8 percent had attended a local meeting, 10 percent had participated frequently or recently, and 6 percent had petitioned the municipality (contrasted with one-third who had spoken with their landlord about a problem). For example, a tailor who had lived in the area for many years and who had at one time been outspoken in his determination to make things better, was precise and articulate in explaining why he no longer took part in such activities:

I have spent much of my life here in Sendas Frutales trying to organize people to see that we are treated fairly by our landlords. Why did I stop? Three reasons: first, too many people move in and out, and it's hard to organize; second, everyone has to work and has no time to meet; and third, the government doesn't give a damn about us. The only hope we have is for SINAMOS to carry through with its plan to declare us a pueblo joven—maybe then we'll have a chance.

Low levels of participation were thus not surprising. In separate questions, only one-third of the respondents said they intended to stay permanently in the area (compared with 88 percent in the squatter communities), less than two-thirds characterized their neighbors as concerned with barrio problems (over 90 percent said so in the squatter communities), and well over one-half said the government was the most important resource for solving their problems (versus 38 percent in the squatter areas).

The data presented in table 10 thus indicate that in 1970 informal poblador involvement—that is, what the pobladores see as rational expenditures of their time and resources—varied widely across communities. Yet despite such interneighborhood differences, the three basic modes identified in chapter 6 still existed in all of the squatter neighborhoods. The reason for this underlying uniformity is, perhaps, that an authoritarian regime will almost always try to control and channel political participation, whether by outlawing, co-opting, or replacing existing parties. Although the Velasco administration did not proscribe parties, it prohibited elections (thereby denying parties their raison d'être) and offered SINAMOS as an alternative vehicle for participation. But the 1971 survey was administered just prior to the initiation of SINAMOS, meaning that poblador participation had not been influenced by the artificial external stimulus of SINAMOS and its uniform implementation and restructuring of local neighborhood organizations.[13] Thus, although the Velasco government limited the modes of participation to nonelectoral problem-solving and petitioning, this probably had little effect on intercommunity differences. Instead, these differences emerged because of the rational responses of pobladores to their neighborhood's unique set of needs, despite (not because of) the policies of the military state.

Whether it is appropriate to classify a local neighborhood association as a social movement is perhaps open to debate, but the data present strong evidence that by 1970, in all communities except Sendas Frutales, the pobladores had created active, autonomous organizations devoted to facilitating and encouraging community resource mobilization to resolve local problems and to petition state authorities. Because these organizations were community specific and did not reach across neighborhood boundaries, it might be argued that they were not in fact true social movements, uniting all or most individuals who were members of a particular social class or who shared a common problem. For example, Primero de Enero and Pampa de Arena both lacked all basic urban amenities (water, sewerage, electricity) as well as other infrastructure (streets, sidewalks, trash collection, police protection), but these common needs did not bring the two communities together in any way. Quite the contrary: neighborhoods that were close to one another sometimes intentionally chose not to collaborate in petitioning state agencies. Each community perceived that state resources had to be viewed from a zero-sum perspective, that is, if Community A got something from the state, then Community B would not get it. This perception of state resources as being limited may well have been accurate and thus one basic reason that truly collective organizing and petitioning coming from some sort of districtwide or citywide federation of all squatter settlements was nowhere in sight.

By the time the second survey was carried out in 1982, such collective experiences had in fact taken place, primarily because the military government had encouraged the formation of supracommunity participatory mechanisms. In addition (and ironically), grassroots opposition to the military and its policies emerged as the military was increasingly unable to keep its promises to the lower classes. Now the question is, How did these experiences in larger-scale movements and protests become manifest in individual patterns of political involvement?

State-Poblador Relations, 1971–1982

The decade between the first and second surveys, from 1971 to 1982, was one of enormous tumult and turbulence for Lima's lower classes. It was also a decade that defies quick or easy analysis. The impact of SINAMOS, growing economic difficulties, the countercoup against General Velasco, the rolling back of many of the revolutionary government's most notable reforms, and the multiple attempts at mobilizing Lima's pobladores (on the barrio, district, and city levels), all came together to create a period of great turmoil that saw some long-term changes as well as many failures. Summarizing either chronologically or topically presents severe obstacles. Nevertheless, a brief synopsis is essential to understand the changes that occurred and that affected the ways in which the pobladores became involved in politics.

Many observers (Gómez Peralta 1990; Tovar 1986; Henry 1981; Centro de Información, Estudios y Documentación 1979; Stokes 1995) have attempted to establish some order over the events of this decade, and although each has his own template, there is some general agreement. As Lima expanded physically, especially during the 1960s, four basic geographic regions of the city became major poles of attraction for new and consolidating pueblos jóvenes. The *cono* or *sector norte* is a large region north of central Lima, which had first started to expand in the 1950s, and which by the mid-1970s contained roughly 350,000 people and more than a hundred *asentamientos urbanos populares* (popular urban settlements).[14] Primero de Enero is part of the cono norte. The *cono este* (eastern sector), east of downtown Lima, is a region of generally older, smaller, and more crowded neighborhoods that actually had more people (380,000) than the cono norte. The pueblo jóven 28 de Julio is in this eastern region. The *sector oeste* (western sector) includes outlying neighborhoods of central Lima (Santiago is an example) and the pueblos jóvenes of Callao, Lima's port city. Finally, the *cono sur* (southern sector) lies south of Lima and is a vast area of generally newer settlements, including Villa El Salvador. Its population in the mid-1970s approached 600,000. Pampa de Arena is situated in the southern sector.[15]

POBLADOR ORGANIZATION AND EXTERNAL STIMULI

At least five factors acted as stimuli for poblador organization and mobilization during the 1970s. These are (1) the sheer numbers of people in the settlements and the magnitude of their problems; (2) the efforts and then especially the shortcomings of the military government in mobilizing the urban lower classes to support the Revolution of the Armed Forces; (3) grassroots organizational efforts by a variety of leftist political parties and groups; (4) the increasingly severe economic conditions facing Peru and Lima's poor; and (5) the rising levels of discontent with military rule in general and a widespread desire to return to civilian governance. Without trying to trace the individual and multiple effects of these factors in detail, the major impacts of each of these can be sketched in as they affected poblador mobilization and participation.

In the first place, the growth of Lima and in particular of its squatter and popular sectors placed enormous strain on the state. As rural-urban migration continued unabated and an ever greater percentage of Peru's population found itself in Lima, the variety and weight of needs, wants, and expectations of the city's poor grew at a seemingly exponential pace. Governmental responses often had counterproductive impacts. For example, when Velasco was confronted in 1971 with a large and embarrassing land invasion near Pamplona in the southern sector, he persuaded the invaders to move to a new vacant area further south, which was christened Villa El Salvador. But this new settlement mushroomed to at least a quarter-million people in less than five years, which meant that the state then had to meet many more demands emanating from what had been labeled a showcase for the Revolution. This demand-making was, in the specific case of Villa El Salvador, intensified by the creation of CUAVES, a highly successful neighborhood association that quickly became a significant pressure group for the entire district.

Pobladores across Lima were willing to try (and often successfully) to supply their communities' needs through their own efforts. But many of the unmet needs, expectations, and frustrations became politicized; that is, the pobladores perceived that certain needs—major infrastructure projects such as running water and sewerage, land titles, police protection, for example—could be provided only by the state. Thus, as demands grew and went unmet, community mobilization became one way of increasing pressures on the state to respond.[16] In addition, in time, a new generation of city-born pobladores began to appear in the pueblos jóvenes. These younger pobladores had not migrated from rural areas, had no awareness of the rural conditions their parents left behind, and had not experienced the satisfaction and vindication of (for example) participating in a successful invasion and of gaining possession of a piece of land. A certain number of this new generation went on to enter universities in Lima, where the prevailing atmosphere was one of extreme radicalism. Others, perhaps raised with similar expectations that were not realized, might have developed high levels of frustration.

In the second place, SINAMOS acted as an overt mechanism by the military government to both encourage and control popular participation by means of corporatist structures, but it produced numerous unanticipated consequences (Dietz and Palmer 1978). SINAMOS personnel were under directives from the state to mobilize and simultaneously control the poor to support the revolution. To accomplish these fundamentally contradictory ends, the agency adopted fundamentally contradictory means. On the one hand, it promised the poor that, if they would organize according to its guidelines, they would receive land titles and all manner of community improvements. Yet sometimes SINAMOS personnel also encouraged the poor to protest and to demonstrate, if the state did not deliver on its promises. The result was an increase in the perception that demonstrative behavior could be efficacious, accompanied by an increased perception that the state could not or would not live up to the expectations it had inflated. One victim of this imbalance was frequently SINAMOS itself. Several times the inhabitants of communities who felt victimized by unkept promises turned militantly against the organization, most spectacularly when a group burned SINAMOS's Rimac headquarters to the ground.

Such protest behavior did not automatically emerge everywhere, of course; a third impetus to neighborhood—and then to citywide—mobilization came from outside organizers, generally belonging to or sympathetic with the left. Although the military government held no elections, it did not outlaw political parties or labor unions, whatever their ideology.[17] Leftist party leaders and would-be leaders, unions, and university groups could all become active in Lima's pueblos jóvenes, and although their specific motives doubtless varied one from the other, the joint effect was one of recruiting new neighborhood leaders, of socializing them with leftist principles (especially social-class consciousness), and of teaching them demonstration and protest tactics.

Stokes (1991, 1995), in particular, argues for the importance of outside groups in the mobilization and radicalization of squatter neighborhoods. She specifically notes that increasingly militant and radical labor and education unions, often labeled *clasista* (class-based), along with a wide variety of outside organizations (new Marxist political parties, Catholic church activists), all tended to add strident and confrontational tactics to poblador demand-making. Although Stokes agrees that the clientelistic tactics so commonly reported in the literature from the 1960s and early 1970s did not necessarily disappear, she argues that a sizable number of community leaders as well as ordinary residents became convinced of the need and the efficacy of demonstrative and confrontational tactics in articulating their needs. Stokes does not give a specific figure, but her data imply that roughly one-third or so of her sample (survey N = 882; Stokes 1991, 1995, chap. 6) could be characterized as being sympathetic with radical tactics or as having a radical worldview.

This whole state of flux found fertile ground as economic conditions started to sour in the mid-1970s. Although SINAMOS had not lived up to its promises, the organization nevertheless had come to symbolize the reformist tendencies of the revolutionary government. When General Morales Bermudez overthrew General Velasco in 1975, most of the reforms that the military had undertaken were either frozen or withdrawn. Morales Bermudez found himself confronted with a number of difficult and politically sensitive economic problems, epitomized by rising inflation, foreign debt payment problems, and pressures from the IMF and the World Bank to put into place strict austerity measures. Lima's lower classes then saw the abandonment of the revolution that had paid at least rhetorical attention to them, along with the imposition of a variety of economic policy measures that created real hardships (rising prices, losses in purchasing power, and the end of subsidies for basic foodstuffs).

The individual and cumulative effects of all these events and processes led to the rapid delegitimation of military rule and to increasing protests against the regime. Throughout the decade Lima and Peru in general saw massive strikes and demonstrations grow increasingly frequent, culminating on July 19, 1977, in a national strike that served resounding notice to the military that they could no longer govern the country (Tovar 1982b). The strikes received a great amount of national and international attention, and (sometimes bloody) land invasions in Lima and in provincial cities, along with marches protesting the lack of basic urban services, all provoked more mobilization of the poor. For instance, invasions such as Puente Huascar in 1976, along with incidents in Condevilla and Campoy (1976) and along Avenida Faucett (1978), were met either (1) with offers to open new land in far outlying areas (as happened with the Pamplona invasion and Villa El Salvador) or (2) with confrontations with the police, who tried forcibly to evacuate the invaders.[18] The former policy simply meant new headaches and demands on the state; the second meant bitter recriminations and a solidifying of mobilization against the military. A march on April 23, 1975, by some twenty thousand inhabitants of Villa El Salvador to protest the cost of water and the absence of schoolteachers and bus service was broken up by the police. The marchers were especially embittered, since General Velasco had visited the area many times during its early years, and it was frequently held up as a showpiece of the revolution.

The difficulties that the Peruvian military encountered in attempting to control participation from the top down were not confined to Peru. Bryan Roberts argues that in general throughout Latin America, authoritarian policies to constrain participation and citizenship failed. "Countering top-down strategies to limit citizenship are popular pressures that, while weakly organized, exercise a cumulative force for change against even the most consolidated authoritarian elite strategies" (1995, 186).

SUPRANEIGHBORHOOD ORGANIZATION

Out of all of this turbulence came what is generally referred to as *centralization barrial* (roughly translated as "barrio centralization"), meaning attempts to build horizontal linkages across individual neighborhoods and thereby create districtwide, citywide, even nationwide federations. According to most accounts (Circulo de Estudios Alejandro Quijano 1983?; Henry 1981), the first attempt to create a Lima-wide association of pueblos jóvenes occurred in September 1975 at the Second Assembly of Pobladores in Villa El Salvador, followed by similar organizational meetings in early 1976, when a Convention of Pueblos Jóvenes of Lima and Callao took place with the support of SINAMOS. This attempt failed (Tovar 1982b, 39) as did others, frequently because of factional divisions among various leftists and government supporters.

The sweeping national strike of 1977 and the prominent roles played in supporting that strike by the pobladores gave renewed impetus to centralization attempts, however. In addition, the success of various leftist parties in the 1978 Constituent Assembly elections led the left to believe that it was in a position to form an alliance with labor and with the urban popular sectors, which could mount a challenge for the presidency.[19] With much urging from leftist political parties, therefore, and with the support of leftist unions such as SUTEP (the public schoolteachers' union), in November 1979 a convention of a new Federation of Pueblos Jóvenes of Lima and Callao (FEDEPJUP) took place in El Hermitaño in the north sector of Lima.[20] As if this effort were not ambitious enough, in July 1980 the first meeting was held in Lima of the General Confederation of Pobladores of Peru. These two organizations thus came into existence just as the country as a whole was returning to civilian rule (May 1980).

The immediate goals of FEDEPJUP were to push the newly elected President Belaúnde to revoke legislation passed under the military that deprived the pueblos jóvenes of rights guaranteed earlier, to carry the fight for basic services throughout Lima and Peru's provincial cities, and to support groups in their struggles to obtain land.[21] But with these goals and with this level of organization came immediate and sometimes intractable problems. First, the struggle for basic services is almost always a local problem; moreover, different communities have different levels of service. A community with potable water, for example, no longer sees that problem as a priority and, given its remaining unfulfilled needs, may well be unwilling to dedicate itself to another community's water problems. In addition, the state informed the many neighborhoods petitioning separately for water or sewerage that such services could not be installed one neighborhood at a time. The state argued (with good reason) that water lines and water treatment plants required large amounts of capital, and that installing services piecemeal was impossible. Second, FEDEPJUP found it difficult to support would-be land invaders, primarily because land invasions are spontaneous affairs that depend in large part upon secrecy to succeed.

FEDEPJUP made immediate efforts to strengthen itself by organizing sub-federations in the squatter-intensive sectors to Lima's north, east, and south. FEDEPJUP realized that without such intermediate support, a citywide federation could not claim to act as a legitimate representative for the entire city's poblador population. But FEDEPJUP faced enormous problems. Financial concerns were, of course, present from the start. Local neighborhoods were distinctly unwilling to donate their scarce resources unless they felt sure it would be worth their while, whereas FEDEPJUP could not reasonably guarantee results unless it had the backing and the trust of its hundreds of separate community members (not to mention the hundreds of thousands of pobladores).

The most intractable problem, perhaps, for FEDEPJUP and for leftist parties and groups in general, was that—regardless of how much mobilization there had been during the 1970s and of how exhilarating that mobilization and centralization might have been—the pueblos jóvenes and their inhabitants were not homogeneous in their support of the left, of protest, or of citywide centralization. Henry (1981, 35–37) suggests there were at least five different levels of poblador social consciousness: (1) newer and often younger political leaders strongly committed to an ideologically driven leftist agenda; (2) older-generation leaders whose power base lay with traditional parties and clientelistic relations; (3) new pueblo jóven cadres more or less committed to either level 1 or level 2 above, but not leaders; (4) the active masses, who were willing to participate and who might have sympathies but not commitment to the left; and (5) the passive masses, who might at one time or another have participated in mobi-

lization efforts but whose energies for participation were low and whose political and ideological sympathies were unclear or absent.[22] Henry makes no
effort to estimate percentages or numbers for each group, but the important
point is that the left's declarations, following the 1978 Constituent Assembly
elections, that the urban poor were the natural and automatic basis of support
for the left were (as was made brutally clear in 1980) wildly naive and opti-
mistic.[23]

As the 1980 presidential elections drew near the leftist parties and FEDE-
PJUP gave one another as much ideological, rhetorical, and financial support as
was feasible. But the left basically did itself in when personal and ideological
differences produced five different candidates for the presidency. This splintering obviously discouraged potential supporters, many of whom were reluctant
to cast a vote for what was bound to be a loss (not to mention the wide popularity of Belaúnde, who carried all of Lima by comfortable margins, regardless
of social class).[24]

THE TRANSITION TO DEMOCRACY

The return to democratic governance in 1980 had numerous effects on Lima's
lower classes. In the first place, Belaúnde was initially a highly popular president whose win was seen not only as a victory for civilian rule in general but as
a vindication for Belaúnde himself, since he had been ousted by the military in
1968. One reason for his high level of popular support in the 1980 elections lay
in the widespread perception that Belaúnde was the best candidate of the four
to manage the transition to democracy and to keep the military at bay.

The change in regime type from authoritarian to civilian doubtless had its
own impact on political participation. First and foremost, the intense level of
poblador mobilization in Lima in the late 1970s could not be sustained indefinitely. Despite their achievements and sense of vindication, the pobladores
were still poor and many of their communities still lacked many basic services.
As Peru's economic conditions began to tighten in the early 1980s, thanks in
large part to worsening world commodity prices and increasing external debt
problems, Lima's pobladores found that economic recession and lack of employment inevitably meant retrenchment, and what Tovar (1986, 135) labels the
"individualization" of an economic crisis. As unemployment, underemployment, malnutrition because of increasing food costs, and basic survival needs
all became increasingly acute, the poor necessarily became so preoccupied with
their own problems that collective action (although not ignored altogether) became ever more expensive in terms of time, money, and effort.

Thus the centralization movement of the late 1970s stumbled, in many cases

either remaining stagnant or collapsing into nothing more than paper federations and agreements. It became clear that progress for Lima's pobladores as
political actors in municipal, city, and national arenas was not and could not be
linear or steady or homogeneous. It would have moments of spontaneity that
would at times give the appearance of acting as a monolithic, collective block,
only to fall back and lose momentum. In addition, the mobilization of the
pobladores and of their pueblos jóvenes was, as Tovar (1986) observes, first and
foremost more a demonstration of anger and frustration and less the manifestation of a real collective movement, much less of a true Marxist social class.
The late 1970s thus constituted a specific and perhaps unique conjunctural historical moment when a whole range of processes and developments happened
to coincide (Tanaka 1997). That so many factors had to come into play simultaneously meant that this mobilization and centralization had as many limitations as strengths.[25]

In addition, the presence of electoral politics had a tendency to defuse mobilizational and confrontational politics, which by definition meant high risk
and no guarantee of success. As a (mandatory) alternative or addition to
protest activities, voting was a much less threatening individual act, which also
carried the promise that, with luck, mobilization—translated into electoral politics—might produce progress as well. As electoral politics became one important way of gaining power, all political parties and leaders, not just the left,
made efforts to capture the very large numbers of votes represented by the
pueblos jóvenes.[26]

The 1980 presidential election was a major victory for Fernando Belaúnde.
But just six months later, when municipal elections were held, it was already
becoming clear that Lima's poor had developed reservations about supporting
candidates from his party. This was the first inkling that politicians and parties
searching for votes from Lima's masas populares might have difficulty in convincing the pobladores that it would be rational for them to continue to vote
for the same party time after time.

The Context for Poblador Participation, 1982

By 1982 Belaúnde's administration was showing signs that it could not correct
or reverse Peru's economic problems, especially those that affected the poor.
Shortly after taking office AP resurrected Cooperación Popular, its community
development organization from the 1960s. CoopPop, as it was universally known,
did some community organization work but was underfunded from the start

and never really took hold. A series of land invasions in Lima following Belaúnde's inauguration doubtless were the reason for CoopPop's reemergence (Ferradas 1983, 122–28). The pobladores also showed that the massive centralizing and protest activities of the 1970s were no longer perceived as having the same efficacy they once had. Finding and holding employment, coping with rising prices, simply making a living, all took time away from what were now seen as perhaps less rational expenditures of time. Strikes and marches did take place, in protest against the cost of living or in support of a land invasion, but on nowhere near the same scale as before. One middle-aged bus mechanic who had lived in 28 de Julio for fifteen years found a good deal to say about the changes that had occurred:

> Here in 28 de Julio during the 1970s we used to have all sorts of activities going on. People would go to meetings here in the Zone to discuss strikes and marches, and when the national strikes took place, lots of us went out and shut down traffic on the Central Highway [a nearby major feeder from the highlands into Lima]. And then when the 1978 elections came along, all kinds of politicians and parties came here as well. But now elections are being held regularly, and the military is gone, and there really isn't the need to go into the streets. Some people still do, of course, but with the economy the way it is today, who has time? I spend all my evenings and weekends looking for *cachuelo* [part-time work].

FEDEPJUP called for its members to vote for the left in the 1980 municipal races, but although this announcement had some symbolic importance, it did little to alleviate the day-to-day struggles faced by the pobladores.

When the 1971 survey was replicated in mid-1982, therefore, involvement in protest activities still went on in Lima but had subsided greatly from a few years earlier. Yet the local community development and the local- and state-directed petitioning activities that had been so noticeable in the 1971 survey were still a major part of the pobladores' repertoire of political activities. The Belaúnde government still operated many of the same state agencies (primarily the Ministry of Housing, along with CoopPop) that had existed in one form or another earlier, and many pobladores doubtless saw that the presenting of petitions and grievances was still one way to obtain things needed by their communities.

The data presented in table 11 reflect much of the development associated with the late 1970s, the onset of democratization in 1980, and the overall specific pueblo jóven context of 1982. The three participatory factors identified in chapter 6 (a blend of local and state petitioning, voting, and campaigning) were present in all of the squatter neighborhoods. For those pobladores who confined their political activities to one mode only, that mode was voting, overwhelmingly the most common of the three modes. This should be no surprise, of

Table 11. Intercommunity Differences in Participatory Activities, 1982

	Community				
	Primero de Enero (N=170)	Pampa de Arena (N=107)	Santiago (N=150)	28 de Julio (N=101)	Total (N=528)
Modal Involvement					
1. Problem-solving/ petitioning	3.1	0.7	—	1.2	1.2
2. Voting	38.1	43.7	65.3	41.2	47.0
3. Campaigning	—	—	0.6	—	0.2
Participant Types					
1. Total activists	16.3	9.4	0.6	4.9	7.8
2. Inactives	3.1	4.7	4.8	2.3	3.7
3. Cross-modal participants	41.2	32.1	17.8	36.3	31.9
Participation Items					
1. Recent involvement	56.4	54.4	55.3	53.1	54.8
2. Frequent involvement	47.3	47.7	21.3	70.1	46.6
3. Attended local meeting	24.0	37.2	9.5	33.6	26.1
4. Petitioned local organization	25.9	45.3	21.9	12.9	26.5
5. Member of local organization	31.5	32.1	19.7	34.0	28.1
6. Petitioned Ministry of Housing	34.7	54.0	18.1	38.7	36.4
7. Petitioned SINAMOS	9.4	26.4	15.1	70.1	30.3
8. Voted 1980 presidential election	96.4	88.7	91.9	88.1	91.3
9. Voted 1978 Constituent Assembly	87.5	87.6	93.9	88.8	88.3
10. Voted 1980 municipal election	89.2	89.5	91.6	86.1	89.1
11. Political party member	13.5	10.3	8.6	15.0	11.9
12. Attended political rally	32.3	20.8	30.6	29.2	28.2
13. Campaign activity	7.8	8.5	5.1	3.1	6.1

Note: Figures are percentages.

course, since voting is mandatory. In sharp contrast, to find pobladores who were exclusively either petitioners or campaigners (not voters) was rare; indeed, individuals who were uniquely campaigners were almost nonexistent. As is more predictable many pobladores, especially in neighborhoods such as Primero de Enero and Pampa de Arena that in 1982 still lacked many basic services, were cross-modal participants. These individuals generally voted but also took part in petitioning work. Rates of cross-modal participation rose compared with 1970 (see table 10), but again, the presence of obligatory voting made such an outcome predictable: voting was mandatory, and neighborhoods still needed assistance. As one initial invader and twelve-year resident of Primero de Enero said: "Everyone votes—of course—it's easier to vote than not, and if you don't vote, then you can't complain about who wins. But elections don't pave streets and dig trenches [for water pipes]; you have to pressure the government for things like that." Total activist percentages fell off by half from 1970 to 1982 (from 13.2 to 6.5 percent), since over the span of a decade even Primero de Enero and Pampa de Arena had accomplished much of what their inhabitants could do for themselves, and problems readily resolved with neighborhood resources had been confronted as much as was possible. Nevertheless, it is worth noting that Primero de Enero and Pampa de Arena still ranked above the overall mean in percentage of complete activists, and that Santiago, the old, most highly developed community, had virtually no complete activists.

THE IMPACT OF THE LOCAL NEIGHBORHOOD, 1982

In order to show interneighborhood contrasts most clearly and to draw comparisons readily with 1970, the data set forth in table 11 break down the modal results of 1982 into the individual items making up these modes. One remarkable result when compared with 1970 is the overall reduction of intercommunity differences, especially in petitioning activities. Whereas in 1970 variations across the four squatter areas were substantial, by 1982 many of these differences had faded, especially if Santiago is set aside. Primero de Enero, Pampa de Arena, and 28 de Julio all had approximately the same percentages of their residents participating in recent and frequent involvement, such as attending meetings and petitioning activities. Santiago, with its high level of community development, its full absorption into Lima Cercado, and its loss of designation as an official pueblo jóven, had in 1982 (as it had in 1970) much lower levels of involvement all round. Insofar as voting and campaign involvement was concerned, neither the age of the community nor any other community-specific factor made any impact at all; people reported voting in high numbers right across all neighborhoods. Attending a political rally was something that less than one-third of the respondents did anywhere, and actual campaigning was rarer still, attracting well less than one-tenth of the pobladores in any community.

Yet these emerging similarities in behavior should not be taken to mean that the pobladores viewed their communities in similar ways. For example, 63 percent of the respondents in Primero de Enero saw their community as united, compared with 36 percent in Santiago. More telling, perhaps, were the answers to the question as to whether the community was more united or less united in 1982 than it had been ten years previously. Fully three of five (60.8 percent) of Primero de Enero said that neighborhood unity was higher, easily the highest proportion in all four neighborhoods (no other was over half). In contrast, two out of five in 28 de Julio said that barrio unity was lower, and the same proportion of Santiago's inhabitants saw their community's level of unity as not having changed. Reflecting the same sorts of differences, the ratio of pobladores in Primero de Enero who said that hard work by the community was more important than governmental aid was 5:3 (50 versus 30 percent), and in 28 de Julio it was almost 2:1 (57 versus 29 percent). In Santiago, it was 1:1 (42 percent even). Finally, in response to a question as to whether the neighborhood had changed from 1971 to 1982, respondent answers basically offered an accurate reflection of reality. Well over 90 percent of both Primero de Enero (the youngest invasion site, which had seen much rapid early development) and 28 de Julio (which had seen broad-scale remodeling) responded affirmatively. But only three-quarters did so in Pampa de Arena, where physical change had been more incremental, and only slightly more than one-half did so in Santiago, where fundamental changes had in fact not occurred.

Yet, in contrast to these rather remarkable attitudinal and perceptual differences, behavioral differences across the squatter communities were in 1982 much less dramatic than they had been in 1970. Perhaps the reason for this seeming discrepancy is that, regardless of how different community attitudinal and perceptual profiles might be, the rational ways of addressing community problems were strictly limited in number. With the passage of time (and all other things being equal), tasks that could be done readily enough through local self-help efforts had in fact been done in all of the neighborhoods—and over time (again, all other things being equal) and regardless of the specific community, a certain base level of community participation seemed to emerge. All other things are never equal, of course, and at no point will every community come to resemble every other. But the wide variation so evident in 1970—when the relative ages of the neighborhoods varied so greatly—had diminished over the course of a decade and would probably never be seen again.[27]

As for Sendas Frutales, its inhabitants continued to struggle against extraordinary odds to make something of their little neighborhood. Their struggle was less spectacular than that of the pobladores in the squatter areas, since the inhabitants of this neighborhood—and others like it throughout the older, blue-collar areas of Lima—operated much more as spectators than as participants in the events of the late 1970s. This was because of the area's legal status, or rather, lack of it. Insofar as the poor neighborhoods of Lima were concerned, the squatter areas occupied center court. The squatters were seen by the left as the most natural constituency; they were much more obvious as a target, physically and juridically speaking; and they had across time received far more publicity and notoriety than the poor living in rental slum apartments of Lima, who were much more scattered and deemed by the left far less ready to mobilize. Unless the individual residents of Sendas Frutales had links into organized labor, therefore, it was unlikely that the firestorm of activities engulfing the pueblos jóvenes would make much heat for the residents of Sendas Frutales's callejones and correlones.

Even though the confused and interminable wrangle over Sendas Frutales's legal status that began in the 1970s was still unresolved in 1982, simply the possibility that something might happen apparently struck a responsive chord over the years. Of paramount importance by 1982 was the existence of a local organization that, despite huge obstacles, had managed to gain the support of a good deal of the neighborhood. In fact, in 1982 over one-third (35 percent) of Sendas Frutales's respondents said they were members, a figure slightly higher than the mean (29 percent) for the four squatter settlements. The same two factors of local involvement and petitioning first identified in Sendas Frutales in 1971 still existed in 1982, but what was most remarkable was the level at which political participation went on. In contrast to the minimal involvement in 1971, local and state involvement and petitioning in 1982 attracted sizable numbers of residents. Frequent (47 percent) and recent (28.5 percent) involvement, attendance at meetings (20 percent), and petitioning the local neighborhood association were all roughly comparable to the squatter communities (compare with table 11). As one ten-year resident of Sendas Frutales who operated a small bodega (convenience store) with his wife said:

> When I came here about 1971, I promised myself and my family that we would stay for a year or two—no more, because conditions were terrible. Landlords used to throw out tenants with no warning; you'd come home and find the door locked and your stuff in the street. And there was nothing to do about it! But when SINAMOS said that we were officially a pueblo joven [a much-disputed claim], this gave us a reason to try to work together somehow and to come up with some way to make the landlords obey the law. Besides, my job is close by here now, and although my house isn't everything I want it to be, my children are close to school. All in all, we decided to stay; I guess it was the right thing to do. God only knows . . . [Sabe Dios, pues . . .].

Sendas Frutales still had its problems, of course; two out of five classified the area as either a "quite bad" or a "very bad" place to live (compared to 14 percent of respondents in squatter communities); over three-fifths said it had not changed in the past ten years (compared to 19.6 percent in squatter areas); more than one-third classified overall government performance in providing basic services as "poor" (compared to 16 percent of squatter residents); only one-third said they saw Sendas Frutales as a permanent residence (compared with 61 percent of the other four communities). But in the light of these relatively pessimistic figures about the area in 1982, and of its perceived overall stagnation over the course of a decade, the rise in political participation was impressive.[28]

The decade of the 1970s was thus one of great turmoil for Lima's poor, but by the time the Belaúnde administration had reached its second year, the great mobilization and centralization efforts of the 1970s had run their course and had either reached their limits or retreated. The recession of the early 1980s forced many individuals to channel their political energies back into more mundane, incremental ways of coping with poverty. Stokes (1991, 1995) claims that a certain significant minority developed and practiced much more confrontational participatory tactics than had been common prior to the mid-1970s. But such tactics and worldviews did not automatically or necessarily replace the more traditional modes of becoming involved in community development efforts or in state-directed petitioning activities. Regardless of how much the late 1970s may have brought radical and clasista tactics to the pueblos jóvenes, it was clear that mobilization and confrontation had not contributed materially to the alleviation of the endemic poverty of Lima's poor (Parodi 1993), and that the bulk of the pobladores continued to take part in traditional neighborhood affairs.

In the final analysis, there may be no precise or satisfactory way to measure how much impact all of the mobilization and radicalization of the 1970s had on the pobladores. But it may be worthwhile to undertake at least one estimate. Assuming that the sample squatter communities were in 1970 and 1982 roughly representative of Lima's squatter population, perhaps one way to suggest the level to which radical attitudes had been internalized would be to ask the pobladores why poverty exists. For Lima's poor, poverty was perhaps their paramount daily reality and obstacle, and their explanations as to its existence—individual shortcomings, fate, the labor market, clasista differences, or whatever—could indicate their degree of radicalism, or lack thereof. Since both the 1970 and the 1982 survey instruments contained an appropriate open-ended question ("What do you think is the principal reason for poverty?"), comparing responses across the decade 1971–1982 can show if the pobladores showed any increase in what could be interpreted as radicalization.

In 1970, well over one-half of the total sample (57.4 percent) blamed lack of work for the existence of poverty. As a young father of six children in Pampa de Arena said: "Poverty comes from not having a good job—a job that pays well and that you can count on. Everyone wants a good job; if everyone here had good jobs, there wouldn't be any poverty, and anyone who was poor would just be lazy." Another one-fifth (20.6 percent) blamed lack of education; a few (3.2 percent) specifically mentioned cost-of-living problems. These three reasons (totaling over 80 percent) include what might best be called structural causes; they are also probably the reasons with which the pobladores themselves are most personally familiar. Far fewer respondents (13.7 percent total) offered explanations of an individualistic or fatalistic nature: lack of ability (3 percent), laziness (10.1 percent), or bad luck (.6 percent). Finally, "other" responses or a combination of factors came to 2.5 percent, for a total of 97.4 percent. Only 2.6 percent gave any response blaming class differences, bad government, or anything else that could be interpreted as overtly radical or clasista in any way whatsoever.

With these data as a baseline, repeating the same question in 1982 can show if the mobilizational and radical atmospherics of the late 1970s had any influence on poblador perceptions. If they had, then responses mentioning clasista or radical interpretations should have increased. But the 1982 results are strikingly similar to those of 1970. Structural reasons (lack of work 55.5 percent, lack of education 15.4 percent, cost of living 2.7 percent) came to 73.6 percent; fatalistic or individualistic responses (laziness 7.5 percent, lack of ability 2.8 percent, bad luck .7 percent) totaled another 11 percent; other and multiple responses came to 10.2 percent, leaving 5.2 percent who offered specifically clasista explanations. On the one hand, this percentage is double that of 1970, but the total is still very low—lower than, for example, laziness.

Little evidence emerges, therefore, that the general poblador population believed that specifically radical (or class-based) explanations could best explain the existence of poverty in 1970, or that the environment of the late 1970s had changed those perceptions and beliefs by 1982. The structural reasons articulated by such an overwhelming majority of the pobladores both in 1970 and in 1982 were, probably more than anything else, reflections of poblador reality. Lack of work (especially well-paying jobs) and of education were in fact major causes of poverty, no doubt about it, but these answers can only with much distortion be interpreted as a conscious, radical critique of Peru's socioeconomic system.[29]

To conclude that the 1970s reshaped poblador perceptions of the world in any massive and inclusive way is, at least on the basis of the survey evidence, probably not warranted. To be sure, political participation, especially political tactics, may well have become more confrontational by 1982 than they had been in 1970. But the evidence does not support any claim of a sea change in attitudes or in patterns of quotidian problem-solving.

State-Poblador Relations in Lima, 1982–1985

One of the difficulties in comparing the 1970 and 1982 data sets is, rather obviously, the time between the two surveys. So much happened to individual pobladores, to their immediate neighborhoods, to Lima, and to Peru and its social, economic, and political fabric that two surveys are in many ways insufficient to capture and portray changes in anything less than the broadest of brush strokes. A third survey was carried out in 1985, only three years later, immediately following the election of Alan García and the triumph of the APRA party. And although it might first be thought that this intervening period of three years would, in contrast to the 1971–1982 period, be too short for significant changes to have occurred, these three years saw a great deal happen that affected the pobladores directly.

Although nothing as fundamental as a regime shift occurred, or nothing as sweeping as the mobilizations of the late 1970s took place, it must be said again that the decade 1971–1982 was from almost any point of view exceptional in Peruvian history. Thus the more compressed time period from 1982 to 1985 between surveys—during which elections occurred as scheduled, economic conditions (though harsh) did not take on crisis proportions, and Sendero Luminoso was at least for Lima still a rural phenomenon—offers the chance to see how much of the late 1970s had a lasting impact and how much was, over time, more ephemeral. Much of what happened in the 1982–1985 period affected the pobladores directly; reciprocally, a fair amount of what happened came about because of the pobladores.

First, and briefly, on the electoral front, the year 1983 saw municipal elections held nationwide. These elections were widely viewed, especially by the opposition, as a referendum on Belaúnde's performance in office, and if so, the results must have given him many long wakeful nights. AP finished last among the four parties, APRA showed considerable resurgence, and IU under Barrantes won the city's mayoral race. By 1985 all polls showed that AP was done with; Belaúnde's once triumphant party again finished last while APRA swept into the presidency with García taking almost half the popular vote.

Whatever the results of a particular election, and regardless of whether an individual poblador saw his candidate win or lose, the electoral process per se did two things. First, it gave every citizen the chance (and mandatory duty) to voice his opinion. Second, in so doing, it tended—however mildly or indirectly —to atomize political participation, making participation more of an individual than a collective activity and persuading at least some of the citizenry that voting was the most important political act and obligation a citizen had, and that having done it, he had done all he really could do to influence the selection and policy-making of government personnel.

Yet elections were, of course, only one of the vehicles used by the pobladores in the early 1980s to become involved in politics. Elections were at best only an indirect means for the pobladores to supply themselves and their communities with public goods (the working definition of informal political participation). Under electoral politics, other ways of obtaining goods became available, not the least of which were policies implemented by elected authorities sympathetic with the conditions of the city's lower classes. After winning the mayoral race in 1983, for example, Alfonso Barrantes and the left instituted a variety of programs designed to reach Lima's lower classes. The most notable of these was the Vaso de Leche (Glass of Milk) program, designed to make a glass of milk available to a million children per day in Lima. Although the program had start-up problems, the long experience of the left in working in the pueblos jóvenes helped to organize the more than seventy-five hundred committees formed to implement the program throughout Lima (see Parodi 1993, 62). At the same time, the left also started to work with the comedores populares or communal soup kitchens program that had begun as a grassroots effort in the earlier 1980s. The left also collaborated with the many women's groups that had appeared in the pueblos jóvenes. Not only did these latter programs provide material assistance to women and their families but they also allowed women to exercise a certain amount of independence and to gain leadership and empowerment skills. Although these different groups had a variety of separate goals, they played critical roles in developing coping strategies (and, later on, survival skills) as the economy crumbled in the late 1980s.

Such activities, both formal and informal, were fragile bulwarks against the economically difficult times of the early 1980s. Approximately one-quarter of Lima's popular masses were by 1985 earning at or below the official minimum wage of $30 a month (Tovar 1986, 131); at the same time, open unemployment had reached 10.9 percent, and severe underemployment was 36 percent (Webb and Fernandez Baca 1992, 485). Given such circumstances the early 1980s showed marked increases in the number of people in the informal sector, rising from 32 percent in 1981 to 40 percent in 1985. In the specific case of Villa El Salvador, which by 1985 had become a separate legal district of Lima, CUAVES, its districtwide association, contracted for a survey that showed that two-thirds of its labor force reported itself either as *dependiente no estable* (unstable employee) or as "self-employed" (Tovar 1986, 132). As would be expected, wages slipped badly in real terms; taking 1979 as a base year of 100, by 1985 purchasing power had slipped one-third. In socioeconomic terms, falling wages and purchasing power also produced gradual rises in infant mortality, malnutrition, and of diseases such as tuberculosis and gastroenteritis (Tovar 1986, 133, 158). Finally, the rising cost of housing materials (bricks, cement, reinforcing bars) meant that individual house construction and remodeling became more costly and slower for Lima's lower classes.

Under such conditions, it would be easy to predict that the pobladores might well revert to the mobilizational involvement of the late 1970s. But no such mobilizations occurred on any scale like that of the late 1970s. Several reasons explain this fundamental difference. First, it cannot be overemphasized that what had happened in the late 1970s had required a unique confluence of processes and events—including economic hardship; a political crisis of governability and of multiclass opposition to and dissatisfaction with military rule; a high degree of social polarization and a widespread recognition by the poor of their status and of their poverty; the dawning of elections after an absence of ten years; the massive presence of the left in the barrios populares; enormous labor unrest; the eruption of massive social demonstrations, especially national strikes—all of which *jointly and only jointly* made possible the mobilization and involvement of very large numbers of lower-class individuals.

Second, and in the absence (or very much diminished presence) of several of these factors, the economic difficulties of 1980 often led to an involution or turning inward that sought and utilized intraneighborhood resources as coping mechanisms rather than broad-scale mobilization. For example, as falling wages and rising prices started to create serious nutritional problems, one innovative response became the comedores populares. These kitchens were in most instances created by women's groups (mothers' clubs, women's associations) that organized themselves to procure foodstuffs and equipment to make one hot and reasonably nutritious meal available to as many families as possible in a neighborhood. Families and households also looked to themselves for assistance; more people reported having (or looking for) second jobs of whatever description, and women and children did everything possible to increase household incomes.

Strikes and demonstrations continued after 1980, of course; both labor and the masas populares knew that putting large numbers of people in the streets or amassing pobladores in front of a ministry could get the attention of state authorities. But between 1982 and 1985 the number of strikes and the number of man-hours lost to strikes nationally both diminished, from 809 to 579 strikes and from 22.7 to 12.2 million man-hours (Webb and Fernandez Baca 1992, 511). In the view of the labor unions, such a decrease was probably because of the overwhelming need to protect jobs. A strike against a factory paying low wages was one thing, but a strike against a factory that had shut down or that—in a time of high unemployment—had fired its workers in response to a strike was quite another.

Thus, in 1970, the unwieldy citywide and districtwide federations of neighborhood organizations were not only weakened by the individualization (to the level of the neighborhood and to the individual citizen) of coping and survival but were also to an extent replaced by a preference in the pueblos jóvenes for fights and petitions focused on specific needs (water, for example) or by and for specific groups (women, for example). This heterogeneity became both a strength and a limitation. A specific group from a neighborhood might band together and petition the state or might unite with other similarly focused groups from other neighborhoods to do so, thus allowing those groups perhaps to increase their chances of success. As a strong community leader in Pampa de Arena said:

> During the Velasco years I could go with a few other delegates to SINAMOS and we could talk face-to-face. But now there are a lot of ministries and agencies to go to, and there's the municipal government as well, depending on what you want to do. And there are a lot more groups here [in Pampa de Arena], and each one sometimes decides to do by itself. No one person or group can be a spokesman any more. It used to be easier . . .
>
> [Q: And so today it's better or worse?]
>
> I guess it's better, but it's harder to know what's going on here and to act in any unified way.

As this individual noted, the targets of such sectoral groups also expanded during the 1982–1985 period. With electoral democracy back on-line, and then with the sweeping IU district-level victories of 1983, municipal leaders and their bureaucracies became (at least theoretically) a source of aid and assistance. But the social-class homogeneity of most of Lima's districts (see chapter 4), and especially of its poorer districts, dictated that the mayor of a district such as Comas (where Primero de Enero is) had more than three-quarters of its populace living in pueblos jóvenes. This fact alone meant that such a municipality could collect very little in the way of taxes by itself and that it would have to depend on metropolitan Lima or the state for anything more than the smallest projects. The mayors of such districts recognized the situation; one declaration by the mayors of San Martin de Porras, El Agustino, Ate-Vitarte, and Villa El Salvador said as much: "the poor districts of Lima, where the majority of our city lives and works, are the fruit of the work and the sacrifice of the inhabitants themselves" (Tovar 1986, 145). Although the leftist-controlled district municipalities as well as the Barrantes administration did what they could to develop some sort of safety net, resources at all levels simply could not meet the increasing demands and needs of the city's masas populares.

The Context for Poblador Participation, 1985

By 1985 and the third survey, Lima's lower classes had come through five years of electoral rule and were in the midst of economically hard times. It is not surprising, perhaps, that the same three modes of participation that had appeared in 1982 (local/state problem-solving and petitioning, voting, and campaigning) were still in place in 1985. Voting was still the most common activity for an individual poblador who became involved in only one mode (43 percent), but cross-modal participants followed close behind (36 percent), which argues that most of the respondents in the sample saw voting as not enough and that spending time in more immediately useful activities was still a rational thing to do.

Compared with 1982, matters had changed little. The percentages of cross-modal participants dropped off somewhat, and people doing nothing but campaigning disappeared. As in 1982 the squatter neighborhoods had more or less reached a base level of participation that might remain quite constant until and unless some major change occurred.

INTERNEIGHBORHOOD DIFFERENCES, 1985

The data presented in table 12 show that the process of eroding the significant variations across the four neighborhoods, first observed between 1971 and 1982, continued on into 1985. For example, about the same percentage of respondents in all squatter neighborhoods thought that their neighborhoods had changed over the past five years (70 percent mean). On a different dimension, approximately three-quarters of the entire sample characterized Belaúnde's presidency as negative, and when asked to rank in order the three most recent presidents (Velasco, Morales Bermudez, and Belaúnde), an overwhelming 87 percent picked Velasco first; only 3.7 selected Belaúnde. These evaluations of Belaúnde did not vary across neighborhoods.

Table 12. Intercommunity Differences in Participatory Activities, 1985

	Community				
	Primero de Enero (N=70)	Pampa de Arena (N=74)	Santiago (N=71)	28 de Julio (N=128)	Total (N=343)
Modal Involvement					
1. Problem-solving/ petitioning	4.1	1.8	—	3.6	2.4
2. Voting	42.3	37.6	58.2	29.3	41.9
3. Campaigning	—	1.2	—	—	0.3
Participant Types					
1. Total activists	7.4	9.6	2.1	8.7	7.0
2. Inactives	0.6	3.9	9.1	6.1	4.9
3. Cross-modal participants	37.1	24.6	11.1	27.6	25.1
Participation Items					
1. Recent involvement	48.6	40.5	36.6	39.1	41.2
2. Frequent involvement	81.6	81.4	68.0	86.7	79.4
3. Attended local meeting	50.0	35.1	26.8	36.5	37.1
4. Petitioned local organization	35.7	31.1	40.8	48.5	39.0
5. Member of local organization	50.0	36.5	40.8	41.4	42.2
6. Petitioned Ministry of Housing	11.4	16.2	8.5	20.4	14.1
7. Petitioned SINAMOS	15.7	13.5	15.5	21.1	16.5
8. Voted 1980 presidential election	80.0	91.9	88.7	92.2	88.2
9. Voted 1985 presidential election	95.7	94.6	98.6	96.1	96.3
10. Voted 1983 municipal election	87.1	85.1	87.3	93.0	88.1
11. Political party member	15.7	9.5	31.0	12.2	17.1
12. Attend political rally	11.4	18.9	8.5	26.6	16.4
13. Campaign activity	11.4	8.1	14.1	9.4	10.8

Note: Figures are percentages.

To be sure, some cross-neighborhood differences still emerged from the data. Santiago's respondents had the lowest levels of participation, falling below the mean in almost every instance. The two poorest and least developed neighborhoods (Primero de Enero and Pampa de Arena) were still highest in total activists, although the differences between them and 28 de Julio also markedly decreased. Again, these differences were doubtless because the settlements that in 1971 had been young and newly invaded, that had lacked everything and had manifested very high levels of community spirit, had over the years resolved the problems that could be readily solved through their own efforts. By 1985 they confronted large-scale difficulties that would eventually require state assistance. A semiretired electrician in Pampa de Arena whose children were grown said:

> What do we need here? We need paved streets and sidewalks; we need more medical posts with doctors in them, and policemen; we need another secondary school, and vocational training. We also need jobs and better pay, like everyone else does. *Pampa de Arena really isn't that different from other parts of Lima in what it needs now, since so much of Lima is pueblos jóvenes and they all want help for the same things.* (my emphasis)

Still, some cross-neighborhood differences were revealing. The area 28 de Julio showed much higher levels of perceived neighborhood unity (over 40 percent of 28 de Julio thought it "high"); no other neighborhood surpassed 25 percent, and Primero de Enero, the exuberant and tightly unified neighborhood of 1970, was now the lowest (17 percent). Primero de Enero also ranked last in respondents who thought that hard work was the answer to their neighborhood's problems, again a noticeable decrease over the years. In 1985, 28 de Julio ranked highest in the perceived efficacy of hard work (almost half). One area of steady decline across all four neighborhoods that started between 1970 and 1982 concerned the neighborhood as a permanent residence. Between 1970 and 1982, the mean positive response fell from nine out of ten (88 percent) to two-thirds (68 percent). Between 1982 and 1985 it fell again, to half (50 percent), indicating perhaps that the poverty and way of life in the pueblos jóvenes did eventually start to wear people down, causing them to think (rightly or not, given the total lack of alternatives) that somewhere else to live had to be better than where they were.

The residents of Sendas Frutales in 1985 were continuing their own rather lonely struggle. Recent and frequent petitioning activities dropped off somewhat compared to 1982, but not much; the same modes of participating still were in place. Perhaps such stability was predictable; when asked about their most important neighborhood problems, 40 percent (a huge plurality) chose land titles, something that received virtually no mention in any of the pueblos jóvenes; another 25 percent chose crime. Legal status had been paramount in Sendas Frutales for years (see Dietz 1980, 61–64), as had crime and delinquency. Given the nature of these problems, the residents could do little except organize themselves to petition anyone who might listen for police protection and for a final adjudication of legal problems.

Still, some developments had occurred. Three out of five of the Sendas Frutales sample said they belonged to the neighborhood association, higher than for any of the squatter areas, and two-thirds said they had attended a meeting of the association within the past year (compared with 40 percent of the squatter inhabitants). Perhaps most remarkable of all was the claim by over half of the respondents that they planned to make Sendas Frutales their permanent place of residence, a figure at the same level as the pueblos jóvenes inhabitants. Not only does this show a substantial rise over previous years (about one-third in both 1971 and 1982), but it seems to fly in the face of the two-thirds of the sample who said that the neighborhood had not changed in the past five years. Obviously the developments and changes noted in 1982 by the bodega owner cited above had had an effect on some of his neighbors. But if by 1985 Lima's poor, whether in squatter areas or in a slum, thought that a combination of economic hardships, a less than successful president, and other difficulties had placed them in hard times, they unfortunately had no idea of what was waiting for them as Alan García and APRA prepared to take power on July 28, 1985.

State-Poblador Relations, 1985–1990

The first two years or so of García's administration were full of hope. The economy registered substantial gains in gross national product and real increases in purchasing power because of a raise in wages. The 1986 municipal elections saw the APRA machine continue to roll; although Alfonso Barrantes of IU ran as a relatively popular and respected incumbent seeking reelection, APRA and García won a tight race (37.5 to 34.7 percent) for Jorge del Castillo, the party's candidate.

What happened in Peru and in Lima following mid-1987 has already been discussed (see chapters 3 and 4). Suffice it to say that Peru's economy went from a tailspin into free fall, as unpaid debt problems, vertiginous inflation, and plummeting wages and salaries came together to create Peru's worst economic crisis of the twentieth century. Mixed with all these economic disasters and their social repercussions was the spread of fear and intimidation that Sendero Luminoso gradually brought to Lima. Lima's poor found themselves caught in a situation where petitioning the state became an exercise in futility. The state had no resources, since the tax revenues fell from 15 percent of GDP in 1985 to

3 percent in 1990 (Graham 1994, 93). Demonstrating was a highly risky activity because of suspicions that Sendero Luminoso might be involved (the state might respond repressively). Survival became a daily, oppressive, all-consuming goal.

Governability became a struggle for García and APRA. As public opinion polls in 1988 and 1989 showed him dropping into the teens and even single digit levels of support, the results of the 1989 municipal elections were a foregone conclusion. APRA took a humiliating 11 percent of the popular vote and failed to win a single district mayoral race. What is more surprising, however, is that all the major parties did poorly against the independent candidacy of Ricardo Belmont, a popular television personality who easily won the city's mayoral race.

Less than six months later the 1990 presidential race attracted worldwide attention for several reasons: first, for the presence of Mario Vargas Llosa, whose early concern was whether he would be able to take half the popular vote and avoid a second-round runoff; second, for the continued weakness of APRA and the left and for all the parties that had so dominated the 1980s; and third, for the emergence in the six weeks prior to the election of Alberto Fujimori, a complete political newcomer whose vague campaign slogan ("Honesty, Work, Technology") and whose campaign style (deadpan and unemotional) somehow propelled him in four weeks from less than 2 percent public support to, on election day, 29 percent of the popular vote (to Vargas Llosa's 32.6 percent). Eight weeks later Fujimori won a runoff with 62 percent of the vote.

While the elections were going on, Lima's poor continued to suffer the ravages of a full-blown economic crisis.[30] The gross national product dropped 25 percent from 1988 to 1990; overall government expenditures fell 43 percent and social expenditures by a full 50 percent, with the result that, "By 1990 social expenditures in per capita terms was at 21 percent of its 1980 real value, at US$12 per person per year" (Graham 1994, 92). In 1985 about one-half of Lima's population was fully or adequately employed, and about one-eighth was in poverty (a household was defined as poor if per capita food expenditures were less than the value of the minimum food basket). By 1990 about 5 percent of Lima's workforce was fully employed, and over one-half of the city was in poverty (Graham 1994, 92–94).[31]

Many pobladores in the sample had seemingly passed beyond outrage and anger over economic conditions to something approaching a state of shock. A schoolteacher in Santiago expressed himself in almost philosophical terms:

> What can you say? Things are so terrible that I don't know where to start. My wages are now about [U.S. equivalent] $35 a month, prices go up from morning to afternoon, the government's a total waste [*una vaina total*], and nobody can

do anything about it. It's as if all of the plagues of the Old Testament were occurring at the same time. Poor Peru! Should any country have to suffer so much?

Nevertheless, individual and collective poblador attempts to confront such cat-
astrophic conditions were widespread. Although Barrantes lost his bid for reelection to an APRA candidate, the Vaso de Leche program remained in place,
both because of its popularity and because of the overwhelming need for it.
But APRA seized upon the program as a political tool, and as Graham (1994, 98)
succinctly put it:

> [APRA] policies were characterized by an unprecedented degree of sectarianism
> and were implemented in a centralized, authoritarian manner. . . . Because of
> the lack of attention to details and to local (i.e., neighborhood-specific) needs,
> the work of most (existing neighborhood) . . . organizations was soon disrupted
> and the groups eventually alienated.

As the economic debacle deepened, the APRA government tried to implement
several emergency assistance programs in Lima's pueblos jóvenes. Primary
among these were the Programa de Apoyo Directo (PAD; Program of Direct
Support) and the Programa de Apoyo de Ingreso Temporal (PAIT; Program of
Temporary Income Support). PAD was designed to help equip and organize
comedores populares, educational programs, and community public health
outreach and to assist and supervise women's clubs and other neighborhood
groups. But from the start PAD was run from the top down, and even APRA
district mayors complained that the program did not coordinate with local
groups and was insensitive to existing neighborhood groups. PAD also tried to
insist that its neighborhood leaders be APRA sympathizers. "The party's attempts to impose external control on autonomous community organizations
so as to channel popular demands were [viewed] as a direct threat to their autonomy" (Graham 1994, 100). PAD thus was in many ways strikingly similar to
the SINAMOS experiment of the early 1970s under the military government.

PAIT was grandly announced as a means of increasing domestic capacity for
consumption. It was an employment program aimed directly at the pobladores
in the pueblos jóvenes who were either unemployed or severely underemployed. PAIT's aim was to pay residents to contribute to public works projects
in their communities. Some aspects of PAIT were beneficial. Many desperately
poor people, especially women (75 percent of PAIT employees were female),
received at least temporary employment at full minimum wage, and some
badly needed construction and maintenance was carried out. And overall, the
program was highly popular among those who received employment. Yet PAIT
had some clear local drawbacks; it disrupted family community life by its un-

certainty and temporary nature, and it interfered with neighborhood group stability (members employed by PAIT no longer had time to remain involved).

It was as political organizations, however, and as state policy ostensibly designed to combat and alleviate poverty, that PAIT and PAD were the greatest failures. APRA administered the programs in a highly sectarian, centralized, hierarchical way. Promises of vast funding for new PAIT positions were made just prior to elections and then were not kept; PAIT officials made little effort to coordinate with local officials, especially in municipalities under IU control; PAIT itself became a substantial bureaucracy for APRA members and supporters; PAIT employees were sometimes required to work for the party or to attend APRA rallies. The partisan nature of PAIT, its tendency toward extravagant and ill-advised pharonic monuments (olympic-sized swimming pools without water, high-tech training centers with no equipment), and its inability to mount anything resembling a true poverty alleviation program, all created much frustration among Lima's poor. A middle-aged plumber who had lived in Pampa de Arena for twenty years and whose wife had worked with PAIT for a few months had mixed feelings:

> What she earned was really important to us; I've been having no luck at all in getting steady work and her little bit *(propinas)* saved the family. But it was never anything you could count on; sometimes she'd go after being told to come to work and they'd tell her to come back again. She never learned a skill that she could use. And the people running PAIT always talked about how wonderful García was and how wonderful his government was. We heard that crap all the time.

The mistakes made by PAD and PAIT clearly contributed to the poor's massive desertion of APRA in the 1989 municipal and 1990 presidential elections. By 1990 both APRA and García were thoroughly discredited; the economy had hit bottom; Sendero Luminoso had begun to make serious incursions into Lima, especially into the pueblos jóvenes; and life in general was as grim and desperate for the poor as it had been in living memory. The fourth survey was administered in the weeks immediately following Fujimori's startling election and just prior to his announcement of a draconian structural readjustment shock treatment for the economy.

The Context for Poblador Participation, 1990

The acute nature of the economic crisis in 1990, coupled with the utter delegitimation of the García administration, produced highly pessimistic attitudes, especially about the nature of the Peruvian state and its ability to act in their behalf. Respondents were asked if they agreed or disagreed (on a seven-point scale) to a series of questions; those who answered one or two (or six or seven) were labeled strongly in agreement or disagreement. Two-thirds agreed that the Peruvian judicial system could not guarantee a fair trial (10 percent said it could); more than one-half said that basic human rights were not protected, and that they had no pride in the nation's political system. Three-quarters said that solving Peru's problems would require radical change; the same number thought that money had more influence in politics than anything else.

What was most unfortunate, however, was that this deeply cynical and despondent view of the state was also, from the pobladores' perspective, accurate.[32] The state could not guarantee a fair trial or protect basic human rights; money and manipulation did define politics; and radical change might indeed be essential for Peru's problems to be overcome. Therefore, taking pride in and supporting the state and the political system was untenable. Democracy was still preferred over military or revolutionary rule by three-quarters of the pobladores, but dealing with the economic crisis was still far more important (four to one) than preserving democracy.

By 1990 the pobladores in my sample had lived in their neighborhoods for a long time. Three-quarters had been there for more than ten years; only 7 percent had been there less than five; 44 percent worked in skilled manual jobs; one-quarter were unskilled manual laborers, although these mean figures varied significantly across neighborhoods. About one in eight was a union member; one-quarter said they held at least two jobs. The sample was therefore composed of Lima's working poor and working-lower to lower-middle classes. The majority had arrived in Lima prior to 1970 and thus had barrio memories built on Velasco and SINAMOS, the swell of mobilization and confrontation as the military withdrew from power, the return to civilian rule and the vindication of Belaúnde, the brief appearance of a united and victorious electoral left, the thunderous rebirth of APRA, and the fall into the abyss of economic collapse and the real threat of a violent, radical insurgency. An extraordinary history indeed, yet underneath it all lay the fundamental substructure of the predictable, routine, day-in-day-out struggle to keep body and soul together, to cope with only partially understood economic forces, and to search for ways to make a neighborhood just a little bit better.

INTERNEIGHBORHOOD DIFFERENCES, 1990

The four surveys reveal that despite the shifting of large-scale economic and social mobilizational tides, much of what the pobladores did remained remarkably stable. When the data presented in table 13 are compared with those in tables 10, 11, and 12, the core ways in which the pobladores faced the challenge of improving themselves and their neighborhoods changed little during the 1980s. Intracommunity development efforts and local and state petitioning were as identifiable in 1990 as they had been in 1971; the addition of voting and campaigning in 1982 did not replace them but simply provided the poor with additional options and alternatives. Everyone voted dutifully as expected, and in the aggregate the poblador vote made a considerable difference in some elections, especially in the 1983 municipal contest, where the lower-class vote swept Barrantes into power, and in 1989 and 1990, where pobladores voted in massive numbers for independent unknowns such as Belmont and Fujimori.

But although the weight of the poblador vote had an impact on national and municipal outcomes, voting as a participatory act did not and could not deal directly with neighborhood problems. So the pobladores kept up their own efforts year after year. As in 1982 and 1985, campaigning barely survived as a mode practiced exclusively, although more people undertook campaign activities in 1990 than previously (the percentage doubled between 1982 and 1990 from 6.1 to 13.6 percent).

Levels of involvement did change in response to local as well as citywide and national conditions, even though intercommunity differences were, in accordance with the trend already noticeable in 1982 and 1985, increasingly small. The percentage of total activists and of cross-modal participants rose to all-time levels in every neighborhood, as the pobladores tried everything they could to ease their situation. By 1990 the state had become so unreliable a source of aid that petitioning directed at state agencies had become a separate (and much less rational) mode of participating. A part-time construction worker, a fairly recent arrival in Primero de Enero, had strong feelings about the whole situation: "No one living here has ever seen anything worse than what we are living through today. We all do what we can for ourselves and for the kids, but what can we really do? If some neighbors are starving we all chip in whatever we can, but that doesn't solve anything." It is not surprising that recent involvement in community activities remained strong; frequent involvement dropped off, probably as available time was dedicated to work and survival; attending meetings in the neighborhoods rose to all-time levels, however. Barrio unity was the same as it had been in 1985; those seeing their present neighborhood as a permanent residence rose to 62 percent (over 1985 levels of 50 percent). Given the economic circumstances, any ideas of moving were probably lost to much more pressing concerns about surviving.

The pobladores were evenly split as to whether hard work (48 percent) or government help (47 percent) was the more important source of assistance for resolving community needs. One clear indication that many pobladores thought

Table 13. Intercommunity Differences in Participatory Activities, 1990

	Community				
	Primero de Enero (N=70)	*Pampa de Arena (N=73)*	*Santiago (N=98)*	*28 de Julio (N=113)*	*Total (N=437)*
Modal Involvement					
1. Problem-solving/ petitioning	6.7	9.0	—	8.1	6.0
2. Voting	45.8	30.7	58.3	39.6	43.6
3. Campaigning	—	—	3.1	—	0.8
Participant Types					
1. Total activists	14.4	10.2	2.3	17.3	11.1
2. Inactives	2.3	4.7	6.1	2.8	4.0
3. Cross-modal participants	46.2	38.6	16.5	40.0	35.3
Participation Items					
1. Recent involvement	55.6	42.4	40.0	41.1	44.8
2. Frequent involvement	33.3	32.2	23.2	46.0	33.7
3. Attend local meeting	50.7	62.5	26.5	45.0	46.2
4. Petitioned local organization	50.7	52.2	28.1	39.3	42.6
5. Member of local organization	43.5	36.6	26.0	36.1	35.6
6. Petitioned Ministry of Housing	24.6	14.3	8.7	18.3	16.5
7. Petitioned PAIT	16.1	15.9	3.2	18.2	13.4
8. Voted 1985 presidential election	94.3	94.4	90.7	94.8	93.6
9. Voted 1990 presidential election (first round)	92.9	93.2	90.8	87.6	91.1
10. Voted 1990 presidential election (second round)	95.7	89.0	91.8	92.9	92.4
11. Voted 1989 municipal election	97.1	98.6	94.9	95.2	96.5
12. Political party member	40.0	43.8	35.7	44.3	41.0
13. Attended political rally	30.1	27.3	18.4	21.1	24.2
14. Campaign activity	16.1	17.8	11.9	8.6	13.6

Note: Figures are percentages.

they had done about all they could do on their own appeared in two sets of questions. First, two-thirds of the pobladores who said that they had seen improvements in their neighborhoods uniformly ascribed these changes to the efforts of the residents and not to the government. Yet when asked what groups were best suited to resolving the neighborhood's most pressing needs, two-thirds said the government; only one in five (22 percent) said they could do the job themselves. These findings parallel those of Parodi, who concluded that "The pobladores have high expectations from the State but, on the other hand, the State has for them very poor legitimacy" (1993, 66).

Fully four out of five pobladores said that the economic crisis (simply *la crisis*) was Peru's most important problem. And although terrorism finished in second place, only 12 percent saw it as more important than the economy. It says a good deal about the impact of Sendero Luminoso that so few people saw terrorism as paramount. Most strikingly, 28 de Julio, a neighborhood that had been publicly targeted for penetration by Sendero Luminoso, had the fewest number of residents (4.7 percent) that classified terrorism as most important, as well as the highest number that saw the economy as first priority (91.7 percent). An informant living in 28 de Julio as a retired security guard classified Sendero Luminoso as

> something out of Larco Herrera [Lima's largest insane asylum]. Those people are totally crazy. Almost no one here has anything to do with them, but you can't talk about them at all. They're here, all right, but it's just a few people who paint slogans on the walls. Most of them are youngsters [*juventud*], but they just don't care what they do, and that's what makes them so dangerous.

Only 9 percent of the pobladores classified García and his presidency as good or very good; nearly one-half said they were bad or very bad. When asked to give a rank order for García and his three predecessors (Velasco, Morales Bermudez, and Belaúnde), only one in ten placed him first; two-thirds made Velasco their first choice. Only one in five of the pobladores said García had any beneficial impact on the neighborhood; slightly more than one in ten (13.4 percent) had ever spoken with PAIT about their problems, despite that organization's high profile. In contrast, almost one-half had at least visited SEDEPAL, metropolitan Lima's water company, about their community's lack of water.[33]

The residents of Sendas Frutales continued to have their own distinctive ways of doing business. The degree to which the neighborhood had developed a sense of community was quite remarkable by 1990. Recent (within the past year) involvement in local affairs was higher in Sendas Frutales than in any squatter area. Likewise, attendance at local meetings (three-quarters of the respondents) and membership in the local association (50.6 percent) was higher than the means (46 and 35.6 percent, respectively) for the four pueblos jóvenes. Petitioning a state ministry was higher in Sendas Frutales, although contact with PAIT was a good deal lower, since PAIT never targeted slum neighborhoods.

Sendas Frutales still had its problems. Nearly half its residents classified it as a bad place to live (less than one-tenth of the other communities did so), which, frankly speaking, was an accurate assessment of the neighborhood's enormously crowded housing conditions, insufficient basic services, high crime rate, and interminably tangled legal status. This latter problem constituted, as it had in 1985, the neighborhood's most pressing problem, according to nearly one-half of the sample. Yet the same percentage of its residents as in the squatter neighborhoods (three out of five) saw themselves as permanent residents, double the number in 1971 and 1982. Whether because of its central location, its closeness to work and transportation, or a widely shared reluctance to move, Sendas Frutales had come a long way from the pessimistic, unorganized, anomic neighborhood it had been twenty years earlier. Its inhabitants had apparently decided to make the best of things, regardless of the extraordinary difficulties that confronted them.

Conclusions

This account of informal participation over twenty years offers several conclusions. Lima's poor persevered against frequently overwhelming odds; they made, from their own perspectives, slow, incremental progress in their neighborhoods through a combination of working together using local resources and petitioning local, municipal, city, and state agencies. As the years passed, confidence in state-directed petitioning eroded, and by the mid- and late 1980s the number of individuals who saw such activities as rational had dropped. By 1990, confidence in the state to perform its most basic functions had reached dismal levels. Indeed, it might well be said that what Figueroa (1993, 1995) labels a crisis of distribution had set in.

The transition to democracy that took place between 1978 and 1980, culminating in the 1980 presidential elections, added to the ways pobladores could participate in the political arena. The poor, it is evident, voted from 1978 onward, as they were required to do. Voting (and campaigning), as participatory indicators of democracy, quickly came to constitute distinct modes of participation. Yet voting and campaigning were not intrinsically related to one another (or to petitioning), and they clearly did not replace the informal activities of the poor during the military period of the 1970s.

The upheavals of the 1970s and the economic hardships of the 1980s left the pueblos jóvenes (and Sendas Frutales as well) more complex neighborhoods and environments than they had been. More kinds of local associational life existed; most important, women had clearly become a major source of community leadership. Generational, ideological, and neighborhood-specific factors also helped to create more political stimuli as well as a more heterogeneous organizational participatory milieu (Ballón 1986, 26). Other forms of participation (in mass mobilizations, for example, or in strikes or in other demonstrative activities) occurred at times as well. Yet certain patterns of involvement held across time, primarily because the poor thought that investing time and energy into them was, on balance, an appropriate and rational investment, given the constraints and bounds that so tightly limited and channeled their behavior. Active individual involvement in demonstrative or mobilizational activities was more evanescent, primarily because the sociopolitical conjuncture of events that had enabled and encouraged such participation was itself much more amorphous than the concrete, daily problems that defined poblador existence.

The model I am using argued that two preference dimensions—the political preference for democracy and the economic preference for material well-being —influence how a lower-class individual will participate in politics. How the individual evaluates well-being at a particular time (as well as over time) may have a great deal to do with whether the importance he gives to democracy stays the same or changes. This chapter has clearly shown that, as the poor saw their modest material well-being deteriorate, their informal behavior in the 1970s became for a relatively short period demonstrative and aggressive. With the transition from authoritarianism to procedural democracy, however, voting and campaigning as distinct modes joined with informal participation, and the latter in turn became a diffuse amalgam of local community involvement and state-directed petitioning. By 1985 the state had lost relevance as a dependable resource, and state-directed petitioning declined over the second half of the 1980s, as economic deterioration and poverty intensified even further. In Hirschman's (1970) terms, loyalty both to the state as a resource and to the tactic of petitioning the state for aid diminished. Voice as an option certainly increased in scope and in intensity in the late 1970s and early 1980s, but by 1985 this also had decreased as more pobladores saw state-directed petitioning and demand-making as irrational activities.

Perhaps the single best way of indicating how the two preference dimensions of politics and economics interacted is to use a few specific questions from the 1982, 1985, and 1990 surveys. In 1982 respondents were asked if they preferred civilian rule over military. Three-fifths answered affirmatively; only 17 percent expressed a preference for military, whereas one-quarter saw no difference between the two—all in all, a solid if not resounding show of support for democratic rule.[34]

The 1985 and the 1990 surveys went directly to the heart of how preferences for democracy and for well-being counterbalance one another by asking not

only whether democracy was preferable to military rule, but also whether maintaining democracy or resolving the economic crisis was the more important. In
1985 almost four out of five preferred democracy to military rule; however, precisely the same ratio said that confronting the economic crisis was more important than maintaining democracy. In 1990 the same percentage again said
that well-being was more important than democracy; the number expressing a
preference for democracy over military rule had dropped to three out of five.

Lima's poor had a clear preference for democratic over military rule. But
they wanted economic well-being more than anything else, and they did not
care a great deal about who delivered it.[35] It is worthwhile here to recall the discussion in chapter 2 about how an underdeveloped capitalist democracy must
try to confront the provision of political rights inherent in democracy with the
scarcity of resources that restricts the provision of public goods and services.
The findings here do not mean that the poor were not as interested in the political rights of democracy as much as in the economic rights or public goods
(health, education, employment) that capitalist democracy promises. Quite the
contrary: they were very much interested in these rights and goods, perhaps
more so (and logically so) than any other segment of society. But the poor were
necessarily more concerned with survival. As Figueroa (1995, 69) puts it, if economic goods and services can be delivered through democracy as rights instead
of through the paternalistic generosity of a clientelistic or authoritarian political system, so much the better. But if the choice must be either democracy and
nothing or clientelism-authoritarianism and something, then the poor (along
with every other group faced with such a choice) will of course choose the
latter.

Lima's poor were willing to do everything they could do to help themselves
during the 1970–1990 time period. In times of great economic stress they did
not see the state as very relevant to solving their problems. Yet they still looked
to the state, primarily because they had no other truly viable alternative.
Sendero Luminoso was perhaps an alternative for a few, but the fear and intimidation it so successfully instilled in people worked against its establishing a
large popular following. Thus by 1990 the poor were left with highly limited,
unattractive alternatives: their own resources, which were extremely restricted;
the state, which under both Belaúnde and García had largely failed them; or a
radical alternative (the Shining Path) that was not only illegal but terrifying.

Once again using Hirschman's (1970) terms, petitioning the state became for
many pobladores an irrational act, and so they ceased to do it. In a word, they
exited. For some, voice remained another but less viable option. For the majority of the poor, loyalty to the state also remained, although in a grudging, un-

enthusiastic fashion. The state was not seen as a viable resource, perhaps, but in the starkest of choices—between the state and Shining Path, for instance—the state won out. Disloyalty to the state, at least as expressed in exit toward the Shining Path, was too costly because of the risks involved (fear of the organization itself and its tactics, and fear of state reprisals for members and sympathizers of the group).

It is clear that the pobladores saw participation in social movements (if local neighborhood associations are seen as social movements) as rational and vital investments of time for trying to obtain collective goods.[36] As economic conditions became especially severe in the late 1980s, the pobladores clearly turned inward to their own devices, unwilling to depend upon the state for resources or aid. With the possible (and, I would argue, short-lived) exception of the late 1970s, the great majority of Lima's poor saw long-term participation in neighborhood activities as a strategy for material gain, as contrasted with the construction of a social identity of some sort.[37]

Under which conditions do exogenous or endogenous factors influence social movements and lower-class behavior? In partial answer to this question, the period of the late 1970s was, quite obviously, a time when a wide range of external actors worked within Lima's pueblos jóvenes, doing their best to stimulate and often to socialize community leaders (as well as the rank and file) along partisan, sectarian, or ideological lines. But we have yet to understand the precise impact of such external agents and to examine under which conditions external actors have their best success. The best general statement we can make is that, at certain times and under certain conditions during the period from 1970 to 1990, external actors (state and nonstate) had some impacts on mobilizing the poor, but that long-term effects were unpredictable and uneven. Whether of the state or of political parties, or of other (religious, charitable) groups, virtually all agencies (especially SINAMOS) found that an appeal to the pobladores to participate in an activity for the sake of participating quickly floundered. Informal participation, which I have characterized as most accurately reflecting what the poor see as rational expenditures of their very scarce resources, started off as highly instrumental in 1970 and remained that way throughout the next two decades. Most exogenously inspired participation, especially if it called for what the poor saw as participation for participation's sake, was short-lived. But while these shifts and changes in informal participation were going on, the poor also had, from 1978 onward, the formal political arena where they could vote and hope thereby at least indirectly to affect how the state would act on their behalf and how those in power would govern.

8

....

FORMAL PARTICIPATION

The Transition to Democracy

and Economic Crisis

EXAMINING PATTERNS OF informal political participation offers perhaps the most direct means of identifying what the poor consider rational expenditures of time and effort (see chapters 6 and 7). Neighborhood involvement, local grassroots activities, and local and state petitioning are, after all, activities that the poor either create out of whole cloth on their own or (in the case of state-directed petitioning) decide for themselves to do or not do. Since these activities are not mandated by the state, they reflect most precisely what the pobladores themselves see as rational ways to provide material goods and improvements for themselves and their communities.

Our two-dimension model of democracy has served as a framework for analyzing how the individual citizen decides to involve himself in certain modes of participation and how he changes his involvement in these modes over time and in response to macro conditions. The two preference dimensions help clarify individual behavior in the informal arena as well as changes in that behavior. But the interest now is in formal or electoral behavior, which is behavior mandated by the state, meaning that the individual cannot choose whether to participate or not.[1]

Thus the question of *why* to vote is not of particular interest, but individual decisions about *whom* to vote *for* are. These decisions are influenced by a wide range of factors. People may identify with a particular candidate or with a party; they may decide to vote sincerely or strategically; they may vote for their pocketbooks or their ideology; they may or may not be well informed about a particular race.

One question I would like to address here concerns whether community leaders in Lima's barrios populares are able (as has been claimed in studies from other countries) to deliver their neighborhood's votes in some sort of block in support of a particular party, for which in return that party facilitates access to state resources for the community. Cornelius (1975) among others has argued that urban *caciques* in Mexico City establish (or at least used to establish) such arrangements with the PRI. It may be, however, that such figures can function successfully only if a strong party system exists, which has not been the case in Peru, especially in the latter part of the 1980s.

For citizens whose most obvious concern and constraint is poverty, economic matters may well come to override all others, especially during times of crisis. Nevertheless, decisions made to translate these concerns into a choice for a party or candidate in any single election are still likely to consider some or all of the factors mentioned above. And across elections—for example, presidential to presidential, municipal to municipal, or presidential to municipal—the relative preferences or weights of these factors may shift, causing changes in voting behavior.

Despite these confounding variables, the model of democracy and its two preference dimensions offers a useful means of addressing the most salient issues. In order to understand how these preference dimensions aid the individual in making his first decision, that is, about what issues are most pressing, I assume that, following the establishment of democracy with its utility and its marginal costs at T_1, time passes and material well-being declines. The preference for democracy may remain relatively high in the short run, although steady increases in marginal costs involved in preferring democracy may produce one of several rational responses, however bounded these may be by incomplete information, structural constraints, and institutional (such as party system) idiosyncrasies. If more time passes and well-being deteriorates further or more rapidly, an individual voter's dissatisfaction may cause him to look for more extreme alternatives.

This search may involve a move away from support for traditional parties toward more antiestablishment candidates, parties, or movements. Such a candidate can be a populist figure, a candidate on either extreme of the ideological spectrum, or a candidate who is unidentified with any party but whose lack of identification is his most appealing feature. If conditions become bad enough and generate an overall decrease in the general legitimacy of the state, a preference for authoritarian leadership or for revolution may emerge. Whatever the specifics, the greater the concern over the loss of well-being, the greater the tendency not only to switch votes but to move from one extreme position to another in the search for improvement or (at worst) survival.[2]

Such vote-switching would be equivalent to Hirschman's (1970) exit, one of three alternative courses of action (exit, voice, and loyalty) all present in the informal political arena. But in the formal arena these same behavioral alternatives operate even more cleanly than in the informal. Electoral choices tend to be clear-cut: to vote or not to vote, or to vote for Party A instead of Party B or Party C. In such an arena, a voter can choose to show loyalty to a candidate or party, even if that candidate or party has been unable to slow or reverse a decline in the voter's well-being. Or a voter may also voice dissatisfaction by attempting to change, rather than escape from, an objectionable state of affairs.[3] A member of a political party can attempt to practice voice through complaints, or through threats to take over a party or rework its platform if it does not or cannot do better. Or finally, a voter may choose to exit or to desert a party or candidate for an alternative.

Exit is the most dramatic response for the dissatisfied citizen. As material well-being decreases, an individual can manifest the exit option by switching his vote from one party to another. In a stable party system where two dominant parties compete with one another, vote-switching may be nothing more than the mutual luring over of one another's voters (Hirschman 1970, 28). But large-scale vote-switching in a nonstable, nondominant multiparty system can fundamentally reorder the relative size and power of parties in the system.

The frequent or widespread presence of Hirschman's exit option as manifested in vote-switching can be facilitated or hindered by structural and institutional factors in the economic as well as the political party system. Structurally, changes in economic conditions and poverty influence individual perceptions of well-being and, thereby, decisions about how to vote and whether to be loyal, to complain, or to exit. Institutionally, basic features of the political party system also come into play. For example, in a country with a dominant one-party system (such as, until the 1990s, Mexico's PRI), vote-switching may not occur until very broad discontent with the dominant party arises and voting for an opposition party becomes something more than just a wasted protest vote. Or as another example, in a nation with a highly institutionalized or hegemonic party system or with strong party identification (such as Chile prior to 1973 and subsequent to 1989, or Colombia and Venezuela before the 1990s), vote-switching may occur across two or three (or more) parties, but support for antiestablishment, populist-led political movements may be forestalled by difficulty of entry of such movements into the formal political arena.

Peru in the 1980s was a country with a highly fluid, noninstitutional, multi-party system with broad ideological representation. In such a system, if material well-being is perceived as threatened, vote-switching as an exit option may become easy, frequent, and wide-ranging, especially among low-income voters, whose search for a suitable candidate, party, or movement may well be driven by desperate circumstances. Widespread vote-switching (exit) will make it difficult for an incumbent party to retain office. Yet a rapid alternation of parties in power may paradoxically work against implementing long-term policies to improve well-being, especially if these policies (as is usually the case) require severe structural readjustments. Such policies, while often inevitable, can generate greater tension between the preference dimensions of politics and material well-being, especially for low-income sectors who may react with even more marked tendencies in vote-switching.[4]

In analyzing the pobladores and their participation in the electoral arena I examine some of the ideas and hypotheses in Hirschman. But before proceeding with the analysis of voting behavior itself, there is a need for a quick chronological sketch of the elections that took place starting in 1978. As each of these elections is described, I include the overall results for Lima as a whole and then the results for the poblador sample (see table 14).

Peruvian Elections, 1978–1990

CONSTITUENT ASSEMBLY ELECTIONS, JUNE 18, 1978 (1978-CA)

The 1978 elections were held to select one hundred representatives to form a constituent assembly and to write a new constitution to replace the one that had been in force since 1933. All parties that entered the election submitted lists of one hundred individuals; seats for the assembly were awarded on the basis of proportional representation by percentage of the popular vote per party. The elections were also a means for the military government to effect the transition back to civilian rule. (Upon completion and ratification of the new constitution in 1979, civilian and military elites agreed that nationwide elections for the presidency and the legislature would be held in 1980.) Three major parties participated in the 1978 elections: APRA, led by its aging leader, Victor Raul Haya de la Torre, who was determined to lead his party to victory; PPC, headed by Luis Bedoya Reyes, a former mayor of Lima who represented Peru's business sector and its moderate right in general; and an often fractious coalition of leftist par-

Table 14. Urban Poor Sample Voting Results in Lima, 1978–1990

	Left/IU	APRA	AP	PPC	FREDEMO	CAMBIO 90	OBRAS
1978CA (N = 419)	24.7	59.2	b	16.1			
(Lima)[a]	35.2	25.4	—	30.2			
1980P (N = 518)	12.2	24.9	54.6	8.3			
(Lima)	12.5	22.9	47.2	15.5			
1980M (N = 500)	18.4	22.2	50.6	18.8			
(Lima)	28.3	16.4	34.7	20.6			
1983M (N = 342)	54.4	29.2	10.8	5.6			
(Lima)	36.8	27.2	11.9	21.2			
1985P (N = 366)	22.1	69.4	3.8	4.7			
(Lima)	23.9	50.6	4.4	19.2			
1986M (N = 417)	46.8	42.7	b	10.3			
(Lima)	34.8	37.6	—	26.9			
1989M (N = 402)	15.4	17.9	c	c	13.2		53.5
(Lima)	13.7	11.5	—	—	26.8		45.2
1990P1 (N = 399)	13.0	17.3	c	c	29.6	39.9	d
(Lima)	11.0	13.8	—	—	39.5	34.4	—
1990P2 (N = 406)	—	—	—	—	33.9	66.1	d
(Lima)	—	—	—	—	53.3	46.7	—

Sources: Surveys from 1982, 1985, and 1990. Lima vote from Tuesta 1994.

    a. Total valid aggregate vote for metropolitan Lima.

    b. AP did not run in 1978CA or 1986M.

    c. AP and PPC ran under Fredemo in 1989M, 1990P1 and 1990P2.

    d. OBRAS did not run in 1990P1 or 1990P2.

ties. The great absence was of AP and Fernando Belaúnde, who refused to participate in the whole process.

APRA won nationally with a substantial plurality with 35.4 percent of the popular vote; Haya de la Torre was elected head of the assembly. The left finished second with 29.4 percent, PPC took 23.8 percent, and several other minor parties gathered a total of 11.4 percent.[5] In Lima, the results were not only closer but at something of a variance: the left took 32.9 percent, PPC took 32.4 percent, APRA took 25.6 percent. These results reflected APRA's traditional difficulty in carrying Lima, and the relative strengths of the left in the barrios populares and of PPC in middle- and upper-class Lima. Absenteeism totaled 16.3 percent of registered voters. During late 1978 and early 1979 the assembly hammered out a new constitution that was subsequently ratified, thus clearing the way for the transition election of 1980. The surveys of 1982, 1985, and 1990 were conducted subsequent to the restoration of civilian rule in 1980, and all of them elicited much information about formal political participation.

The 1982 survey was carried out slightly more than two years after Fernando Belaúnde had been reelected president. Reported voting levels within the sample were high: close to 90 percent of the respondents said they had voted in the 1978 constituent assembly elections and in the 1980 presidential and municipal elections.[6] In areas other than voting, participation occurred on much lower levels. Less than one-third said they had attended a rally for any of the three elections, only one in ten said they were members of a political party, only 7 percent said they had campaigned for a party or candidate. Four out of five said there had been no change in their neighborhood since Belaúnde's election (15 percent cited a positive change, 5 percent cited a negative change).

The 1982 sample showed certain notable idiosyncracies in the voting behavior of Lima's poor. For example, APRA in the 1978 constituent assembly elections won first place nationally but finished a close third in Lima. Yet APRA carried the poblador sample overwhelmingly. Almost 60 percent of the sample voted for APRA as against only one-quarter for the left. As would be expected for low-income voters, the PPC, which represented Lima's business interests, took 16 percent, well under its Lima total of almost 24 percent.

PRESIDENTIAL ELECTIONS, MAY 18, 1980 (1980-P)

The 1980 elections came only two years after those for the Constituent Assembly, but Peru's political scene had changed considerably in the interim. First, Haya de la Torre had died, only days after seeing his constitution ratified, and APRA went through a fierce internecine struggle between the old guard and the young turks over leadership and the ideological direction of the party. As a result, the party's usual discipline and organization unraveled. Second, Belaúnde returned as a hero from exile. Third, the left (living up to its old stereotype as internally riven) split badly, and five separate candidates ran for the presidency.

The 1978 constitution went into effect for the 1980 elections, and several of its provisions had a major impact on electoral politics. The new constitution lowered the voting age from twenty-one to eighteen, for instance, and dropped all literacy requirements. These changes meant two things. The first was that the size of the electorate expanded quickly. In 1978 Peru had 4.9 million registered voters, but that number rose to 6.4 million in 1980 and then to over 10 million by 1990. The second effect of these changes was to diminish Lima's electoral dominance. In 1978 the Lima metropolitan vote was 38.4 percent of the national total; by 1990 that percentage had dropped to 30.8 percent of the total cast nationally. The new constitution also required that a candidate for the presidency take a simply majority of the valid popular vote to win; if no candidate succeeded in doing this, then a second round would pit the two highest candidates against one another.

The results in 1980 were a stunning victory and vindication for AP and Belaúnde, who swept all opposition and won with 45.2 percent of the popular vote nationally (47.2 percent in Lima). Armando Villanueva, APRA's old guard candidate, fared badly, pulling in only 27.4 percent (22.3 percent in Lima). PPC and Bedoya Reyes did reasonably well in Lima (15.4 percent) but poorly elsewhere (9.7 percent). The left, hopelessly splintered, took an embarrassing total of 13.8 percent of the vote nationally (12.5 percent in Lima). Other parties took less than 4 percent. Absenteeism totaled 28.9 percent nationally and 15.6 percent in Lima.

Table 14 shows that Belaúnde more than matched his strong showings nationally and in Lima with the poblador sample (using the 1982 survey). Although taking something less than half the vote overall, AP captured about 55 percent of the poblador sample, almost all as a result of lower totals for PPC. Relative to Lima totals, the left and APRA held their own with the voters in sample.

Belaúnde benefited not only from the death of Haya de la Torre and the fractured left but also from his status as a civilian president who had been overthrown but who had returned. This image gave him and AP a highly symbolic, antimilitarist appeal to many voters. However, Peru had changed dramatically since his overthrow twelve years earlier. The country's population was larger, and so was the electorate; the political spectrum had widened and become more complex; widespread political mobilization had affected many people. Winning the election was one thing, governing was another.

MUNICIPAL ELECTIONS, NOVEMBER 23, 1980 (1980-M)

Six months later nationwide municipal elections were held for mayors and city council members. Nationally, AP retained a solid if somewhat diminished lead, as the party took 35.8 percent of the popular vote and won 104 of 148 mayoral posts around the country. AP won the mayoral race in Lima with 34.7 percent of the vote and captured 22 of the city's 38 district mayoral races. The left, which had pulled itself together in the IU coalition under the leadership of

Alfonso Barrantes, improved its showing by taking 23.3 percent nationally and by winning 14 mayoral posts. In Lima Barrantes ran as IU's mayoral candidate and finished second with 28.3 percent of the vote. IU also captured 9 district races. APRA did poorly. Nationally its candidates took 22.5 percent of the vote and only 22 mayoral positions. In Lima, it did far worse, taking 16.4 percent of the vote and 2 district races. PPC showed its usual national-Lima difference. Nationally, PPC garnered 11.1 percent but in Lima won 20.6 percent and 2 district races. Overall, absenteeism was 30.9 percent nationally and 23.6 percent in Lima.

The pobladores in the 1982 sample followed national and Lima trends, but again with some variations. Eduardo Orrego, the AP candidate, did much better within the sample than he did in the aggregate citywide vote.[7] This result may be because the electorate was removed from military rule by only six months and, as a consequence, was perhaps hesitant to cast votes for an unknown or for a candidate or party that might be perceived as a threat, either to the military or to the recently restored democratic system. In the terminology of the model, a vote for AP was a vote to sustain democracy and civilian rule, whereas a vote for the new IU coalition or for APRA was a warning to AP that its ability to manage the economy was suspect.

MUNICIPAL ELECTIONS, NOVEMBER 13, 1983 (1983-M)

The 1983 elections were widely perceived as a referendum on AP and Belaúnde's first three years in office. As such, they must have given him and his party little comfort. In addition to the widespread dissatisfaction with Belaúnde's performance, APRA had started to pull itself back together under the leadership of Alan García. IU and Barrantes continued to gather strength as they demonstrated their ability to act as a functioning coalition as well as a viable and electable alternative to the center, the right, and (perhaps most important) to Sendero Luminoso.[8]

The results were a disaster for AP and a triumph for the opposition. APRA took 33.1 percent of the national vote and won 78 of the 155 mayoral races contested, although in Lima it took only 27.2 percent and won only 6 of the 40 district races. IU showed the opposite tendency; although nationally it captured 29 percent of the vote and 31 races, in Lima it took 36.5 percent of the vote, making Barrantes mayor of the city, and won 19 district races, including every district mayoral race in the city's low-income districts. PPC took 13.9 percent nationally and 2 mayoral positions; in Lima it surged to 21.2 percent and 11 district mayoral wins (all in upper-income districts). AP finished poorly; it barely beat out PPC, never a national threat (17.5 percent of the vote and 36 races nationally). In Lima AP fell to 11.9 percent overall and only 2 district wins. Absenteeism was 35.8 percent nationally and 26.3 in Lima. The pobladores in the 1985 sample gave APRA about the same level of support it received in the city overall (29.2 percent sample, 27.2 percent citywide), but they deserted AP in vast numbers, giving Belaúnde's party only one in ten votes. As a result, IU took more than half of the poblador vote, indicating the extraordinary degree to which IU and Barrantes could generate support and the equally extraordinary degree to which AP had lost it, losing 80 percent (from 50 to 10 percent) in only three years. The overall results gave APRA and IU, AP's opposition, nearly two-thirds of the popular vote—both nationally and in Lima—and served as a precursor for the upcoming presidential elections eighteen months later.

PRESIDENTIAL ELECTIONS, APRIL 14, 1985 (1985-P)

The 1983 municipal results were reinforced in 1985. A rejuvenated APRA led by Alan García swept to an enormous victory, taking 53.1 percent of the popular vote nationally and 50.6 in Lima. APRA also won a simple majority in each chamber of the legislature, thereby giving Peru's oldest party its first presidential victory ever and a firm lock on political power. IU with Barrantes as its candidate had the doubtful distinction of finishing a distant second (24.7 percent nationally and 23.9 percent in Lima), while CODE (a new acronym for PPC) did poorly across the board (11.9 percent) but relatively better in Lima (19.2 percent). Belaúnde, who could not succeed himself, saw his party go down to a crushing defeat as it took only 7.3 percent of the national popular vote and a minuscule 4.4 percent in Lima. Absenteeism was much lower than usual: 9.5 percent overall and 7.6 percent in Lima.

The 1985 survey was administered immediately following the election of García and APRA. Ninety-six percent of the sample reported having voted in the presidential race; 89 percent said they had voted two years earlier in the 1983 municipal elections. Working in a campaign (11 percent) or being a party member (19 percent) were still relatively rare activities. When asked if government affected their daily lives, 31 percent said the national government had much effect, 36 percent said it had none. On the metropolitan and district levels, over one-half said that neither had any effect. Belaúnde himself was ranked as a good president by only 7 percent of the respondents, and as poor or very poor by almost one-half, a massive decline from his 45 percent popular vote total five years earlier. The pobladores from the 1985 survey gave APRA and García an enormous advantage: seven in ten voted for APRA. The left faded to less than one-quarter of the vote; both PPC and AP virtually disappeared, taking less than one-tenth of the poblador vote.

The swing from the left vote in 1983 to the APRA vote in 1985, as well as the collapse of AP, did two things. First, it provided García with an unbeatable margin of victory. When it won, therefore, APRA not only gained a lock on both houses of the legislature but also showed that its decades-old enmity with the military was definitively a relic of the past.

MUNICIPAL ELECTIONS, NOVEMBER 9, 1986 (1986-M)

Nineteen months later APRA finally won something it had desperately wanted for years but had never won: municipal power, especially in Lima.[9] Although its margin of victory was something less than in the 1985 race, APRA's ability to win individual mayoral races across the entire country was remarkable. APRA took a total of 47.6 percent of the national popular vote in local races and won an extraordinary 161 of all 174 races contested. In Lima APRA candidates won 18 of 40 district races and managed to pull off a hard-fought narrow win (37.6 percent) over IU and Barrantes (34.8 percent), who ran for reelection. Nationally, IU finished second in number of votes polled (30.8 percent) but won only 9 mayoral races. PPC (now having discarded its CODE acronym), took 14.8 percent of the vote but only 1 mayoral contest; in Lima, as was customary, PPC did better, taking 26.9 percent of the vote and winning 12 district races. AP, so badly defeated in the 1985 presidential race, did not participate in 1986. Absentee levels rose considerably (21.8 percent nationally, 14.7 percent in Lima).

The 1990 survey (see table 14) shows that among the pobladores the left rebounded vigorously. Indeed, Barrantes carried the sample by a narrow margin (46.8 to 42.7 percent) over APRA's mayoral candidate. PPC, as usual, did far less well among the low-income sample than it did citywide. The 1985 presidential and 1986 municipal elections thus gave APRA something that no civilian political party had ever won: true dominance in all centers and on all levels of power, and an assurance from the military that it would be allowed to govern. In the first few months following this rise to power, various signs of confidence (or arrogance, depending on the point of view) emerged briefly, such as discussions about amending the constitution so that García could run for direct reelection, or speculation about how many times García might be able to be president even if he respected the no-direct-reelection rule.[10]

MUNICIPAL ELECTIONS, NOVEMBER 12, 1989 (1989-M)

Few chief executives in Peru (or anywhere) have started off as universally popular as García (he had approval ratings well in excess of 80 percent in the first year), only to fall to single digit levels within three years. By the 1989 municipal races, Peru's economy had collapsed, and García's popularity with it. The right

—united in Fredemo, a coalition supporting Mario Vargas Llosa and made up of independents as well as of AP and PPC—showed considerable strength nationally, taking 31.6 percent (a plurality) and winning 70 of 161 mayoral races. In Lima Fredemo slipped somewhat (26.8 percent of the vote) but won 29 of 40 district races. Yet all other candidates in Lima were swept aside by Ricardo Belmont, a popular television personality and political novice who took 45.2 percent of the citywide vote, easily winning the city's mayoral race. His political movement, Obras (Works, as in public works), ran no district-level candidates. The left, dispirited and disputatious after its bitter defeat in 1986, reversed its historic tendencies and did better nationally (17.9 percent of the popular vote and 47 mayoral wins) than it did in Lima (11.5 percent of the vote and only 7 district victories). APRA, stricken by García's disastrous performance, could manage only 19.7 percent of the national vote and 27 races; in Lima the party did abysmally, taking 11.5 percent of the vote and failing to win a single district-level race.

The 1990 poblador sample mirrored Lima's overall results, but again with its own twists and peculiarities. Belmont, the Obras candidate, gathered over half of the poblador vote. Fredemo, the left, and APRA all took less than one in five votes, indicating two things: first, that Vargas Llosa's attempts to convince Lima's low-income voters that Fredemo had their best interests at heart met with little success, and second, that APRA had lost virtually all its credibility.

There was one other important straw in the wind. Nationally, independent candidates won 30.8 percent of the vote and 17 races. These results, coupled with Belmont's win in Lima, signaled that the traditional parties were losing their grip and that the party system itself was vulnerable to challenges from candidates unaffiliated with what had been the dominant political contenders in the political arena.

PRESIDENTIAL ELECTIONS, APRIL 8, 1990, FIRST ROUND (1990-PI)

By 1990 Peru's economy was one of the worst in the world, and the nation's populace was in desperate straits. Sendero Luminoso had spread throughout the highlands and was starting to move toward the cities, toward Lima in particular. APRA was in internal disarray and was headed for a clear defeat. The left was irretrievably split. In sharp contrast, Fredemo and the neoliberal right were poised for victory with Mario Vargas Llosa as its candidate, and for many observers in early 1990, the only real question was whether Fredemo would win an outright majority in the first round.

The 1990 election has gone through many analyses (Schmidt 1996, forthcoming; Torres 1989; Daeschner 1993; Vargas Llosa 1993; Cameron 1994), but its re-sults are still astonishing. Five weeks prior to the elections, Alberto Fujimori's Cambio 90 (Change 90) movement was included among one of several "oth-ers," since it was receiving less than 2 percent support in the polls. Yet starting in early March, Fujimori began an unprecedented surge that closed to within less than 3 percentage points of Fredemo by the first week of April. The results of the first round showed Fredemo finishing first, with 32.6 percent of the na-tional popular vote and 39.5 percent in Lima. But Fujimori took 29.1 percent nationally and 34.4 percent in Lima. APRA fell, and although it did manage to hang on to respectability nationally (22.5 percent), it dropped precipitously to 13.8 percent in Lima. IU was a shadow of its former self, nationally (8.2 per-cent) as well as in Lima (6.1 percent). Independent candidates showed marginal strength (7.3 percent nationally, 6.2 percent in Lima), but nowhere near their to-tals from the 1989 municipal races. Absenteeism in the 1990 first round was 21.7 percent overall, 12.4 percent in Lima.

Of the poblador 1990 sample, 90 percent said they had voted in that election, and 93 percent said they had done so some six months earlier in the 1989 mu-nicipal elections. The García administration was seen by only a quarter of the respondents as having done something positive for their neighborhoods; more than half said his administration had had no impact. By 1990 the pobladores in the sample were deeply pessimistic about the ability of the Peruvian state to act in their behalf. Two-thirds said the Peruvian judicial system could not guaran-tee a fair trial (10 percent said it could); more than one-half said basic human rights were not protected and that they had no pride in the nation's political sys-tem. Three-quarters said that solving Peru's problems would require radical change (the same number who thought that money had more influence in pol-itics than anything else). Such depressing and probably accurate perceptions of the nation's political system in general meant, among other things, that a can-didate or party viewed as representing the status quo or the established powers would have great trouble in carrying the poblador vote. In addition and for the first time, race and ethnic identity became issues in a presidential race, espe-cially in Lima, where the race-ethnicity-class distinctions between Lima pituco (upper-class, Western, white European Lima) and Lima chicha or Lima cholo (lower-class, mestizo, migrant-origin Lima) emerged as a distinct undercurrent in the campaigns.

The pobladores surveyed in 1990 showed that their 1989-M tendencies to support an independent candidate and to turn their backs on the candidates of traditional parties were no passing whim (see table 14). Fujimori, the exemplary independent, defeated Vargas Llosa, himself an independent and nontraditional candidate, 4:3 in the first round. APRA and the left were left with 30 percent of the vote between them.

PRESIDENTIAL ELECTIONS, JUNE 10, 1990, SECOND ROUND (1990-P2)

Eight weeks later, the amazing occurred. Alberto Fujimori, a political nobody in early 1990, soundly defeated the establishment candidate Mario Vargas Llosa and Fredemo by more than a 3:2 margin. Fujimori took 62.4 percent of the total popular vote. That he took 53.3 percent in Lima meant that his margin of victory outside the capital was substantial indeed. The pobladores in the 1990 sample voted 3:2 for Fujimori. This margin meant that Vargas Llosa and Fredemo lost among Lima's poor by a much greater margin than in the city overall, and that the traditional strength of PPC in Lima's wealthier districts was more than offset by the sheer weight of numbers of voters in the barrios populares.

CONCLUSIONS

Since 1978 the results from three presidential and four municipal races make it clear that Peru managed to reestablish and maintain democratic governance and procedures more successfully than it ever had previously in its history, and to do so under the worst conditions it had experienced in the twentieth century. Judged by any standard definitions of democracy (Dahl 1971), Peru was from 1980 through 1992 a procedural democratic success. Its political system legally permitted and in fact encouraged broad participation, and all parties that wished to compete electorally could do so. In addition, the system and its players supported successful contestation. Incumbents as well as challengers accepted uncertainty; parties that were voted out of office accepted their defeats; no candidate or party ever claimed or made a convincing case for voter fraud.

Such accomplishments need to be placed in historical context. Since World War II, the cycle of power whereby a civilian president completes his term in office and turns power over to a civilian successor had happened in Peru only once, in 1945. On the local level, Peru had only a fleeting experience with municipal elections, in 1963 and 1966. Before those years and after them up until 1980, all local officials had been appointed in Lima, regardless of whether the regime in power was civilian or military.

Yet the success of contestation and the rejection of incumbents on both national and Lima levels also implies there was a great deal of vote-switching by individual citizens in their search for a solution to the social and economic problems plaguing Peru. By the late 1980s aggregate electoral data indicate that vote-switching from one party to another had been replaced by movement toward independent candidates. More voters abandoned the traditional parties altogether in support of nontraditional candidates and movements, such as Belmont in Lima in 1989 and again in 1993 and, as a more extreme case, Fujimori in 1990.[11]

The surveys from 1982, 1985, and 1990 reveal certain marked patterns. The most notable is that, if the aggregate Lima totals show that a presidential candidate received strong support and was a runaway victor, the pobladores showed the same tendency, but in a more exaggerated form. Likewise, if a shift occurred across elections for the city's voters overall, the poblador totals showed the same movement, but the shifts were again more exaggerated. These tendencies occurred across the decade. Belaúnde's victory in 1980-P was larger in the sample than nationally or in Lima. The left's margins in 1980 (and certainly in 1983) were likewise larger, as was Belaúnde's collapse from 1980 to 1985, APRA's rise in 1985 and its fall by 1990, and Belmont's and Fujimori's victories in 1989-M, 1990-P1, and 1990-P2. Right across the decade, the pobladores swam with the electoral tides but did so in a more extreme fashion than the populace as a whole.

It is clear that Lima's lower classes participated fully in the formal political process. Their (reported) voting levels are as high as anyone else's, although they did not take part in other formal activities such as campaigning or attending political meetings and rallies. And while they had a preference for civilian rule, they did not seem to care much who resolved the country's economic problems, so long as someone did. They thought that government had relatively little effect on their neighborhoods for good or bad, although they viewed both outgoing incumbent presidents—Belaúnde and García—in highly negative terms. Toward the end of his study of the García administration, John Crabtree noted that the informal sector

> is a sector whose political preferences have not been the subject of extensive or systematic study. While it is clear that in the 1983 and 1986 municipal elections the Izquierda Unida drew support from the informal sector and from the *pueblos jóvenes,* it also appears as a sector whose political preferences tend to be highly volatile. (Crabtree 1992, 183)

My purpose in this chapter is to provide the systematic study Crabtree calls for, and in particular, to investigate the volatile political preferences of Lima's low-income residents that Crabtree noted.

Vote-Switching Across Time and Elections:
Some Preliminary Considerations

The discussion thus far has shown clearly that the pobladores changed their votes from one party to another, from one ideological position to another, and toward the end of the decade from traditional institutional parties to unaffiliated, antiestablishment candidates and their movements. But examining the survey data in this aggregate fashion does not provide any knowledge about how *individual* voters changed their votes, which parties or candidates they deserted, or to whom they gravitated. The survey data can address these and related questions, but I first need to identify which variables can affect formal political participation, and how and why these variables might not be the same ones that often influence informal participation.

The modes and levels and intensities of informal involvement by the pobladores varied significantly by neighborhood of residence (see chapter 7). This variation was frequently and intimately related to the profile of material needs of a specific local neighborhood. Patterns of participation changed over time as the neighborhood's profile of needs was satisfied, or otherwise resolved, or not.

Variations in formal participation may not depend anywhere near as much on neighborhood conditions as does informal participation, however. In the first place, specific neighborhood conditions (whether young or old; whether formed by invasion or accretion; its level of internal development) will presumably have little effect on voting turnout. But there are three important institutional reasons why formal behavior will be influenced by a different set of factors.

First and foremost, the rules and sanctions concerning how and when to participate formally come from the state, and unless the individual decides not to vote, there is no choice as to whether or when to vote.[12] Second, citizens vote individually and secretly. No one need know (or be able to determine) whether his neighbor votes as he does. A concerned individual citizen may try to persuade his neighbors to vote a certain way, as may a local neighborhood leader, but community pressures can have only a limited effect on the (secret) vote of an individual member of that community. Thus no community leader can make a convincing case to a political party or candidate that he can deliver his community's votes en masse.

Moreover, although a political party may try to appeal to particular groups of voters (defined, for example, by income, social status or class, gender, ethnicity), no party can specifically cast its appeals to different segments of any one such group. The left, for example, might concentrate on the urban poor, but the left cannot tailor a campaign to specific community needs, nor can residents of a particular neighborhood approach a party or candidate and ask that it focus its campaign specifically on the needs of that neighborhood. Neighborhood residents can (and do) tailor their modes of informal participation to address specific needs, but they cannot do so formally. There is only one opportunity and time to vote, and this is determined by the state; the individual citizen (especially the individual poor citizen) in general has no role in determining what parties will run or who the candidates will be. In terms of formal behavior, therefore, the state and/or the political party system has a great deal to say about who can participate, when participation can occur, what parties and candidates can participate, and how and when participation can take place. All of these external constraints make the formal arena and formal participation much less likely to be a direct reflection of neighborhood needs or of individual poblador preferences for becoming involved.

In addition to the legal mandate to vote, there is a third major reason that factors important for explaining informal behavior may not exert equal influence in the formal arena. This is, ironically, poverty itself, and the differential influence of poverty on informal and formal political participation. Poverty can be in effect decomposed (or, in a real sense, deconstructed) to the level of the individual residents of a neighborhood and/or on the level of the neighborhood. For example, the residents of a neighborhood may all recognize that their neighborhood is, as a collectivity, poor; they may also perceive themselves as poor. But a single resident can decide to address his individual poverty or his neighborhood's poverty in any number of ways, ranging from doing nothing (nothing, that is, outside of his own individual efforts to survive or cope or improve himself) to becoming involved in one or more of a wide variety of community-based efforts. Specific neighborhood poverty profiles exert a strong influence on an individual resident's informal behavior (see chapter 7). A resident can choose to lend a hand on a neighborhood construction project, or to work in a soup kitchen, or to petition municipal or state authorities for basic infrastructure or for land titles or for any other number of collective goods. Whatever his choice, by choosing to concentrate on a specific facet of his or his neighborhood's poverty, an individual has in effect decomposed poverty into manageable subcomponents that are (at least theoretically) more amenable to resolution than is poverty in its disaggregated, holistic entirety.[13]

In sharp contrast, formal behavior requires the individual citizen to perform a single act, that is, to vote. In so doing the individual must estimate which political candidate or party is most likely to make a difference in his or his neighborhood's poverty.[14] In the formal arena, both voters and candidates are forced to confront poverty in holistic terms. That is, the voter necessarily makes a judgment as to which single party or candidate he will support through the single act of casting a vote, and the candidate necessarily addresses poverty in the aggregate while addressing other national problems, not to mention other voters for whom poverty is not a paramount concern.

Recall that political participation is defined, informally, as activity designed to supply public goods by obtaining a favorable distribution of government resources and, formally, as activity designed to influence the selection and/or policy decisions of state personnel. For low-income individuals, informal participation allows a personal choice of when and how to become involved. Informal activities are at the same time costly, in terms of time, money, and energy expended, and risky, in terms of such activities having no guarantee of success. In contrast, formal political participation is a cruder, less selective, and far less direct means toward obtaining material improvements. Yet voting is a much easier, less time-consuming act that the state actively promotes and facilitates.

One additional aspect of electoral behavior and of vote-switching may come to have particular significance, and that involves different *levels* or *types* of elections. This is to say that a voter who in fact changes his mind over time may use one set of criteria about whom to vote for in a presidential race but may use different and additional criteria for a municipal race. Or, in terms of the model employed throughout this study, the two preference dimensions—one favoring democracy and the other favoring material well-being—may vary in their importance, depending on the type of election being held. For example, in a transition election (such as 1980-P), where political power was being shifted from a military to a civilian regime, a voter may vote for Party A because he views Party A as most likely to be acceptable to the military or as most likely to consolidate democratic rule. Five years later, however, in the next election (in this case 1985-P), if economic conditions have worsened or if democracy appears reasonably well established, then the voter may switch to Party B to demonstrate his dissatisfaction with his material well-being.

Moreover, other criteria may come on-line in local races. For instance, the voter may decide that Party B has a sounder or more sympathetic appreciation of local matters, or that an opposition victory may alert the president that he should pay attention to local problems and discontent. In addition, an opposition party can develop local strength that it may not have on a national level. Whatever the specifics, some voters who switch their votes may do so using different criteria that will vary by the type or level of election being held.[15] (This hypothesis will come under constant scrutiny as I proceed through the analysis of the 1980s elections.)

Both individual pobladores and Peruvian political parties recognized from the outset that Lima's poor in the aggregate represents a huge block of votes (roughly 15 percent of Peru's total electorate reside in Lima's low-income districts). Party reactions to this sheer weight of numbers varied, of course. Radicals saw a marginalized mass, the electoral left saw a natural and automatic constituency, the center and right saw a group to be coopted or defused, and nontraditional populist candidates saw a possible source of support. But the fact that every party and candidate running for the presidency had to develop some stance toward Lima's poor went hand in hand with two others facts: the city's poor could (and would) choose among a variety of contenders, and they could (and would) move their support from one party to another if they became dissatisfied.

Vote-Switching Across Elections

Since Peru between 1978 and 1990 had one constituent assembly election (1978-CA), three presidential elections (1980-P, 1985-P, 1990-P1 and -P2), and four municipal elections (1980-M, 1983-M, 1986-M, and 1989-M), an overwhelming number of cross-election comparisons could potentially be investigated. But there is no need to do a comprehensive analysis. Examining how voters might have shifted their votes from 1978-CA to 1989-M would not be especially enlightening or productive. A purposive choice of combinations of elections can be used to reveal different things. One obvious choice is to compare vote-switching across presidential elections or across municipal races, thereby maintaining a constant level of comparison. But a presidential-municipal comparison could highlight how a president or his party is doing, how long a president's coattails might be. I thus compare all possible consecutive presidential races and all consecutive municipal races, and I will also examine some other pairings of intrinsic interest.

FROM 1978-CA TO 1980-P

The data presented in table 15 show the results of vote-switching from 1978-CA to 1980-P. Table 15 shows how the 1982 sample vote in 1978-CA for the three main parties that participated—i.e., the left, APRA, and PPC. Table 15 then shows how the individuals who voted for each of these parties in 1978-CA split their votes in the 1980-P election for the four parties involved in that race. For example, of those who voted for APRA in 1978-CA, 45.1 percent voted for APRA in 1980-P. Or again, for those who voted for the left in 1978-CA, 50.2 percent voted for AP in 1980-P. (Tables 16 and 17 are constructed in the same manner.) The 1978-CA—1980-P comparison is of particular concern because it shows what happens when a previously powerful player (Fernando Belaúnde Terry of AP) who did not participate in one race presents himself for another. Such circumstances allow for a first glimpse into the intensity with which party identification is held among Lima's poor.

In this case the answer is quite clear. Party identification was weak. All three of the parties that competed in 1978-CA saw voters in large numbers desert them for AP. APRA could hold onto slightly less than half of its 1978 voters, whereas PPC and especially the left saw dramatic desertions toward AP. The reasons given for such shifts were fairly straightforward and could be classified as either a "push away from" their original party or a "pull toward" Belaúnde.

The pull factor was most commonly expressed as sympathy or admiration. Respondents said they were pulled toward Belaúnde because of his willingness to return after being overthrown and exiled, or because they saw him as best suited for reestablishing democratic governance. They also saw a certain irony and vindication in AP's win. For example, a thirty-eight-year-old bricklayer from 28 de Julio said, "I thought that Belaúnde deserved the chance to come back and to finish his term, and that it would serve the military right if he did. It's only right that he's the one to let Peru become a democracy again." And his neighbor, a shoe repairman who operated his business on the sidewalk of 28 de Julio's main street, said, "AP didn't run in 1978, and so APRA was the second best choice that year. But Belaúnde was a candidate in 1980, and he's the best person."

The push explanations were more specific and dealt with problems particular to a specific party. For example, 1978-CA voters who deserted APRA were clearly upset with the death of Haya de la Torre and that he would never have

Table 15. Vote-Switching Across Two Elections, 1978–1980

1978-CA Vote											
LEFT = 24.7				APRA = 59.2				PPC = 16.1			
(N = 103)				(N = 247)				(N = 67)			
1980-P Vote											
LEFT	APRA	AP	PPC	LEFT	APRA	AP	PPC	LEFT	APRA	AP	PPC
24.7	16.3	50.2	8.7	9.6	45.1	40.5	4.7	—	8.6	60.2	30.1

Source: Survey, Lima, 1982.

Notes: Figures are percentages. N = 417. Excluded: other parties, blank ballots, did not vote, no answer. Totals do not necessarily sum to 100 percent.

Table 16. Vote-Switching Across Three Elections, 1980–1985

	1980-P Vote		
IU = 11.4	APRA = 27.6	AP = 52.6	PPC/CODE = 3.9
(N = 41)	(N = 99)	(N = 189)	(N = 14)

1980-M Vote															
IU	APRA	AP	PPC	IU	APRA	AP	PPC	IU	APRA	AP	PPC	IU	APRA	AP	PPC
76.8	2.8	11.1	5.2	8.3	67.9	8.1	2.3	18.2	5.6	64.7	3.9	9.1	9.1	18.2	63.6

1983-M Vote															
IU	APRA	AP	PPC	IU	APRA	AP	PPC	IU	APRA	AP	PPC	IU	APRA	AP	PPC
89.7	4.1	—	5.0	36.1	63.9	—	—	59.0	13.3	19.1	6.6	60.5	14.4	7.7	15.4

1985-P Vote															
IU	APRA	AP	PPC	IU	APRA	AP	PPC	IU	APRA	AP	PPC	IU	APRA	AP	PPC
46.7	44.6	—	5.0	7.0	91.8	—	—	18.2	63.0	5.6	6.1	—	63.3	7.1	20.4

Source: Survey, Lima, 1985.

Notes: Figures are percentages. N = 343. Excluded: other parties, blank ballots, did not vote, no answer. Totals do not necessarily sum to 100 percent.

Table 17. Vote-Switching Across Four Elections, 1985–1990

	1985-P Vote	
IU = 21.0	APRA = 65.8	AP/PPC = 8.0
(N = 81)	(N = 254)	(N = 31)

1986-M Vote								
IU	APRA	PPC[a]	IU	APRA	PPC	IU	APRA	PPC
87.9	9.9	1.2	16.2	74.3	3.8	23.8	32.3	43.3

1989-M Vote											
IU	APRA	FREDEMO	OBRAS	IU	APRA	FREDEMO	OBRAS	IU	APRA	FREDEMO	OBRAS
47.3	12.3	11.3	39.4	16.4	29.6	13.4	36.6	—	—	44.0	56.0

1990-P1 Vote											
IU	APRA	C90	FREDEMO	IU	APRA	C90	FREDEMO	IU	APRA	C90	FREDEMO
12.6	17.3	48.5	19.7	4.3	19.0	60.7	14.0	—	—	32.6	67.4

1990-P2 Vote					
CAMBIO 90	FREDEMO	CAMBIO 90	FREDEMO	CAMBIO 90	FREDEMO
84.3	15.7	77.1	22.9	50.7	49.3

Source: Survey, Lima, 1990.

Notes: Figures are percentages. N = 366. Excluded: other parties, blank ballots, did not vote, no answer. Totals do not necessarily sum to 100 percent.

a. AP did not participate in the 1986M elections.

the chance to be president of Peru. They were also dismayed with the internal squabblings of the party. As a barber in Santiago with his own shop, a self-described die-hard APRA supporter, said, "Haya was still alive in 1978 and so I voted for him, but by 1980 he had died and the party was a mess [*una pachamanca*]; anyway, the military liked Belaúnde and I wanted to be sure that those sons of bitches [the military] had no excuses not to accept the elections."

In similar fashion, leftist voters from 1978-CA expressed feelings of impatience and even betrayal by the inability of the left to maintain a coherent identity and by the presence of five candidates running against each other. A part-time truck driver from Pampa de Arena said, "I would have supported a leftist candidate, but when five of them appeared I knew that the left would lose badly. Why vote for something that won't win?" A retired factory worker from Sendas Frutales, a longtime leftist supporter and union worker, was a good deal more outspoken: "Not one of them [the leftist candidates] deserved my vote or anyone else's. After the 1978 assembly elections we finally had a chance to show solidarity and maybe even win or at least do well. And what happens? They [the five candidates] are so selfish that they can't even struggle together. What a waste!" Whatever the case, push and pull factors together and separately combined to rout the left and to create a landslide for Belaúnde and AP.

Although Peru was going through difficult times in the late 1970s, almost no one in the sample voiced support for Belaúnde because he thought that Belaúnde would be capable of turning around the economy. In terms of the model, the material well-being dimension played little effect in deciding how to vote in 1980-P or in the decision to switch votes from 1978-CA to 1980-P. Rather, the motives mentioned were much more heavily weighted toward the political dimension, either in order to put military rule firmly aside or because Belaúnde was perceived as best suited to restore civilian rule. Thus respondents in the sample who switched votes from 1978-CA to 1980-P referred almost exclusively to political reasons for their decision.

FROM 1980-P TO 1980-M

Although only four months intervened between Belaúnde's inauguration (July 28, 1980) and the November municipal elections, this pair of elections deserves a brief comparison, since some of the results were a straw in the wind for 1983-M. AP won readily (see table 14), although its margin of victory among the pobladores was less robust than it had been in the presidential race in May. One factor in this race that deserves particular attention is the coming together of IU as a viable leftist coalition under the leadership of Alfonso Barrantes. This development helped bring about some significant vote-switching (see table 16). About one-fifth of APRA and AP voters in 1980-P moved to the left, more than offsetting the one-tenth of IU voters that supported AP's candidate.

Almost all respondents who switched from AP or APRA to the left again cited political reasons for their change. For example, a middle-aged long-term resident of Primero de Enero who operated a store in his house said, "I voted for Barrantes and also for Medina [the local district IU mayoral candidate] after voting for Belaúnde for president because Medina is a schoolteacher here in Comas and he lives here. He knows about Primero de Enero and people here identify with him."

Some voters showed a highly developed sense of what might be called tactical voting. A longtime informant in 28 de Julio spelled out his reasoning in detail:

I voted for Belaúnde for president, but for IU in Lima's mayoral race and for the mayor here in 28 de Julio. Belaúnde had the best chance to win [and to avoid a runoff election in 1980-P], and besides I thought he could keep the military out once he got in. But since Belaúnde hasn't done anything for us here since he took office, I thought that leftist mayors would be able to get more done. First, the left say that they care about people like us; second, they say that they have new ideas about decentralizing power and letting the districts run themselves.

But I really thought that if we could elect a leftist mayor here in 28 de Julio, the central government would have to pay more attention to us, because we would show them that they can't take us for granted. The same thing if AP won Lima's citywide race, but IU won here in 28 de Julio.

I know that it might work the other way around—if 28 de Julio didn't support AP by electing an AP mayor, then we might not get anything from Belaúnde here at all. But I still think that I did the best thing for me and my family and for the barrio. We'll just have to wait and see. Who knows?

This response illustrates what the different elections stand for, how preferences can change over these different elections, and a clear willingness to weigh alternative strategies and outcomes vis-à-vis specific goals. The goal was to obtain goods or services from the state, but the tactics to do so were purely political.

FROM 1980-M TO 1983-M

The 1983 municipal election was widely viewed by almost everyone—voters and observers alike—as a referendum on the first half of Belaúnde's term in office. If so, it must have been a sobering experience for AP. Well over one-half of the poblador sample voted in favor of IU (see table 14); about 30 percent voted for APRA, whereas AP and PPC combined for less than one-tenth of the vote.

Of those pobladores in the 1982 sample who had supported AP in 1980-P, less than one-fifth voted for AP's Lima mayoral candidate in 1983-M. A full three-fifths moved their vote to IU and Alfonso Barrantes. At the same time, IU won back 90 percent of its 1980-P voters, while it was also able to attract 60 percent of 1980-P PPC voters. Only APRA held on reasonably well to its 1980-P voters, losing slightly more than one-third to IU. The move to IU and to Barrantes was widespread across the political party spectrum; the left took in excess of half of the sample's votes (see table 14).

Yet outright anti-AP and anti-Belaúnde sentiment was seldom given by the pobladores as the major reason in deciding how to vote. Indeed, only one in ten of the sample said that rejecting the incumbent was the principal reason for voting as they did. Instead, the candidate's party was the most common reason (40 percent of the sample), followed by the speeches of a particular candidate (30 percent), and then by the personal characteristics of the candidate (20 percent).

Open-ended explanations for the substantial move to the left came under one of two general headings. The first was broad dissatisfaction with (and rejection of) Belaúnde's administration, and in particular his economic policies. A carpenter in his early thirties, a recent migrant from a rural setting who rented a room in Sendas Frutales, was blunt in his views: "I had no reason to vote for AP in 1983. AP has brought nothing but misery to me, whether here in Lima or back in Chincha [his hometown]. He's surrounded with fools [tontos] and crooks, and as for helping out people like me, there are no jobs that pay well or that are steady."

The second, and more generally expressed, motive was active support for IU and/or Barrantes. As a candidate, Barrantes was widely viewed, even by his opponents (grudgingly so), as being responsible, not some fire-breathing radical. This image was remarked upon repeatedly. As a retired policeman living in Pampa de Arena put it:

> Finally we had the chance [in 1983] to vote for someone who cares about us, the pobladores and the poor. Barrantes knows what we need and will find ways to help out. The left has been working here in all kinds of ways for years; they deserve our votes and our support. They are people I can work with in my spare time because they have my best interests at heart.

One theme that was reiterated time and again dealt with the investment the left had made in the local neighborhood. Whether in assisting in local affairs or in organizing demonstrations or political rallies, or in having representatives and spokesmen living in the community, by 1983 the left had clearly become a salient and personal presence for many pobladores. This effort was repaid in votes and in general support.

FROM 1980-P TO 1985-P

The 1985 presidential elections revealed as nothing else could the hollow shell that AP had become. With Belaúnde unable to succeed himself, AP's nomination of a party hack, and the economic conditions that had been delivered upon the country, all polls indicated that AP would go down to a crushing defeat, and that APRA would stand once again dominant—this time guaranteed not only to win the election but also to take power. The data presented in table 14 show, in the starkest terms, the dimensions of AP's collapse and of APRA's reemergence under García within the poblador sample: APRA took 70 percent of the vote, AP took 4 percent.

The question of vote-switching across presidential elections is, of course, of fundamental interest. Vote-switching across types of elections (from presidential to municipal, for example), although intriguing, has some built-in problems, the most notable precisely the difference in type. Not only can different salient issues emerge in municipal as compared with presidential elections, but local elections can give small, non-national parties the chance to put up candidates, which makes any direct comparison across elections difficult. Presidential campaigns can, at least in this regard, be more readily compared with one another.

The vote-switching that occurred from 1980 to 1985 was enormous. In gross terms, the poblador sample deserted AP in huge numbers; support dropped from more than one-half (54.6 percent in 1980-P) to a minuscule 3.8 percent five years later. APRA gained accordingly, moving from one-quarter of the sample vote in 1980-P to over two-thirds in 1985-P. IU voters in 1980-P split evenly; about half remained loyal to IU, and the same percentage switched to APRA. It is not surprising that APRA gathered over 90 percent of its 1980-P voters back into the fold. Both AP and PPC, in sharp contrast, saw two-thirds of their 1980-P voters move to APRA. What AP had done in 1980-P, APRA did in 1985-P, and in each case IU was left a distant second, despite its huge margin of support in 1983-M.

The reasons given by the respondents for such a massive redistribution of the vote fall into two major categories. The first (as it was in 1983-M) was a rejection of AP and Belaúnde, especially his economic policies and performance. Of those voters who switched support from AP in 1980-P to APRA in 1985-P, over one-third (37.9 percent) cited bad government and/or the economy as the principal motive for changing their vote. The discontent voiced in 1983-M simply grew deeper and more bitter. As a bus driver from Santiago put it:

These past five years have been terrible. Prices have gone up and my wages haven't; repairs to my bus are eating me alive, and I don't make enough to buy the necessities of life. Belaúnde may have kept the military out of power, but I'll tell you that things were better under Velasco. I voted for García, but more to make sure that AP wouldn't win than because I like APRA.

The second main reason for the groundswell of movement toward APRA was García himself and a rejuvenated APRA party. More than 20 percent of the sample who supported APRA but who had voted for another party earlier said simply that APRA—especially with García at its head—represented a new hope and new leadership for Peru and for them personally. A widowed father of five children who was an elementary schoolteacher in Primero de Enero and who normally voted for the left as a matter of course gave a typical response:

I voted for APRA; almost everyone did that I know. He's the best man for the job, and APRA is well organized. And now that APRA controls [both houses of] the Congress, maybe somebody can do something about the economy and about raises for people like me. I almost always vote for the left, and SUTEP [a strong, militantly leftist teachers' union] told us all to support the left in the election, but APRA had the best chance to win.

It is worth pointing out that respondents from the sample who voted straight ticket between 1980-P and 1985-P (that is, across two presidential and two municipal elections) were very rare. IU did the best in holding on to its voters over time, but perhaps only because it started off so poorly in 1980-P, when it won only 11.4 percent of the sample vote (see table 14). This low total meant that its supporters in that race were most probably its hard core who would be unlikely to change. Of this nucleus, close to half (43.9 percent, or N = 18) voted IU in every election. APRA, which also started at a disadvantage in 1980, did less well, despite its traditional ability to generate extreme party loyalty and identification. Only 28.3 percent (N = 28) of APRA voters in 1980 stayed with the party. PPC, which had negligible support in the sample, saw only straight-ticket voters. AP, given its record, fared the worst, not surprisingly, but the extent of its inability to hold on to support was astonishing. It started with over half of the poblador vote (N = 189 out of 343) in 1980-P, but it had retained only two (1.1 percent) of its voters by 1985-P. In Hirschman's (1970) terms, IU and APRA managed to cope reasonably well with their "customers," convincing a fair portion of them to practice at least loyalty, if not voice. But overall, every party encountered difficulties in convincing its customers not to exit. AP clearly failed utterly in this task as it saw vast numbers of previous supporters desert the party.

Halfway through the decade, therefore, AP had been virtually discredited, and the left had enjoyed considerable municipal success in Lima but had been soundly defeated on the presidential level. APRA had shown remarkable recovery and broad national support. The rest of the decade lay ahead.

FROM 1985-P TO 1986-M

APRA's sweeping national victory in 1985 left it hungry for local power as well, and the party and President García pulled out all the stops to help their candidate, Jorge del Castillo, win Lima's mayoral race. At the same time the left, which had seen Barrantes fall far short in his presidential challenge against García, hoped desperately to see Barrantes reelected. Both parties recognized that the city's lower-class populations, with their hundreds of thousands of votes, would be critical.

How close the IU-APRA race was within the poblador sample can be seen in the data (see table 14): IU won by only a 4 percent margin.[16] But this edge within the sample was not enough, and del Castillo won in Lima thanks in large part to the organizational strength of APRA and to President García's personal (and, by Peruvian standards, unprecedented) involvement in the election. According to the respondents in the 1985 survey, there was no single dominant motive for deciding how to vote. The speeches of the candidate, the party of the candidate, and the candidate himself as an individual were each given as the principal reason by 30 percent of the sample (the remaining 10 percent said they voted as they did to oust the incumbent).

Both APRA and IU managed to hold on to the bulk of their 1985 supporters (see data from the 1990 survey, presented in table 17). IU did somewhat better in this respect, maintaining the loyalty of almost nine-tenths of its 1985-P voters, whereas APRA held on to three-quarters. The major difference here is that in 1985-P far fewer people voted for IU than voted for APRA; in addition, APRA was much better in attracting substantial numbers of Lima's huge independent or floating electorate, many of whom were drawn to APRA by its well-organized and flashy campaign tactics.

FROM 1985-P AND 1986-M TO 1989-M

Given the disastrous performance of the García administration following mid-1987, describing the shifting nature of voting from APRA's triumphs in 1985-P and 1986-M to the end of the decade assumes great importance. Tracing the deterioration of the APRA vote is especially critical for understanding how and why Peru's best organized political party so completely alienated the urban lower-class voter. It will be recalled that by 1989 Peru's economy was bordering on collapse. The country's gross domestic product was to lose one-eighth of its value during the year, and inflation was approaching 2,000 percent (about 35 percent monthly). These losses in purchasing power and in wages and salaries were making daily life ever more difficult. In the political sphere, the left during 1988 and 1989 went through an enormously divisive and ultimately irreconcilable power struggle. APRA, desperately searching for a way to halt its slide in public opinion, conducted rancorous party meetings and conventions in frantic efforts to find a recovery strategy. Meanwhile, a resurgent right under Fredemo —and with the leadership of Vargas Llosa and the support of AP and PPC— was becoming a major political player.

The 1989 municipal elections were therefore viewed as a referendum on APRA, as a chance for the right to reestablish itself, and as a precursor for the 1990 presidential race. Over half the pobladores in the 1990 sample (see table 14) voted for Ricardo Belmont, a political novice but an attractive television personality. APRA (17.9 percent), the left (15.4 percent), and Fredemo (13.2 percent) all trailed far behind Belmont as they split the remainder of the vote more or less evenly. Insofar as APRA was concerned, the results of 1989-M were abysmal. The poblador sample repudiated APRA and deserted the party. Indeed, 36.6 percent of APRA voters from 1985 voted for independent candidate Ricardo Belmont, compared with only 29.6 percent who voted for the party's mayoral candidate in Lima. Fredemo (13.4 percent) and the left (16.4 percent) attracted much smaller percentages of the APRA voters.

The left had its own problems with desertion. It did fare somewhat better than APRA; almost half its 1985-P voters stayed with it in 1989-M. Nevertheless, four out of ten IU voters moved to Belmont. These results generated even further bickering and recriminations within the left, which led to deeper splintering and more electoral problems in 1990-P. For the much smaller number of pobladores who voted in 1985-P for AP or PPC, Fredemo and Belmont split their votes more or less evenly.

The pobladores who changed their votes from 1985-P or 1986-M to 1989-M voiced one overwhelming concern—the state of the economy and of their own lives. With few exceptions, they voiced one source of blame—the APRA government. As a hotel doorman living in 28 de Julio put it, on a personal level:

> Things have never been so bad. I work at a tourist hotel and there aren't any tourists! Who's going to come to Peru to go to Cuzco and Machu Picchu when the economy's a total mess and when there's subversive violence [Sendero Luminoso]? And that all means no business at the hotel and no tips for me.

A secondary public schoolteacher who lived with his family and taught school in Primero de Enero was even more blunt:

Goddamn Apristas [the APRA government]! They complain for sixty years about how they've never been given the chance to win an election or to govern, and when they finally do, look what happens! This poor screwed-up country doesn't deserve what's happening to it. I see the youth that's supposed to lead this country; what can they do?

The attraction of Ricardo Belmont as a candidate was straightforward. He was new, and he was not the candidate of one of the traditional parties. These strengths, along with his personal charm, brought him votes from all sides. Meanwhile, by 1989 the left had frustrated all but its most fervid supporters. Its inability to hold together, its endless public wranglings about ideology, and the somewhat tattered public image of Barrantes, all made it difficult indeed for the left to maintain enthusiasm among its erstwhile supporters (Roberts 1996).

So the 1989-M elections made three points abundantly clear. First, APRA's 1985-P and 1986-M strength was hugely volatile and fragile. Second, the left had seen many of its gains from 1983-M seriously eroded. Third, independent candidates—as compared with candidates standing for the traditional parties—had a great potential appeal, at least in Lima. Whether and how this potential could be mobilized on a national level could only be tested in a national election, which was, as matters stood, only five months away.

FROM 1985-P TO 1990-P1

The 1990 presidential race will be remembered in Peru for many reasons. Economically, the elections occurred while Peru was at the very nadir of its crisis. Socially, Sendero Luminoso had begun to make serious moves toward Lima, and its campaign to instill fear and intimidation throughout the country was becoming more a realizable fact. Politically, APRA and García had failed themselves, their party, and the country as a whole. All these ills fed upon one another, although from the point of view of the poor, what mattered most was abundantly clear: the economy and, most of all, inflation. When asked to identify the two most important problems facing Peru at the time of the 1990-P elections, the poblador sample was absolutely clear: eight out of ten named *la crisis* (the economic crisis in general; unemployment, inflation, prices, the cost of living, in particular) first. Terrorism finished a distant second with 12 percent.

Although the disgrace of APRA, the fragmentation of the left, and the emergence of Mario Vargas Llosa as a would-be politician were all important factors, the year 1990 was most clearly the year of Alberto Fujimori and his extraordinary climb from obscurity to the presidency. The Fujimori phenomenon has been analyzed many times, and although this election was indeed complex and fascinating, it is not the focus of this book. It was clear from the start, however, that both Fujimori and Vargas Llosa devoted much attention to Lima's masas populares. One of Vargas Llosa's principal reasons for entering politics in the first place was his interest in Hernando de Soto's *El otro sendero,* an international best-seller that extolled the virtues of Lima's informal urban sector. Vargas Llosa had written the preface, and during the presidential campaign, he spent a fair amount of time visiting Lima's squatter communities and central city neighborhoods, despite his reluctance and personal aversion to doing so.[17] Fujimori, on the other hand, promised repeatedly in his campaign appearances that, if elected, he would be *un presidente como Ustedes* (a president like yourselves) and claimed to represent all of Peru, not just its European, urban, educated minority.

By April 1990 and the first round, Vargas Llosa and Fredemo had slipped somewhat from their earlier position in the polls, which showed them with almost half the vote. It was clear that Fredemo's loss was Fujimori's gain. In the polls Fujimori climbed almost one percentage point a day during the month of March and closed with a rush to finish a strong second (29.1 percent nationally, 34.4 percent in Lima) to Vargas Llosa (32.6 percent nationally, 39.5 percent in Lima). Overall both Vargas Llosa and Fujimori did better in Lima than they did nationally, primarily because APRA did so poorly in the capital city (22.8 percent nationally versus 13.8 percent in Lima).

Lima's masas populares provided Fujimori with the bulk of his vote total in the capital. First, using aggregate data and summing the percentages of valid votes cast in the five districts in which the survey neighborhoods were located, we can see that the residents of these districts voted four to three (40.1 to 30.7 percent) in favor of Fujimori. Second, using aggregate results from the five districts of Lima that are arguably the city's poorest (and excluding the five above that contain the survey communities)—namely, Independencia, San Juan de Lurigancho, San Martin de Porres, Villa Maria del Triunfo, and Villa El Salvador—we can produce an even greater difference: 42.7 percent for Fujimori and (more notably) 22.7 percent for Vargas Llosa, or basically a 2:1 margin for Fujimori. It should also be noted that Fredemo carried twenty-six (or 63 percent) of Lima's forty-one districts; Fujimori took the remaining fifteen, most of which were poor or blue-collar districts. But in terms of the aggregate total vote Fujimori trailed Fredemo by only five percentage points, which is another way of underscoring the vast numbers of people living in Lima's lower and working-class districts.

The poblador sample certainly mirrored these tendencies (see table 14). Reflecting the aggregate totals of their districts, 40 percent of the respondents voted for Fujimori, whereas 30 percent supported Vargas Llosa (the left and APRA gathered in 13 and 17.3 percent respectively). For Cambio 90 voters, Fujimori's main attraction was that he was perceived as an independent candidate (see below) and that he stood for the poor. This latter perception emerged vividly in the comments of the pobladores. When asked, for example, which groups in Peruvian society Fujimori and Cambio 90 represented, over half answered "the poor"; the second most common response was, tellingly enough, "all Peruvians." In dramatic contrast, almost eight in ten respondents (78.6 percent) said that Fredemo and Vargas Llosa stood first for "the rich and powerful" and second for "businessmen."

Overall, the single most common reason (37 percent) given by the respondents, when asked why they voted as they did, was "the candidate." It is striking to note, however, that of the pobladores who were Fujimori supporters, 46 percent mentioned the candidate himself as most important, in contrast to 28 percent of Fredemo supporters. The second most important factor in deciding the vote (29 percent of the sample) was the candidate's platform, but once again, Fujimori–Vargas Llosa differences are notable. In all, 21 percent mentioned the platform for Fujimori as the primary reason for deciding how to vote versus 35 percent for Vargas Llosa.[18] For both candidates, ideology and party were each given much less weight as major factors. Almost no respondents in the sample (3 percent) said the major reason for voting as they did was to prevent another candidate from winning (cf. Schmidt, 1998).

In addition to personalist effects and other general motives for deciding how to vote, various other factors had mixed but apparently little impact on the decision-making processes of the pobladores. For example, respondents were given a list of several factors (television, radio, newspapers, public opinion surveys, family, workplace, neighborhood, the church) and were asked whether these had much, some, or no effect on how they voted. What was most notable about the responses was that none stood out, and that none was ranked high. Television was first; about one-quarter credited TV with having much influence on them, although 43 percent said it had no influence. No other factor ranked over 20 percent as having had much influence. The workplace (with 18.8 percent giving it much influence) was second highest; the church (at 9.7 percent) was the lowest.[19]

The pobladores who switched their vote from 1985-P or 1986-M to 1990-P mentioned several reasons why they changed. Many cited the failures of the García administration (inflation and bad government, for example) as driving them away from APRA. A middle-aged recent migrant from Chimbote who lived with his brother's family in Sendas Frutales said, "I have always been an

Aprista [APRA] supporter, but the rise in prices and the inflation of the past couple of years forced me to look for a change." And a retired bus driver who lived with his daughter's family in Santiago said, "Well, APRA promised a whole lot of things, but didn't do what it said it would, and even though I guess García wanted to help the country, his party and his government cheated us all." Those who switched from the left to another party often mentioned the splits within the left and equated a vote for the left with a throwaway vote. As a longtime resident and leftist activist in Primero de Enero put it, "with all of the divisions in the left, I preferred to vote for an independent candidate."

The great majority of pobladores who switched their votes from 1985-P or 1986-M to 1990-P1 did so to vote for Fujimori. And regardless of the party they had voted for in 1985-P or 1986-M, the primary reason for switching—voiced again and again—was not only that Fujimori was a new face but that he was an *independent* candidate. That Fujimori did not belong to any of the traditional parties worked enormously in his favor among the respondents in the sample. As a plumber from Sendas Frutales who searched for business every day by wearing a placard around his neck that advertised his skills said:

> Fujimori is independent and new. He's not a traditional politician who only wants us [the poor] to vote for him and then he'll forget us a day later. He seems sincere and honest, and I'm tired of all of the traditional parties who got us into this mess; APRA failed and the left failed and Belaúnde failed and so why should anyone vote for them?

The theme of independence, of not being connected to the traditional parties, ran throughout the survey responses as well as throughout informant interviews. Ironically enough, the pobladores who had switched their 1985-P or 1986-M votes to support Fredemo said the same thing, though not as often. They saw Vargas Llosa as a newcomer in politics and not tied to the traditional parties. Whether this latter perception was objectively true, both Vargas Llosa and Fujimori clearly were nontraditional candidates and both of them benefited from this status.[20]

FROM 1990-P1 TO 1990-P2

The six weeks or so between the first and second rounds of the presidential election in 1990 simply delayed the inevitable. All polls predicted a substantial Fujimori victory; indeed, immediately following the first round and then again during the truncated campaign, Vargas Llosa seriously considered dropping out and conceding victory to Fujimori (Vargas Llosa 1993). In any case, he did not do so, and he was soundly defeated, especially on the national level (62.4 to 37.6

percent). In Lima, results were much closer (53 to 47 percent), but again, Fujimori's hold was firm on the lower-class districts of the city. As in the first round, the aggregate totals from the five districts of the sample neighborhoods showed a 3:2 difference (61 to 39 percent), while the city's five poorest districts showed a better than 2:1 (70 to 30 percent) difference. The 1990 sample virtually matched the results in these poorest of Lima's districts (see table 17), with the pobladores voting 2:1 for Cambio 90.

With only two candidates running, of course, vote-switching took on an exaggerated form, since anyone who had not voted for one of the two finalists had to change his vote. Yet even given these somewhat artificial circumstances, the move to Fujimori was massive indeed. Fredemo gained only four percentage points (29.6 percent in 1990-P1 to 33.9 percent in 1992-P2), but Cambio 90 gained 27 percentage points (39.9 percent in 1990-P1 to 66.1 percent in 1990-P2, a jump of 26 percentage points). Leftist and APRA supporters, not surprisingly, went 4:1 and 3:1 for Fujimori, and even AP and PPC voters from 1985 split evenly between Fredemo and Cambio 90.

Given the widespread nature of vote-switching, individuals who voted a straight ticket from 1985-P to 1990-P1 were rare indeed. In the first place, AP did not participate at all in 1986-M and later did so as part of the Fredemo coalition in 1989-M and 1990-P1. Obras came into being in 1989-M and operated only in Lima. Therefore straight-ticket voting related only to IU and APRA voters, which after all are the parties (ideologically speaking) that should have the greatest appeal for the urban lower classes. Yet for these two parties, the results over 1985–1990 cannot help but be frustrating and disturbing. Of IU supporters in 1985-P, only 11 percent (N = 9) voted for IU across all elections, a disappointing figure for a coalition whose future had looked so promising in the Barrantes win in Lima in 1983-M. APRA did only slightly better: only 17 percent (N = 44) of its 1985-P voters stayed with the once proud party that had appeared so dominant when García led it to victory.

By the end of the decade, Peru was into a nightmare that showed no signs of ending. The economy was in a state of collapse, traditional political institutions and parties and their candidates of all ideological stripes had been discredited at the polls, and Sendero Luminoso had become a viable presence and threat in Lima. Lima's low-income voters moved from one candidate to another, from one party to another, and then away from all parties to populist, independent, and antiestablishment political movements. What had seemed to be quite precise calculations about weighing presidential voting decisions off against municipal races disappeared as economic conditions went from bad to worse and as surviving grimly replaced hoping for improvement.

Conclusions

There can be little doubt that Lima's poor participated in their country's (and city's) formal political arena during the 1980s. Most pobladores saw voting simultaneously as a civic duty, as an act (especially at the beginning of the decade) that would help move Peru away from military rule (of which they were heartily tired), and as a chance (indirect as it might have been) to influence, or to try to influence, the distribution of collective goods to themselves and their neighborhoods. Thus Hirschman's (1970) loyalty option—loyalty to Belaúnde and to democracy as a political way of life—held sway at the beginning of the decade.

As Peru's economy went from bad to worse, and to worse still, thoughts of voting to preserve democracy or to support traditional parties and candidates gave way to coping and then surviving brutal economic circumstances. Loyalty gave way to voice (complaints) and then—as far as AP and then other parties were concerned—to exit, as many of their supporters deserted them. The voting patterns of Lima's poor show this shift with remarkable clarity. First, across the period 1978 to 1986 and its five elections, Lima's poor shifted their votes from one party to another for what they saw as pragmatic and (from their perspective) rational motives. In 1980-P, the principal goal of the election was to ensure the transition to civilian rule, and Belaúnde was overwhelmingly perceived as the most able to manage that task. The left was widely seen as splintered and not worth wasting a vote on; APRA was viewed as disorganized and uncertain following the death of Haya de la Torre.

By 1983-M the left had reorganized itself around Barrantes, and APRA was reemerging from its post-Haya difficulties under the aggressive leadership of Alan García. Both APRA and the left had thus become viable political contenders. Meanwhile Belaúnde had shown himself an uninspired leader whose policies helped usher in what were then seen as grave economic conditions. The exclusively political goals of 1980 concerning the transition to civilian rule thus became increasingly replaced with economic concerns. By 1985-P disenchantment with and exit from AP was almost total, and despite a good record in managing Lima, on the national level Barrantes and IU came up against an invincible juggernaut in García and APRA. The combination of dissatisfaction with AP and the attraction and discipline of APRA made 1985-P no contest. APRA managed by use of García's still powerful coattails to wrest the Lima mayoral race away from the left in 1986-M, although Lima's pobladores split narrowly in favor of Barrantes's reelection. The poblador vote-switching that went on during the first half of the 1980s therefore consisted of exiting from one party to another over time (from one presidential or municipal election to the next, for example) or over type of level of election (from presidential to municipal, for example).

In 1989-M, however, Ricardo Belmont swept Lima's low-income districts. A combination of APRA's disastrous economic performance and a fractured left, as well as the emergence of Fredemo, drew poblador support away not only from the left side of the political spectrum but also from candidates of the traditional parties in general. This tendency became a tsunami or tidal wave in 1990-P1 and 1990-P2, which Alberto Fujimori rode to spectacular victory. Vote-switching thus came to signify not simply changing votes from one party to another but, instead, an exit and rejection of all institutional parties for independent figures and their individual movements.

This large-scale vote-switching meant that, at almost every turn, Lima's poor followed, supported, and propelled the winning candidates. Seldom did the poblador sample back a losing candidate. Indeed, it is strikingly obvious that one vital reason every winning candidate won was because of his ability to attract large numbers of poor voters. The vote-switching found across 1980–1990 indicates that Lima's poor exercised Hirschman's exit option repeatedly, and on a massive scale. Loyalty was obviously a quality that no party developed in any meaningful way with Lima's poor, since each party had in turn showed its inability to manage the economy (AP, APRA) or to hang together as a viable party (the left). And voice—an option whereby complaining could be a means to notify the various parties that they were ineffectual—was for the poor perhaps never a viable mechanism, since the electoral process by definition allows and encourages exit over voice, especially in elections with more than one party participating.[21]

Formal political participation (it will be recalled) consists of involvement in activities directed at influencing the selection of and/or the policy decision-making of government personnel. Given this definition, Lima's poor behaved rationally throughout the decade in their search for some candidate or some party that could address their most fundamental social and economic needs. When they found one party after another seriously wanting, they subsequently deserted all parties and supported antiestablishment candidates whose major attraction was often the lack of any connection to established parties. For the poor, exit included not only moving from one party to another but also moving away from the established parties toward noninstitutional alternatives.

Did the pobladores consider voting a viable means of expressing their demands or of addressing their most pressing and material grievances? The survey data offer strong evidence not only that Lima's poor thought their votes mattered but also that individually and in the aggregate they realized their votes could make a difference in who was elected. The Fujimori election of 1990 was perhaps the first presidential election in Peru where a novice political candidate rode to victory on lower-class support. Undercurrents of class, race, and ethnicity that circulated throughout the 1990-P election helped define the differences between *Lima pituco* and *Lima chicha* more sharply than ever in the formal political arena. The bulk of Fujimori's support came from the cholo populace of Lima, whose overwhelming numerical presence was the reason he did so well in Lima, where Fredemo and Vargas Llosa had their principal electoral strength.[22]

In general Lima's poor participated in the electoral process much as most people do anywhere: some with pride and enthusiasm, some with strong partisan feelings, some in total ignorance of the candidates and their platforms. But virtually all of them voted, in hopes that the electoral process would bring some sort of improvement to their lives. For the most part they appear to have been disappointed. The great majority changed their votes over time on both presidential and local levels, as one and then another party left them no better and sometimes even worse off. Perhaps the linkage between an electoral outcome and changes in physical and economic well-being is a tenuous one at best, and nonexistent much of the time. For Lima's endemically poor, the linkage seemed for the decade of the 1980s to be direct and one way: whoever was elected brought or continued harsh economic and social times. The only rational response was to vote for someone else, which is precisely what they did.

Neither strategic voting nor block voting played much of a role in the 1990 presidential elections. Strategic voting (here understood to mean a vote cast not for a favorite candidate but instead against a candidate to prevent his winning) was not a common phenomenon among Lima's poor (see Schmidt 1996, 1998). In 1990-P1 and 1990-P2, only a small handful of respondents said that their principal reason for voting as they did was to prevent a candidate from winning. As for block voting and the ability of a neighborhood leader to control and to deliver the votes of his community, no evidence of any kind (quantitative data, informant interviews, anecdotes) supports the argument that leaders could or did exercise such control. Undoubtedly the absence of strong, durable parties contributed to this lack of urban *caciquismo*, as did low levels of labor union membership. In general, it may well be oxymoronic to talk of urban machines and local neighborhood bosses on the one hand and of poorly institutionalized political parties on the other.

In somewhat parallel fashion, the local community itself played a negligible role in deciding how to vote—in sharp contrast to its key role in shaping informal political participation. The sample neighborhoods did not vary significantly from one another in how their residents voted in any of the elections. The only pattern that appeared consistently was that Santiago, the oldest and certainly the most developed of all the barrios, voted in a modestly more conservative fashion than did the others, but this pattern has much more to do with the socioeconomic status of its residents than with the physical needs of the community itself.

The vote is the quintessential individual political act compared to grassroots community participation and state-directed petitioning. There can be little doubt that the decisive factors in the poblador vote were pocketbook and the state of the economy. The behavior of the poor was thus from the poblador perspective highly and consistently rational, given the vicissitudes of the Peruvian economy and their effect on the daily life of Lima's poor. The question of whether voting was itself a rational act for the individual citizen is not an issue, since voting was mandatory. But the individual decision-making process of how to vote, which resulted in consistent vote-switching over time and across types of elections, was highly rational given the macro contexts that constrained the pobladores, the extreme limitations under which they operated, and the poverty that enveloped them.

9

....

CONCLUSIONS

THIS STUDY BEGAN with a number of basic notions and concepts to orient the whole discussion of political participation among low-income urban dwellers in Lima from 1970 to 1990. But two major questions have dominated from the start. The first overarching question—which deals with the dependent variable of the whole effort, namely, political participation—asks in what ways Lima's urban poor participated in politics, and whether these ways changed over time. This basic query gave rise to many subsidiary questions. What advantages accrue by conceptualizing participation as formal and informal? What are the benefits gained by using the idea of modes of participation? How useful are Hirschman's three different options for each type of participation?

The second overarching question deals with those factors—that is, the independent variables—that guided, limited, or encouraged participation in the political process. It was posited that four macrolevel factors (the economy, poverty, the state, and state–civil society relations) and three intermediate-level factors (the urban setting of Lima, the district setting, and the specific neighborhood) constitute important influences on arenas, modes, and options of micro behavior. Throughout the study, a whole range of questions based on these seven variables emerged. For example, did economic trends in general, and changes in the level and intensity of macrolevel poverty in particular, influence participation, both formal and informal? How was participatory behavior altered by a state-level regime shift from authoritarianism to democracy? Did the specific neighborhood affect different types of participation? If various economic or political institutions rose or fell in importance, did political behavior change as regards those institutions? What influence did various constraints (or bounds, in Simon's terminology) have on individual behavior?

Political Participation: Elements for Analysis

INFORMAL AND FORMAL PARTICIPATION

The primary concern of the book is political participation: how, in what ways, and with what intensities, did Lima's poor take part in politics from 1970 to 1990? By borrowing from and building on scholars such as Verba and Nie (1972), Booth and Seligson (1978), and more recently Brady, Verba, and Schlozman (1995), I initially considered and adopted a general definition of political participation as those activities designed to influence government and its policies and/or personnel in some fashion. But in the course of the twenty years spent collecting the data, it became clear that such a definition was not sufficiently sensitive to the context in which it had to operate. The definition was, in effect, simultaneously too vague and too narrow: too vague in that words such as "influence," "government," and "personnel" lacked ready empirical referents, and too narrow in that it did not explicitly take into account multiple levels or arenas of government. That is, adopting or insisting upon a conceptualization of political participation as exclusively made up of citizen-state interactions would have meant missing a great deal, for two reasons. First, field observation and the existing literature of the 1970s both made it immediately obvious that Lima's lower classes carried on a vigorous, local-level associational life that had to be incorporated definitionally as well as empirically into the study. Fortunately, beginning fieldwork in 1970 during military rule meant concentrating exclusively on informal political participation. After all, had my fieldwork started after 1980 and after the return of civilian rule, the study might have focused exclusively on voting behavior as political participation. Although such a focus would have had intrinsic interest and be quite justifiable, it would in no way have been a complete examination of political participation by Lima's lower classes.

Since the study did carry over twenty years, the definition of political participation I employed had to retain its usefulness and relevance across a period of time during which the nation's economy, its degree of poverty, the nature of the regime of the state, and the structure of civil society and its relationship with the state, all underwent fundamental change. Still, the omnipresence of poverty throughout the period called for a view of participation that was essentially both rational and instrumental in nature. *Rational*, in that a key as-sumption of the whole study was that people in general, and poor people in particular, will participate in politics when there is a reasonable expectation that some material benefit may eventually be forthcoming, either directly (through local efforts) or indirectly (through petitioning or through the election of a sym-pathetic candidate). And *instrumental*, in that the whole conceptualization of participation concentrated on activities aimed at obtaining, directly or indirectly, public goods or services that would improve neighborhood well-being. With such rational and instrumental goals in mind, both informal (neighborhood-originated) and formal (electoral) involvement became the two components of full political participation.

MODES OF POLITICAL PARTICIPATION

While informal and formal arenas of participating in politics were essential com-ponents of the definition of participation, the notion of modes of participation —that is, of separate sets of activities that differ systematically in how they re-late individuals to their government(s) of participation—became an additional integral part of the whole investigative scheme, for two major reasons. First, when the questionnaire for the 1971 survey was being constructed, Verba and Nie had just introduced their concept of modes of participation (Verba, Nie, and Kim 1971), and testing its analytic and empirical replicability in the some-what exotic setting of lower-class Lima seemed a provocative idea.[1] In addition, when the survey was replicated in 1982, and again in 1985 and 1990, the presence of electoral politics in Peru made continuing the use of modes of participation especially compelling. Verba, Nie, and Kim (1978) had found that voting consti-tuted a distinct mode of participation in each of the seven countries they stud-ied; seeing if it would be a separate mode in Peru following the transition to democracy was an intriguing question. But the primary attraction of modes of participation as an analytical tool came from the longitudinal nature of the in-vestigation. As the survey was repeated, seeing if changes took place in the exist-ence, strength, and stability of modes became, for the first time in any context, empirically feasible.

INDIVIDUAL OPTIONS OR CHOICES

Hirschman's argument (1970) that three options—exit, voice, and loyalty—con-stitute basic choices for individuals confronted with an organization (for exam-ple, a firm or a political party) whose performance is deteriorating appeared well worth testing, especially since the data available on political behavior (microlevel and longitudinal) offered the chance of seeing when citizens resorted to one or more of these options. What sorts of performances or conditions by salient macrolevel organizations would provoke the widespread choice of a specific option? And if that choice did not resolve a deteriorating situation, then what sorts of subsequent choice might ensue?

Political Participation: Empirical Conclusions

These three major areas of inquiry concerning political participation—informal and formal arenas, distinct modes of participation, and available behavioral options—shaped the contours of the study since its inception and constitute much of this book. What conclusions, substantive as well as analytic, can be formed? In the first place, it is obvious that the two-part notion of political participation employed here was essential for comprehending how Lima's pobladores became involved in politics between 1970 and 1990. Without incorporating both formal and informal arenas into the analysis, any treatment would have been incomplete at best, and reaching an understanding of any one of the arenas would have been impossible, since changes in one were frequently reflected in another.

For example, to know that widespread electoral involvement followed the resumption of democratic rule is to know little, since voting was mandatory and people were at the outset enormously frustrated with military rule. But to know that the onset of democracy and of voting did not replace the informal activities that had been in place for many years is to know a good deal more about how the pobladores thought their scarce resources could best be invested. Likewise, this same finding illuminates the less than total confidence the pobladores had that the state would make their own individual neighborhood efforts unnecessary. Or as another example, to know that the level of involvement in state-directed petitioning fell during the mid- and late 1980s may be of some interest (see chapter 6), but to discover that this decline was accompanied by steady or increasing levels of intraneighborhood cooperation and collaboration says a great deal more about what sorts of participatory choices the poor saw as rational during periods of economic crisis.

Joining the arenas of formal and informal participation with the notion of modes of participation allows for even further dissection and understanding of political participation. Formal participation becomes not just a grab bag of electoral activities but instead an orderly set of distinct activities—voting, campaigning—from which individual citizens choose. Likewise, the informal arena is not composed willy-nilly of random acts but is composed of discrete possibilities, most commonly communal activity and particularized contacting (Verba, Nie, and Kim 1978, 53–54).

In the case of Lima, the 1970 data revealed three separate modes of informal behavior: community problem-solving, local involvement, and state petitioning. But as electoral politics reemerged in 1980, what happened to these informal modes? Some of these modes of informal participation remained constant throughout the 1970–1990 period (see chapters 6–8). Involvement in neighborhood activities (collaborating on local projects and being involved with the local organization), for instance, constitutes a strongly defined mode of participation across all four surveys. The pobladores clearly view such activities as being a rational investment of their principal resources (time and energy, if not money). In contrast, petitioning state agencies for aid decreased as time passed, becoming not only a separate, barely discernible mode by 1985 and 1990, but also what might be best labeled a tangential mode in which only small numbers of people participated.

In the formal arena voting was, subsequent to 1980, the single most common political act for the pobladores, and it comprised a highly discrete and stable mode of involvement right across the decade of the 1980s. Such a finding was no surprise, since it matched results from many other nations (Verba, Nie, and Kim 1978; Milbraith and Goel, 1977).[2] Campaigning, however, did not emerge in Lima as a separate mode of participation; rather, it was one behavioral component of what might be best described as an "associational" mode (see tables 5, 7, 9) present in 1982, 1985, and 1990.

Finally, when Hirschman's (1970) behavioral options are brought in as well, both the arenas and the modes of participation are themselves further refined, thanks to the longitudinal nature of the data. That is, it would not be especially useful or accurate to conclude from one survey that the pobladores' use of the exit option was high or that their loyalty was low, since there would be no basis for comparison. But with multiple data points, such statements become meaningful, since changes in the choice of options reveal how the pobladores shifted in their perceptions of what was a rational investment of time in terms of political participation.

In the informal arena, for example, over time the pobladores maintained significant loyalty to local community involvement. Not only did this appear as an empirically separate mode over all four data sets, but it was also a mode of involvement that attracted relatively large numbers of people, given that these were voluntary acts in which people could choose to participate (in contrast to voting, which was mandatory; see tables 2–9). Similarly, the pobladores showed their loyalty by attending local meetings and belonging to neighborhood associations in relatively stable fashion over the years. In addition, it can be intuited that these local activities involved a fair amount of voice involvement. That is, people who were involved in community projects and who attended meetings and belonged to local associations presumably voiced their support or expressed their concerns or made complaints. They also presumably were listened to by local leaders, or else the pobladores would not keep on participating. Yet other voluntary acts showed high levels of desertion or exit over time; petitioning state agencies is a case in point. While petitioning (going to ONDEPJOV and asking for assistance, for example) was in 1970 an activity that involved one-third or more of the respondents (see table 10), by 1985 and 1990 involvement in equivalent acts had dropped into the midteens.

It thus appears that the combination of these three elements—arenas (informal and formal), modes, and options, all analyzed over an extended period of time—provides a powerful set of tools for describing, analyzing, and explaining political participation. In a political setting where different modes of involvement depend in part upon the type of regime in power and in part upon whether, over time, citizens have the opportunity as well as the need to make choices about how they will act, a political setting where involvement in politics operates simultaneously on several levels, ignoring or leaving out any one of these elements would provide a less than complete picture of how people participated in the political process, the dependent variable of the investigation. Yet the picture is still incomplete, for although different kinds of behavior become clear, microlevel participation is in turn affected by a variety of independent macrolevel variables, which not only influence behavior but do so in ways that vary over time.

Factors Affecting Political Participation

I spent some time at the beginning of this study not only in defining microlevel political participation but also in identifying those macrolevel and intermediate factors that could affect lower-class participation, especially over time. Four such factors suggested themselves a priori: the economy; the presence and intensity of poverty; the state, especially its policies and resources; and state–civil society relations.[3] In turn, each of these had to be investigated to see how it might be mediated by the general setting (in this case urban), by the legal status of the individual's dwelling place (whether the individual resided in a legally recognized part of the city, for example), and by the idiosyncracies of the specific neighborhood in which the individual lived.

THE ECONOMY

The macrolevel data offer all the evidence necessary to conclude that Lima's poor went through some extraordinarily difficult times during the period in question (see chapter 3). The devaluation and inflation that began during the latter part of military rule, which helped give rise to the regional and national strikes of the late 1970s, were followed by increasingly hard times in the early to mid-1980s, which were in turn followed by a brutal and unprecedented economic collapse in the late 1980s. The crisis suffered by the country's urban poor obviously had political repercussions.

Informally, Lima's pobladores turned toward self-help solutions to survive the nation's economic travails. Petitioning the state continued, but in much reduced and less coherent form. Economic crisis thus had a direct impact on poblador involvement in certain modes of participation and on the options the pobladores chose to employ in both formal and informal arenas. It was rational for the poor to remain loyal to those tactics that had worked (local community involvement) and to discard those that did not (state petitioning). Formally, on the other hand, the poor first voted for and then rejected one party after another, in what was largely a fruitless search for candidates and parties that could alleviate the crisis. The economic crisis for Lima's poor generated classic issues of the pocketbook, but in one of the most extreme forms that Peru or any Latin America country had ever experienced.

This study concentrates exclusively on the urban poor, and this focus presents the chance to observe these pocketbook effects as they became especially acute. Whereas Peru's rural campesinos or peasantry caught in the economic crisis might have had self-sufficiency agricultural alternatives they could turn to in order to survive, their urban counterparts had no such options. Moreover, as members of the urban labor force who received a monetary income, Lima's lower classes were much more intimately and immediately affected by inflation, devaluation, and rises in the cost of living than were the rural poor. And although it may be true that infrastructure in general—transportation, education, health care, communication—is more highly developed in urban than in rural settings, such infrastructure is also far more essential in the city than in the countryside. The data from several chapters show that in times of economic crisis this urban infrastructure either was inadequate or simply could not function properly; at the same time it became more essential to the poor for it to work. One result was that, as matters continued to worsen, the poor turned to their own devices, such as they were. And although some might praise the poor for their resourcefulness, the degree to which the city of Lima physically deteriorated delegitimated the state to a considerable degree.

By the time the first survey was conducted in 1970, all the neighborhoods selected as research sites were within one or another of the legal districts of the city of Lima. Yet Lima's districts always have been, with few exceptions, extremely homogeneous (see chapter 4). Its wealthy districts tend to be uniformly wealthy, its poor districts uniformly poor. Such homogeneity has meant across the years that poor districts have little to work with; their municipal authorities are hamstrung by a lack of financial and fiscal autonomy and must constantly look to Lima or to the state for resources. This lack of resource capacity is reflected in the low numbers of people who petitioned their local municipalities for assistance.

Finally, the specific neighborhood of residence played a fundamental role in patterns of informal political participation (see chapter 7). Differences existed across the sample neighborhoods in several ways—age, manner of formation, degree of internal development, location, squatter versus slum origin—and all of them influenced at one time and in one form or another how their inhabitants involved themselves in the informal arena. Yet over time these differences tended to smooth out. In 1970 differences in rates and modes of participation were sometimes dramatic across neighborhoods (see chapters 6, 7). But the passage of time saw the younger and needier communities provide—and receive assistance in providing—themselves with many basic goods and services, meaning that after some years or even decades the neighborhoods reached a rough equivalency, and that patterns of informal participation came more or less to resemble one another.[4]

In contrast, patterns of formal involvement showed little variance across the survey neighborhoods. Especially in voting, turnout levels were consistently high across all neighborhoods (campaign involvement was also consistent, but minimal). Even how people voted did not vary significantly in most instances, as old and new residents, slum dwellers and squatters, migrants and natives, all voted with few exceptions along the same general lines in both presidential and municipal elections. Lima's poor reacted strongly to the country's economic turmoil, and they reacted more or less in the same fashion insofar as the candidates and parties they supported were concerned.

POVERTY

Separating the state of the economy from a discussion of poverty is more easily done analytically than it is in real life, since the two are so intertwined. Yet poverty is much more than a discussion of economic ups and downs. A downturn in the overall economy inevitably makes life more difficult for the poor, whereas an upturn may not benefit the poor, either relatively or absolutely.[5]

Early in the study I drew a distinction between macro and micro poverty (see chapter 2). Macrolevel poverty is characterized by a lack of resources, inadequate distribution of those resources, inequalities, and an economic system that cannot or does not address these inequalities. Micro poverty has as its principal economic feature a low or inadequate income, which limits or distorts access to the market economy, to consumer goods, to private sector medical care and education, and to the state and its resources. Politically, micro poverty can produce isolation from the formal political process, often forcing citizens to turn to their own means to confront their individual and collective needs.

Lima's poor went through two cycles of macroeconomic populism, each followed by significant downturns, and poverty in both instances deepened in intensity and broadened in scope. More people found themselves unable to purchase a minimal basket of goods, as purchasing power eroded and inflation took hold. Full-time employment that paid more than a minimum wage and that provided even minimal benefits became scarcer; *buscando cachuelo,* that is, looking for odd jobs or part-time work, became a necessity even for middle-class households, and the informal sector became swollen with Lima's traditionally poor, its newly poor, and its recent immigrants.[6]

One repercussion of the first economic downturn, in the late 1970s, was an upsurge in a variety of demonstrative, frequently ideological, informal activities that involved many of the pobladores and their neighborhoods. But, I argue, many of the effects of such participation—especially the presumed ideological shift of the masas populares to the left—appear in hindsight to have been short-lived (see chapter 7). By the midpoint of Belaúnde's second term, economic conditions had clearly worsened, but this downturn did not reproduce the large-scale participatory mobilization of the late 1970s. And when mid-1987 ushered in virtually total economic collapse and profound levels of poverty, once again broad, ideologically motivated mobilization did not occur. Rather, given the severity of the crisis, the poor banded together as best they could, producing as they did so a variety of largely informal survival mechanisms.

In formal terms, the pobladores did indeed support leftist candidates in 1978-CA, then again in 1980-M, and especially in 1983-M. But by the mid- and late

1980s such support just as clearly had eroded. Extreme macro and micro poverty gave rise to voting patterns that showed a desperate search on all levels (presidential and municipal) for candidates, traditional or otherwise, who could alleviate the crisis.

The context of metropolitan Lima had certain effects on both the presence and the impacts of poverty. Although Lima has a lower percentage of extremely or chronically poor people than other regions of the country, the absolute numbers of poor people are considerable, given the size of the city (almost 7 million in 1990) and the growth of the percentage of poor Limeños across the decade of the 1980s (Webb and Fernandez Baca 1992, 449; Instituto Cuánto 1995, chap. 2). In addition, of course, Lima is the national capital. It is overwhelmingly the nation's largest city, is still the largest pole of attraction for migrants from all other regions, and contains the single largest concentration of voters in the country. The combination of these and other factors made poverty and the poor in Lima highly salient and highly political. By 1990, with close to half of Lima's population residing in its pueblos jóvenes, poverty was never far away.

Informally, Lima's poor have been remarkable for decades for their abilities to cooperate on individual and communal undertakings, especially housing. Much of the city's growth since World War II has been uncontrolled by formal planning, and the creation of new districts has been largely in reaction to such growth. These new, poor districts need a great deal of assistance, and since all the national ministries and state agencies are located in Lima, they become visible symbols (and sometimes targets) for the grievances and petitions of the city's poor. Collaborative neighborhood-level participation remained one of the most predictable of all modes of involvement from 1970 to 1990.

Formally, national candidates for office necessarily spend a good deal of time and money campaigning in Lima, and the race for mayor of Lima is widely viewed as the second most important electoral contest in the country after the presidency. No presidential or municipal candidate was able to win without the support of the city's lower-class voters. Indeed, the pobladores in the samples frequently voted for winning candidates in numbers larger than shown in aggregate district-level data.

The presence and influence of poverty on the neighborhood level emerged most clearly longitudinally. The younger and less developed a neighborhood (Primero de Enero and Pampa de Arena, for example), the greater the level of informal participation, whether it be involvement in local undertakings, in the neighborhood association, or in state-directed petitioning. Over time, as immediate needs susceptible to self-help were addressed, these differences diminished, not because all needs were satisfied but because those that remained were more intractable and required external assistance. Both local involvement and state petitioning approached similar levels across all the research sites, with two exceptions. The first exception was Santiago, the older, well-established neighborhood with the lowest levels of individual and household poverty of all the research sites. Informal participatory levels in Santiago were lower, right from the start, and stayed that way. The other exception was the opposite: 28 de Julio, an equally old neighborhood, but one that had severe problems with high population densities and that, overall, was by all estimates among the two or three poorest in Lima. Across the 1980s, 28 de Julio had somewhat higher levels of state petitioning, since many of the problems its residents faced could not be resolved without state aid. But even including these exceptions, interneighborhood differences so notable in 1970 had been smoothed over considerably by 1990 (see tables 10–13).

In the formal arena, the specific neighborhood made little difference at any time. Voter turnout was for all intents and purposes the same, which is not surprising, perhaps, given mandatory voting. Ideological patterns of voting varied but little across presidential and municipal elections, with the exception of Santiago, the least poor of the neighborhoods, which voted somewhat more conservatively than did the others. In other areas, such as involvement in campaigning, cross-neighborhood differences were minimal.

During those periods that macrolevel poverty spread and deepened, political involvement among the poor changed. In the informal arena, as state relevance and legitimacy diminished, state-directed petitioning also dropped off and local involvement either remained steady or increased. In formal behavior, poverty played a major role in the vote-switching that manifested first as the pobladores moved from party to party and later as they moved from supporting established parties to supporting independent candidates, regardless of specific neighborhood.

THE STATE

One essential function of the state is its ability to order a society, by which is meant the capacity of a state to penetrate a society, respond to that society's needs, and distribute resources within that society. This characterization parallels Huntington's argument that a state is developed to the degree that its responsive and distributive capacity is roughly equivalent to the demands, needs, and expectations generated within a society (Huntington 1968). As a state seeks to increase its capacity to meet society's demands, one key demand-capacity linkage lies in what mechanisms or means the state puts in place for society to articulate its needs.[7]

Across the two decades covered by this study, one fundamental aspect of the Peruvian state changed, while another equally basic characteristic persisted. The first occurred in 1980 when a transition election saw the military step down and the reestablishment of civilian rule. This transition obviously affected political participation. The new institutions or rules of the game, embodied in the 1978 constitution, mandated universal suffrage and obligatory voting or (in the terminology of this study) formal participation. Yet the data from the post-1980 surveys clearly demonstrate that this formal arena for political participation was an addition to, not a replacement for, the informal arena. The new rules allowed Lima's lower classes to have what sometimes became a key voice in who would govern them, but this formal articulation and aggregation of preferences was from the start a mode of participation empirically separated from the informal activities that had been present during the 1970s.

As much as this regime change signaled a change in available modes of participation, however, another characteristic of the Peruvian state remained stable, indeed became even more noticeable. This was its inability both to generate adequate resources for its citizenry, especially its poor, and to distribute even these inadequate resources efficiently or equitably. The macroeconomic populist policies of both the Velasco and the García administrations produced severe and (in the case of García) profound economic crises, which tragically and starkly revealed this incapacity in rampant inflation, crumbling infrastructure, totally inadequate health care, and the virtual absence of any social safety net.

Under such macro conditions, the poor reacted rationally. On one hand, they continued to participate in the formal arena by voting, because they realized that in the aggregate they could make a difference in the outcome of an election, and especially on the municipal level. Voting was also mandatory, of course. But their highly volatile voting behavior (see chapters 6, 8) argues that Lima's poor saw vote-switching (the exit option) as more rational than party or ideological loyalties.

On the other hand, through their informal behavior the poor showed that they recognized the state could not or would not provide for them. The decline in the number of pobladores who petitioned the state (most notably the drop between 1985 and 1990) provided compelling evidence that the poor viewed such activities as inefficacious and irrational. The state as a source of assistance became tragically irrelevant to the poor, just as the needs of the poor for assistance were becoming increasingly desperate because of economic breakdown and deepening poverty. In addition, Lima's poor saw weakness not just in the national government. The minimal levels of interaction with district or municipal authorities showed that the sample saw little reason for spending time in requesting aid from authorities whose resources were so limited.

The pobladores were thus left to their own resources, and they acted accordingly. As the García years took their toll, for instance, the numbers of pobladores involved in problem-solving activities (measured by frequent involvement, recent involvement, petitioning neighborhood leaders) rose in every neighborhood. The post-1980 presence of formal political participation (voting), an activity sanctioned and encouraged by the state, did not replace the informal tactics pobladores had utilized during authoritarian rule, especially those operating within the specific neighborhood. When the democratic state was reestablished in 1980, neither its electoral mechanisms nor its agencies reduced the need of Lima's poor to depend upon their own resources for material aid.

THE STATE AND CIVIL SOCIETY

A transition from authoritarian to democratic rule not only means that the citizenry will have new avenues to aggregate and articulate their needs. It also inevitably means that society will be able to organize itself autonomously, free of a repressive state that prohibits organization at all or of a corporatist state that restricts social organizations to state-sanctioned and controlled groups. In a word, a society becomes *civil,* insofar as this term suggests a society in which independent self-generated organizations voluntarily engage in activities to pursue their interests. The poor citizens of a poor nation will join in this process as best they can, and many of their efforts will be dedicated to organizing themselves to influence the distribution of material goods and resources through electoral and nonelectoral ways.[8]

A multiplicity of organizations aimed at providing goods or at electing sympathetic leaders does not necessarily raise the probability that such goods or leaders will appear, however. If the capacity of the state does not increase, or if the political willingness of state leaders to make goods available does not increase, then the poor may become frustrated. Frustration can potentially lead to a variety of possible outcomes: civil unrest, impatience or alienation, loss of legitimacy by the state, increasing electoral support for antiestablishment political leaders, or the creation of defiantly autonomous organizations.

During the authoritarian rule of the 1970s, the state attempted to control political participation through a variety of corporatist agencies, most notably SINAMOS. To put it bluntly, SINAMOS was understaffed, underfunded, counterproductive, short-lived, and resented by its client groups. As the military began its withdrawal and as the economy suffered in the mid- and late 1970s, nonstatist ideological, radical, and class-based organizations penetrated into Lima's pueblos jóvenes, giving rise to most of the outcomes just mentioned.

Yet such activities were short-lived. By 1982 a combination of repressive and demobilizational policies enacted at the end of military rule, economic hardship (especially unemployment and underemployment), increasing party attention to campaign and electoral activities, and an overall desire to implant and sustain civilian rule discouraged broad, continuing protest behavior. Yet the poor's voting behavior certainly revealed protest against the status quo and any party that was perceived to represent it. Widespread vote-switching by Lima's lower classes on both presidential and municipal levels meant not only that none of the political parties established any sort of firm support among the city's poor, but also that the poor would discard one party after another until they were convinced someone could and would help them (Fujimori, for example), whom they then supported in substantial fashion.

Informally, the city's poor played a major if sometimes unappreciated role in re-creating Peru's civil society after 1980. Respondents in the samples belonged to a variety of organizations; many were neighborhood-based organizations that allowed the poor to pursue their immediate interests as best they could. That these organizations were largely and relatively successful is revealed in their staying power across such difficult social and economic circumstances. The poor would not participate in—and contribute their extremely scarce resources of time, money, and energy to—such activities unless they perceived that it was worth their while to do so.

Lima's Poor Across Twenty Years

From 1970 to 1990, Lima's poor experienced two regimes, two military and two civilian presidents, several metropolitan and district mayors, three economic downturns (one of which was unprecedentedly brutal in its consequences), significant social protest, and a serious attempt at violent insurgency. Throughout it all the poor survived, endured, coped, and persevered. They hoped for something better, a hope that was frequently denied them; when improvement did occur, this was generally a result of their own efforts. Yet improvements did in fact take place. One has only to compare the state of housing in either Primero de Enero or Pampa de Arena over twenty years, for example, to see how much the poor individually and collectively invested money, time, and effort in their neighborhoods. Moreover, anecdotally and in the aggregate, some basic socioeconomic conditions changed within Lima's lower classes. Education levels rose, for example; so did occupational status; and even the overall provision of services expanded slowly. All these gains were basically modest and frequently suffered from false starts and real declines. Perhaps the best that can be said is that Lima's poor *managed*—they managed to survive and endure on their own, frequently in spite of the state and not because of it.

What final conclusions emerge from these twenty years? Two separate but related questions suggest themselves, one macro and one micro. The first deals with the poor and democracy, while the second deals with the poor and participation.

THE POOR AND DEMOCRACY

Adam Przeworski (1991) has proposed that any democracy, but especially a new one, must convince its citizens they have some specific minimum probability of benefiting from their involvement in it. If citizens are persuaded that this is so, it means among other things that citizens accept democracy above other possible alternative political choices because they perceive their interests are better met being on the losing side in a democracy than are their probable gains (material and nonmaterial) of winning in a nondemocracy. Insofar as material gains are concerned, in order for a democracy to be convincing to its citizenry, it must provide its members not only with a higher minimum welfare floor than its nondemocracy alternatives but also with the possibility of a higher ceiling, whereby citizens can have "real opportunities to improve their material benefits" (Przeworski 1991, 13). In cases where one or other of these provisions is missing or perceived to be missing, then one or more alternatives to democracy (populism, authoritarianism, revolution) may become attractive options to different societal groups.

One major nonmaterial gain that democracy offers its citizens is the chance to influence the distribution of power, either directly by winning an election or indirectly by being able to influence those who do. Yet democracy demands that all groups in society accept the possibility that they might lose an election and power. Indeed, Przeworski defines democracy in large part as a system in which parties lose elections (1991, 10).[9] Democracy thus offers all its members (at least in theory) a chance to attain power, since the outcome of elections is indeterminate ex ante and since the winner of one election is not guaranteed to win the next. Uncertainty is therefore not only desirable in a democracy; it is essential.

While uncertainty about political outcomes is definitionally essential for a democracy, uncertainty about economic outcomes may be harmful or fatal. If economic uncertainty (especially in the form of a sustained crisis) occurs in a democratic system, and if the minimum floor and ceiling postulated by Przeworski collapse, then frustration or desperation, especially within low-income groups, may rise to such levels that incumbents will lose elections to the opposition, who in turn will lose to other opponents, until all existing party alternatives have been elected and have lost. At such a point, several outcomes are possible: (1) independent, nonpartisan, and likely populist candidates may win but may have trouble governing; (2) the military may become restive and move against not only the government but the system; (3) revolutionary groups dedicated to constructing an entirely new (nondemocratic) system may gain strength.

Any one of these outcomes could eliminate a central core of democracy: providing its citizens with "security from arbitrary violence" (Przeworski 1991, 31). Democracy certainly claims to offer its citizens freedom from arbitrary arrest, for example, and other forms of capricious violence. However, democracy may be helpless to prevent its own collapse when it is confronted by a polarizing populist figure gaining power, for example, or a military bent on seizing control, or an insurgent movement utilizing violence.

A much more intimate and crucial relationship between the poor and the success of a democracy lies in the need for a widespread belief that democracy is in the long run conducive to economic development. Przeworski (1991) argues that "if some important political forces have no chance to win distributional conflicts and if democracy does not improve the material conditions of losers, those who expect to suffer continual deprivation under democratic institutions will turn against them" (32). But are matters quite so clear-cut?

Precisely what, for example, constitutes an "important" political force or group? Is importance to be measured in numbers? Or in economic strength? If such a group feels continued deprivation, will that group necessarily turn against democracy? Might not recent failures by alternatives (the military, for example, or a populist regime), or the presence of a violent and radical insurgent group, persuade even dissatisfied groups to continue to support a democratic regime, if not a particular party, in the belief that democracy represents the *mal menor* (least worst) option available? Peru's political history since 1970 provides considerable evidence that, although democracy may not have been able to deliver sometimes even minimal resources and services to its poor majority, that majority was still willing to back democratic rule in spite of its shortcomings, precisely because the other alternatives either had recently failed (the military, populism) or were otherwise unacceptable (the Shining Path).

The experience of Lima's poor in this study during the 1970s and 1980s thus

appears to offer some instructive empirical modifications to Przeworski's generalization about economic performance, democracy, and the behavior of groups
(and individuals within them) unlikely to win distributional battles. Lima's poor
participated in many ways in the political process under both military and civilian rule. They cooperated with one another; they joined a variety of groups;
they petitioned authorities (neighborhood as well as municipal and national);
they voted. Few of these activities had, however, any real chance of fundamentally affecting the allocation of resources, regardless of whether these were direct assistance in the form of attention, technical assistance, public works, or
more remote and abstract objectives such as policies aimed at job creation or
income redistribution.

Yet despite these real limitations, over the past twenty years Lima's lower
classes may well have made a substantial contribution to the consolidation of
democracy in Peru. (Whether other actors or elements or structures in Peru
can or will match their contribution is very much an open question.) To justify
this claim, consider that many scholars have pondered what sorts of conditions
are necessary if not sufficient for a democratic regime to become consolidated.
Most agree that these conditions include the need for elite accords and agreements, economic growth and development, rising levels of socioeconomic well-
being, the creation of new institutions (political parties, electoral systems), an
appropriate political culture, a thriving civil society, certain religious traditions,
state legitimacy, and a rule of law (Lipset 1994; Dahl 1971; Diamond, Linz, and
Lipset 1990). While all these conditions are essential for democratization, they
all have one crucial shortcoming for the Peruvian case under discussion and for
Third World societies in general: they focus on elite attitudes and behavior, and
on structures and rules that elites initiate or control. Few pay more than cur-
sory attention to the roles and influences of the masses in the democratization
process.

The subject of civil society requires that society at large be considered. Civil
society, as employed in the democratic consolidation literature, refers to those
groups, networks, or organizations in a society that are free and voluntary (not
mediated, sanctioned, or created by the state), that are generally horizontal in
nature, that address public interests (the family is not included, for example),
that develop a relationship or orientation toward the state, that are plural in
nature (not the product of a corporatist system), and that exhibit "partiality"
(they do not include organizations such as political parties that are exclusively
political in nature). They act as a buffer between the state and the individual
members of society and are critical for the consolidation of democracy (Lipset

1994; Gellner 1991; Cohen and Arato 1992, esp. chap. 10). Putnam (1993) has, in a widely cited study, argued that the viability of democracy depends upon the presence of a local civil culture. Lipset (1994, 13) argues that

> certain democratic values and rights have evolved primarily through conflict among groups in society. Instead of struggling to attain elite political power, various groups—class, religious, economic, professional and the like—compete with one another and the state for popular attention, for power to carry out their own agendas. . . . *these groups form an alternative to the state and its control of society.* (emphasis added)

Lima's poor compete for popular attention, they do not aspire to elite power, and their neighborhood organizations form an alternative to the state. They have come to constitute, in fact, a vital part of Peru's civil society and are, and will continue to be, critical to the consolidation of democracy in Peru, since they have for twenty years and more been building, as best they can, what are clearly viable civil organizations. What has been missing is an equally clear and valid analogue by the state that can integrate and cooperate and mesh with what the poor have done.

The question therefore lies not with Lima's poor but with the Peruvian state and with its elites, who may not realize the richly beneficial aspects of what the city's masas populares have created. It is ironic, of course, that Lima's lower-class civil society has come into existence not because of state and elite policies but out of necessity and because of the willingness of the poor themselves to create their own ad hoc problem-solving and state-petitioning mechanisms. As would be expected, the poor have more faith in their own devices. They certainly are willing to petition and demand resources from the state, and to vote so as to have an influence on who makes policy and who might respond to them. But in times of crisis, they fall back on their own initiatives and organization, unsure as they are (because of much experience) that the state will have anything to offer them.

Lima's poor intentionally and unintentionally have done their part and more to consolidate democracy in Peru. Formally, they vote and accept the uncertain outcome of elections. Informally, they sustain a rich civil society and develop mechanisms that link them to the state. All these activities comprise essential ingredients for democracy, regardless of whether the poor think of them in such a way. But until and unless elites recognize these contributions, especially the informal, democracy may continue to be imperfectly joined and differentially perceived by its constituents.

THE POOR AND RATIONAL PARTICIPATION

Perhaps the most essential micro concern that underlies the whole study is linked to eternal questions about people in general. Do they react passively to conditions that are beyond their control? Or do they have the will to respond to such conditions and, in responding, create opportunities for themselves?

One side of this issue has argued that the dependent status of the Third World generates processes and institutions that create an endemic poverty, and that the masses ensnared in that poverty can only struggle helplessly. The other side has countered that human agency can modify society in the face of overwhelming odds, and that change is possible even under broad structural constraints. In simplified terms, the argument revolves around determinism versus free will.

Lima's poor have been characterized throughout this study as operating under conditions of bounded rationality. The bounds that constrain the poor are all too obvious: unpredictable economic conditions, endemic poverty, a frequently stultifying state, and state–civil society linkages that for the poor border on irrelevance. As Bryan Roberts (1995) puts it: "Above all, perhaps, the exigencies of daily life in the face of poverty, an inadequate material infrastructure and an unresponsive state . . . engender vigorous, if piecemeal, grass roots organization to demand new and defend old rights" (187).

But here exists, I would argue, an additional, ambiguous, nonstructural, micro constraint on behavior: namely, Lima's poor know they are poor. They know that what they can do individually and collectively to survive or transcend their poverty is distinctly limited. They realize that the state is limited by its resources; they know they have strictly limited means to influence the state and its leaders. This knowledge might be viewed, especially by an outside observer, as an overwhelming constraint.[10] Such knowledge is likely to be seen, especially from an external perspective, as inherently and enormously self-defeating: why even try to do anything? On the other hand this knowledge, from the poor's perspective, prevents behavior that is inefficient, wasteful, or risky. The realization of limitations defines rational behavioral responses for individuals, groups, and nation-states.

Under such constraints and realizations, what sort of behavior is rational? My approach to this question has been to assume that the actual behaviors by the poor to improve their material lot in life are rational, especially if these behaviors are not mandated and if they persist over an extended period of time. This assumption rests on the simple notion that people, especially poor people, will not consistently behave in ways that they perceive as harmful to their own well-being or as a waste of time and scarce resources. Rather, they become involved in activities that have at least a minimal chance of helping them survive and cope. It also means that the poor can and will modify their behavior over time as circumstances and constraints change.

Across twenty years in Lima, the poor behaved as they could, and in ways they deemed appropriate. Informally, if their participation in an activity produced some material benefits, and if their well-being or liberty was not threatened, then their behavior was rational. If their involvement paid no benefit or became too risky, or if circumstances changed, then their reaction was also rational: their behavior changed. Formally, they voted because they wished to do so, because they had personal, ideological, or partisan preferences, and because they wished to avoid sanctions. But dynamically, they decided whom to vote for on the basis of who they thought would best represent them and favor them, and who would attempt to make their poverty bearable if not ameliorated. If their selection did not live up to these really rather modest expectations, then they changed their votes. Exit became far more rational than either voice or loyalty.

Yet neither their informal nor their formal participation resolved their problems. The poor knew better than anyone else that nothing they could do would by itself produce better economic times, eliminate poverty, create a responsive state, or make state-society relations efficacious. But such knowledge did not produce inaction; quite the contrary, Lima's pobladores were proactive in a variety of activities and modes across the twenty years in question.

Changes in how they participated did not have to do simply with the passage of time. Rather, changes in participation occurred in reaction to what happened around them. And a great deal happened over the twenty years covered by this study. Enormous economic vicissitudes, enduring and frequently worsening poverty, and a weakening state meant that the poor constantly had to decide what kind of behavior would be rational. Poverty was, broadly speaking, constant for the poor, over the two decades in question (that is, it never disappeared), but its severity and behavioral ramifications were not constant. And as poverty varied, so did its impact on the poor, on their behavior, on the state, and on state–civil society relationships.

As economic conditions deteriorated first in the late 1970s, then again in the mid-1980s, and again most profoundly in the late 1980s, all the many macro aspects of poverty (inflation, cost of living, lack of jobs) deepened as well. In turn, micro or individual poverty also worsened, as people tried desperately to find ways to survive, to obtain ever more costly food and other necessities, to hold on to jobs, and to look for more work. For the state, deepening poverty meant increasing demands from increasing numbers of increasingly desperate people, just as state resources were not only diminishing but were also being stretched beyond capacity.[11] As a result, civil society—and especially, but by no means exclusively, its low-income members—often saw the state as irrelevant.

Under such circumstances, and in rational response to them, the poor changed their participatory behavior. Formally, the poor voted but, across time, showed wide swings as to whom they voted for. Incumbents in national and municipal elections found that once-strong support often evaporated in only a few years. Ideological stances and party identifications came to count for less, ultimately becoming liabilities as independents (whose primary claim to office was no experience and no partisan affiliation) won on all levels. Informally, the poor participated more in local neighborhood groups and tactics than anything else; they perceived dependence on the state or petitioning the state for assistance as being a waste of time, or largely useless, or, in a word, irrational.

It is equally clear, however, that formally as well as informally Lima's poor did not become marginalized or alienated, at least from one another or as neighbors, because such behavior would also have been irrational. They tried to do what needed to be done with their own resources, and sometimes (surprisingly so, considering the obstacles) they succeeded. Take one single fact: Lima's pueblo jóven population grew by 160 percent from 1971 to 1993. It was the poor's ability and willingness and their involvement that occupied land, built housing, created neighborhoods, and in general added to the physical and cultural expansion of Lima, in spite of laws and other obstacles against such activities. It was their behavior that created informal alternatives to the formal economy and to formal employment when the latter (and the state) could not or would not do what they needed done. It was their neighborhood and local organizations that contributed immensely to Lima's civil society under both authoritarian and democratic regimes. And it was their electoral weight that almost always made the difference in citywide races.[12]

These behaviors and their quite remarkable accomplishments bring us once again to the conclusion offered earlier. The poor have done far more than their fair share in creating and maintaining a democratic society. If the presence of non–state sanctioned organizations indeed comprises one essential component of democracy, then Lima's pobladores may be owed an incalculable debt—if and when the state and Peru's political elites and their parties can ever carry out their share.

10

EPILOGUE

This study formally ended in 1990. I completed the survey and my in-depth interviews, I visited the neighborhoods one last time, and I decided to call it quits on the research. It would have been possible to extend the project, but I thought twenty years a good round number. Yet, for a variety of reasons, completing the manuscript took longer than I anticipated, and now almost a decade has passed since the final survey was done.

Fujimori's Administrations, 1990–1998

Peru, Lima and its urban poor, their political involvement, and politics in general have not stopped, of course. Indeed, the past eight years have been tumultuous and in many ways unprecedented. Alberto Fujimori's first term started bluntly when he informed the Peruvian people that the country was in disastrous shape (which everyone knew) and that he had a plan for overcoming the nation's problems (which not everyone knew or believed). Two weeks after taking office, Fujimori unleashed one of Latin America's most sweeping and draconian neoliberal economic reforms. It was clear from the start of his administration that he focused on two all-important goals: to put the country's economic house in order (primarily, to halt its 7,600 percent inflation and to reinstate Peru in the good graces of the international financial community), and to confront and overcome the Shining Path.

For the first goal, Fujimori became (in part because he had no choice) a neo-liberal true believer. State resources had been exhausted, budget deficits were uncontrollable, and international watchdog agencies such as the IMF, the World Bank, and the Inter-American Development Bank had all made it clear that Peru would receive no further credit unless it could bring some order out of chaos. As a result, Fujimori began a drastic cutback on state expenditures, many of which directly hurt Peru's lower classes. Government subsidies disappeared without warning on basic food items and other essentials (in one instance, the cost of gasoline rose about 3,000 percent in a matter of a few days) as the market was allowed to determine prices. Critics claimed that, within a few months, the number of poor people in Peru rose to an all-time level of two-thirds of the populace, as families could no longer afford even a minimal basket of food. The state itself was slimmed down drastically as thousands of state employees were let go and privatization became a mantra.

Much has been written on Fujimori's social policies, and I do not intend to summarize or recapitulate that literature here.[1] On one hand, something drastic had to be done in Peru; the economy was in free fall, and hyperinflation (inflation greater than triple digits) had enormously severe effects on low-income groups (Cardoso 1992). But whether Fujimori's policies had to be as brutal as they were has been the subject of much debate. Regardless of the debate, the effects on the poor were dramatic.

As for the Shining Path, Fujimori had only a few options. He could negotiate (a nonstarter, as the movement was completely unwilling to talk). He could try a military solution, which under García had not only failed but been counterproductive. He could infiltrate (difficult, risky, and slow). Or he could attempt, through hard police work and intelligence, to capture Abimael Guzmán and thus decapitate the movement. Fujimori concentrated his scarce resources on this last possibility, and on September 12, 1992, Guzmán was captured without a shot being fired in a house in middle-class Lima. The results were dramatic. Peru experienced immense, delirious relief, and Fujimori's popularity soared, never to reach below 50 percent for the rest of his first term.

Given the condition of Peru when he assumed office, there can be little surprise that Fujimori's policies toward the economy and terrorism enjoyed huge support. The Peruvian citizenry was willing to ignore—or at least put up with —any of the high costs of his first term. Such costs ranged across the economic (the dramatic rise in the cost of living, the consistently high underemployment rates in the economy), the social (continued deep-seated poverty, social inequality, questionable human rights policies), and the political. This last included Fujimori's surprise *autogolpe* (literally, "self-coup"), which occurred on May 4,

1992, when he announced he was shutting down the congress and the Ministry of Justice and that he would rule singlehandedly.

Domestic reaction was mixed; the military made no effort to prevent or contest the coup, and polls showed that his action produced only a mild drop in his support (the upper classes showed higher disapproval ratings than did the poor). International reaction was stronger or at least more united in its opposition. Fujimori strongly defended his act, but a few months later called for congressional elections and for the new congress to rewrite the constitution. Several main opposition parties boycotted the elections, which meant that Fujimori supporters won a majority. A new constitution was produced, voted on, and approved in a national referendum on October 31, 1993. Although Fujimori saw the new constitution approved, the margin of victory (52.3 percent in favor to 47.7 percent against) was much less than his opinion polls. The new constitution contained two major departures for Peru: it allowed for the direct reelection of the president, and it created a unicameral legislature. Both these changes came at the specific behest of Fujimori. The autogolpe postponed the municipal elections scheduled for 1992; they were later held on January 29, 1993. By 1990 most of the major political parties had lost support (see chapter 8), and during his first term Fujimori did little or nothing to prevent their disintegration or the withering away of many other social and political institutions.

In the formal (electoral) political arena, such deinstitutionalization meant several things for Peru as it continued to struggle toward a democratic way of life. In the first place, the collapse of the party system meant an upsurge in candidates who were avowedly nonpartisan and indeed antipartisan, including most notably Fujimori himself, who owed a good deal of success to not being affiliated with the traditional parties, and Ricardo Belmont, who won two consecutive terms as Lima's mayor (1989–1993 and 1993–1996). For Fujimori, the fluid nature of party politics meant a divided opposition, a state of affairs very much to his liking. In addition, with a weak and splintered congress, Fujimori could also continue to centralize power in the executive branch, either into his own hands or into those of the Ministry of the Presidency, a position first created during the García administration and then revived by Fujimori in 1992.[2]

Fujimori's first term in office had its ups and downs, but there can be little doubt that society, with regards the economy and terrorism, was in many ways in far better shape in 1995, when he ran for reelection, than it had been in 1990. The economy showed robust signs of recovery, at least in macro terms. Inflation fell from 7,600 percent in 1990 to about 12 percent in 1995, and the gross national product grew by more than 12 percent in 1994, the highest of any country in the world. The capture of Guzmán seemed to support Fujimori's 1990 claim that terrorism would be a thing of the past by 1995. Yet even so, he faced some fourteen opponents in 1995, and the leading opposition candidate, Javier Perez de Cuellar, was the former secretary general of the United Nations and arguably the best-known Peruvian in the world.

Fujimori nevertheless won in an enormous landslide, taking almost three votes to Perez de Cuellar's one (64 to 22 percent). Such totals not only were a huge personal win but offered overwhelming evidence that the traditional party system was in complete disarray. IU, APRA, AP, and PPC took a total of less than one-tenth of the popular vote; not one of them took more than 5 percent. But even as Fujimori won, numerous signs indicated that his second term might be more difficult than the first. For one example, although macroeconomic signs were favorable, poverty, social inequality, unemployment, underemployment all remained deeply rooted problems. And as another, Fujimori showed signs shortly after taking office that he was determined to interpret the 1993 constitution's reelection clause as allowing him to run again in the year 2000.[3]

Yet the 1995 municipal elections revealed that Fujimori's popularity might in fact be fragile, and certainly nontransferable. In these elections Jaime Yoshiyama, a close friend and potential heir apparent to Fujimori, was opposed by Alberto Andrade, twice a highly popular mayor of the district of Miraflores. After a seesaw campaign Andrade was able to pull off a somewhat surprising 54–46 percent victory. His victory immediately put Andrade in the role of very early favorite to oppose Fujimori in the presidential race for the year 2000.

Although the ultimate end of the hostage crisis precipitated by the Tupac Amaru Revolutionary Movement (MRTA) in Lima in 1996 gave Fujimori a significant bounce in the polls, this spike proved short-lived indeed. A month or two later public opinion had returned to an approval rating of between 30 and 40 percent. Various scandals in Fujimori's administration with the high-handed and questionable tactics to cover them up kept the political fires burning. In a move reminiscent of Roosevelt's packing of the Supreme Court in the United States, Fujimori dismissed three judges on the Constitutional Court when it appeared the court would rule against his running in 2000. A Lima television channel revealed that Vladimiro Montesinos, a close but particularly noxious advisor to Fujimori with close ties to the military and the intelligence communities, was receiving an annual salary approaching $600,000.[4] In response, Fujimori declared that Baruch Ivcher, the owner of the television station and an Israeli-born Peruvian citizen, would have his citizenship revoked and would be deported. Still other scandals involved the misuse of intelligence for partisan purposes. The result was, in mid-1997, street demonstrations the likes of which Peru and Lima had not seen for years. Although the 2000 elections were still some time off, Fujimori's plans for a third term seem premature, risky, and anything but secure.

Lima's Urban Poor, 1990–1998

As this brief account suggests, Lima's poor bore a highly disproportionate burden of Fujimori's economic policies in the early 1990s. Although Fujimori perhaps did not have much choice about implementing severe readjustment policies, he also made little or no effort to provide a safety net for those who were bound to be hurt the most. Just what was done, and what happened, in both the formal and the informal political arenas?

THE URBAN POOR, THE STATE, AND INFORMAL POLITICAL BEHAVIOR

Fujimori created a Programa Social de Emergencia (Social Emergency Program) in the first few months of his term that was ostensibly designed to provide emergency employment, but the program had a minimal budget and was directly under the president's control, presumably so Fujimori could benefit from the distribution of urgently needed social resources. This program spent only 14 percent of what was originally programmed in its first year, which was a total of $89 million, for a target population of at least 7 million people. It should be noted that Fujimori was spending $60 million per month to repay Peru's external debt arrears (Graham 1994, 106–07). The Fondo Nacional para el Desarrollo y Compensación Social (Foncodes; National Fund for Development and Social Compensation) was a more ambitious program created in 1991, and although it received international backing and had more success it was still inadequate and politicized. Fujimori from the start resisted any policy that he could not personally control or that would not redound to his personal political credit.

As inflation came under control, the gross national product began to regrow and investment reappeared. Fujimori then added to Foncodes in 1992 by creating two more state agencies, one with a direct effect on the poor (Pronaa) in general and another (Fonavi) with a direct effect on the urban poor in particular. The Programa Nacional de Asistencia Alimentaria (Pronaa; National Nutritional Assistance Program) was established to provide food and nutritional supplements for poor children in both rural and urban areas. After a slow and much criticized start (Burgos 1994), Pronaa by 1994 was dispensing almost three thousand rations daily to Peru's poor, generally with the direct assistance of the military, and not through the multiple autonomous neighborhood or NGO (nongovernmental organization) channels created in the 1980s. For example, Pronaa skirted the Vaso de Leche programs as well as the thousands of communal kitchens and mothers' clubs already in place. As Kay (1996–1997) concludes: "rather than working with or complementing organizations already in existence, Pronaa . . . sought to compete with them and to weaken their influence" (80) primarily so that Fujimori could maintain control over the process and take credit for whatever successes occurred.

The Fondo Nacional de Vivienda (Fonavi; National Housing Fund) was created to make low-cost loans available to the urban poor in Peru for subsidizing house, school, and other construction and improvement projects in economically marginal areas, especially in Lima's pueblos jóvenes. Kay (1996–1997) notes that to label these programs purely public relations gestures because of the political motivation behind them would be at least partially erroneous. Loans did reach thousands of marginal homeowners in Lima and elsewhere, through Fonavi, as did access to formal education and medical care through the construction of schools and medical posts.

Yet all these programs—Foncodes, Fonavi, and Pronaa—were controlled and directed by Fujimori himself or by the Ministry of the Presidency, which became an increasingly important centralized source of patronage for Fujimori as his first term unfolded. By the middle of 1994 the Ministry of the Presidency, through Foncodes, "was responsible for the management of 4,760 support projects, most of which (54 percent) were public works that kept an estimated 25,000 employed in new jobs (on a monthly basis) throughout the year" (Kay 1996–1997, 80). Most of Foncodes social assistance expenditures went to highland departments, which had the greatest poverty levels, while public works projects were concentrated in those departments with the highest levels (over 20 percent) of unemployment. Fujimori issued a decree in September 1993 that allowed him to control Fonavi funds more easily through the Ministry of the Presidency and that gave him discretion over how to spend more than $15 million monthly. The Ministry of the Presidency thus became the vehicle for launching a broad personalist program that had Fujimori flying all over the country in a helicopter, descending on pueblos jóvenes, small towns, and villages and asking what people needed—roads, schools, and the like—and then seeing to it that such projects were provided. As Kay noted, however,

the program was of crucial importance in allowing Fujimori to shuttle back and forth from the shantytowns that ring Lima to peasant communities in the war-torn *sierra,* inaugurating new projects at every stop along the campaign trail. It allowed the president to continue to fulminate against *partidocracia* ("party democracy"), contrasting it with the effectiveness and efficiency of his "direct democracy, without intermediaries." (1996–1997, 81)

Despite all these programs and expenditures, however, by the middle of his second term it was clear that Fujimori's public opinion ratings had taken a beating (his July 1997 level fell below 30 percent approval, for example). Most polls cited consistently high unemployment and underemployment levels as well as human rights abuses as the major cause of these poor showings. In clear response to these polls, in June 1997 Fujimori announced yet another set of policies aimed at low-income groups, saying he would invest \$2.7 billion for social programs, the creation of jobs, and measures to combat extreme poverty between mid-1997 and the year 2000. Most opposition observers and analysts immediately claimed that this new initiative was nothing more than an obvious attempt to reverse low approval ratings.

Looking back over the first eight years of the Fujimori period, perhaps the most surprising aspect of the whole shock treatment policy of the early 1990s was that it produced virtually no popular protest. This lack of demonstrative or violent response was in sharp contrast to similar circumstances in other countries, most notably the Caracas riots in Venezuela of 1989, where hundreds of people were killed as the military and police responded to widespread rioting.[5] Although the policies instituted by President Carlos Andres Pérez were severe by Venezuelan standards, they were nowhere near as extreme as those implemented in Peru.

Why this remarkable difference? and why the lack of protest in Peru? Several explanations are likely. First, when Fujimori announced his shock treatment and then implemented it as quickly as he did,[6] the poor were not only unprepared (as was most of Peruvian society) to respond but were also so intent on trying to cope with the horrendous state of affairs that demonstrating or rioting was simply unthinkable. Moreover, given the state of the economy in mid-1990 with its ravenous inflation, many people doubtless thought that, as bad as escalating prices and the cost of living might be, they would be preferable to continued four-digit inflation.

Perhaps more important, I would suggest (in substantial part from the evidence in this book), the urban lower classes had long since given up much hope that the state and its policies could or would truly work on their behalf. As a result they had over the years created elaborate and enduring self-help mechanisms to which many of them contributed time, money, and effort. In the late 1980s Lima had an estimated eighteen hundred communal soup kitchens, serving approximately seventy thousand individuals daily, and some thirty-five hundred Vaso de Leche neighborhood committees delivering some 1 million glasses of milk a day in Lima. The number of kitchens may have more than doubled shortly after—and as a result of—the shock. Indeed, a USAID official calculated that the agency was feeding one of three Peruvians (Graham 1994, 110). As a result, "the lack of popular protest and the remarkable autonomous efforts on the part of the urban poor and the NGO community to organize into communal kitchens and other self-help organizations on a wide scale eliminated the government's primary incentive—fear of popular unrest—for organizing a program" (Graham 1994, 106). Thus the widespread self-help efforts that have played such a prominent role throughout this book ironically provided Fujimori with some badly needed breathing room as well as the chance to avoid having to implement a comprehensive social safety net program.

Graham (1994, 110) notes another unanticipated and, in this case, unfortunate result of this successful grassroots organization in the early 1990s. The Shining Path viewed such autonomous associations as threats to its attempts to establish a beachhead in Lima, especially in the city's low-income barrios. In late 1991 Sendero Luminoso launched a wave of intimidation and assassinations against scores of soup kitchens and neighborhood organization leaders in Lima. The most notorious of these involved the cold-blooded murder of Maria Elena Moyano, the popular and widely respected vice mayor of Villa El Salvador. The Sendero leadership hoped through these acts to persuade neighborhood leaders as well as the rank and file to join them. In fact, just the opposite occurred as such atrocities provoked massive public condemnation, often in the form of citywide peace marches, and drew most neighborhoods closer together against the Shining Path.

When Guzmán was captured in 1992, the economy was starting to show signs of coming around. These two accomplishments gave Fujimori enormous and relatively sustained popularity, and he capitalized on it repeatedly. But Peru's economy slowed dramatically after his reelection in 1995 and although the MRTA hostage crisis was resolved, again with Fujimori claiming much of the credit, opponents still criticized the three months the crisis had dragged on and questioned some of the human rights aspects of the rescue itself.[7]

For a variety of reasons, therefore, much of the broad support that Fujimori had enjoyed through his first term showed serious signs of erosion by 1997. In June 1997 five of Fujimori's cabinet members resigned, including one of his closest advisors and confidants, Foreign Minister Francisco Tudela. News accounts said that Tudela, who had been held hostage by the MRTA and who was widely admired, was upset by reports that the government had spied on leading

Peruvian journalists, politicians, and businessmen by tapping their telephones and by using military intelligence for political ends. Tudela was also reported as being troubled by the attempted deportation of Baruch Ivcher, which was widely criticized as a vendetta undertaken at Fujimori's express orders. June and July 1997 saw numerous demonstrations in downtown Lima, led largely by university students, in protest against all these developments.

The extent to which Lima's urban poor were aware of or involved in these activities is unknown. That many of them might have benefited in some fashion from Foncodes, Fonavi, Pronaa, or from other social policy initiatives goes without saying. However, the degree to which such benefits would persuade the poor to support Fujimori remained uncertain.[8] In 1996 a long-term resident of 28 de Julio acknowledged that he had received assistance from Fonavi to help finish his house, primarily by making a loan available so he could complete his roof:

> Fonavi helped me, that's for sure, and that's fine. But that doesn't mean I think Fujimori himself is a great president or that I'd vote for him or for Cambio 90. All of us here in 28 de Julio are poor, and the government has never done anything for us much at all. So when Fonavi gives me a loan, I don't owe anything to Fujimori or the government or anyone else. The government should have made agencies like Fonavi available to us long ago. What I got with the loan was just what I should have always had. So I took it and finished the house, and that's all. Why should I automatically vote for Fujimori?

Why indeed? The question deserves an answer.

THE URBAN POOR, THE STATE, AND
FORMAL POLITICAL BEHAVIOR

Discussing the informal, neighborhood-based behavior of Lima's urban poor can be done only indirectly without detailed survey data. Hence, the preceding summary of 1990–1997 concentrated heavily on state policies directed toward the poor, not on the poor's reaction to these policies, and certainly not on individual patterns of behavior. But discussing formal or electoral behavior is easier, since good electoral data exist for all the elections that have taken place since 1990.[9] Briefly put, in the presidential elections of 1990 and 1995 Lima's urban poor voted heavily for Fujimori. Fujimori carried Lima's poor districts in both first and second rounds, winning by sometimes substantial margins. In the first round of voting, with five major parties competing, Fujimori took more than 40 percent of the vote in twelve low-income and populous districts.[10] In the second run-off round (Fujimori versus Vargas Llosa), Fujimori won twenty-five of

Lima's forty-two districts, sometimes by overwhelming margins such as 3:2, 2:1, and even 3:1. The sample surveyed in the six neighborhoods gave Fujimori very strong backing in both rounds (see chapter 8).

The same levels of support were abundantly present in the 1995 presidential race. Fujimori won an astonishing 61.4 percent of Lima's popular vote over more than a dozen opponents. His nearest rival, Javier Perez de Cuellar, took 18.7 percent, a 3:1 margin. Breaking down Lima's districts by social class reveals that, although Fujimori did well across the board, his totals in upper- and middle-class districts (59.6 and 59.1 percent, respectively) were less than in the city's lower-class districts (65.4 percent). For example, Fujimori took over two-thirds of the popular vote in four such districts. In the districts where the six sample neighborhoods are located, Fujimori's total ranged from a low of 55.6 percent in Cercado de Lima to over 65 percent in Pampa de Arena, 28 de Julio, and Primero de Enero.

Fujimori, while still successful, could not match these totals in municipal and other contests. On November 22, 1992, a Constituent Assembly congressional election took place to replace the congress that Fujimori had dismissed some months earlier. The Cambio 90 slate (pro-Fujimori) just missed taking an absolute majority of the valid vote nationally (49.2 percent) but did win 53 percent in metropolitan Lima, where it took fifteen districts outright with absolute majorities and won nothing less than 45 percent in any district. These were obviously impressive totals (especially in a nine-party race), but they were still something less than two years earlier. The Fujimori slate won in all of the districts where the surveys had been administered, with totals ranging from 58.7 percent (Comas) to 50.1 percent (Cercado de Lima).

A little less than a year later (October 31, 1993), the country voted in a yes/no referendum to decide if the new constitution produced by the Cambio 90–dominated Constituent Assembly should be accepted or not. At the time of the referendum, Fujimori's approval ratings were running well above 60 percent, so most observers expected a runaway vote in favor of the new constitution. And, although Fujimori won his referendum, the final results were no landslide: 52 percent in favor, 48 percent against. The provinces were considerably less supportive than was metropolitan Lima, where the vote to approve totaled 60 percent. In general Lima's middle- and upper-class districts tended to support the referendum more strongly. For example, the highest levels (in excess of 70 percent) came uniformly from upper-class districts (San Isidro 70 percent, Miraflores 68 percent, La Molina 67 percent), whereas the city's poor district totals were lower. The districts where the sample neighborhoods were located all voted in favor, but their vote totals ranged only from 55.8 percent to 62 percent, and in fact in three of them (El Agustino, Comas, and Cercado de Lima), the totals were less than the citywide average (60 percent).

Peru has seen two municipal elections since 1990, one on January 29, 1993, postponed from the scheduled time of November 1992, and the other on November 24, 1995. The 1993 elections revealed little about support for Fujimori, since his party ran no candidates in Lima, either in the metropolitan race or in the separate district races. Yet it is worthwhile to examine the results of these municipal elections. Nationally, of the traditional parties, AP finished first with 12.3 percent of the vote and 42 victories out of 183 races. APRA finished second (11.7 percent, 26 races). PPC finished third (5.3 percent, 9 races), and IU finished fourth (4 percent, 26 races). Other small parties took 3.8 percent and 4 races. But nationwide, independent lists took 25.6 of the vote and 66 races, to far outdistance all rivals.

In Lima, Ricardo Belmont, a television personality who had first won in 1989, won handily with about 45 percent of the total vote. Other Obras candidates won 21 district races. AP (8.2 percent, 3 races), APRA (3.3 percent, no races), PPC (2 percent, 5 races), and IU (1.2 percent, no races), all did very poorly. Independent candidates (excluding Obras) fared well, on the other hand, especially a movement called Lima 2000, which took 28.3 percent of the popular vote. All told, independent candidates (apart from Obras) won thirteen district races.

In 1995, however, another round of municipal elections was held, and this time Fujimori wanted very much to capture the mayoral race in Lima. Jaime Yoshiyama, a close advisor and presumed heir apparent of Fujimori who had been a major figure in the Congress, was nominated and Fujimori threw all the weight of office behind him. Yoshiyama's principal opposition came from Alberto Andrade, twice a highly popular mayor of the wealthy district of Miraflores who ran on an ad hoc *Somos Lima* (We are Lima) ticket. The campaign was hard fought; in the end, Andrade won a 52–48 percent victory.[11] Yoshiyama won 19 districts and Andrade 20 (one AP candidate won, as did two independents). Clear-cut patterns were hard to discern. For instance, Cambio 90 (Yoshiyama's party) won most of Lima's lower-class districts, but not all, and in those it did win its victories were relatively narrow. Yoshiyama's margins in districts such as San Martín de Porres (50–48), Villa Maria del Triunfo (54–46), Comas (53–43), Independencia (45–41), San Juan de Miraflores (51–43), and San Juan de Lurigancho (55–43) all fell far short of the 3:2 and 2:1 victories Fujimori had enjoyed in his presidential races. In Villa El Salvador, the huge squatter area in the southern cone of Lima, Yoshiyama lost as Andrade took 59 percent of the vote cast. Yoshiyama won in all the sample neighborhood districts, but in only two did his margin of victory exceed 10 percentage points. Close as it was, Andrade's victory accomplished several things. It provided Fujimori with something of a black electoral eye, it put Yoshiyama's political future in serious doubt, and it gave some new hope to Fujimori's tattered opposition, and to Peru's party system in general.

New elections are not due until 1998 (municipal) and 2000 (presidential), and a great deal of political maneuvering must take place before they occur. However, given his low public opinion ratings in July 1997 (23 percent approval), along with the furious and unresolved debate over his status in 2000, Fujimori clearly has a great deal to do to become a viable candidate. All observers agree that the Peruvian electorate is notoriously fickle and that the current state of the party system makes predicting political outcomes a risky venture indeed. In the late 1980s many politicians and party leaders found to their dismay that the electorate could voice its discontent and then exit, turning against them with frightening suddenness, and that party or personal loyalty could be blindingly evanescent.

Meanwhile, throughout the changes and crises of the past quarter-century, one generalization has stayed firmly in place. The urban poor have continued to be poor. State policies have come and gone, as have candidates and parties, sometimes helpful but more often not; and the poor, repeatedly thrown back on their own resources, have relied upon themselves and little else—not because they necessarily have preferred matters this way but because they have learned, and it has been demonstrated to them time and again, that to do otherwise would be risky and irrational. Believing that this state of affairs might change has remained a dream; actually believing that matters would and could change has remained, unfortunately, ill-advised and foolish. The ancient injunction "The poor you shall always have with you" seems as true and as unrelenting in Peru as it always has.

APPENDIX

Selecting the Research Communities

I selected the survey communities by combining (like many other studies) what Przeworski and Teune (1970) call "most similar" and "most different" strategies. Verba, Nie, and Kim (1978) and Barnes and Kaase (1979) use this same two-step strategy, although both of them claim to use a most-different strategy only. For example, Verba, Nie, and Kim selected only nations that provided universal participatory rights, which in the early and mid-1970s meant excluding a large number of countries. Once this basic decision was made, then Verba, Nie, and Kim maximized variation in terms of individual-level and group-level forces that shape political participation (1978, 20–21). Barnes and Kaase (1979) made an initial decision to work only in Western industrialized democracies that had in the 1960s undergone great waves of political protest, in effect limiting their universe to perhaps two dozen countries. Both studies make much of how they use the "risky" strategy of most-different systems comparison, but make rather less of how they first limited their universes.

My first stage of selection was to decide to focus on low-income segments of Lima's population. In so doing I opted for a most-similar strategy, i.e., all of the survey communities selected would be low-income areas. Having made that decision, however, I then maximized variation within this universe by selecting five squatter communities that differed markedly along three basic dimensions: age of the neighborhood, manner of formation (incremental, state sponsored, large-scale land invasion), and overall development of the community, including (1) materials used in house construction, (2) population density, (3) terrain, and (4) internal cohesion of the community, meaning level or intensity of intraneighborhood conflict, efficacy of the local association, the success of communitywide activities. I also decided to conduct work in a *tugurio* (rental slum) area, a qualitatively different kind of neighborhood because of the presence of the landlord-tenant relationship. I describe each of the neighborhoods in chapter 5.

Over the twenty years of the research project, I found that the four surveys elicited much detailed information about voting behavior, a variety of politically relevant attitudes and opinions, past political involvement and voting, as well as information regarding a range of social, economic, and demographic factors. I carried out the survey interviews at the same addresses each time, although the generally precarious nature of housing and the appearance and disappearance of streets over time in all six neighborhoods prohibited exact replication. I thus made no real effort to conduct a strict panel survey over the twenty-year period. People move in and out of these neighborhoods with great frequency, and tracing the same individuals over two decades would have been logistically impossible. Nevertheless, these four surveys provide more detailed information about both formal and informal political participation by low-income groups than has previously been available for Lima or for any other Latin American city.

The population initially considered was the universe of people inhabiting the officially recognized pueblos jóvenes of Lima (the Sendas Frutales area was added as a means of comparing the squatter areas with a central-city slum). At the time of the first survey in 1970, there were approximately 250 squatter settlements, with a total population of at least a million people. (The number of slum neighborhoods and their population was and still is impossible to estimate.) But I never attempted to draw a strictly representative sample from the squatter universe. In the first place, in 1970 drawing such a sample would have been impossible, since there was not enough information from censuses or any other source to develop a reliable sampling frame. Secondly, I assumed from the start that the neighborhood itself was essential and that drawing a sample of individuals with no regard for their neighborhood of residence would be counterproductive. I therefore concentrated on a few research neighborhoods selected deliberately (see Walton 1973) and not randomly, since gathering information about the communities themselves would be as important as gathering information about their inhabitants.

Given the aims of the original study, I would argue that the five squatter neighborhoods and one slum area constitute representative samples of Lima's working classes. As the study progressed over two decades, my decision not to incorporate new settlements in my sample meant that I could not compare the settlements in my sample with newer areas or their inhabitants with newer migrants (e.g., those who might have moved into Lima because of the Shining Path). However, I could follow how neighborhoods and their inhabitants develop and change over time and generate the longitudinal data base found in this study.

Sampling Procedures

Sampling was generally not difficult, since I was not drawing a stratified sample but instead a simple random sample. If a comprehensive list of inhabitants was available (which it was in most cases), I used that. However, each neighborhood presented its own peculiarities and problems.

THE 1970 SURVEY

Primero de Enero. This settlement was the most difficult to work in, since 1970 the whole area was less than three years old. Of the 1,080 families listed in the local association's rosters, about 800 had fixed lots, and drawing random sample from this was straightforward. The questionnaires carried the name and address of the respondent selected, and once I located the street (not always an easy thing to do, since the only existing lot map was a year and a half out of date), interviewing could proceed. For the other names that had no fixed lot number or address, however, the only thing to do was to determine as best I could in what approximate part of Primero de Enero my respondent lived, and then track him down by knocking on doors.

Pampa de Arena, all four subsections. Lots maps from ONDEPJOV provided me with a means for drawing a sample of about thirty households per subsection. In the two larger subsections I first drew a random sample of blocks and then another sample of lots.

28 de Julio, Zones A and B. I obtained a copy of most recent censal listing carried out by ONDEPJOV in these two zones. This listing carried names and full addresses, from which I drew a random sample.

Santiago. I used the same technique in Santiago as in Pampa de Arena: a sample of blocks and then of lots.

Sendas Frutales. I had no other way to select a sample than to walk the entire street and make a complete map of lots and households in the various alleyways, and from that to draw a sample.

THE 1982 SURVEY

Twelve years later, much of the 1970 information used for drawing samples was hopelessly outdated. However, for the 1982 sample, I obtained access to the original materials gathered for the national census in 1981. All of the communities were divided into blocks, which in turn were divided into individual lots. I drew a random sample of blocks and then of lots. The initial goal was to have a sample of 150–200 individuals per neighborhood, in anticipation of a certain number of individual addresses or dwellings not locatable, or refusals. The goal was again to have simple random samples, not stratified or weighted in any fashion.

Given this comprehensive data set, it was not difficult to draw samples. I nevertheless visually inspected all the research communities to see if the census data checked with reality, and I found little deviation. Even for Sendas Frutales, the census data included all the alleyways and lots on the street where the survey was carried out.

THE 1985 AND 1990 SURVEYS

I used the same sample when I replicated the survey in 1985 and 1990. By 1982, all the research communities were consolidated, in the sense that none grew appreciably after that date, meaning that the overall size of the communities remained largely unchanged over the 1980s. I could therefore use the same addresses and lot plans as in 1982. Yet over time conditions change in areas like the sites of my survey. In one neighborhood street names had been changed, which caused some momentary problems; in another, some new streets had been cut through the neighborhood.

I should perhaps note that anyone wishing to draw a sample using the 1993 census would find it a far easier task than I did. Data from that census are all available for purchase on disk. In fact, the amount and accessibility of Peruvian census and other demographic and socioeconomic data is today quite remarkable and sophisticated.

This book does not include copies of the questionnaires, largely to save space. Anyone wishing to obtain the complete survey instruments should contact the author at Department of Government, University of Texas, Burdine 536, Austin, TX 78712.

Interviewer Training

A detailed discussion of the process by which interviewers were selected, hired, and interviews verified for the 1970 survey can be found in Dietz (1980, 201–05). Briefly, at that time I hired fourth- and fifth-year students from the School of Social Work at the Universidad Richardo Palma in Lima. All were used to doing survey research and all had worked previously in areas similar to the research neighborhoods. They all went through three lengthy training sessions before undertaking a pretest and another debriefing session. The survey itself took about two months to complete in all six areas. I hired a young sociologist from the Catholic University to assist me and to help coordinate the surveys.

For subsequent surveys (1982, 1985, 1990), the process was much the same. I hired advanced students from the School of Social Work at the Catholic University. All of them had previous experience working in neighborhoods similar to the survey sites, and all had previous experience as survey interviewers. For each survey I hired as field supervisor Fernando Tuesta, a Peruvian social scientist with much experience in urban research. Tuesta and I conducted the training sessions, which consisted of three two-hour sessions that not only went through the questionnaire item by item but also explained the nature of the investigation. He and I accompanied the interviews into the field for the pretests, did the debriefing from the

pretests, and then accompanied the team into the field again during the actual interviewing. After each survey, either Tuesta or I returned to the communities returned
to the communities and did a systematic spot check of the houses and individuals
interviewed to ensure that the interview had been carried out with the individuals
listed on the completed questionnaire.

Completion Rates

I always drew a sample that was about 20 percent larger that the minimum number
I hoped to obtain, assuming (correctly) that in every neighborhood some individual
names, houses, or addresses would never be located. Due to their persistence and
hard work, the interviewers eventually found all but a handful of individuals selected in the random samples. Given the nature of the research sites, there was
sometimes a less than perfect correspondence between the census data and actual-
ity. People move in and out of these neighborhoods with some frequency, and lo-
cating the precise dwelling from census descriptions was not always easy. Yet across
all four surveys and six neighborhoods, there were never more than 10–12 percent of
specific individuals or dwellings or lots "not found." (This was even true in Sendas
Frutales, the rental tenement environment.) But once specific dwellings and individuals were located, refusal rates were very low (less than 2 percent).

In 1970 I was in the field for a year (from September 1970 to August 1971). The actual interviewing went on from early February 1971 through April 1971, although I
refer to the survey throughout as the 1970 survey. Primary funding for this work
came from the Social Science Research Council Foreign Area Fellowship Program,
with some additional support from the Stanford University Center for Research in
International Studies. In 1982 I was in the field from very late December 1981 through
mid-August 1982. Interviews were done on weekends in mid-February 1982 through
late April 1982. A grant from the Tinker Foundation provided primary funding. I was
again in the field from late May 1986 through the end of July 1995. Interviews were
carried out on weekends between late June through July; funding came from the
Institute of Latin American Studies and the Hogg Foundation, both at the University of Texas. Then I did field work in 1990 from early June through mid-August
1990, largely on weekends. Primary funding came from the Heinz Foundation as
well as the Institute of Latin American Studies at the University of Texas. In every
instance, the interviewing was conducted during university vacation periods so that
the students could concentrate on their interviewing full time.

All Male Samples

I should comment on using all male head-of-household samples. When I first started this project in graduate school, I did so in close cooperation and collaboration with Wayne Cornelius, who went to Mexico City to do similar work just a few months before I left for Lima (Cornelius 1975). He and I decided at that time that we would do all male head-of-household samples for three basic reasons. First, we hoped to avoid the necessity of drawing male-female comparisons throughout the study. While gender comparisons are obviously worthy of inquiry, our studies were not focusing on sociology as much as on politics. A second and related point is that we both were forced to keep the size of the samples (and the cost of interviewing) under control. Doubling the sample size would have meant considerable extra expense, which neither of us could afford. Third, we both intended to explore the relationship between type of occupation outside the home and political participation. That is, Cornelius and I wished to see if and how work outside the home (formal as well as informal), as well as membership in organizations such as labor unions, might affect political participation. In 1970, the great majority of low-income women were not formally employed, for a variety of sociocultural as well as economic reasons, although this pattern has changed substantially since that time. In addition, spot census counts in 1970 indicated that the number of households headed by women (i.e., where no employed man was present at all) was small.

When I returned to replicate the survey in 1982, I decided to maintain the all-male sample for the sake of consistency and comparability, but certainly not because the role of women was trivial or had not changed. On the contrary, women in the research sites have become much more involved in the formal and especially the informal economies of Lima since the early 1970s, due in large part to the vicissitudes of the Peruvian economy and the need for low-income households to have as many wage earners as possible. Indeed, the study of low-income urban women has become a recognized field unto itself, especially since the early to mid-1980s and the emergence of the neighborhood *comedores populares* that have spread throughout the city. The number of sources now available on women is now very large (Andreas 1985; Ballon et al., 1986a; Barrig 1982, 1988; Blondet 1986, 1991, 1995a, 1995b; Escobar and Alvarez 1992; Galer and Nuñez C. 1989; Grandón and García Rios 1984; Lafosse 1984; Paredes and Tello 1989; Ruíz-Bravo 1996).

Thus, all things considered, several reasons justify the decision to draw an initial all-male sample and to continue with similar samples over time. Were I to start out fresh today (and were funding available), I would certainly incorporate women into the samples. Nevertheless, the all-male sample in this study remains the largest and most detailed longitudinal comprehensive data set of political participation available for Peru or for any country in Latin America.

NOTES

1. Third World Urban Poverty and Political Participation

1. The basic intent of this book is not to provide a narrative treatment of Lima's poor over twenty years. Although some historical discussion is desirable and indeed necessary, the focus of the book is on individual-level political participation among the urban poor and how participation patterns responded to changes in the several macrolevel factors mentioned in the text.

2. Examples of the sorts of public goods and services I have in mind here include buildings (a community center, school buildings, a chapel or church building), amenities (paved sidewalks or streets), infrastructure (water and sewerage lines, electricity), services (mail service, transportation, police protection), and legal benefits (legal recognition, land titles). Informal participation can be aimed either at directly providing some of these goods and services or at mobilizing the community to petition or demand such goods and services from the appropriate authorities.

3. These definitions parallel Roberts's (1995, 184) definition of participation and citizenship: "an individual citizen has the right to vote, but the broader definition of citizenship focuses on the ways in which and the extent to which people exercise that right collectively to make changes in the way resources are allocated. Citizenship is, from this perspective, always negotiated since by their participation citizens can change their rights and obligations and, equally, governing elites may seek to limit or influence these changes as a means of consolidating their power." The choice of terminology is always subjective: I use "formal" and "informal" whereas others might use "national-level" and "local-oriented," or "electoral" and "communal." Any of these alternatives would serve my purposes.

4. Most social scientists concern themselves with procedural rather than substantive democracy, including Joseph Schumpeter (1976), whose definition has been repeated many times: "the democratic method is that institutional arrangement for arriving at political decisions in which individuals acquire power to decide by means of a competitive struggle for the people's vote" (260). Procedural and substantive definitions are not the only schools of thought on the topic; for example, Nagel (1987) contrasts the instrumental, developmental, and intrinsic benefits from participation.

5. These two dimensions are analogous to Margolis's (1982) "fair share" model, which proposes a dual preference structure for individuals, wherein an individual acts as a vector of S (self-interest) and G (group-interest). Without pursuing the point further here,

Margolis's S is analogous to the well-being dimension and his G to the political dimension. Although well-being can be a social as well as an individual concern, it is arguable that most individuals will be concerned with self well-being before group well-being. On the other hand, the benefits that derive from democracy concern group or social utilities at least as much as individual.

6. Sanctions are not severe enough to ensure that everyone always votes. Rates of abstention vary by type of election: presidential races have the highest turnout whereas municipal elections are lower (see chapters 6, 8). For complete results on blank and spoiled ballots as well as abstention rates in Lima, see Tuesta (1994).

7. The term *rationality* is used here in a fairly loose and informal fashion. I make no pretense of offering and testing a formal model of political participation. Rather, I use *rationality* more in the way Verba and Nie employ it in *Participation in America* (1972), for example, or in the way Barry and Hardin use it in their "Epilogue" (Barry and Hardin 1982). Barry and Hardin argue that "we should not attach very much attention to the kind of formal rationality embodied in [Arrow]. . . . Substantive rationality—whether or not there are reasons that can be publicly supported for doing one thing rather than another—is much more important" (385–86).

8. How such circumstances might work themselves out depends, at least in part, on the size of the political party in question. A large, well-established party with a viable chance of winning an election may be reluctant to respond to the voice option from a small group, since such a response might disquiet those members already onboard. A smaller party, on the other hand, with a low probability of winning an election may respond more positively to voice from an aggregate of individuals in hopes that the marginal gain of new voters will be greater than the potential loss of other members.

9. If politicians or parties do succeed in creating better conditions, then of course they are likely to be rewarded with loyalty from their adherents when the next round of elections is held. They may also attract new supporters who abandon their previous loyalties to other candidates and parties.

10. Collier and Norden (1992) support structuration and urban praxis theories with their idea of strategic choice analysis. Although Collier and Norden concentrate on elite actors, their argument—that actors are not fully bound by their structural positions— clearly echoes the stance I take here.

11. It should be stressed that it is the individual and his individual behavior that is under discussion here. The urban poor in the aggregate can have a major effect on any or all of these macro levels whether by formal (voting) or by informal means (see chapters 7, 8).

2. Macrolevel Contexts and Participation

1. Vega-Centeno (1995, 30), using 1992 World Bank data, compared income distribution in six Latin American nations. Brazil and Peru were highest in disparities between top and bottom quintiles. In Brazil the top 20 percent of the population received 66.6 percent of the income (the highest percentage for the top quintile of any of the six

countries), whereas the bottom 20 percent received 2 percent. In Peru the figures were 61 and 1.9 percent (the lowest percentage of any country) respectively. All others (Argentina, Chile, Mexico, and Venezuela), along with Latin America as a whole, were less skewed.

The ratio between the top and bottom quintiles in Brazil was 33.3:1, in Peru 32:1. For the other four countries and for Latin America in general the ratio was less than 20:1. Finally, Peru had the lowest absolute figures for any of the six nations, calculated on the basis of 1982 U.S. dollars. Peru's top quintile averaged $2,460 annually and its bottom quintile $77, far and away the lowest averages for the six nations. The average top and bottom quintile figures were $5,696 and $304 for Latin America as a region, for example.

2. This is not the place to examine the many propositions contained in Sachs or in Dornbusch and Edwards, or to explore some of the inconsistencies in these propositions. For example, as Figueroa (1995, 69) notes, if inequality is the source of conflict in a society (as Sachs argues), why do many of Sachs's own policies prescribe economic efficiency, foreign debt repayment, and macroeconomic equilibrium, all independently of their consequences for inequality?

3. It should be made clear here that not every individual who belongs to Lima's lower classes is a member of the city's civil society. There are undoubtedly individuals, as well as whole neighborhoods, that lack virtually all the organizational or associational characteristics of civil life. Empirically, the residents of Lima's central city slum areas may as a rule be far less well developed as a civil society than the residents of its squatter settlements. The data from the 1970 and 1982 surveys (see chapters 5–8), show that Sendas Frutales was nowhere near as well organized as the four squatter communities in the sample. But the 1985 and 1990 data also reveal that Sendas Frutales's participation profile developed markedly over the 1980s, providing evidence that even the most anomic and unorganized neighborhood can, under certain conditions, develop an associational life.

4. The literature on the Shining Path is immense and can only be hinted at here. Useful sources include Palmer (1992), Strong (1992), Goritti (1990), Wickham-Crowley (1992), and Tarazona-Sevillano (1990), as well as innumerable journal articles. Chronologies and statistics dealing with the Shining Path can be found in DESCO (1989). Stern (1996) is a comprehensive annotated bibliography.

5. Much of this general formulation of macro-micro linkages comes from the work of James Coleman (1987; 1990, chaps. 14, 28, 29). See in general Alexander et al. (1987). Bryan Roberts (1995, 197–201) also discusses the interrelationships between macro socioeconomic processes and micro behaviors.

3. The Political Economy of Peru

1. The $ symbol throughout indicates U.S. dollars.

2. The Shining Path also started its public insurgency in 1980, when movement activists seized and destroyed ballot boxes in Chuschi, a remote Andean village in rural Ayacucho. Although the party was to become an increasingly violent political actor throughout the 1980s, it never participated in elections. Quite the contrary: one of its

basic aims was to subvert the whole electoral process by encouraging a boycott of elections through propaganda and intimidation.

3. The following account draws upon Pastor and Wise (1992), Handelman and Baer (1989), and Thorp and Whitehead (1987), among other sources.

4. Sources on the 1990 presidential campaigns and elections include Daeschner (1993), Jochamowitz (1994), and Schmidt (1996; forthcoming). Vargas Llosa wrote his own account of his campaign (Vargas Llosa 1993).

4. Metropolitan Lima and Its Districts

1. The primacy of Lima has been the subject of an immense literature in Peru. Perhaps the classic inquiry appeared in 1929 in Jorge Basadre's treatment (1980), which, although obviously dated in some ways, is still required reading on the subject.

2. The term *Lima* applies to several different entities. Most broadly it applies to the *departamento* (state) of Lima, which is one of twenty-three states that comprise the nation of Peru. But Lima is also the name of a province within the departamento; this province is sometimes used to refer to metropolitan Lima, since it contains the city proper as well as several outlying areas. Finally, *Lima* refers as well to a district of the city that comprises the old heart of the city (its actual name is Cercado de Lima). For my purposes, metropolitan Lima includes those districts that are inherently urban in nature and that form an integral urban part of the city. This definition excludes outlying seaside vacation districts (San Bartolo and so on) that have a permanent population of perhaps a few hundred people. The 1981 census counted thirty-nine total districts within metropolitan Lima; in the 1993 census the total had risen to forty-three. New districts have been created because of the physical expansion of the city or because old districts have been subdivided.

3. Books and Prysby (1991) define social class as a compositional contextual factor (21-25), which in turn they operationally define as a mathematical construct (mean, for example) about a discrete geographically bounded social unit such as a neighborhood. Such an operationalization of social class is, of course, quite different from most traditional social science definitions, whether by Marx or Weber or many others. The Books and Prysby treatment of social class is useful here since the major effort is to see not only whether Lima's districts (geographically bounded social units) contain individuals of one class but also whether the districts themselves as units can be classified as being of a distinct social class.

4. ILD data should be used with some caution, since there have been claims that their accuracy leaves something to be desired (Rossini and Thomas 1990; also ILD 1990). Riofrio (1991) in particular argues that ILD's calculations and conclusions about Lima's housing problems are suspect (129-52).

5. Data dealing with Lima finances are notoriously difficult to gather and interpret, and district-level finances are even worse. Allou (1989), the basic source used here, is convenient and is as accurate and neutral as any source can be.

6. One of the most pathetic individual examples of inflation run amok occurred when a fire destroyed a few houses in El Agustino in 1990, forcing the inhabitants into the street. One elderly couple, who had clearly lost everything, were interviewed on local television; the man had rescued his "savings," which consisted of some bills he clutched in his hat. Most of them were old soles from the early 1980s; the new inti currency introduced in 1985 was worth 1,000 soles, and by 1990 the exchange rate was about 435,000 intis to the dollar. The couple's savings were literally not worth the paper they were printed on.

7. The two most important studies of Lima's informal sector are undoubtedly de Soto (1986) and Carbonetto et al. (1988). De Soto is the best known and probably the most controversial (Bromley 1990; Rossini and Thomas 1990); any summary of his work and that of his critics would take an enormous amount of space. Carbonetto's work is more thorough and empirical and constitutes by any measure a truly pathbreaking study. Carbonetto's central concern is with the contribution of the informal sector to Lima's economy; although this is a vital consideration, it is tangential to the focus of this book. Carbonetto does discuss the quality of life and the political attitudes of members of Lima's informal sector, but these discussions are brief and relatively unenlightening.

8. Several studies rank Lima's districts. These include Dietz (1985), Dietz and Dugan (1995), García (1985), Cameron (1991a), Driant (1991), Gonzales de Olarte (1992), Durand (1996), and the Banco Central de la Reserva (1984). The latter study utilizes some twenty variables to identify five distinct clusters, based on intragroup homogeneity within Lima/Callao's then forty-five districts. The first two clusters together contain only 11 percent of the city's population; they are rural, outlying, sparsely populated districts. Cluster 3 contains twelve districts with about 48 percent of Lima's total population; all were formed during the 1950s and 1960s and all contain sizable squatter housing. Cluster 4 contains eleven older core districts, most of which have significant slum housing. Cluster 5 contains six districts, all of which are wealthy residential areas. Three of the districts discussed here (Comas, El Agustino, San Juan de Miraflores) are in cluster 3; two (Lima and Surquillo) are in cluster 4.

9. Villa El Salvador was created by the Velasco military government in 1971 in the aftermath of a large-scale land invasion that occurred on the edges of part of San Juan de Miraflores; see Dietz (1980) and Zapata (1997) for details of the highly political nature of the land invasion itself and the creation of Villa El Salvador. Villa El Salvador has been the focus of considerable national and international attention over the years. It made headlines throughout the world when members of the Shining Path brutally assassinated Maria Elena Moyano, its assistant mayor, in 1992. I was in Lima when the 1970 invasion occurred and witnessed Villa El Salvador's early days from a very close vantage point. But its size and the subsidies it received from the Velasco government from the moment of its creation make it in many ways atypical.

10. The 1993 census shows that San Juan de Lurigancho had a population of almost 600,000, which is more than the total population of metropolitan Lima in 1940. Yet San Juan de Lurigancho was not an official district of Lima until 1967.

11. There are various sources for Peruvian electoral data, including the official results from the Jurado Nacional Electoral (JNE) or national electoral board. The most complete source available, and the one used here, is Tuesta (1994).

5. Six Poor Barrios and Their Inhabitants

1. It should not be concluded that inner-city slum environments uniformly and necessarily deteriorate, or that squatter communities always improve. Sánchez Leon et al. (1979) noted years ago that squatter neighborhoods could, over time, become increasingly *tugurizados* (or "slummified"). Likewise, the data and description of Sendas Frutales in this book indicate that an inner-city slum area can sometimes recover. See also Eckstein (1990).

2. For more detailed descriptions of these neighborhoods in the 1970s, see Dietz (1980, chap. 4). One extraordinary development that has occurred in Peru since the 1960s is the growth in social sciences and the amount of research done on Lima. In the early 1960s, survey data were rare indeed, census materials were insufficient, published studies were infrequent and for the most part unsophisticated. A glance at the bibliography demonstrates how matters have changed.

3. A good deal has been written about Pampa de Arena, including Boggio (1970), Centro de Estudios y Publicaciones (1971), Riofrio (1978), and Villalobos and Vega (1982). Other studies dealing with Lima in general and with low-income housing and the squatter phenomenon frequently include some mention of Pampa de Arena as a classic invasion-consolidation site.

4. Materials dealing with the creation of La Parada and of its impact on the surrounding neighborhoods of Lima are now considerable. Ponce Menteza (1994) is an excellent socioeconomic analysis of an area near La Parada known as Gamarra and of its phenomenal growth as the primary textile and clothing producer for both Lima and Peru. Patch (1967) contains a fascinating view of La Parada itself, its inhabitants, and their lifestyles both legal and illegal.

5. A good deal has been written in the past twenty years or so on 28 de Julio. One useful source on the history of the neighborhood is Calderón (1980). Other sources include Grandón and García Rios (1984), Blondet (1986), Grandón and García (1990), and SEA (1995).

6. In the 1990 presidential campaign both major candidates—Mario Vargas Llosa and Alberto Fujimori—made frequent and extravagant claims to be speaking for los informales of Lima. Indeed, Hernando de Soto, author of *El otro sendero* (1986), was a close advisor to Vargas Llosa during the late 1980s before Vargas Llosa announced his candidacy. Several of Vargas Llosa's major political speeches during this time were aimed directly at eliciting support from los informales—an effort that was ultimately to fail, as low-income Lima went very heavily for Fujimori.

7. It should be remembered that Peru requires its citizens to vote and that a fine is levied against those who do not. Thus these reported levels may be exaggerated because respondents did not want to report they had not voted (if indeed they had not).

8. This term has generated vast and even violent discussions and arguments in Peru

for decades insofar as it touches on the highly sensitive questions of race and ethnicity in Peruvian society. Such questions were for Vargas Llosa major themes and personal preoccupations in his campaign for the presidency (Vargas Llosa 1993, 5). Nugent (1992) is among the more recent and provocative essayists to analyze the concept of the cholo, although such ruminations go back at least to the 1920s. More recent sociological and ethnographic studies include Portocarrero (1993) and Panfichi and Portocarrero (1995). Pride in being labeled a cholo has emerged in many ways, including a song from the 1980s entitled "Cholo soy, y no me compedezcas" (I'm a cholo, and don't you pity me).

6. Modes of Participation

1. These five variables were: attending a local meeting, general community efforts to solve problems, petitioning the landlord about a problem, visiting the local municipality (for any reason), and petitioning municipal authorities.

2. The reader will note that only the principal solution is shown here. Although I did carry out a rotated solution (as discussed for table 3), there was no need to show the results here, since the principal solution reveals no single common dimension. In other words, in 1970 the three modes—local involvement, neighborhood involvement, and state petitioning—are all varieties of a single dimension of participation. In 1982 and subsequently, petitioning, voting, and campaigning are all separate activities that have no common underlying dimension.

3. For example: recent involvement 47 percent, frequent involvement 29 percent, meeting attendance 20 percent, petitioning local organization 22 percent, petitioning SINAMOS 6 percent, membership in a local organization 35 percent (compare with table 4). Moreover, by 1982 it was relevant to include "member of local organization" as a question in Sendas Frutales, whereas in 1971 it had not been so, since none existed.

4. Parodi (1993, 70) found in his study of pobladores in Lima that party membership was very low (1.5 percent), and that two-thirds of his sample called themselves independents. My survey did not ask if the respondent preferred "independent" to any party affiliation, but I would guess that perhaps a majority of my sample might have chosen this alternative in 1990. Aside from APRA, which traditionally has had enduring party adherents, party identification has never been strong in Peru.

5. The district 28 de Julio was in fact one of the districts of Lima where Sendero Luminoso made a sustained effort to establish a foothold. During the late 1980s painted Sendero slogans and symbols appeared on walls throughout the district, and Lima newspapers commonly referred to the area as one where Sendero infiltration was supposedly highest. When the military discussed the notion of declaring certain districts of Lima as *zonas de emergencia* (zones officially recognized as under Sendero threat), 28 de Julio was among them. The military eventually dismissed this idea, recognizing that this would have been to admit publicly that it could not control parts of the capital city.

6. Specifically: recent involvement 70.4 percent, local meeting attendance 74.4 percent, petitioning local authorities 48 percent, petitioning ministry officials 32.5 percent (compare with table 8).

7. Moreover, other sorts of activities emerged as coping mechanisms. The most fa-

mous of these was the proliferation of *comedores populares* (soup kitchens) throughout Lima's pueblos jóvenes. These kitchens not only functioned to make hot meals available to thousands of families in the late 1980s and early 1990s but also served as a means for thousands of women to become involved in community affairs even more than they had over the decades. For accounts of these and related developments see Galer and Nuñez (1989) and Lafosse (1984).

7. Informal Participation

1. Olson and many others are vague about specifying small and large. Although he talks about a group of five as ideal for a committee (Olson 1965, 54), he also acknowledges only that a group should be small enough to allow for face-to-face interaction. Hardin (1982) admits freely that "the meaning of small is somewhat indeterminate and probably variable according to context" (48).

2. It should be clear at this point that "informal" political participation means informal from the point of view of the state. For the urban poor, the kinds of activity involved in informal modes of participation can in fact be quite formal. That is, being a member in the local association, being a delegate or local association leader, or forming part of a delegation from a neighborhood to petition a state agency are all, from the point of view of the poblador, formal (that is, organized, not ad hoc) sorts of participatory activities. Whether the state looks upon neighborhood associations as formal or legally representative groups often depends on the particular government in power. For example, during military rule neighborhoods often held their own "formal" (that is, organized and from the pobladores' point of view binding) elections to select local leaders, despite "formal" (that is, state-generated and legal) injunctions against all such electoral activities.

3. It should be clear that not everyone will participate in an activity simply because it has a good probability of providing a good. Some people will not become involved at all, regardless of the "rationality" of the involvement in terms of material success, simply because they refuse to do so, or because they do not have the time, or because they behave like Olson's (1965) rational individual who sees that if a collective good is provided he will be able to enjoy it, whether or not he contributed to its provision. What is under discussion here are tendencies and probabilities, not claims that all people will participate if there is a significant likelihood they will obtain something from such participation. A certain percentage will always be free riders, regardless of all inducements or threats, primarily because it is rational to let others provide a public good.

4. This is not to imply that political participation must be seen as irrational if it is not directed exclusively and always toward the provision of material goods. It *is* to say, however, that instrumental behavior is defined here as rational, especially for low-income groups.

5. Virtually all observers and writers on new social movements note the division of strategy versus identity within the literature. Yet the most productive perspective on the whole issue does not and cannot involve any sort of forced dichotomous choice, or that

one is always correct and the other always incorrect. The collection of essays edited by Foweraker and Craig (1990), for example, concentrates on resource mobilization among social movements in Mexico. This emphasis is doubtless due in part to the political as opposed to the ethnographic orientation of the volume and its contributors; it is also because of Foweraker and Craig's focus on strictly popular sector actors, low-income rural as well as urban. Escobar and Alvarez (1992, 6) imply that social movements involving indigenous status, race and ethnicity, gender, the ecology and environment, and feminist identity construction may involve middle- and upper-class elements rather than (or at least in addition to) *clases populares.*

6. Salman (1990) offers one of the more accessible and comprehensive guides to the nature of these arguments.

7. It should be clear that the dates used here are approximate; obviously history does not unfold in neatly defined packages. The periods presented here are an amalgam of several accounts, including Driant (1991), Circulo de Estudios Alejandro Quijano (1983?), Ballón (1986), Ballón et al. (1986), Henry (1981), Valdeavellano (1980), Tovar (1982a, b), Gomez Peralta (1990), and Collier (1976). The periodization here makes no attempt to be a full history of the physical or socioeconomic growth of Lima during the time under consideration.

8. See Matos Mar (1966, 1968) for a historical description and a useful compilation of statistics dealing with these years.

9. Collier (1976, 59) reports that, of a sample of eighteen squatter settlements formed during the Odría years about which there is reasonably complete information, only three showed no evidence of state/political involvement of one sort or another.

10. Many studies by Peruvian observers and scholars label such money and aid as *asistencialismo,* a word with no direct English equivalent that connotes paternalistic and even imperialistic aims and tactics and is applied equally to domestic as well as to international aid. See, for example, Circulo de Estudios Alejandro Quijano (1983?), Riofrio (1978), and Rodriguez et al. (1973).

11. What is contained here makes no pretence of being a full account of the Velasco years. For attempts to cover this tumultuous period, see Lowenthal (1975), McClintock and Lowenthal (1983), and Pease (1977, 1978). On Lima's poor, SINAMOS, and the state, see Collier (1976), Tovar (1982a, b, 1985), Dietz (1980), and Stepan (1978), among many others.

12. The discussion here separates the squatter-origin pueblos jóvenes from the rental slum neighborhood of Sendas Frutales. The squatter neighborhoods and the slum environment are fundamentally different in that the former encourages communal participation whereas the latter, because of the nature of the landlord-tenant relationship, discourages communal involvement and tends to atomize its inhabitants.

13. SINAMOS started its program of uniform neighborhood organization in mid-1971. This program imposed a standard template of local organization structure, along with regulations about who could stand for office or be elected in neighborhood elections. For fuller descriptions of the program, see Dietz (1980, chap. 8), Stepan (1978), and Delgado (1975).

14. This term is used in several sources as a catch-all label that includes officially rec-

ognized pueblos jóvenes; *urbanizaciones populares de interés social* (social interest popular settlements), a special category that came into existence in the 1950s, which refers approximately to low-income housing settlements officially sanctioned by the state; *urbanizaciones irregulares* (unrecognized irregular settlements); and similar settlements (Henry 1981, 39). It is not especially important here to differentiate these types either legally or colloquially.

15. Sendas Frutales, being a rental slum neighborhood in Surquillo, is not included under the general heading of a popular urban settlement. The district of Surquillo is located south of downtown Lima but is not part of the cono sur.

16. This imbalance between increasing demands and static state capacity is a vivid illustration of Huntington's (1968) prediction that social mobilization and modernization do not necessarily lead to political development but can instead bring about what he terms political decay. Although this label is not one I would choose, the Peruvian case exemplifies how unmet needs and demands can produce increasing mobilization, if the state capacity or political will to respond is insufficient.

17. With SINAMOS the revolutionary government tried instead, in true corporatist fashion, to undermine both labor unions and parties, or to replace them with officially sanctioned substitutes. The military did not outlaw the major existing unions but, instead, allowed and encouraged new unions to form as a counterweight to existing ones, many of whom were under the control of various Communist/Marxist groups or of APRA. The decision not to outlaw existing unions was probably a mistake, from the military's point of view. As the revolutionary government tried to generate new and friendly unions, the older unions worked that much harder to recruit new and retain old members. They also, quite naturally, developed considerable animosity toward what they saw as the military's encroachment onto their turf. In 1971, 20 percent of the total sample said they belonged to unions. In 1982, only 14 percent were union members, a percentage that remained more or less constant through 1990.

18. The attempts to occupy land along and near some of Lima's main arterial streets (Avenida Argentina, Avenida Faucett) were a striking departure from previous invasions, which generally had taken place on either unused or commercially worthless land or on site far outside the downtown areas. These invasions of valuable commercial land met with considerable resistance and with offers to make lots available outside Lima, but the invaders' main objective was to "rescue" land from commercial interests and give it to the poor. Indeed, these particular land takeovers were universally known as *los rescatadores* (the rescuers or redeemers). Eventually there appeared a Frente de Rescatadores (Rescuers' Front) across some thirteen squatter areas along the left bank of the Rimac River (Valdeavellano 1980).

19. In the 1978 elections a group of some four leftist parties took a total of 29.35 percent of the popular vote and finished in second place behind APRA as a force in the Constituent Assembly (Tuesta 1994). It should be noted, however, that these four did not commonly act or vote as a united body in the deliberations of the assembly.

20. Reconstructing a complete list of all pueblos jóvenes that attended this first convention would today be difficult. The most reliable information I have seen is in Henry, who reports that some 230 delegates from 110 pueblos jóvenes from all of Lima attended

the convention. Henry also reports that at least fourteen leftist political parties attended, not to mention a wide variety of other leftist unions and groups sympathetic to the cause (Henry 1981, 67–72).

21. Law 20066, which prohibited land invasions (as had Law 13517 earlier), and Law 22250, which was the new municipal law, were targets of poblador dissatisfaction throughout the 1970s. Law 22250 supposedly gave more power to district and municipal authorities, but the pobladores complained that the state was simply trying to avoid the responsibilities given it in earlier legislation. But it was Law 22612 that generated the most protest. This law, which the military passed on July 27, 1979, shortly before it was due to give up power, seemed to favor the squatter settlements. It modified previous legislation by allowing the government to award full land titles prior to the completion of neighborhood improvements and the installation of services. But the pobladores (accurately) saw Law 22612 as a way for the government to provide titles (a low-cost good) and then avoid the costs of additional basic services.

22. Stokes (1991, 1995) found three variables positively associated with a radicalized worldview: (1) exposure to labor unions, (2) certain patterns of involvement in local organizations, and (3) education. In contrast, socioeconomic distinctions, along with geographic and life-cycle differences, had no significant association with levels of radicalism. My 1982 sample shows relatively low levels of union membership (see chapter 7, note 17), but marked differences among pobladores in education and in their experiences with local organizational involvement. Stokes's argument, although convincing, also suggests that a wide range of levels of ideological sophistication and commitment would have to exist within any single pueblo jóven. If, for example, ranking high on all three explanatory variables were necessary for radicalism to emerge, then presumably only a small minority of a total population would exhibit such attitudes and behavior patterns.

23. The rise and fall of the left during the 1980s has been the subject of much analysis and speculation. Sources that examine the relationship between the left and Lima's popular classes include Parodi (1993), Roberts (1996), and Roberts and Arce (1998).

24. In the 1980 elections, Belaúnde captured 47.17 percent of the popular vote of metropolitan Lima. He took over 40 percent in all but one district, and over 50 percent in seventeen of the city's thirty-nine districts. The combined left (five parties, five candidates), meanwhile, finished fourth in a four-way race with 12.52 percent of the popular vote (Tuesta 1994, 200–201).

25. Haber (1996) in a recent review essay of the social movements literature in Latin America concludes that social movements in general did not succeed in shaping the civilian governments and state institutions that emerged in the 1980s. He also argues that "The study of social movements has . . . [paid] more attention to identity politics and less attention to analyzing the relatively disappointing political power of the movements as measured by their ability to shape the policy process" (172). In a similar review essay, Roberts (1997) also finds that "the course of events . . . has not been kind to [the] romanticized vision of the transformative potential of grassroots actors" (138).

26. The constitution approved in 1979 lowered the voting age from twenty-one to eighteen and allowed illiterates to vote. Given that Lima's squatter population is a

young one (although by no means an illiterate one), the lowering of the voting age meant that a greater number of people would begin to vote in 1980, meaning in turn that all political parties had to make significant efforts to attract these new and/or un-attached voters.

27. The only way to test this argument would have been to survey a new settlement in 1982 and then again in 1985 and 1990 to see if age by and of itself would reproduce the intercommunity results from the 1971 sample. Costs and logistics did not allow the in-clusion of new settlements each time the survey was replicated.

28. The level of involvement in voting and campaigning in Sendas Frutales was in-distinguishable from the other sample communities, providing even stronger evidence that neither the legal type of neighborhood nor the level of its internal development had any impact on formal political participation.

29. The reader might object by suggesting that leftist parties and candidates did very well in the 1980 and 1983 municipal elections, a result that suggests support for radical ideologies and policies. Chapter 8 discusses voting behavior in detail in these and all other elections of the 1980s.

30. The fact that elections did take place as scheduled throughout the late 1980s was remarkable in itself. In the first place, and against a great deal of historical precedent, the military showed no sign of intervening or of taking power. The joke at the time was that the military would have taken power if things had not been so bad. Second, Sendero Luminoso made every attempt possible to subvert the elections by threatening and assassinating mayors and candidates and by ordering people not to vote. By and large their efforts were not successful. It is true that absenteeism rose across the decade, especially in municipal races (Tuesta 1994, 34; Pareja Pflucker and Gatti Murriel 1993), and that elections could not be held in some isolated rural districts because the state could not guarantee voter safety. Nevertheless, all things considered, Sendero Lumi-noso's attempts to shut down or discredit elections and to keep people from the polls failed.

31. Much of this account draws upon Graham (1994), whose data and interpretations are scrupulous and comprehensive.

32. Parodi found many of the same attitudes and perceptions of the government and of state institutions in his survey of Lima's poor (1993, 66–68).

33. It should be understood that, by the late 1990s, many of Lima's squatter areas had potable water systems installed, either through public spigots and standpipes or through individual household connections. Yet this infrastructure did not mean that the water supply was dependable. Lima has suffered for decades from insufficient water. The city's complex system of tunnels and aqueducts, many high in the sierra, depends upon rainfall, which is often unpredictable. Thus in times of scarcity (in summer, for exam-ple), water is sometimes severely rationed and is available in low-income areas for only a few hours each day—sometimes, for example, between 3 and 6 A.M. If a household fails to fill containers at that time, it simply has to do without for the rest of the day or borrow from neighbors. Thus water remains a constant problem for the poor, whether a water system has been installed or not.

34. Parodi (1993, 76–77) found much the same in his survey. His sample preferred

democracy over military rule by large margins (about 3:1 overall). Moreover, Parodi also included "popular revolution" as an option to democratic and military. Few of the pobladores chose this third option (3–10 percent, depending on level of education).

35. Figueroa (1995, 69) characterizes this incongruence through adapting Mazlov's hierarchy of needs. From this perspective, democracy is not among the primordial necessities of the poor. Simply put, only after people have full stomachs will they concern themselves with democracy or with other high-level, more abstract human values.

36. This is a major "if." Considerable argument exists over whether local neighborhood organizations should be classified as new social movements (Escobar and Alvarez 1992; Assies 1990; Foweraker and Craig 1990).

37. This is obviously a generalization that leaves out numerous specific sectoral cases and instances where popular social movements did have consciousness-raising, empowerment, or identity-creation as a primary or ancillary goal. Women's groups in the pueblos jóvenes, for example, often started as soup kitchens, offering a hot meal once a day to needy neighbors, but frequently became much more than that (Grandón 1990; Lafosse 1984; Blondet 1986). *Debates en Sociología* (1984) contains several articles about low-income women in Lima.

8. Formal Participation

1. As noted elsewhere, the legal requirement to vote does not equate with universal turnout. Depending on the election (that is, presidential versus local), turnout rates during the 1980s ran from a high of 91 percent (1985 presidential) to a low of 64 percent (1983 municipal). These are nationwide turnouts; absenteeism in Lima is a few points lower than the national average for both presidential and municipal elections (see Tuesta 1994).

2. The extreme exit option would come from the individual who has no confidence in any candidate to improve well-being and who therefore renounces democracy and its procedures, either by refusing to vote, or by supporting either an authoritarian or a radical (nondemocratic) solution and becoming disloyal to democracy altogether. In the case of Peru during the 1980s, Sendero Luminoso obviously hoped that increasing numbers of people would turn to it by choice or through desperation as social and economic conditions deteriorated and as the bourgeois parties demonstrated their intellectual and ideological bankruptcy and incapacity to improve those conditions.

3. Hirschman notes that "voice is nothing but a basic portion and function of any political system, known sometimes also as 'interest articulation'" (1970, 30).

4. If a government succeeds in improving material conditions, then of course this government may stand to gain substantial voter loyalty, especially from low-income voters whose well-being might have been severely threatened. If such a government should become associated with a decline in democratic norms (that is, political corruption, restrictions on constitutional guarantees, heavy-handed treatment of the opposition), its gains in loyalty may be enough to withstand voice (complaints) about such problems.

5. All of the electoral results in this chapter come from Tuesta (1994), whose figures are as complete and accurate as any available. Tuesta has become the standard source for Peruvian electoral data. The popular vote totals reported throughout this chapter are, unless otherwise noted, valid votes; they exclude blank and nullified ballots as well as absentee voters. In 1978-CA the left was made up of the Frente Obrero Campesino Estudiantil y Popular (FOCEP; Worker Peasant Student and Popular Front); the Unidad Democrático Popular (UDP; Popular Democratic Unity); the Partido Socialista Revolucionario (PSR; Revolutionary Socialist Party); and the Partido Comunista Peruana (PCP; Peruvian Communist Party), not to be confused with the Shining Path, whose adherents called it the Peruvian Communist Party.

Others parties represented in the assembly included the Frente Nacional de Trabajadores y Campesinos (FNTC; Workers' and Peasants' National Front); the Unión Nacional Odriísta (UNO; National Odría Union); the Democracia Cristiana (DC; Christian Democracy); the Acción Revolucionaria Socialista (ARS; Revolutionary Socialist Action); and the Partido Democrático Reformista Peruana (PDRP; Peruvian Democratic Reformist Party).

6. Reported levels may be exaggerated.

7. IU's citywide total (28.3 percent) was considerably higher than its total among the pobladores (18.4 percent), but this statistic is somewhat misleading. Recall that IU also won 9 district-level mayoral races. If the sample's votes for district-level mayors in 1980 (not shown in table 14) are examined, it becomes clear that it is on the district level that the left showed its strength with the pobladores. IU district mayoral candidates took about 30 percent of the sample's votes, most of which came at the expense of AP (down ten percentage points) and PPC (down eleven).

8. The emergence of Sendero Luminoso in 1980 as an armed and violent leftist movement caused much initial soul-searching among the more moderate parties of the electoral left, that is, those who participated in and abided by elections. When Sendero Luminoso's violence became gradually more evident, however, Barrantes and virtually all members of IU renounced the movement on both ideological and strategic grounds. This stance by Barrantes gained him much credibility across the entire ideological spectrum. In return, Sendero Luminoso saved much of its most vitriolic rhetoric for IU, and for Barrantes personally.

9. APRA was for decades a regional party in Peru. Its iron grip on northern coastal areas (La Libertad, Lambayeque, the city of Trujillo) was unquestioned, but in the central and southern sierra and coast and particularly in Lima the party always did less well.

10. All such speculation soon ceased. Talk of amending the constitution was not popular, in general, and although García was indeed young (thirty-five years old) when he assumed office, assumptions that he could be automatically elected every five years for the next three or four decades soon disappeared.

11. Although my main analysis stops in 1990, see the epilogue for some results of elections since 1990.

12. Abstention occurs in Peru with a good deal of frequency, and although not voting means paying a fine, these fines frequently have not been enforced. Early in the 1980s the requirements to vote were sometimes difficult to fulfill. For example, an indi-

vidual had to vote where he was originally registered. Given the amount of rural-urban migration and of general demographic redistribution that has occurred in Peru in the past three or four decades, such a requirement meant considerable traveling and expense for a great many people, a certain number of whom decided it was more economical not to vote and to take the consequences. Other problems involved the bureaucratic difficulties of registering and the state's problems in maintaining its registration lists.

In the electoral arena, the Peruvian state has put in place what Verba, Nie, and Kim (1978, 6–8) call a compulsory ceiling and compulsory floor. The ceiling consists of a "one person, one vote" law (that is, no one's vote counts more than another's); the floor consists of a mandatory voting law. If fully implemented, such laws would mean that no relationship would exist between individual motivation to vote and resources, on the one hand, and the amount of political activity, on the other. There would thus be legally mandated equality of political activity across all social groups.

13. It might well be claimed here that this line of reasoning means that the poblador is thus resigning himself to piecemeal tactics that can never attack the fundamental structural causes of national (as well as individual and neighborhood) poverty. Although such an argument may from one perspective be correct, the pragmatics of the situation are such that the poor themselves harbor few if any illusions that they can in any way eliminate poverty. Attacking it on an incremental basis is preferable for at least two reasons. First, such a tactic has a realistic chance of working; second, asking or expecting or demanding broad-scale socioeconomic change both entails high risk and has low (if not zero) probability of working.

14. This choice is obviously complicated by party identification, personal ideology, and a whole raft of other factors that can reinforce, cancel, or modify a choice based solely on considerations of which candidate or party has the highest probability of resolving (or at least confronting) poverty. The individual voter, it should be noted, encounters costs involved in gathering information on all these factors.

15. That Peru's constitution calls for nonconcurrent presidential and municipal elections allows and even encourages such switching. In other Latin American nations with concurrent elections, vote-switching and ticket-splitting are much less frequent occurrences, primarily because the presidential race so overshadows the local, and presumably because of the ease of voting a straight ticket (or the difficulty in ticket-splitting).

16. The results from the sample do not differ dramatically from the overall Lima results. Those districts within Lima that are readily classifiable as lower class in general voted for Barrantes and IU, but not by large margins. APRA, on the other hand, certainly held its own in the barrios populares, but it also did extremely well in blue-collar and middle-income districts (see Tuesta 1994).

17. Vargas Llosa (1993), which combines about twenty years of autobiography with a detailed account of the 1990 presidential campaign, is notable not only for the quality of its writing but for its honesty and candor. Vargas Llosa makes no attempt to hide how distasteful he found campaigning to be, in general, and how uncomfortable he frequently felt surrounded by lower-class Lima and its citizens.

18. This latter difference may be due at least in part to the detailed *Plan de gobierno*

that Fredemo developed and distributed widely. This plan drew much favorable attention in the press and served as a major campaign element for Fredemo.

19. This may be surprising, since the Roman Catholic church was seen by some (especially the media) as playing a major role in the campaign. The church found itself faced, on one hand, with Mario Vargas Llosa who was an avowed atheist (or at least agnostic), someone who, early in his career as a writer, had said some definitely unflattering things about the church in his novels and in public. On the other hand, Alberto Fujimori, who was a professed Catholic, had received early in his campaign much grassroots support from Protestant and Evangelical groups and had named a minister from such a denomination as one of his vice-presidential running mates. In the end, although not officially endorsing any candidate, it was clear the church preferred Vargas Llosa to Fujimori.

20. Many Fujimori voters said they did not back Vargas Llosa because he was supported by AP and PPC. But regardless of whether AP's support of Vargas Llosa was important in an individual voter's decision on how to vote, both Fujimori and Vargas Llosa could certainly claim not to be traditional (that is, professional) politicians.

21. In Peru, where party institutionalization is low and where direct re-reelection of the president was not allowed until 1995, parties had particular difficulty in generating or maintaining *party* loyalty (that is, loyalty to the party per se) as distinct from loyalty to a personalist leader of a party or movement.

22. Although the poblador sample in particular—and Lima's lower classes in general —voted for Fujimori, it must be remembered that in 1990 Fujimori finished second in the first round both nationally (32.6 to 29.1 percent) and in metropolitan Lima (39.9 to 34.5 percent, respectively). Two things should be kept in mind. First, in Lima, Fujimori's popularity in the barrios populares (Cambio 90 generally took these areas by 2:1) was the only thing that allowed him to finish as close to Vargas Llosa as he did, since Fredemo took middle- and upper-class Lima by huge margins (as much as 8:1 in some districts). Second, in the second round, Fujimori won by a wide margin nationally (62.4 to 37.6 percent). His victory in Lima, however, was much narrower (53.3 to 46.7 percent). Again, only support from Lima's barrios populares allowed Fujimori to defeat Fredemo in Lima, since Vargas Llosa commanded the same huge majorities in Lima's middle- and upper-class districts in the second round as he had in the first.

9. Conclusions

1. A preliminary report on the 1971 data set (Dietz 1975) reported the presence of discrete modes of poblador involvement. Verba, Nie, and Kim (1978, 336–37) briefly note these results in their seven-nation study published subsequent to their earlier work, which dealt only with the United States (Verba and Nie 1972).

2. Whether voting dominated because it was mandatory is really of little consequence. Verba, Nie, and Kim (1978) found that voting was the most common act in every country they studied, even though it was not obligatory in any of them.

3. Other factors certainly influence Lima's poor and presumably their political be-

havior, directly and indirectly. For example, international forces and events such as slumps in world commodity prices clearly affect Peru's national economy and state policies. At an even further remove, it can be argued, global capitalism has placed Peru in a disadvantageous position as supplier of raw materials and as consumer of manufactured goods. However, although such global processes are undeniably important, they are also undeniably broad in nature. Tracing their direct influence on individual behavior may be asking too much.

4. It should be clear that even if the sample neighborhoods came to resemble each other, as did their aggregate patterns of political behavior, the need profile of the specific neighborhood lost its relevancy. Just because the needs of the neighborhoods became more or less similar does not mean these needs did not provoke and shape political involvement.

5. An overall economic upswing may do one of four things. First, the poor may gain absolutely in terms of real income, as well as relatively in terms of the closing gap between rich and poor. Second, the poor may gain in absolute terms, but not as much or as fast as do the wealthy. Third (less likely), the poor could lose absolutely but not as much or as fast as do the rich. And fourth, the poor may lose in both absolute and relative terms.

6. The Shining Path was operating throughout the 1980s in Peru's rural areas, a fact that contributed to rural-urban migration and to the numbers of poor supporting themselves in Lima's informal sector. Just how many such migrants moved to Lima, and how many of them found themselves in this sector, can only be guessed at.

7. This is not to imply that society cannot create its own means and mechanisms, whether they are approved by the state or not. Such means might include strikes, civil disturbances, insurrections, and a variety of other semilegal and illegal tactics.

8. The poor may prefer to organize themselves rather then be organized (and thereby co-opted) by the state, although autonomous organizations may encounter difficulties in being recognized or received by state representatives or agencies.

9. As an example, for decades one major complaint against Mexico's PRI was that it never lost an election. A system like Mexico's in which one party always (up until recent years) won cannot claim to be democratic, since elections were pre- (or PRI-) determined.

10. An outsider might also consider the realization of these limitations as a motive for mounting frustration, dissatisfaction, and perhaps radical or revolutionary behavior. This question in general terms is too broad a topic here. In the case of Peru, the only truly revolutionary option in existence in the late 1980s was the Shining Path (and, secondarily, the Revolutionary Tupac Amaru Movement). Some lower-class individuals supported the Shining Path, but the great majority of Lima's poor saw the movement more as a violent and brutal threat than as a viable or rational alternative.

11. In the late 1980s, in particular, the Peruvian state not only had to deal with increasing domestic needs and demands but also was under great international pressure to meet its debt obligations (which it could not and did not do, thereby exacerbating problems in the domestic arena as well).

12. The ability of the pobladores to maintain their own generally autonomous neigh-

borhood organizations was an important reason the Shining Path tried to infiltrate these organizations, and why, if they could not, they did everything possible to eliminate the organization and assassinate its leaders. Anything the Shining Path could not control it attempted to destroy.

10. Epilogue

1. One highly useful comparative source in English is Graham (1994), who provides case studies from Chile, Bolivia, Senegal, Zambia, and Poland, as well as Peru. Graham's view on Fujimori's (and García's) policies are aptly summed up in the title of the chapter on Peru: "The Politics of Reform Without a Safety Net: The Case of Peru" (83). Graham's chapter contains numerous sources and personal interview data. Other basic sources include Anderson et al. (1994) and Cameron and Mauceri (1997).

2. The Ministry of the Presidency under Fujimori became a position of considerable power, since most public works and pork barrel projects were under its aegis.

3. Although his election in 1995 was in fact his second term, Fujimori argued that his 1995 election was the first under the new constitution, and that if he were to run and be reelected in the year 2000, taking office then would be only his second term under the constitution. As of mid-1997, the matter remained unsettled, as did the way to resolve it—through the Constitutional Court, a national referendum, or by some other means.

4. This figure, which would be astonishing in any country let alone in Peru, was especially notable in light of the announcement in May 1997 that the new official minimum wage would be $115 monthly.

5. John Walton has argued for an explicit relationship between IMF-sponsored readjustment policies and urban rioting (Walton 1987), citing instances from Peru in support of his general argument, positing a direct cause-and-effect relationship between austerity measures and urban demonstrations. But such an argument may well be overly simplistic and does little to explain those instances where demonstrations did not occur when austerity measures were implemented.

6. Fujimori ran much of his 1990 presidential campaign against Mario Vargas Llosa's ill-advised public declaration that he would implement a shock treatment and his admitting that such a treatment would be painful. From all accounts and analyses, Fujimori gained much ground by warning voters about what Vargas Llosa planned to do, and by his own campaign platform, which was composed of the bland, vague promise of "Work, Honesty, and Technology." However, less than two weeks after assuming office, Fujimori announced his own shock treatment, which was in most respects more severe than Vargas Llosa's plans and which included no provision for a social safety net.

Moreover, Fujimori acted immediately upon taking office. Tactically, it may be best for an executive faced with implementing a harsh and unpopular policy to do so at the beginning of the term in power, in the hopes that the policy will prosper, that the initial pain associated with it will fade, and that the electorate will remember only its success. In the Peruvian case, this sequence appears to have happened with Fujimori in his first term.

7. Critics claimed that several of the hostages had attempted to surrender but had been shot and killed, and that the army had entered the compound with no intention of taking any prisoners. Fujimori and the military responded that the rescue had been extremely tense and that the troops involved (three of whom were killed) could not have been expected to ask questions before opening fire.

8. Manuel D'Ornellas, a widely read and respected journalist in Lima's newspaper *Expreso*, offered the opinion that Fujimori was losing or had lost the support of upper- and middle-class members of Peruvian society, but that lower-class and poor Peruvians gave much less importance to legal and human rights issues and continued to support Fujimori, thanks in large part to programs such as Foncodes and Fonavi (*Resumen Semanal* 1997, 2). His analysis offered little in the way of hard evidence to support it, however.

9. This statement should be taken with a bit of caution. The electoral data that exist do so on an aggregate level (that is, the district level). Although such data are reliable, and much can be learned from them, they are still not individual-level data. Thus the discussion here, which necessarily uses aggregate data, has its limitations. Data for all elections through the 1993 referendum are taken from Tuesta (1994); the results for the 1995 presidential race come from Durand (1996) and from data given to me in Lima by the National Electoral Board. The board also made available to me the results (then unpublished) of the 1995 municipal race.

10. Vargas Llosa actually won more districts in the first round than Fujimori, capturing twenty-five districts to Fujimori's fifteen. But many of Vargas Llosa's victories came in small outlying districts that contained only a few hundred voters. Most of Fujimori's victories came in the largest and poorest districts. For detailed analyses of voting in elections during the 1990s see Dietz and Dugan (1995) and Durand (1996).

11. It is perhaps worth noting that within a day or so following the election, Yoshiyama was named minister of the presidency.

REFERENCES

Abrams, Robert. 1980. *Foundations of Political Analysis: An Introduction to the Theory of Collective Choice.* New York: Columbia University Press.

Abugattás, Javier. 1990. *Estabilización y crecimiento económico en el Perú.* Lima: Fundación Friedrich Ebert.

Actualidad Económica. 1980. Lima. Vol. 27, May.

Adrianzén, Alberto. 1994. "Gobernabilidad, democracia y espacios locales." *Perfiles latinoamericanos: Revista de la Sede Académica de México de la Facultad Latinoamericana de Ciencias Sociales* 3.5 (December): 37–61.

Alarco, German, et al. 1986. *Empleo, salarios y distribución del ingreso: Margenes de política.* Lima: Fundación Friedrich Ebert, Taller de Investigación.

Alexander, Jeffrey, et al., eds. 1987. *The Micro-Macro Link.* Berkeley and Los Angeles: University of California Press.

Allou, Serge. 1989. *Lima en cifras.* Lima: Centro de Investigación, Documentación y Asesoría Poblacional.

Amat y León, Carlos. 1983. *Niveles de vida y grupos sociales en el Peru.* Lima: Universidad del Pacífico and Fundación Friedrich Ebert.

———. 1986. *La familia como unidad de trabajo.* Lima: Universidad del Pacífico, Centro de Investigaciones.

Amat y León, Carlos, and Dante Curonisy. 1981. *La alimentación en el Peru.* Lima: Universidad del Pacífico, Centro de Investigaciones.

Anderson, Janine, et al. 1994. *Pobreza y políticas sociales en el Perú.* Lima: Centro de Investigaciones, Universidad del Pacífico.

Andreas, Carol. 1985. *When Women Rebel: The Rise of Popular Feminism in Peru.* Westport, Conn.: Lawrence Hill.

Apoyo. 1993. "Resultados de las elecciones municipales: Informe de opinión." Unpublished report. Lima: Apoyo. February.

Assies, Willen. 1990. *Structures of Power, Movements of Resistance: An Introduction to the Theories of Urban Movements in Latin America.* Amsterdam: CEDLA.

Badie Bertrand, and Pierre Birnbaum. 1983. *The Sociology of the State.* Chicago: The University of Chicago Press.

Balbi, Carmen Rosa, et al. 1990. *Movimientos sociales: Elementos para una relectura.* Lima: DESCO.

Ballón, Eduardo, ed. 1986. *Movimientos sociales y democracia: La fundación de un nuevo orden.* Lima: DESCO.

Ballón, Eduardo, et al. 1986a. *Movimientos sociales y crisis: El caso peruano.* Lima: DESCO.

Banco Central de la Reserva del Perú. 1978. *Memoria.* Lima: Banco Central de la Reserva del Perú. June.

————. 1984. *Identificación de las diferencias interdistritales en Lima metropolitana.* Lima: Banco Central de la Reserva, Gerencia de Investigación Económica.

Barnes, Samuel, and Max Kaase. 1979. *Mass Participation in Five Western Democracies.* Beverly Hills, Calif.: Sage.

Barrig, Maruja. 1982. *Convivir: La pareja en la pobreza.* Lima: Mosca Azul.

Barrig, Maruja, ed. 1988. *De vecinas a ciudadanas: La mujer en el desarrollo urbano.* Lima: Servicios Urbanos y Mujeres de Bajos Ingresos.

Barry, Brian, and Russell Hardin. 1982. *Rational Man and Irrational Society?* Beverly Hills, Calif.: Sage Publications.

Basadre, Jorge. 1980. *La multitud, la cuidad y el campo en la historia del Perú.* Lima: Ediciones Treintaitrés and Mosca Azul Editores.

Bennett, Stephen, and Linda Bennett. 1986. "Political Participation." In Samuel Long, ed., *Annual Review of Political Science,* vol. 1, pp. 157–204. Norwood, N.J.: Ablex.

Berry, Albert. 1990. "International Trade, Government, and Income Distribution in Peru since 1870." *Latin American Research Review* 25.2: 31–60.

Blondet, Cecilia. 1986. *Muchas vidas construyendo una identidad: Mujeres pobladoras de un barrio limeño.* Lima: Instituto de Estudios Peruanos, Documento de Trabajo 9.

————. 1991. *Las mujeres y el poder: Una historia de Villa El Salvador.* Lima: Instituto de Estudios Peruanos.

Blondet, Cecilia, and Carmen Montero. 1995a. *Hoy: Menu popular—Comedores en Lima.* Lima: Instituto de Estudios Peruanos and UNICEF.

————. 1995b. *La situación de la mujer en el Perú, 1980–1994.* Lima: Instituto de Estudios Peruanos, Documento de Trabajo 68.

Boggio, Klara. 1970. *Estudio del ciclo vital en Pamplona Alta.* Lima: DESCO, Cuaderno A6.

Books, John W., and Charles Prysby. 1991. *Political Behavior and the Local Context.* New York: Praeger.

Booth, John, and Mitchell Seligson. 1978. "Images of Political Participation in Latin America." In John Booth and Mitchell Seligson, eds., *Political Participation in Latin America,* vol. 1, pp. 3–26. New York: Holmes and Meier.

Brady, Henry, Sidney Verba, and Kay Lehman Schlozman. 1995. "Beyond SES: A Resource Model of Political Participation." *American Political Science Review* 89.2 (June): 271–94.

Bromley, Ray. 1990. "A New Path to Development? The Significance and Impact of Hernando de Soto's Ideas on Underdevelopment, Production, and Reproduction." *Economic Geography* 66.1 (October): 328–48.

Burgos, H. 1994. "Gasto social y pobreza: Cada vez menos para cada vez mas pobres." *Cuestion de Estado* 7 (March): 37–43.

Bustamante, Alberto, et al. 1990. *De marginales a informales.* Lima: DESCO.

Calderón C., Julio. 1980. *El Agustino: 33 años de lucha, 1947–1980.* Lima: Servicios Educativos El Agustino, Programa Centro de Estudios y Comunicación Social de El Agustino.

———. 1990. *Las ideas urbanas en el Perú.* Lima: Instituto de Desarrollo Urbano.

Cameron, Maxwell. 1991a. "Political Parties and the Worker-Employer Cleavage: The Impact of the Informal Sector on Voting in Lima, Peru." *Bulletin of Latin American Research* 10.3: 293–313.

———. 1991b. "The Politics of the Urban Informal Sector in Peru: Populism, Class and 'Redistributive Combines.'" *Canadian Journal of Latin American and Caribbean Studies* 16.31: 79–104.

———. 1994. *Democracy and Authoritarianism in Peru: Political Coalitions and Social Change.* New York: St. Martin's Press.

Cameron, Maxwell, and Philip Mauceri, eds. 1997. *The Peruvian Labyrinth: Polity, Society, Economy.* University Park: Pennsylvania State University Press.

Carbonetto, Daniel, Jenny Hoyle, and Mario Tueros. 1988. *Lima: Sector Informal.* 2 vols. Lima: Centro de Estudios para el Desarrollo y la Participación.

Cardoso, Eliana A. 1992. "Inflation and Poverty." Cambridge, Mass.: National Bureau of Economic Research, NBER Working Paper 4006.

Caretas. Lima. April 5, 1977.

Castells, Manuel. 1983. *The City and the Grassroots: A Cross-Cultural Theory of Urban Social Movements.* London: E. Arnold.

Centro de Estudios y Publicaciones. 1971. *Pamplona: Mas all de los hechos—documentos.* Lima: CEP.

Centro de Información, Estudios y Documentación. 1979. *Partidos y conciencia en las barriadas.* Lima: Centro de Información, Estudios y Documentación.

Circulo de Estudios Alejandro Quijano. [1983?]. *Movimiento de pobladores y lucha de clases: Balance y perspectivas.* Lima: Circulo de Estudios Alejandro Quijano.

Cohen, Cathy, and Michael Dawson. 1993. "Neighborhood Poverty and African American Politics." *American Political Science Review* 87.2 (June): 286–302.

Cohen, Jean, and Andrew Arato. 1992. *Civil Society and Political Theory.* Cambridge, Mass.: MIT Press.

Coleman, James. 1987. "Microfoundations and Macrosocial Behavior." In Jeffrey Alexander et al., eds., *The Micro-Macro Link,* pp. 153–75. Berkeley and Los Angeles: University of California Press.

———. 1990. *Foundations of Social Theory.* Cambridge, Mass.: Belknap Press of Harvard University Press.

Collier, David. 1976. *Squatters and Oligarchs*. Baltimore: Johns Hopkins University Press.

Collier, David, and Deborah Norden. 1992. "Strategic Choice Models of Political Change in Latin America." *Comparative Politics* 24.2 (January 1992): 229–43.

El Comercio. 1990. June 1, E.1.

Córdova, Adolfo. 1958. *La vivienda en el Perú: Estado actual y evaluación de las necesidades*. Lima: Casa de la Moneda.

Cornelius, Wayne. 1975. *Politics and the Migrant Poor in Mexico City*. Stanford, Calif.: Stanford University Press.

Crabtree, John. 1992. *Peru Under García: An Opportunity Lost*. Pittsburgh, Pa.: University of Pittsburgh Press.

Cruz Saco, Maria. 1992. "Drawing More Lines: Factor Analyzing and Clustering Poverty in Peru." Paper presented at the 1992 Congress of Latin American Studies Association.

Daeschner, Jeff. 1993. *La guerra del fin de la democracia: Mario Vargas Llosa versus Alberto Fujimori*. Lima: Peru Reporting.

Dahl, Robert. 1971. *Polyarchy*. New Haven, Conn.: Yale University Press.

Debates en Sociología. 1984, entire issue.

Degregori, Carlos Ivan, Cecilia Blondet, and Nicolas Lynch. 1986. *Conquistadores de un mundo nuevo: De invasores a ciudadanos en San Martin de Porres*. Lima: Instituto de Estudios Peruanos.

Deler, Jean Paul. 1975. *Lima 1940–1970*. Lima: Centro de Investigaciones Geográficas.

Delgado, Carlos. 1975. *Revolución peruana: Autonomía y deslindes*. Lima: Libros de Contratiempo.

de Soto, Hernando. 1986. *El otro sendero*. Lima: Instituto de Libertad y Democracia.

DESCO. 1989. *Violencia política en el Perú, 1980–1988*. Lima: DESCO.

Diamond, Larry. 1994. "Rethinking Civil Society: Toward Democratic Consolidation." *Journal of Democracy* 5.3 (July): 3–17.

———. 1996. "Is the Third Wave Over?" *Journal of Democracy* 7.3 (July): 3–24.

Diamond, Larry, Juan Linz, and Seymour Martin Lipset, eds. 1990. *Politics in Developing Countries: Comparing Experiences with Democracy*. Boulder, Colo.: Lynne Rienner.

Dietz, Henry. 1975. "Some Modes of Participation in an Authoritarian Regime." Paper prepared for presentation at the 1975 meeting of the American Political Science Association.

———. 1977. "Bureaucratic Demand-Making and Clientelistic Participation in Peru." In James Malloy, ed., *Authoritarianism and Corporatism in Latin America*, pp. 413–58 Pittsburgh, Pa.: University of Pittsburgh Press.

———. 1980. *Poverty and Problem-Solving Under Military Rule: The Urban Poor in Lima, Peru*. Austin: University of Texas Press.

———. 1985. "Political Participation in the Barriadas: An Extension and Re-examination." *Comparative Political Studies* 18.3 (October): 323–55.

Dietz, Henry, and David Scott Palmer. 1978. "Citizen Participation Under Innovative

Military Corporatism in Peru." In John Booth and Mitchell Seligson, eds., *Political Participation in Latin America*, vol. 1, *Citizen and State*. pp. 172–88. New York: Holmes and Meier.

Dietz, Henry, and William Dugan. 1995. "Urban Social Classes and Voting Behavior in Lima: An Aggregate Data Analysis." Paper presented at the 1995 Congress of the Latin American Studies Association, Washington, D.C.

Dornbusch, Rudiger, and Sebastien Edwards. 1990. "The Macroeconomics of Populism in Latin America." *Journal of Developmental Economics* 32.2 (April): 247–77.

Dornbusch, Rudiger, and Sebastien Edwards, eds. 1991. *The Macroeconomics of Populism in Latin America*. Chicago: University of Chicago Press.

Driant, Jean-Claude. 1991. *Las barriadas de Lima: Historia e interpretación*. Lima: DESCO.

Durand, Francisco. 1996. "El fenómeno Fujimori y la crisis de los partidos." *Revista Mexicana de Sociología* 58.1 (January–March): 97–120.

Eckstein, Harry. 1992. "Rationality and Frustration." In *Regarding Politics: Essays on Political Theory, Stability, and Change*, pp. 378–95. Berkeley and Los Angeles: University of California Press.

Eckstein, Susan, ed. 1989. *Power and Popular Protest: Latin American Social Movements*. Princeton, N.J.: Princeton University Press.

———. 1990. "Urbanization Revisited: Inner-City Slum of Hope and Squatter Settlement of Despair." *World Development* 18.2: 165–81.

ECLAC. See Economic Commission for Latin America and the Caribbean (ECLA).

Economía y Política. Lima. March–April 1980.

Economic Commission for Latin America and the Caribbean (ECLA). 1997. *The Equity Gap: Latin America, the Caribbean, and the Social Summit*. United Nations: ECLAC.

Escobar, Arturo, and Sonia Alvarez, eds. 1992. *The Making of Social Movements in Latin America: Identity, Strategy, and Democracy*. Boulder, Colo.: Westview.

Evans, Peter. 1979. *Dependent Development: The Alliance of Multinational, State, and Local Capital in Brazil*. Princeton, N.J.: Princeton University Press.

Favaro, Edgardo. 1994. "Institutions, the Modern State, and Development: Terrorism in Peru." Washington, D.C.: World Bank, Cross Fertilization Seminars. Unpublished report.

Ferradas, Pedro. 1983. *Ciudad y pobladores de Lima metropolitana, 1940–1983*. Vol. 1. Lima: CELADEC.

Figari Gold, Eduardo, and Xavier Ricou. 1990. *Lima en crisis: Propuestas para la gestión de los servicios urbanos en Lima metropolitana*. Lima: Universidad del Pacífico, Centro de Investigación.

Figueroa, Adolfo. 1993. *Crisis distributiva en el Perú*. Lima: Fondo Editorial de la Pontificia Universidad Católica del Perú.

———. 1995. "Desigualdad y democracia." In Gonzalo Portocarrero and Marcel Valcárcel, eds., *El Perú frente al siglo XXI*, pp. 53–76. Lima: Pontificia Universidad Católica del Perú.

Fitzgerald, E. V. K. 1983. "State Capitalism in Peru: A Model of Economic Development and Its Limitations." In Cynthia McClintock and Abraham Lowenthal, eds., *The Peruvian Experiment Reconsidered*, pp. 65–93. Princeton, N.J.: Princeton University Press.

Flores Galindo, Alberto. 1984. *Aristocracia y plebe: Lima, 1760–1830*. Lima: Mosca Azul.

Fondo Nacional de Salud y Bienestar Social. 1960. *Barriadas de Lima metropolitana*. Lima: Fondo Nacional de Salud y Bienestar Social.

Foweraker, Joe. 1990. "Popular Movements in Political Change in Mexico." In Joe Foweraker and Ann Craig, eds., *Popular Movements in Political Change in Mexico*, pp. 3–22. Boulder, Colo.: Lynne Rienner.

————. 1995. *Theorizing Social Movements*. Boulder, Colo.: Pluto Press.

Foweraker, Joe, and Ann Craig, eds. 1990. *Popular Movements and Political Change in Mexico*. Boulder, Colo.: Lynne Rienner.

Franco, Carlos. 1989. *Informales: Nuevos rostros en la vieja Lima*. Lima: Centro de Estudios para el Desarrollo y la Participación.

Galer, Nora, and Pilar Nuñez C., eds. 1989. *Mujer y comedores populares*. Lima: Servicios para el Desarrollo.

Galín, Pedro, Julio Carrión, and Oscar Castillo. 1986. *Asalariados y clases populares en Lima*. Lima: Instituto de Estudios Peruanos.

García, José María. 1985. "Pobreza, población y vivienda en distritos de Lima metropolitana, 1981." In Narda Henríquez et al., *Lima: Población, trabajo, y política*, pp. 113–34. Lima: Pontificia Universidad Católica.

Gatti Murriel, Aldo, and Pieded Pareja Pflucker. 1995. *Democracia y participación*. Lima: Fundación Friedrich Ebert.

Geddes, Barbara. 1995. "Use and Limitations of Rational Choice." In Peter Smith, ed., *Latin American in Comparative Perspective: New Approaches to Methods and Analysis*, pp. 81–108. Boulder, Colo.: Westview.

Gellner, Ernest. 1991. "Civil Society in Historical Context." *International Social Science Journal* 43: 495–510.

Germaná, Cesar. 1994. "Algunas hypotesis sobre el autogobierno de la `comunidades urbanas' en el Perú." *Revista de Sociología* (Lima) 8.9: 61–83.

Giddens, Anthony. 1984. *The Constitution of Society: Outline of the Theory of Structuration*. Berkeley and Los Angeles: University of California Press.

Gilbert, Alan, and Josef Gugler. 1992. *Cities, Poverty, and Development: Urbanization in the Third World*. 2d ed. New York: Oxford University Press.

Glewwe, Paul. 1988. *The Distribution of Welfare in Peru, 1985–1985*. Washington, D.C.: World Bank, LSMS Working Paper 42.

Glewwe, Paul, and Dennis de Tray. 1989. *The Poor in Latin America During Adjustment: A Case Study of Peru*. Washington, D.C.: World Bank, LSMS Working Paper 56.

Goldrich, Daniel. 1970. "Political Organization and the Politicization of the Poblador." *Comparative Political Studies* 3.2 (July): 176–202.

Gómez Peralta, Oscar E. 1990. *Las poblaciones marginales en el Perú.* Lima: E. F. Gómez e Hijos Editoriales.

Gonzales de Olarte, Efraín. 1992. *La economía regional de Lima: Crecimiento, urbanización y clases populares.* Lima: Instituto de Estudios Peruanos.

Goritti Ellenbogen, Gustavo. 1990. *Sendero: Historia de la guerra milenaria.* Lima: Apoyo.

Graham, Carole. 1992. *Peru's APRA: Parties, Politics, and the Elusive Quest for Democracy.* Boulder, Colo.: Lynne Reinner.

———. 1994. *Safety Nets, Politics, and the Poor: Transitions to Market Economies.* Washington, D.C.: Brookings Institution.

Grandón, Alicia Trinidad, and José Maria García Rios. 1984. "El trabajo doméstico de la mujer de sectores populares urbanos: El caso de la pobladora de El Agustino." *Debates en Sociología* (Lima) 10: 95–120.

Grandón, Alicia Trinidad, and José Maria García Rios. 1990. *Discriminación y sobrevivencia.* Lima: Pontificia Universidad Católica and Fundación Friedrich Naumann.

Grofman, Bernard. 1987. "Models of Voting." In *Research in Micropolitics*, vol. 2, pp. 31–61. Greenwich, Conn.: JAI Press.

Grompone, Romeo. 1986. *Talleristas y vendedores ambulantes en Lima.* Lima: DESCO.

Grompone, Romeo, et al. 1983. *La Lima de los 80: Crecimiento y segregación social.* Lima: DESCO.

Gurr, Ted R. 1970. *Why Men Rebel.* Princeton, N.J.: Princeton University Press.

Haak, Roelfien, and Javier Diaz Albertini, eds. 1987. *Estrategias de vida en el sector urbano popular.* Lima: DESCO and Asociación Fomento de la Vida.

Haber, Paul. 1996. "Identity and Political Process: Recent Trends in the Study of Latin American Social Movements." *Latin American Research Review* 31.1:171–87.

Hadenius, Axel, and Fredrik Uggla. 1996. "Making Civil Society Work, Promoting Democratic Development: What Can States and Donors Do?" *World Development* 24.10: 1621–39.

Hall, John A., ed. 1995. *Civil Society: Theory, History, Comparison.* Cambridge, Mass.: Polity Press.

Handelman, Howard, and Werner Baer, eds. 1989. *Paying the Costs of Austerity in Latin America.* Boulder, Colo.: Westview.

Hardin, Russell. 1982. *Collective Action.* Baltimore: Johns Hopkins University Press.

Harvey, David. 1973. *Social Justice and the City.* Baltimore: Johns Hopkins University Press.

———. 1978. "The Urban Process Under Capitalism: A Framework for Analysis." *International Journal of Urban and Regional Research* 2.1: 101–32.

Henry, Etienne. 1981. *Movimiento de pobladores y centralización.* Lima: Centro de Investigación, Documentación y Asesoría Poblacional.

Herzog, Don. 1989. *Happy Slaves: A Critique of Consent Theory.* Chicago: University of Chicago Press.

Hibbs, Douglas. 1982. "Economic Outcomes and Political Support for British Governments Among Occupational Classes." *American Political Science Review* 76.2 (June): 259–79.

Hirschman, Albert. 1970. *Exit, Voice, and Loyalty: Responses to Decline in Firms, Organizations, and States.* Cambridge, Mass.: Harvard University Press.

Hobsbawm, Eric. 1971. "Peru: The Peculiar Revolution." *New York Review of Books,* December 16, 1971, 19–36.

Hommes, Rudolf. 1995. "Decentralization: Political and Fiscal Problems." In *Development Policy,* pp. 5, 8. Washington, D.C.: Inter-American Development Bank, Newsletter of Policy Research. June.

Hunt, Shane. 1985. "Growth and Guano in Nineteenth-Century Peru." In Roberto Cortés Conde and Shane Hunt, eds., *Latin American Economies: Growth and the Export Sector, 1880–1930,* pp. 8–54. New York: Holmes and Meier.

Huntington, Samuel. 1968. *Political Order in Changing Societies.* New Haven, Conn.: Yale University Press.

ILD. See Instituto Libertad y Democracia (ILD).

INEI. See Instituto Nacional de Estadística e Informática (INEI).

INP. See Instituto Nacional de Planificación (INP).

Instituto Cúanto. 1995. *Retrato de la familia Peruana: Niveles de vida, 1994.* Lima: Instituto Cúanto.

Instituto Libertad y Democracia (ILD). 1989a. *Compendio técnico y estadístico de 'El otro sendero.'"* Lima: ILD.

———. 1989b. *El comercio ambulatorio en Lima.* Lima: ILD.

———. 1990a. *El transporte urbano de pasajeros en Lima.* Lima: ILD.

———. 1990b. "A Reply." *World Development* 18.1: 137–45.

Instituto Nacional de Estadística e Informática (INEI). 1992. *Lima-Callao: Compendio estadístico, 1991–1992.* Lima: INEI, Dirección Nacional de Estadisticas Regionales y Locales.

———. 1994. *Censos nacionales 1993: Resultados definitivos a nivel provincial y distrital, Departamento de Lima, Provincia Lima.* Vol. 1. Lima: INEI, Dirección Nacional de Censos y Encuestas.

Instituto Nacional de Planificación (INP). 1989. *Distribución territorial de la pobreza en el Peru.* Lima: INP, Proyecto Regional para la Superación de la Pobreza RLA/86/004.

Jochamowitz, Luís. 1994. *Ciudadano Fujimori: La construcción de un político.* 2d ed. Lima: PEISA.

Kaska, John. 1993. "Parties, Interest Groups, and Administered Mass Organizations." *Comparative Political Studies* 26.1 (April): 81–110.

Kay, Bruce. 1996–1997. "'Fujipopulismo' and the Liberal State in Peru, 1990–1995." *Journal of Interamerican Studies and World Affairs* 38.4 (winter): 55–98.

Kuczynski, Pedro-Pablo. 1990. "Peru." In John Williamson, ed., *Latin American Adjust-*

ment: How Much Has Happened?, pp. 86–95. Washington, D.C.: Institute for International Economics.

Lafosse, Violeta Sara. 1984. *Comedores comunales: La mujer frente a la crisis*. Lima: Servicios urbanos y mujeres de bajos ingresos.

Lago, Ricardo. 1991. "The Illusion of Pursuing Redistribution Through Macropolicy: Peru's Heterodox Experience, 1985–1990." In Rudiger Dornbusch and Sebastien Edwards, eds., *The Macroeconomics of Populism in Latin America*, pp. 263–323. Chicago: University of Chicago Press.

Leeds, Anthony. 1969. "The Significant Variables Determining the Character of Squatter Settlements." *America Latina* 12.3 (July–September): 44–86.

Lijphart, Arend. 1997. "Unequal Participation: Democracy's Unresolved Dilemma." *American Political Science Review* 91.1 (March): 1–14.

Lipset, Seymour Martin. 1994. "The Social Requisites of Democracy Revisited." *American Sociological Review* 59.1 (February): 1–22.

Llorens, José Antonio. 1983. *Musica popular en Lima: Criollos y Andinos*. Lima: Instituto de Estudios Peruanos and Instituto Indigenista Interamericano.

Lowenthal, Abraham, ed. 1975. *The Peruvian Experiment*. Princeton, N.J.: Princeton University Press.

Mainwaring, Scott. 1986. "Brazil: The Catholic Church and Popular Movements in Nova Iguacu, 1974–1985." In Daniel Levine, ed., *Religious and Political Conflicts in Latin America*, pp. 124–55. Chapel Hill: University of North Carolina Press.

Manaster, Kenneth. 1968. "The Problem of Urban Squatters in Developing Countries: Peru." *Tulane Law Review* 43.1 (December): 94–127.

Margolis, Howard. 1982. *Selfishness, Altruism, and Rationality: A Theory of Social Choice*. Chicago: University of Chicago Press.

Martínez, G. S. 1965. *Ley de barriadas*. Lima: Distribuidora Bendezu.

Matos, Mar, José. 1966. *Estudio de las barriadas limeñas*. Lima: Universidad Nacional Mayor de San Marcos.

———. 1968. *Urbanización y barriadas en América del Sur*. Lima: Instituto de Estudios Peruanos.

———. 1984. *Desborde popular y crises del estado: El nuevo rostro del Perú en la década de 1980*. Lima: Instituto de Estudios Peruanos.

McClintock, Cynthia, and Abraham Lowenthal, eds. 1983. *The Peruvian Experiment Reconsidered*. Princeton, N.J.: Princeton University Press.

Mesa-Lago, Carmelo. 1994. *Changing Social Security in Latin America*. Boulder, Colo.: Lynne Reinner.

Migdal, Joel. 1988. *Strong Societies and Weak States: State-Society Relations and State Capabilities in the Third World*. Princeton, N.J.: Princeton University Press.

Milbraith, Lester, and M. L. Goel. 1977. *Political Participation*. 2d ed. Chicago: Rand McNally.

Miller, Nicholas. 1986. "Public Choice and the Theory of Voting: A Survey." In Samuel Long, ed., *Annual Review of Political Science*, vol. 1, pp. 1–36. Norwood, N.J.: Ablex.

Moore, Richard J. 1978. "Assimilation and Political Participation Among the Urban Poor in Guayaquil, Ecuador." Ph.D. diss., University of Texas.

Muller, Edward. 1980. "The Psychology of Political Protest and Violence." In Ted Robert Gurr, ed., *Handbook of Political Conflict*, pp. 69–99. New York: Free Press.

Muller, Edward, and Karl-Dieter Opp. 1986. "Rational Choice and Rebellious Collective Action." *American Political Science Review* 80.2 (June): 171–89.

Muller, Edward, Henry Dietz, and Steven Finkel. 1991. "Discontent and the Expected Utility of Rebellion: The Case of Peru." *American Political Science Review* 85.4 (December): 1261–82.

Nagel, Jack. 1987. *Participation*. Englewood-Cliffs, N.J.: Prentice-Hall.

Nelson, Joan. 1979. *Access to Power: Politics and the Urban Poor in Developing Nations*. Princeton, N.J.: Princeton University Press.

Nugent, José Guillermo. 1992. *El labyrinto de la choledad*. Lima: Fundación Friedrich Ebert.

Okun, Arthur. 1975. *Equality and Efficiency: The Big Trade-Off*. Washington, D.C.: Brookings Institution.

Olson, Mancur. 1965. *The Logic of Collective Action*. Cambridge, Mass.: Harvard University Press.

Palmer, David Scott, ed. 1992. *The Shining Path of Peru*. New York: St. Martins.

Panfichi, Aldo. 1994. "Los pobres de las ciudades latinoamericanas: Balance y perspectivas teóricas." *Revista de Sociología* (Lima) 8.9: 85–113.

Panfichi, Aldo, and Felipe Portocarrero, eds. 1995. *Mundos interiores: Lima, 1850–1950*. Lima: Universidad del Pacífico, Centro de Investigaciones.

Paredes, Peri, and Griselda Tello. 1989. *Los trabajos de las mujeres: Lima, 1980–1987*. Lima: Asociación Laboral para el Desarrollo.

Pareja Pflucker, Piedad, and Aldo Gatti Murriel. 1993. *Elecciones municipales en las provincias de Lima y Callao*. Lima: Fundación Friedrich Ebert.

Parodi, Jorge, ed. 1993. *Los pobres, la ciudad y la política*. Lima: Centro de Estudios de Democracia y Sociedad.

Pastor, Manuel, and Carol Wise. 1992. "Peruvian Economic Policy in the 1980s: From Orthodoxy to Heterodoxy and Back." *Latin American Research Review* 27.2: 83–117.

Pateman, Carole. 1988. *The Sexual Contract*. Stanford, Calif.: Stanford University Press.

Patch, Richard. 1967. "La Parada, Lima's Market," pts. 1, 2, 3. American Universities Field Staff Reports, West Coast South America, vol. 14, pts. 1, 2, 3.

Paus, Eva. 1991. "Adjustment and Development in Latin America: The Failure of Peruvian Heterodoxy, 1985–1988." *World Development* 19.5: 411–34.

Pease, Henry. 1977. *El ocaso del poder oligárquico*. Lima: DESCO.

———. 1978. *Los caminos del poder*. Lima: DESCO.

Pease, Henry, ed. 1991. *Construyendo un gobierno metropolitano: Políticas municipales*. Lima: Instituto para la Democracia Local.

Perú Económico. 1990. Vol. 13, March 3, 11–13. Lima.

Peterson, George. 1997. "Decentralization in Latin America: Learning Through Experience." Washington, D.C.: World Bank, World Bank Latin American and Caribbean Studies.

Poole, Deborah, and Gerardo Rénique. 1992. *Peru: Time of Fear*. London: Latin American Bureau.

Ponce Monteza, Carlos Ramon. 1994. *Gamarra: Formación, estructura y perspectivas*. Lima: Fundación Friedrich Ebert.

Popkin, Samuel. 1979. *The Rational Peasant*. Berkeley and Los Angeles: University of California Press.

Portes, Alejandro. 1989. "Latin American Urbanization in the Years of Crisis." *Latin American Research Review* 24.3: 7–44.

Portes, Alejandro, and Manuel Castells. 1989. "World Underneath: The Origins, Dynamics, and Effects of the Informal Economy." In Alejandro Portes, Manuel Castells, and Lauren Benton, eds., *The Informal Economy*, pp. 11–37. Baltimore: Johns Hopkins University Press.

Portes, Alejandro, Manuel Castells, and Lauren Benton, eds. 1989. *The Informal Economy*. Baltimore: Johns Hopkins University Press.

Portocarrero, Gonzalo. 1993. *Los nuevos limeños: Sueños, fevores y caminos en el mundo popular*. Lima: SUR Casa de Estudios del Socialismo and TAFOS Talleres de Fotografia Social.

Portocarrero, Gonzalo, and Marcel Valcárcel, eds. 1995. *El Perú frente al siglo XXI*. Lima: Pontificia Universidad Católica del Perú.

Powell, Sandra. 1969. "Political Participation in the Barriadas." *Comparative Political Studies* 2.2 (July): 195–215.

Przeworski, Adam. 1991. *Democracy and the Market: Political and Economic Reforms in Eastern Europe and Latin America*. New York: Cambridge University Press.

Przeworski, Adam, and Henry Teune. 1970. *The Logic of Social Inquiry*. New York: Wiley-Interscience.

Psacharopoulos, George, et al. 1997. "Poverty and Income Distribution in Latin America: The Story of the 1980s." Washington, D.C.: World Bank, World Bank Technical Paper 351.

Putnam, Robert. 1993. *Making Democracy Work: Civic Traditions in Modern Italy*. Princeton, N.J.: Princeton University Press.

Quehacer. Various issues. Lima: DESCO.

Reid, Michael. 1985. *Peru: Paths to Poverty*. London: Latin American Bureau.

Resumen Semanal. 1997. Vol. 19, no. 924, June 18–24.

Riofrio, Gustavo. 1978. *Se busca terreno para próxima barriada: Espacios disponibles en Lima 1940/1978/1990*. Lima: DESCO.

————. 1986. *Habilitación urbana con participación popular: Tres casos en Lima, Perú.* Eschborn, Germany: Deutsche Gesellschaft für Technische Zusammenarbeit.

————. 1991. *Producir la ciudad (popular) de los '90.* Lima: DESCO.

Riofrio, Gustavo, and J. C. Dirant. 1987. *¿Qué vivienda han construido? Nuevos problemas en viejas barriadas.* Lima: Centro de Investigación, Desarrollo y Asesoría Poblacional.

Roberts, Bryan. 1995. *The Making of Citizens.* New York: Halsted Press.

Roberts, Kenneth. 1995. "Neoliberalism and the Transformation of Populism in Latin America." *World Politics* 48 (October): 82–116.

————. 1996. "Economic Crisis and the Demise of the Legal Left in Peru." *Comparative Politics* (October): 69–92.

Roberts, Kenneth. 1997. "Beyond Romanticism: Social Movements and the Study of Political Change in Latin America." *Latin American Research Review* 32.2: 132–5.

Roberts, Kenneth, and Moises Arce. 1998. "Neoliberalism and Lower-Class Voting Behavior in Peru." *Comparative Politics* 31.2 (April): 217–46.

Rodriguez, Adolfo, et al., eds. 1973. *Segregación residencial y desmobilización política.* Buenos Aires: Ediciones SIAP.

Rodríguez Rabanal, César. 1989. *Cicatrices de la pobreza: Un estudio psicoanalítico.* Caracas: Editorial Nueva Sociedad.

Rossini, R. G., and J. J. Thomas. 1990. "The Size of the Informal Sector in Peru: A Critical Comment on Hernando de Soto's *El otro sendero.*" *World Development* 18.1: 125–35.

Rueschemeyer, Dietrich, Evelyne Huber Stephens, and John D. Stephens. 1992. *Capitalist Development and Democracy.* Chicago: University of Chicago Press.

Ruíz-Bravo, Patrícia, ed. 1996. *Detrás de la Puerta: Hombres y mujeres en el Perú de hoy.* Lima: Pontificia Universidad Católica del Perú.

Sachs, Jeffrey. 1990. *Social Conflict and Populist Policies in Latin America.* San Francisco: International Center for Economic Growth.

Salman, Ton. 1990. "Between Orthodoxy and Euphoria: Research Strategies on Social Movements: A Comparative Perspective." In Willem Assises et al., eds., *Structures of Power, Movements of Resistance: An Introduction to the Theories of Urban Movements in Latin America,* pp. 99–161. Amsterdam: Centro de Estudios y Documentación Latinoamericanos.

Sánchez Leon, Abelardo, et al. 1979. *Tugurización en Lima metropolitana.* Lima: DESCO.

————. 1980. *El laberinto de la ciudad: Políticas urbanas del estado, 1950–1979.* Lima: DESCO.

Schmidt, Gregory. 1996. "Fujimori's Upset Victory in Peru: Electoral Rules, Contingencies, and Adaptive Strategies." *Comparative Politics,* pp. 321–54.

————. 1998. *From Tidal Wave to Earthquake: The Fujimori Phenomenon in Peru.* Gainesville: University of Florida Press.

Schumpeter, Joseph. 1976. *Capitalism, Socialism, and Democracy.* London: Allen and Unwin.

Servicios Educativos El Agustino (SEA). 1995. *Hablan los dirigentes vecinales.* Lima: SEA.

Shapiro, Harvey. 1976. "Monitoring: Are the Banks Biting Off More Than They Can Chew?" *Institutional Investor,* October, 1–7.

Sheetz, Thomas. 1986. *Peru and the IMF.* Pittsburgh, Pa.: University of Pittsburgh Press.

Simon, Herbert. 1982. *Models of Bounded Rationality.* Cambridge, Mass.: MIT.

———. 1985. "Human Nature in Politics: The Dialogue of Psychology with Political Science." *American Political Science Review* 79.2 (June): 293–304.

Smith, Michael Peter, and Richard Tardanico. 1987. "Urban Theory Reconsidered: Production, Reproduction, and Collective Action." In Michael Peter Smith and Joe Feagin, eds., *The Capitalist City: Global Restructuring and Community Politics,* pp. 87–110. New York: Basil Blackwell.

Smith, Michael Peter, and Joe Feagin, eds. 1987. *The Capitalist City: Global Restructuring and Community Politics.* New York: Basil Blackwell.

Sobrevilla, Luis, Elsa Alcantara de Samaniego, and Emilia Gartner de Nunez. 1987. *Nacer y morir en la pobreza.* Lima: Universidad Peruana Cayetano Heredia, Instituto de Estudios de Población.

Stallings, Barbara. 1979. "Peru and the U.S. Banks: Privatization of Financial Relations." In Richard Fagen, ed., *Capitalism and the State in U.S.–Latin American Relations,* pp. 217–53. Stanford, Calif.: Stanford University Press.

Stepan, Alfred. 1978. *The State and Society: Peru in Contemporary Perspective.* Princeton, N.J.: Princeton University Press.

———. 1988. *Rethinking Military Politics.* Princeton, N.J.: Princeton University Press.

Stern, Peter. 1996. *Sendero Luminoso: An Annotated Bibliography of the Shining Path Guerrilla Movement, 1980–1993.* Austin, Texas: SALALM Secretariat.

Stokes, Susan. 1991. "Politics and Latin America's Urban Poor: Notes from a Lima Shantytown." *Latin American Research Review* 26.2, pp. 75–101.

———. 1995. *Cultures in Conflict: Social Movements and the State in Peru.* Berkeley and Los Angeles: University of California Press.

Strong, Simon. 1993. *Shining Path: The World's Deadliest Revolutionary Force.* London: HarperCollins.

Suárez, Wilfredo Hurtado. 1995. *Chicha peruana: Música de los nuevos migrantes.* Lima: Grupo de Investigaciones Económicas ECO.

Tanaka, Martin. 1997. "Fujimori's Peru and Popular Organizations: From Electoral-*Movimientismo* to Electoral-Media Politics: The Changing Patterns of State-Society Relationship." Paper prepared for delivery at a conference entitled "Fujimori's Peru: Is It Sustainable?" held at the Institute of Latin American Studies, University of London, June 19–21.

Tarazona-Sevillano, Gabriela. 1990. *Sendero Luminoso and the Threat of Narcoterrorism.* New York: Praeger.

Thorp, Rosemary. 1987. "The APRA Alternative in Peru: Preliminary Evaluation of Garcia's Economic Policies." *The Peru Report* 1.6: 1–5, 23.

Thorp, Rosemary, and Geoffrey Bertram. 1978. *Peru, 1890–1977.* New York: Columbia University Press.

Thorp, Rosemary, and Lawrence Whitehead, eds. 1987. *Latin American Debt and the Adjustment Crisis.* London: Macmillan.

Toledo, Alejandro, and Alain Chanlat, eds. 1991. *Las otras caras de la sociedad informal.* Lima: Escuela Superior de Administración de Negocios.

Torres, Alfredo. 1989. *Perfil del Elector.* Lima: Apoyo.

Touraine, Alain. 1987. *Actores sociales y sistemas políticos en América Latina.* Santiago de Chile: Oficina Internacional de Trabajo.

Tovar, Teresa. 1982a. *Velasquismo y movimiento popular: Historia de movimiento popular, 1968–1975.* Lima: DESCO.

———. 1982b. *Movimiento barrial: Organización y unidad, 1978–1981.* Lima: DESCO.

———. 1985. *Velasquismo y movimiento popular: Otra historia prohibida.* Lima: DESCO.

———. 1986. "Vecinos y pobladores en la crisis (1980–1984)." In Eduardo Ballón, ed., *Movimientos sociales y crisis: El caso peruano,* pp. 113–63. Lima: DESCO.

Tuesta, Fernando. 1991. "Pobreza urbana y participación política: Clases populares y cambios electorales en Lima." In Alejandro Toledo and Alain Chanlat, eds., *La otras caras de la sociedad informal: Una visión multidisciplinaria,* pp. 275–324. Lima: Escuela Superior de Administración de Negocios.

———. 1994. *Perú político en cifras.* Lima: Fundación Friedrich Ebert.

Tulchin, Joseph, ed. 1995. *The Consolidation of Democracy in Latin America.* Boulder, Colo.: Lynne Rienner.

Valárcel, Marcel, ed. 1990. *Pobreza urbana: Interrelaciones económicas y marginalidad religiosa.* Lima: Pontificia Universidad Catolica del Perú, Facultad de Ciencias Sociales.

Valdeavellano, Rocio. 1980. *Historia del movimiento barrial.* Lima: DESCO.

Vargas Llosa, Mario. 1993. *El pez en el agua: Memorias.* Barcelona: Seix Barral.

Varillas Montenegro, Alberto, and Patricia Mostajo de Muente. 1990. *La situación poblacional peruana.* Lima: Instituto Andino de Estudios en Población y Desarollo.

Vayda, Andrew. 1983. "Progressive Contextualization: Methods for Research in Human Ecology." *Human Ecology* 11.3: 265–81.

Vega-Centeno, Máximo. 1995. "Desarrollo, crecimiento e inversiones en el Perú y América Latina." In Gonzao Porto carrerro and Marcel Valcárcel, eds., *El Perú frente al siglo XXI.* Lima: Pontificia Universidad Católica.

Verba, Sidney, and Norman Nie. 1972. *Participation in America.* New York: Harper and Row.

Verba, Sidney, Norman Nie, and Jae-On Kim. 1971. *The Modes of Democratic Participation: A Cross-National Comparison.* Vol. 2 of *Comparative Politics Series.* Beverly Hills, Calif.: Sage.

Verba, Sidney, Norman Nie, and Jae-On Kim. 1978. *Participation and Political Equality: A Seven-Nation Comparison.* New York: Cambridge University Press.

Villalobos, Gabriela, and Gabriela Vega. 1982. *Evolución de la familia: Un estudio de casos en Pamplona Alta.* Lima: DESCO.

Walton, John. 1973. "Standardized Case Comparison: Observations on Method in Comparative Sociology." In Michael Armer and Allen Grimshaw, eds., *Comparative Social Research: Methodological Problems and Strategies,* pp. 173–88. New York: John Wiley.

———. 1987. "Urban Protest and the Global Political Economy: The IMF Riots." In Michael Peter Smith and Joe R. Feagin, eds., *The Capitalist City: Global Restructuring and Community Politics,* pp. 364–86. Oxford, England: Basil Blackwell.

Walzer, Michael. 1995. "The Civil Society Argument." In Ronald Beiner, ed., *Theorizing Citizenship,* pp. 153–74. Albany, N.Y.: State University of New York Press.

Webb, Richard. 1977. *Government Policy and the Distribution of Income in Peru, 1963–1973.* Cambridge, Mass.: Harvard University Press.

Webb, Richard, and Graciela Fernandez Baca. 1991. *Perú en números, 1991.* Lima: Cúanto.

———. 1992. *Perú en números, 1992.* Lima: Cúanto.

Webb, Richard, et al. 1981. *Distribución del ingreso en el Perú.* Lima: Pontificia Universidad Católica, Programa de Ciencias Sociales, Publicación de Proyección Social.

Weiner, Myron. 1971. "Political Participation: Crisis of the Political Process." In Leonard Binder et al., *Crises and Sequences in Political Development.* pp. 159–204 Princeton, N.J.: Princeton University Press.

Wickham-Crowley, Timothy. 1992. *Guerrillas and Revolution in Latin America: A Comparative Study of Insurgents and Regimes.* Princeton, N.J.: Princeton University Press.

Wilson, Patricia. 1987. "Lima and the New International Division of Labor." In Michael Peter Smith and Joe R. Feagin, eds., *The Capitalist City: Global Restructuring and Community Politics,* pp. 199–214. New York: Basil Blackwell.

Zapata, Antonio. 1997. "Society and Urban Planning in Villa El Salvador." Ph.D. diss., Columbia University.

INDEX

27 de Octubre, 144

28 de Julio, 80, 99, 100, 235; in 1970 survey, 261; during 1971–82, 152, 155; in 1982, 165, 166; in 1985 survey, 175, 176; in 1990 survey, 184; in 1995 presidential election, 255; assistance requirements in, 5; level of neighborhood unity in, 112; as research community, 95–97; as target of Shining Path, 271n5; Zones A and B, 95–97

Abugattas, Javier, 58

age distribution, 70, 102

Agency for International Development, 147

Agrarian Reform and Housing Commission, 145, 146

agriculture, 44, 45, 64

Alfonso Ugarte, 78

Alliance for Progress, 46, 147

Andrade, Alberto, 256–57

AP party, 52, 60, 207, 210–12; in 1980 elections, 54, 120, 195; in 1983 municipal elections, 55, 170, 196, 197; in 1985 presidential election, 124–25; in 1989 municipal elections, 199; in 1995 municipal elections, 249; absence from 1978 elections, 193; absence from 1986 municipal elections, 198; under Belaúnde administration, 147, 148; electoral support of, 146; and resurrection of Cooperacion Popular, 162–63

APRA, 52, 206–07, 210–16, 221, 274n17; in 1962 elections, 46; in 1978 elections, 192–94; in 1980 municipal elections, 194, 196; in 1980 presidential election, 120; in 1983 municipal elections, 54, 170, 196, 197; in 1985 presidential election, 55, 124, 197; in 1986 municipal elections, 177, 198; in 1989 municipal elections, 178, 199; in 1990 presidential election, 62, 128–29, 199, 200, 201; in 1995 municipal elections, 249; actions under Belaúnde administration, 147–48; founding of, 45; Odría and, 145; and sup-

port of Prado, 145; and support of Vargas Llosa, 61

APRA-UNO coalition, 147

Arequipa, Peru, 64, 148

Argentina, 25

ASI, 60, 62

assassinations, 54

assistance sources in survey barrios, 113–15

Association of Popular Urbanizations of Arequipa. *See* AUPA

Ate-Vitarte district, 89, 174

AUPA, 148

authoritarian regime, 5, 6

autogolpe, 247–48

Ayacucho, Peru, 148

azoteas. *See* slum housing

Bambaren, Msgr. Luis, 98

Barnes, Samuel, 259

Barranco district, 69–70, 89

Barrantes, Alfonso, 60, 209, 211, 221; in 1980 municipal elections, 196; and 1983 mayoral victory, 170; and 1983 municipal elections, 196, 197; in 1985 presidential election, 124–25, 197; in 1986 municipal elections, 177, 198; and 1990 municipal elections, 179; and Glass of Milk program, 171; renunciation of Shining Path, 278n8

barriadas. *See* squatter settlements

barrio centralization, 159

barrios, survey. *See* survey barrios

Barrios Altos, 89

barrios marginales. *See* squatter settlements

barrio-state relations, 41

Bedoya Reyes, Luis, 60, 192, 195

Belaúnde administration: in 1982, 162–63; dissatisfaction with, 211; inflation during, 72; overview of, 146–49; Primero de Enero and, 92; response to Shining Path, 54; rise of party politics under, 147–48

demise of, 57; failures of, 180; implementation of, 179; problems with, 179–80

Pampa de Arena, 99, 100, 234, 238; in 1970 survey, 261; in 1971, 150–51, 152, 154; in 1982, 164–65, 166; in 1985 survey, 175; in 1995 presidential election, 255; assistance requirements in, 115; compared to 28 de Julio, 96; crime in, 93; education level in, 101; level of neighborhood unity in, 112; level of satisfaction in, 112; neighborhoods in, 78; as research community, 92–93; self-help preference in, 114; white-collar workers in, 103

Pamplona Alta, 77–78

party politics, 147–48

Paseo de la República, 82

Peace Corps, 147

Perez de Cuellar, Javier, 249, 255

Peru: defeat in War of the Pacific, 32; distribution of poverty in, 63; economic crisis in, 25–26; economic distribution in, 23; economic relationship with England, 44; historical background of, 44–47; populist cycles in, 24; post–World War I economy of, 45; post–World War II industry, 64

petitioning, national, 229; as irrational behavior, 187, 245; as mode of participation, 118

Piura, Peru, 44

Plaza de Armas, in Lima Cercado, 78

pobladores: defined, 107; employment by PAIT, 56; relations with state, 142–49

poblador social consciousness, 160–61

political participation: 1970, 117–20; 1982, 120–24; 1985, 124–28; 1990, 128–32; authoritarian regime and, 5; defined, 4–5, 7, 205; democratic, 5; effect of economy on, 231–32; effects of poverty on, 233–35; effects of the state on, 235–37; formal, 2, 7, 17, 28, 37, 105–06, 228–29; informal, 1, 7, 17, 28, 37, 134, 138, 204, 229, 272n2; instrumental view of, 227; and macroeconomic crisis, 26; macro factors affecting, 36; model for examining, 35–39; modes of, 4–5; motives for, 10–11; rational, 8–10, 243–45; rational view of, 227; the state and, 29–30; and state–civil society relations, 31–33; and transition from military to civilian rule, 6; urban setting and, 33–34

political preference dimension, 136, 186–87, 190

political rights, 23

Popular Action. See AP party

Popular Christian Party. See PPC

Popular Revolutionary American Alliance. See APRA

populist cycles in Peru, 24, 44

populist economic cycle theory, 48

populist macroeconomics, 24

Portes, Alejandro: on class polarization, 67; and definition of informal sector, 73–74; on informal economy, 104; on macroeconomic crisis of 1980s, 65–66

poverty, 1; as bounding rationality, 12–13; distribution of, in Peru, 63; effects on political participation, 28, 233–35; macro, 27; as macro factor, 22, 24, 35; macrolevel, defined, 233; and Peruvian history, 44; and vote-switching, 235

PPC, 53, 60, 207, 211, 215; in 1978 elections, 192–94; in 1980 presidential election, 120, 195; in 1980 municipal elections, 196; in 1985 presidential election, 197; in 1986 municipal elections, 198; in 1989 municipal elections, 199; in 1990 presidential election, 201; in 1995 municipal elections, 249

Prado, Manuel, 46, 47, 145

Prado administration, 145–46

presidential elections: of 1980, 194–95; of 1985, 197–98; of 1990, 199–201

primacy, 66–67

Primero de Enero, 99, 100, 132, 234, 238; in 1970 survey, 261; in 1971, 150–51, 152, 154; during 1971–82, 155; in 1982, 164–65, 166; in 1985 survey, 175, 176; in 1995 presidential election, 255; assistance requirements in, 115; compared to 28 de Julio, 96; level of neighborhood unity in, 112, 113; level of satisfaction in, 112; as research community, 90–92; state improvements in, 91–92; white-collar workers in, 103

PROEM, 56, 57

Program of Temporary Income Assistance. See PAIT

Pronaa, 250–51, 254

Przeworski, Adam, 116, 259; on citizen support of democracy, 15; on democratic transitions, 16, 39–40

public schoolteachers' union. See SUTEP

pueblos jovenes. See squatter settlements

rational action theory, 27

rational behavior, 18–19

rationality, 16–18, 266n7, 272n3

rational political participation, 8–10, 189, 243–45